JUSTICE LEAGUE
GODS AND MONSTERS

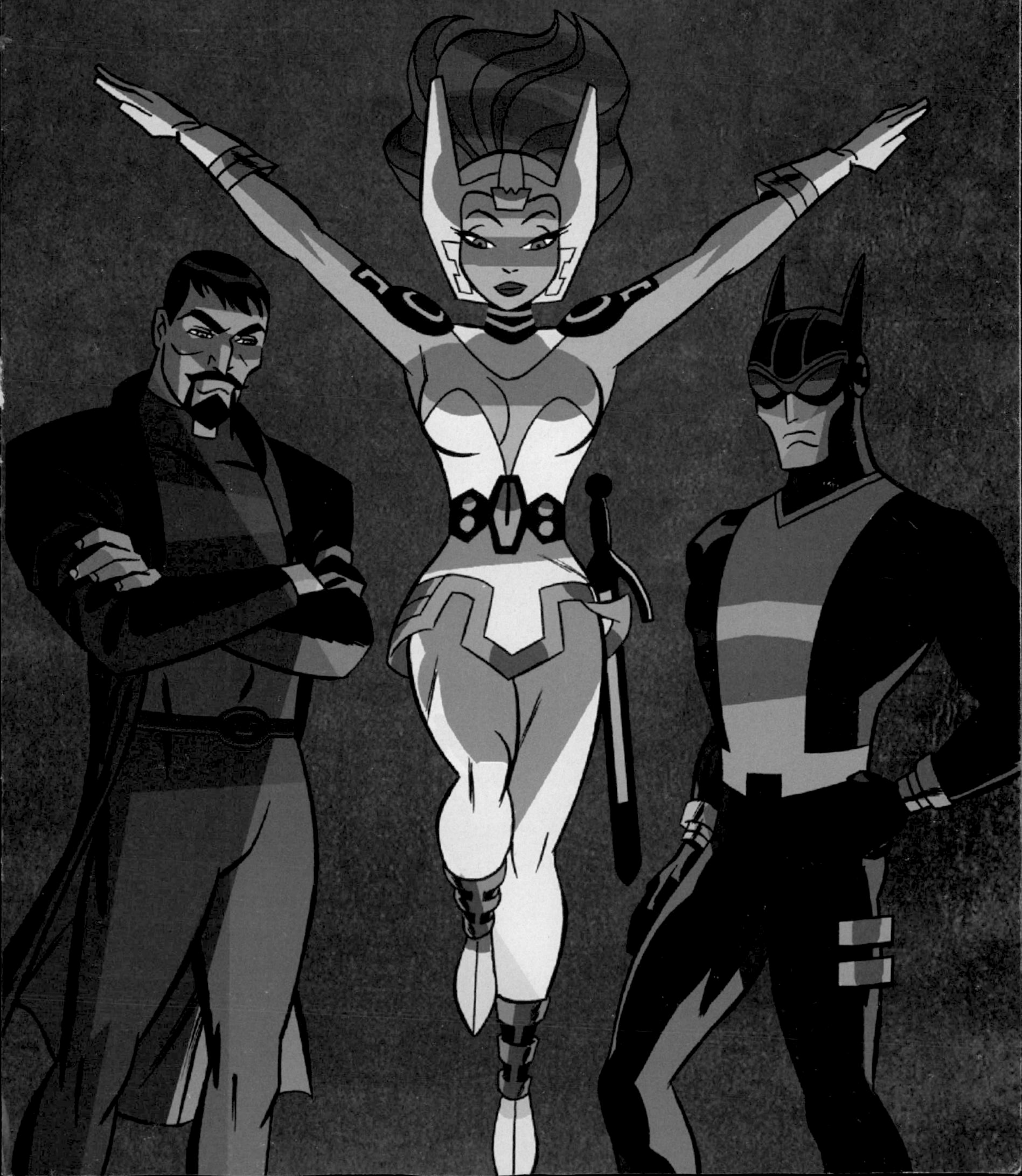

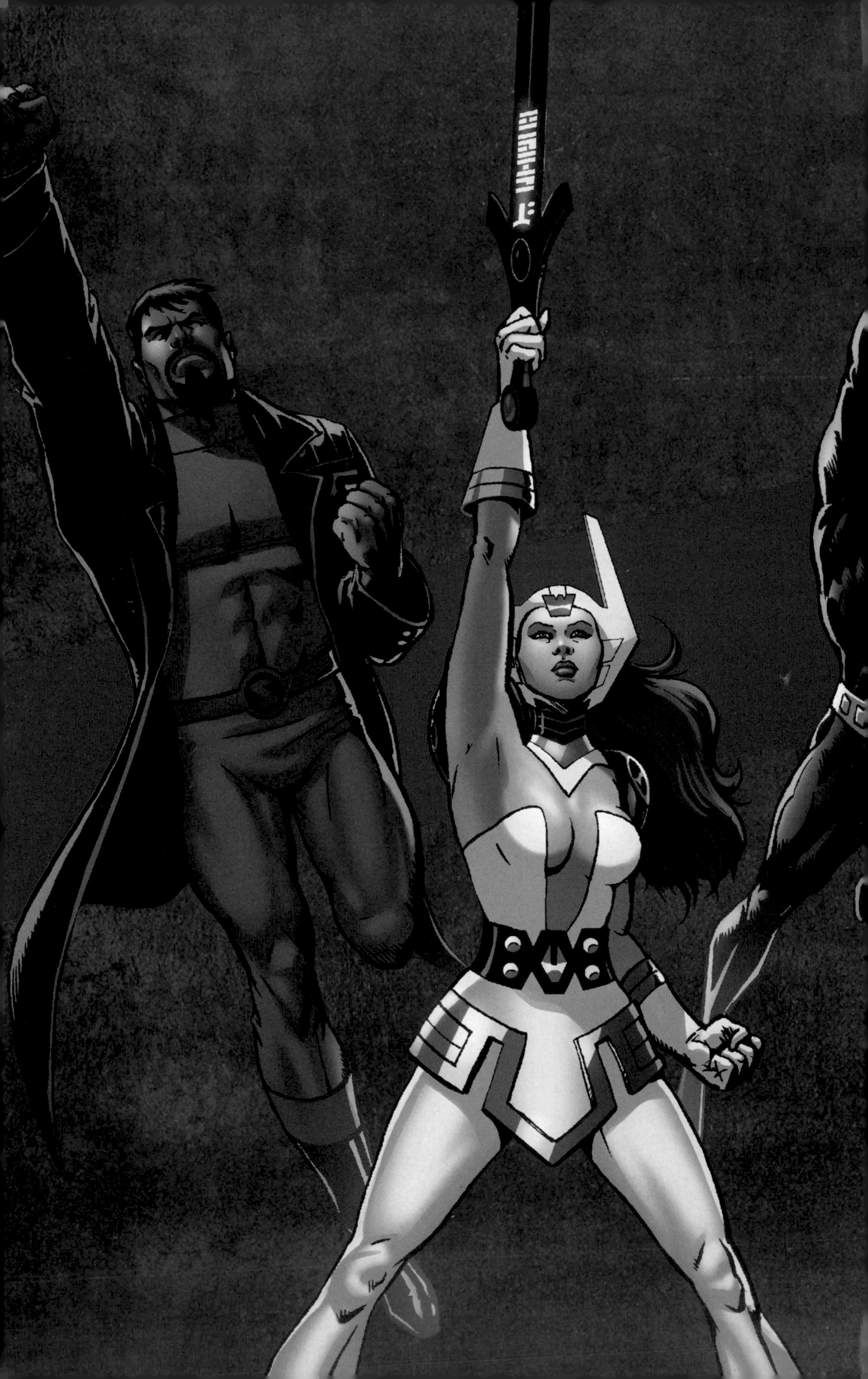

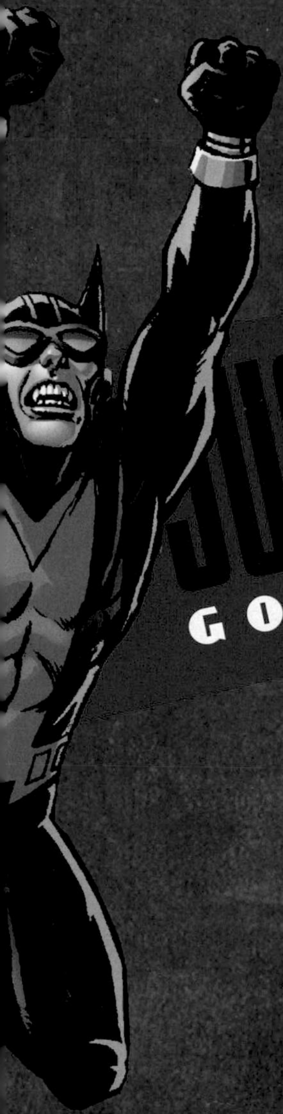

JUSTICE LEAGUE
GODS AND MONSTERS

WRITERS BRUCE TIMM
J.M. DEMATTEIS

ART BY THONY SILAS
MORITAT
MATTHEW DOW SMITH
RICK LEONARDI
DAN GREEN

COLORS BY TONY AVIÑA
MORITAT
JORDIE BELLAIRE
ALLEN PASSALAQUA

LETTERS BY SAIDA TEMOFONTE

COLLECTION COVER BY DARICK ROBERTSON AND DIEGO RODRIGUEZ

SUPERMAN created by JERRY SIEGEL and JOE SHUSTER.
By Special Arrangement with the Jerry Siegel Family.

KRISTY QUINN Editor – Original Series JESSICA CHEN Associate Editor – Original Series JEB WOODARD Group Editor – Collected Editions
PAUL SANTOS Editor – Collected Edition STEVE COOK Design Director – Books SARABETH KETT Publication Design

BOB HARRAS Senior VP – Editor-in-Chief, DC Comics

DIANE NELSON President DAN DIDIO Publisher JIM LEE Publisher GEOFF JOHNS President & Chief Creative Officer
AMIT DESAI Executive VP – Business & Marketing Strategy, Direct to Consumer & Global Franchise Management
SAM ADES Senior VP – Direct to Consumer BOBBIE CHASE VP – Talent Development MARK CHIARELLO Senior VP – Art, Design & Collected Editions
JOHN CUNNINGHAM Senior VP – Sales & Trade Marketing ANNE DEPIES Senior VP – Business Strategy, Finance & Administration
DON FALLETTI VP – Manufacturing Operations LAWRENCE GANEM VP – Editorial Administration & Talent Relations
ALISON GILL Senior VP – Manufacturing & Operations HANK KANALZ Senior VP – Editorial Strategy & Administration
JAY KOGAN VP – Legal Affairs THOMAS LOFTUS VP – Business Affairs JACK MAHAN VP – Business Affairs
NICK J. NAPOLITANO VP – Manufacturing Administration EDDIE SCANNELL VP – Consumer Marketing COURTNEY SIMMONS Senior VP – Publicity & Communications
JIM (SKI) SOKOLOWSKI VP – Comic Book Specialty Sales & Trade Marketing NANCY SPEARS VP – Mass, Book, Digital Sales & Trade Marketing

JUSTICE LEAGUE: GODS AND MONSTERS

DC Comics, 2900 West Alameda Avenue, Burbank, CA 91505
Printed by LSC Communications, Salem, VA, USA. 1/6/17. First Printing.
ISBN: 978-1-4012-6786-5

Library of Congress Cataloging-in-Publication Data is Available.

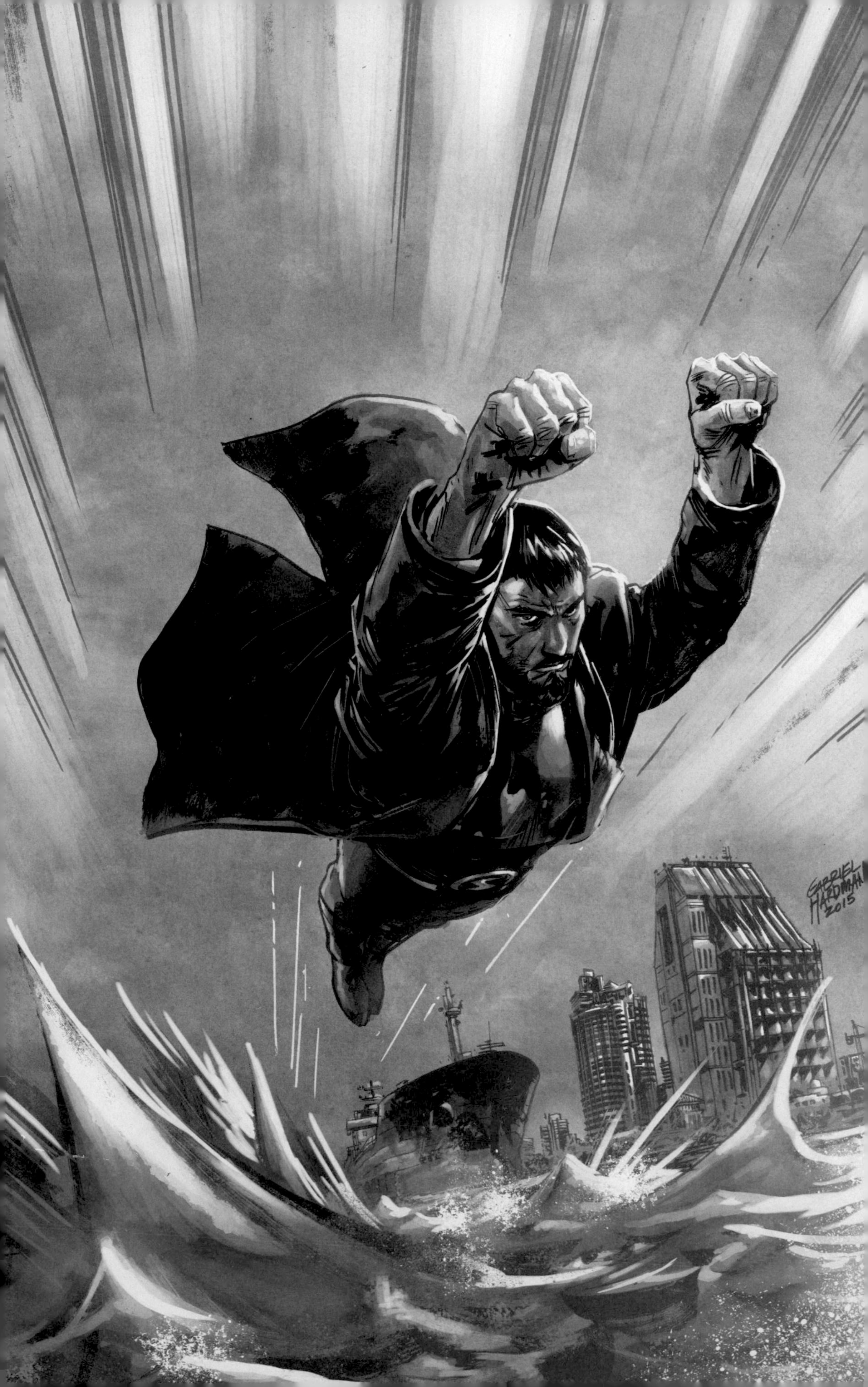
GABRIEL HARDMAN 2015

FALLEN

ART BY MORITAT

COVER ART BY GABRIEL HARDMAN
AND JORDAN BOYD

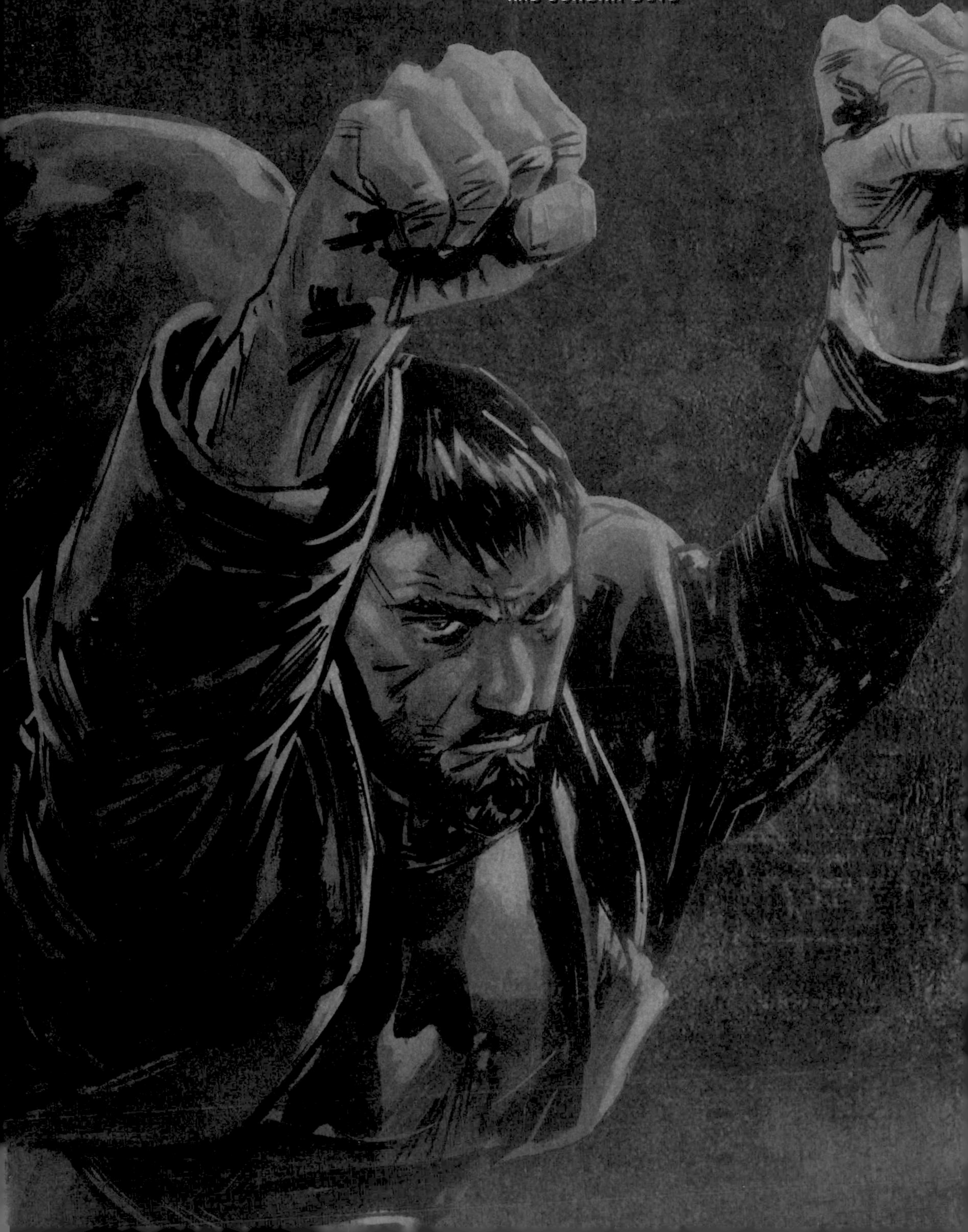

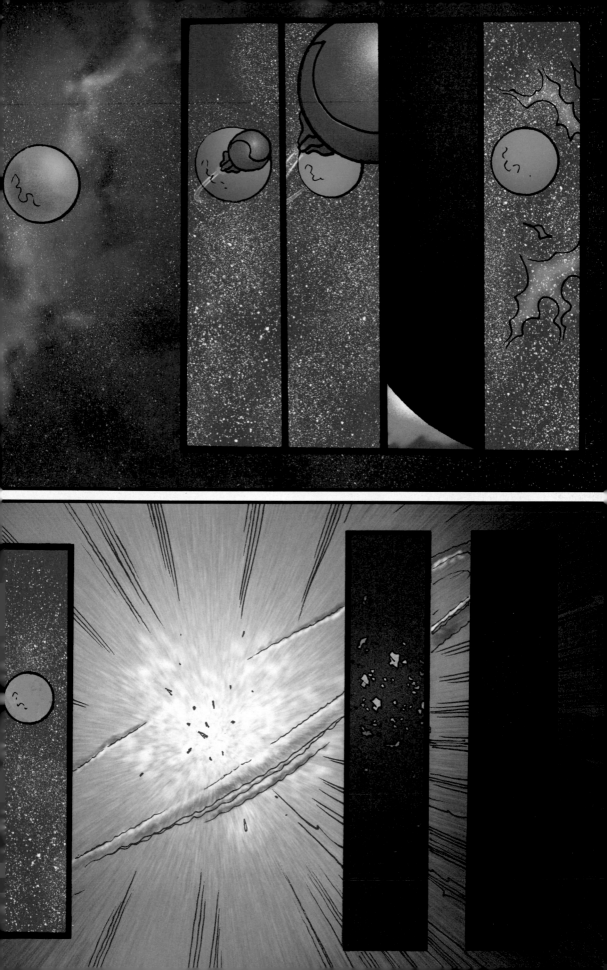

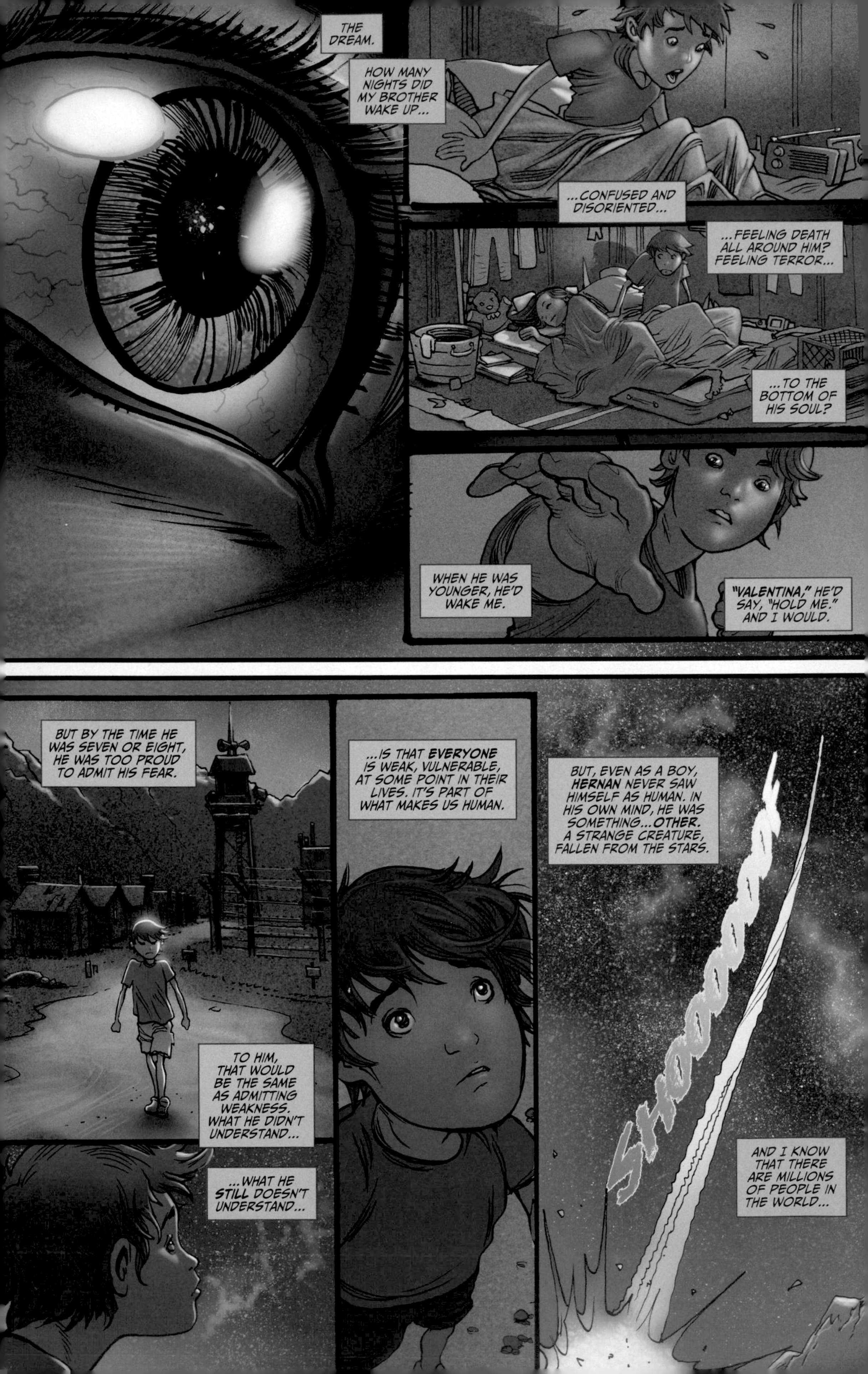
THE DREAM.
HOW MANY NIGHTS DID MY BROTHER WAKE UP...
...CONFUSED AND DISORIENTED...
...FEELING DEATH ALL AROUND HIM? FEELING TERROR...
...TO THE BOTTOM OF HIS SOUL?
WHEN HE WAS YOUNGER, HE'D WAKE ME.
"VALENTINA," HE'D SAY, "HOLD ME." AND I WOULD.
BUT BY THE TIME HE WAS SEVEN OR EIGHT, HE WAS TOO PROUD TO ADMIT HIS FEAR.
TO HIM, THAT WOULD BE THE SAME AS ADMITTING WEAKNESS. WHAT HE DIDN'T UNDERSTAND...
...WHAT HE STILL DOESN'T UNDERSTAND...
...IS THAT EVERYONE IS WEAK, VULNERABLE, AT SOME POINT IN THEIR LIVES. IT'S PART OF WHAT MAKES US HUMAN.
BUT, EVEN AS A BOY, HERNAN NEVER SAW HIMSELF AS HUMAN. IN HIS OWN MIND, HE WAS SOMETHING...OTHER. A STRANGE CREATURE, FALLEN FROM THE STARS.
SHOOOOOOM
AND I KNOW THAT THERE ARE MILLIONS OF PEOPLE IN THE WORLD...

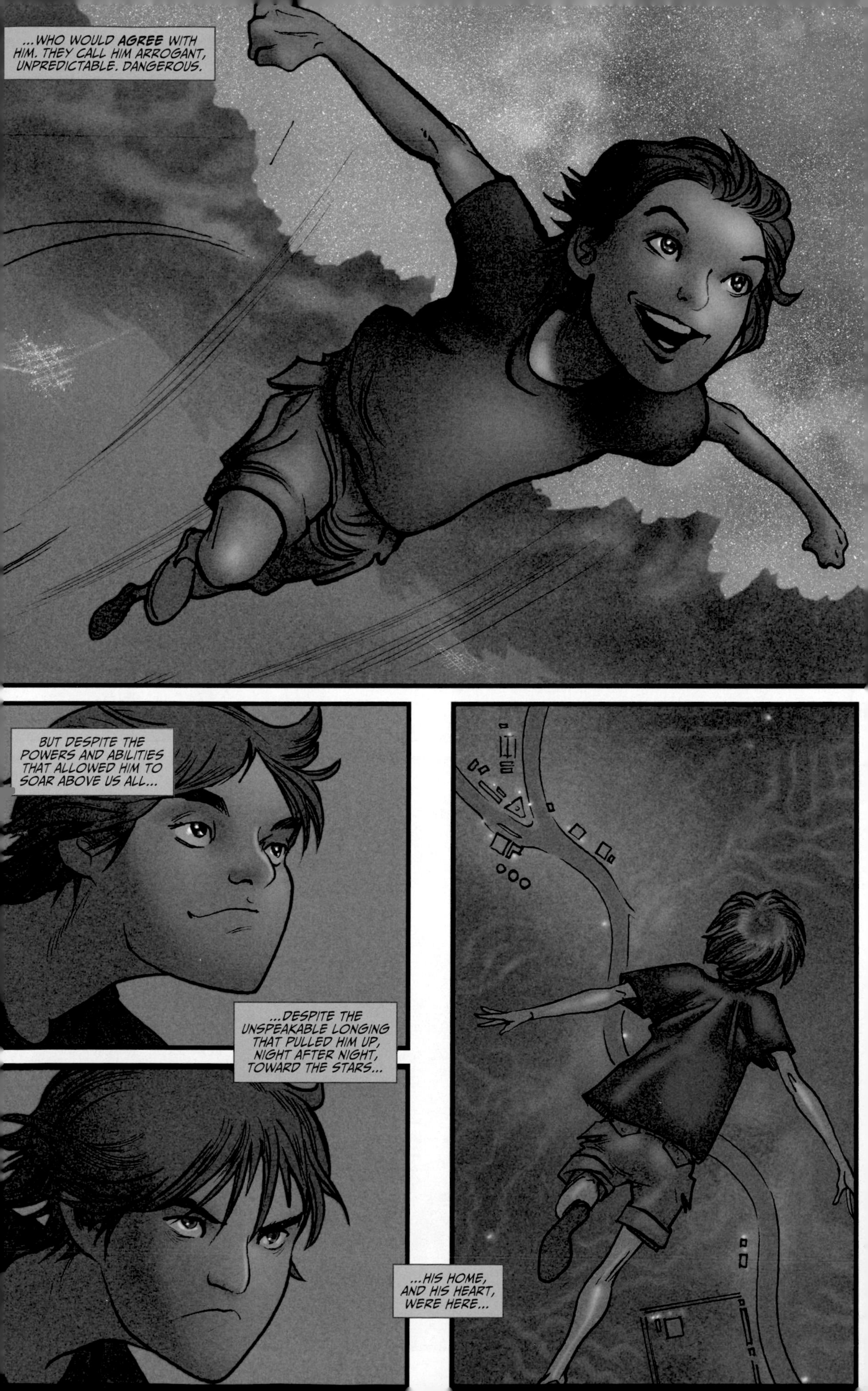
...WHO WOULD AGREE WITH HIM. THEY CALL HIM ARROGANT, UNPREDICTABLE. DANGEROUS.
BUT DESPITE THE POWERS AND ABILITIES THAT ALLOWED HIM TO SOAR ABOVE US ALL...
...DESPITE THE UNSPEAKABLE LONGING THAT PULLED HIM UP, NIGHT AFTER NIGHT, TOWARD THE STARS...
...HIS HOME, AND HIS HEART, WERE HERE...

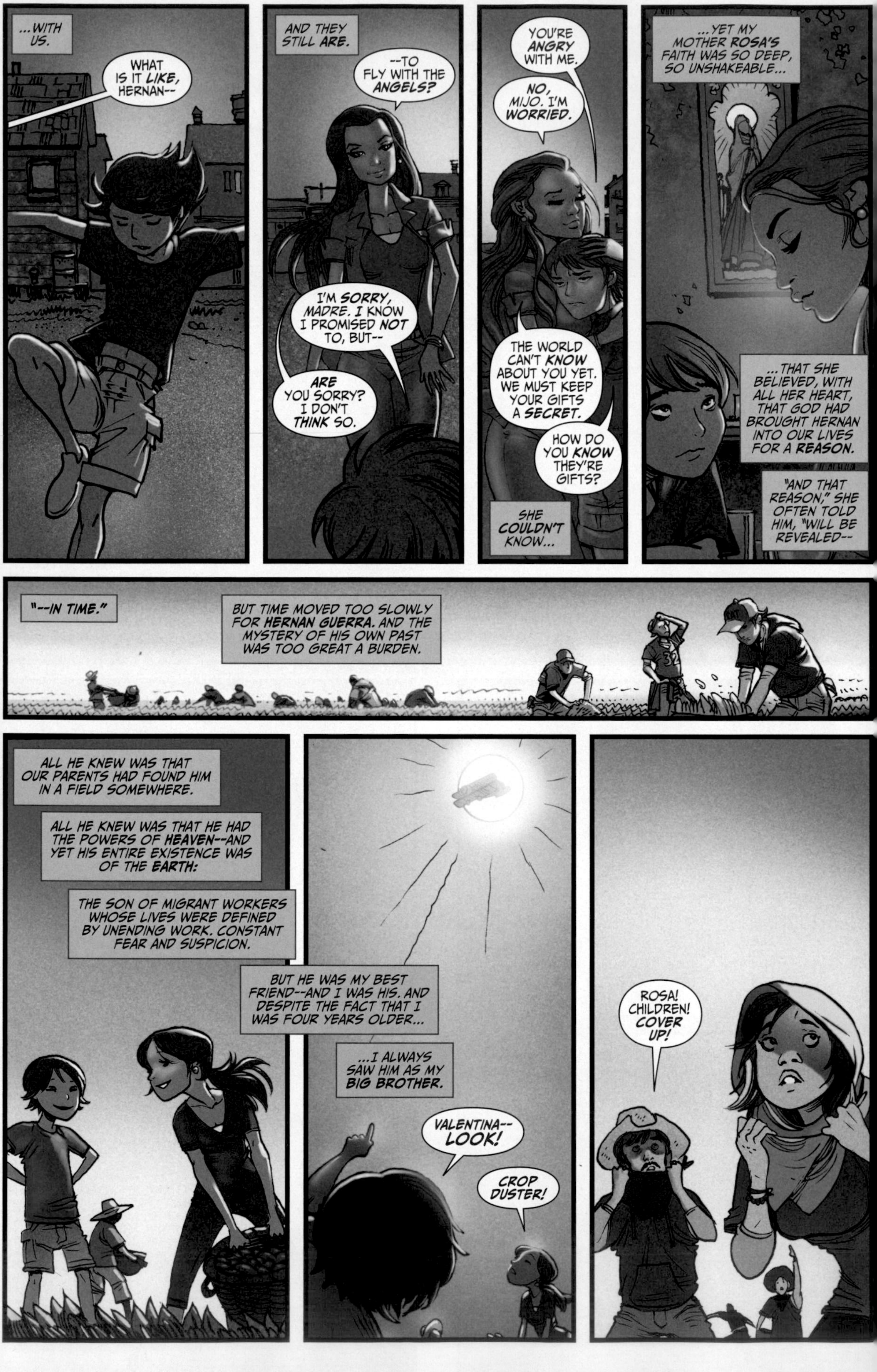

...WITH US.
WHAT IS IT LIKE, HERNAN--
AND THEY STILL ARE.
--TO FLY WITH THE ANGELS?
I'M SORRY, MADRE. I KNOW I PROMISED NOT TO, BUT--
ARE YOU SORRY? I DON'T THINK SO.
YOU'RE ANGRY WITH ME.
NO, MIJO. I'M WORRIED.
THE WORLD CAN'T KNOW ABOUT YOU YET. WE MUST KEEP YOUR GIFTS A SECRET.
HOW DO YOU KNOW THEY'RE GIFTS?
SHE COULDN'T KNOW...
...YET MY MOTHER ROSA'S FAITH WAS SO DEEP, SO UNSHAKEABLE...
...THAT SHE BELIEVED, WITH ALL HER HEART, THAT GOD HAD BROUGHT HERNAN INTO OUR LIVES FOR A REASON.
"AND THAT REASON," SHE OFTEN TOLD HIM, "WILL BE REVEALED--
"--IN TIME."
BUT TIME MOVED TOO SLOWLY FOR HERNAN GUERRA. AND THE MYSTERY OF HIS OWN PAST WAS TOO GREAT A BURDEN.
ALL HE KNEW WAS THAT OUR PARENTS HAD FOUND HIM IN A FIELD SOMEWHERE.
ALL HE KNEW WAS THAT HE HAD THE POWERS OF HEAVEN--AND YET HIS ENTIRE EXISTENCE WAS OF THE EARTH:
THE SON OF MIGRANT WORKERS WHOSE LIVES WERE DEFINED BY UNENDING WORK. CONSTANT FEAR AND SUSPICION.
BUT HE WAS MY BEST FRIEND--AND I WAS HIS. AND DESPITE THE FACT THAT I WAS FOUR YEARS OLDER...
...I ALWAYS SAW HIM AS MY BIG BROTHER.
VALENTINA--LOOK!
CROP DUSTER!
ROSA! CHILDREN! COVER UP!

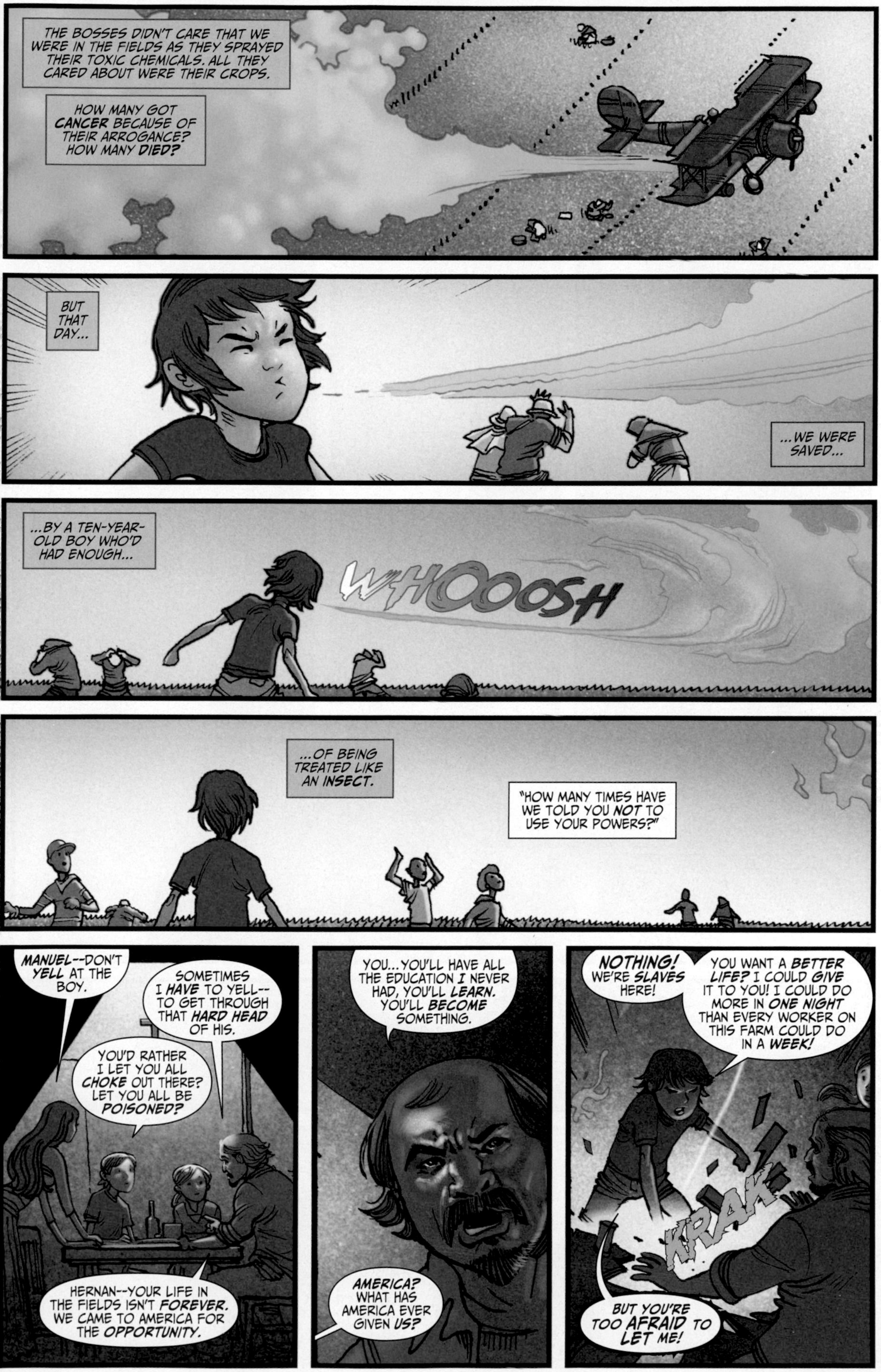
THE BOSSES DIDN'T CARE THAT WE WERE IN THE FIELDS AS THEY SPRAYED THEIR TOXIC CHEMICALS. ALL THEY CARED ABOUT WERE THEIR CROPS.
HOW MANY GOT CANCER BECAUSE OF THEIR ARROGANCE? HOW MANY DIED?
BUT THAT DAY...
...WE WERE SAVED...
...BY A TEN-YEAR-OLD BOY WHO'D HAD ENOUGH...
WHOOOSH
...OF BEING TREATED LIKE AN INSECT.
"HOW MANY TIMES HAVE WE TOLD YOU NOT TO USE YOUR POWERS?"
MANUEL--DON'T YELL AT THE BOY.
SOMETIMES I HAVE TO YELL--TO GET THROUGH THAT HARD HEAD OF HIS.
YOU'D RATHER I LET YOU ALL CHOKE OUT THERE? LET YOU ALL BE POISONED?
HERNAN--YOUR LIFE IN THE FIELDS ISN'T FOREVER. WE CAME TO AMERICA FOR THE OPPORTUNITY.
YOU...YOU'LL HAVE ALL THE EDUCATION I NEVER HAD, YOU'LL LEARN. YOU'LL BECOME SOMETHING.
AMERICA? WHAT HAS AMERICA EVER GIVEN US?
NOTHING! WE'RE SLAVES HERE!
YOU WANT A BETTER LIFE? I COULD GIVE IT TO YOU! I COULD DO MORE IN ONE NIGHT THAN EVERY WORKER ON THIS FARM COULD DO IN A WEEK!
KRAK
BUT YOU'RE TOO AFRAID TO LET ME!

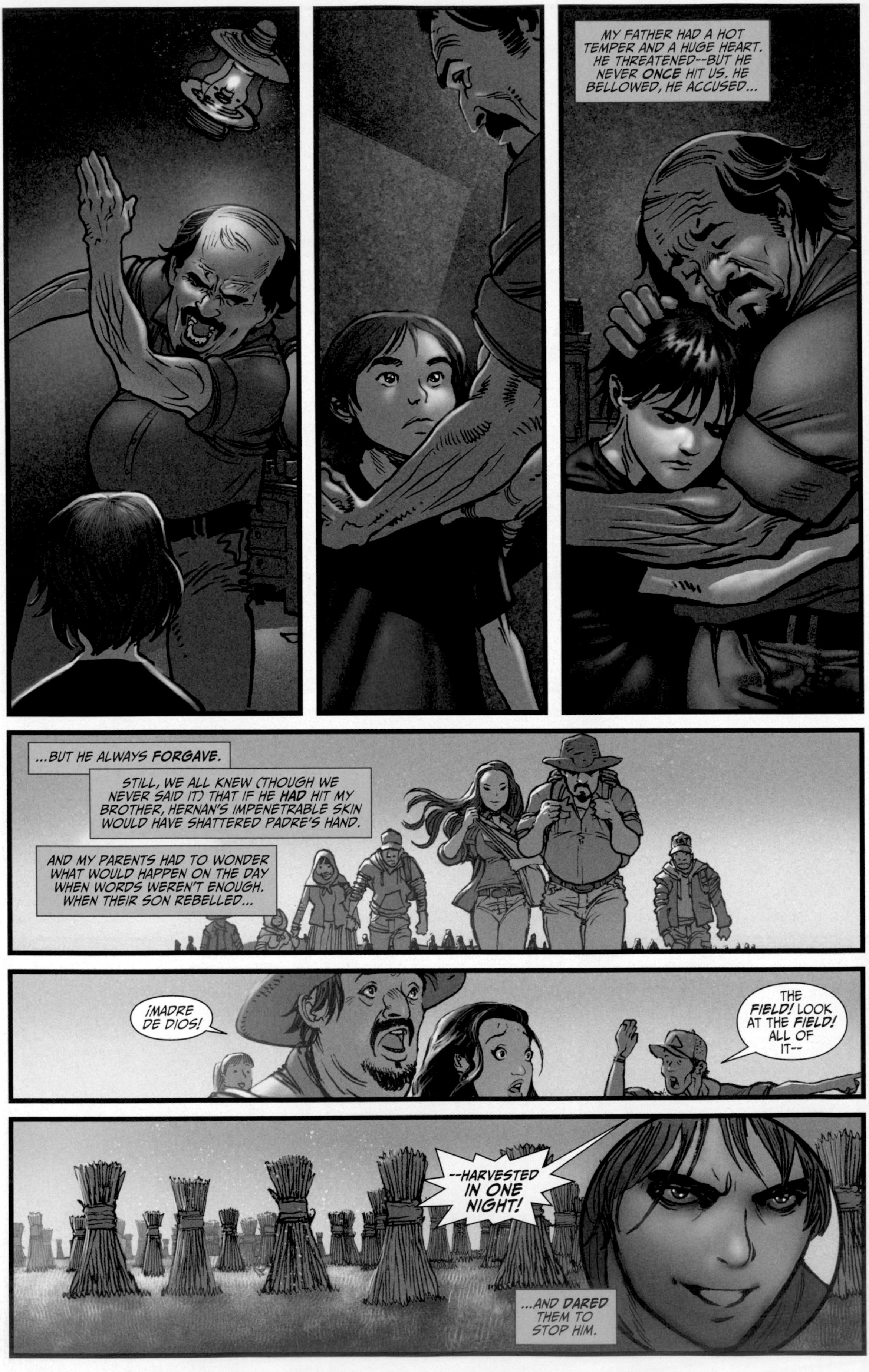
MY FATHER HAD A HOT TEMPER AND A HUGE HEART. HE THREATENED--BUT HE NEVER ONCE HIT US. HE BELLOWED, HE ACCUSED...
...BUT HE ALWAYS FORGAVE.
STILL, WE ALL KNEW (THOUGH WE NEVER SAID IT) THAT IF HE HAD HIT MY BROTHER, HERNAN'S IMPENETRABLE SKIN WOULD HAVE SHATTERED PADRE'S HAND.
AND MY PARENTS HAD TO WONDER WHAT WOULD HAPPEN ON THE DAY WHEN WORDS WEREN'T ENOUGH. WHEN THEIR SON REBELLED...
¡MADRE DE DIOS!
THE FIELD! LOOK AT THE FIELD! ALL OF IT--
--HARVESTED IN ONE NIGHT!
...AND DARED THEM TO STOP HIM.

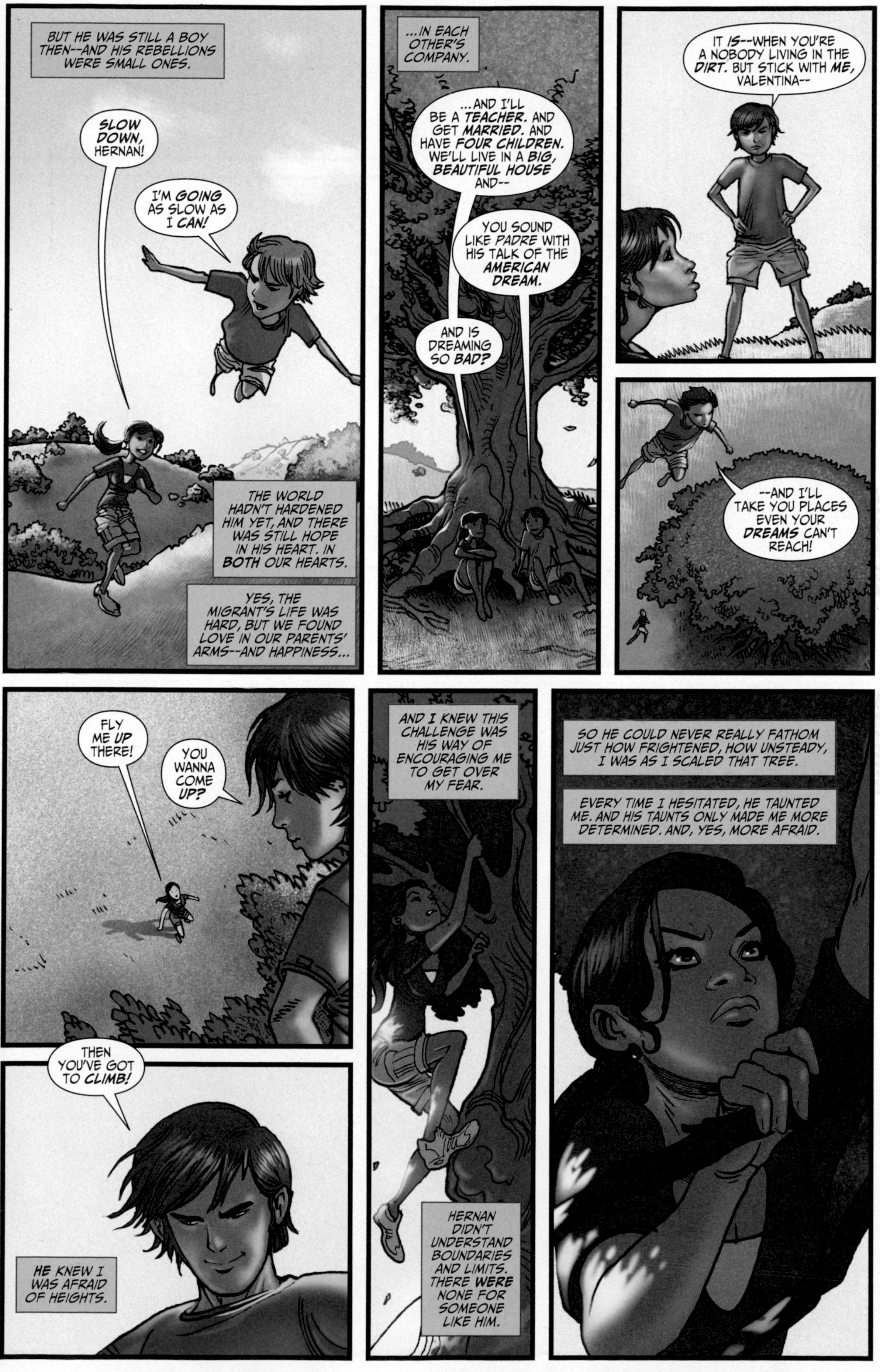
BUT HE WAS STILL A BOY THEN--AND HIS REBELLIONS WERE SMALL ONES.
SLOW DOWN, HERNAN!
I'M GOING AS SLOW AS I CAN!
THE WORLD HADN'T HARDENED HIM YET, AND THERE WAS STILL HOPE IN HIS HEART. IN BOTH OUR HEARTS.
YES, THE MIGRANT'S LIFE WAS HARD, BUT WE FOUND LOVE IN OUR PARENTS' ARMS--AND HAPPINESS...
...IN EACH OTHER'S COMPANY.
...AND I'LL BE A TEACHER. AND GET MARRIED. AND HAVE FOUR CHILDREN. WE'LL LIVE IN A BIG, BEAUTIFUL HOUSE AND--
YOU SOUND LIKE PADRE WITH HIS TALK OF THE AMERICAN DREAM.
AND IS DREAMING SO BAD?
IT IS--WHEN YOU'RE A NOBODY LIVING IN THE DIRT. BUT STICK WITH ME, VALENTINA--
--AND I'LL TAKE YOU PLACES EVEN YOUR DREAMS CAN'T REACH!
FLY ME UP THERE!
YOU WANNA COME UP?
THEN YOU'VE GOT TO CLIMB!
HE KNEW I WAS AFRAID OF HEIGHTS.
AND I KNEW THIS CHALLENGE WAS HIS WAY OF ENCOURAGING ME TO GET OVER MY FEAR.
HERNAN DIDN'T UNDERSTAND BOUNDARIES AND LIMITS. THERE WERE NONE FOR SOMEONE LIKE HIM.
SO HE COULD NEVER REALLY FATHOM JUST HOW FRIGHTENED, HOW UNSTEADY, I WAS AS I SCALED THAT TREE.
EVERY TIME I HESITATED, HE TAUNTED ME. AND HIS TAUNTS ONLY MADE ME MORE DETERMINED. AND, YES, MORE AFRAID.

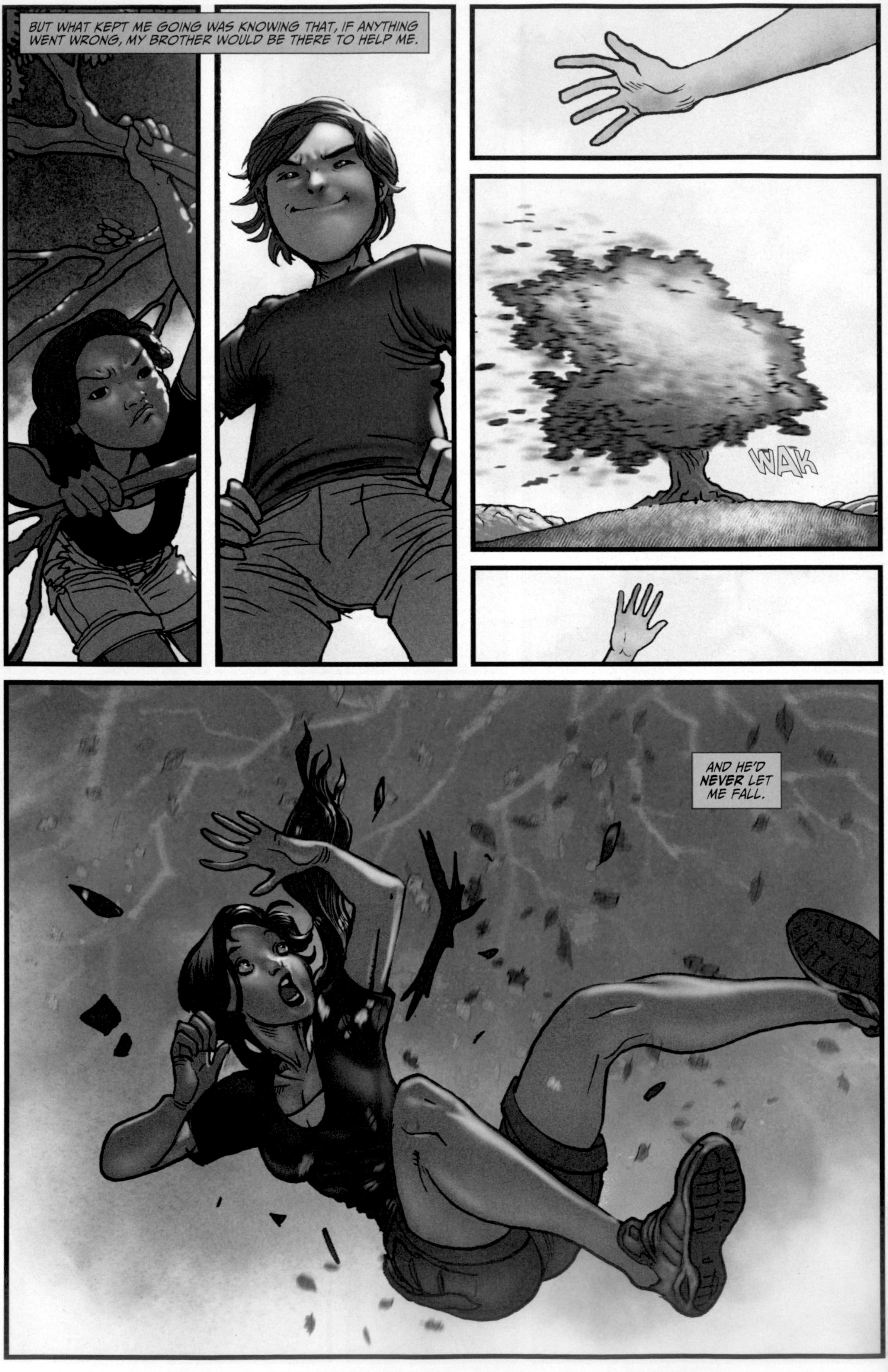
BUT WHAT KEPT ME GOING WAS KNOWING THAT, IF ANYTHING WENT WRONG, MY BROTHER WOULD BE THERE TO HELP ME.
WAK
AND HE'D NEVER LET ME FALL.

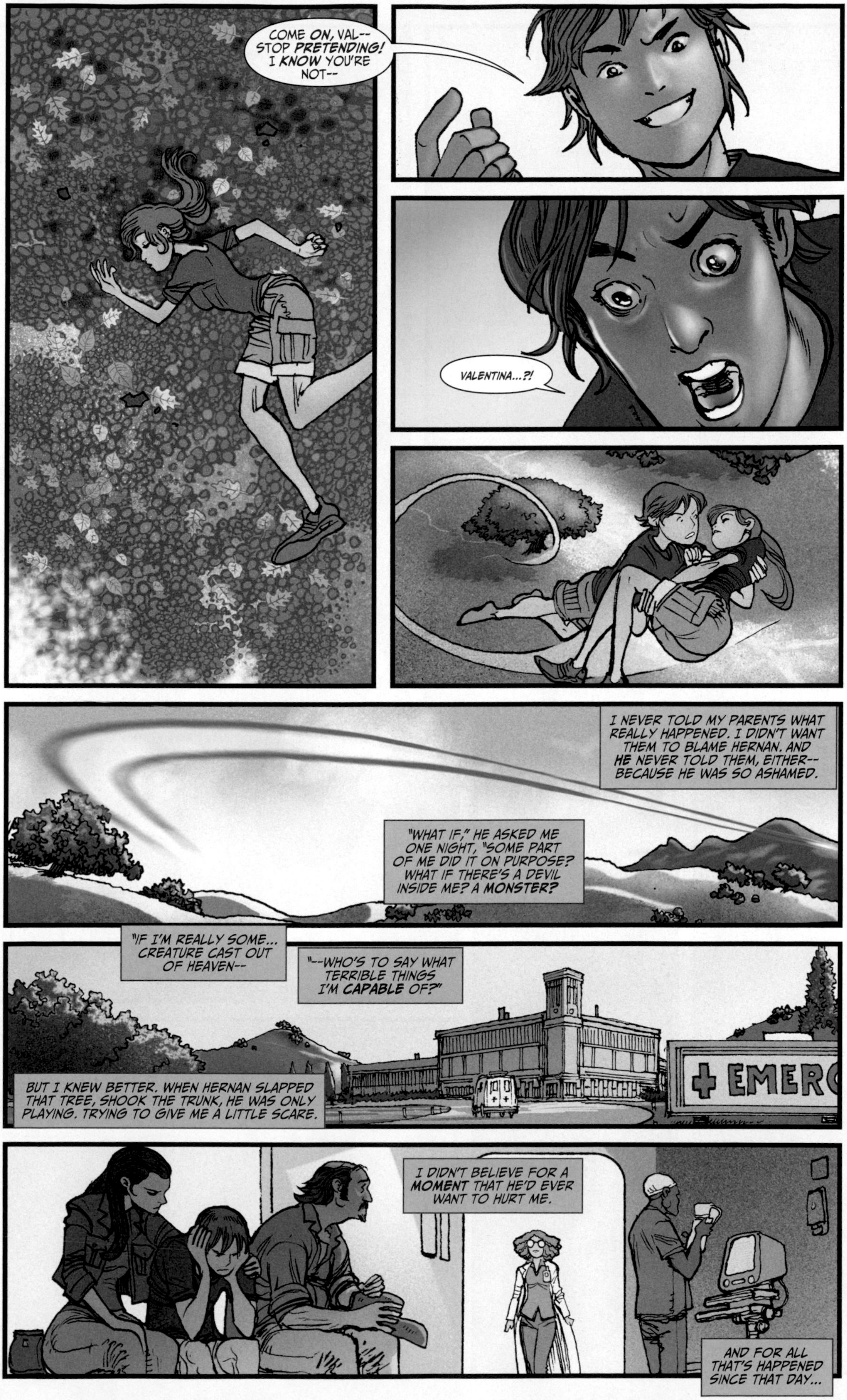
COME ON, VAL-- STOP PRETENDING! I KNOW YOU'RE NOT--
VALENTINA...?!
I NEVER TOLD MY PARENTS WHAT REALLY HAPPENED. I DIDN'T WANT THEM TO BLAME HERNAN. AND HE NEVER TOLD THEM, EITHER-- BECAUSE HE WAS SO ASHAMED.
"WHAT IF," HE ASKED ME ONE NIGHT, "SOME PART OF ME DID IT ON PURPOSE? WHAT IF THERE'S A DEVIL INSIDE ME? A MONSTER?
"IF I'M REALLY SOME... CREATURE CAST OUT OF HEAVEN--
"--WHO'S TO SAY WHAT TERRIBLE THINGS I'M CAPABLE OF?"
EMERG
BUT I KNEW BETTER. WHEN HERNAN SLAPPED THAT TREE, SHOOK THE TRUNK, HE WAS ONLY PLAYING. TRYING TO GIVE ME A LITTLE SCARE.
I DIDN'T BELIEVE FOR A MOMENT THAT HE'D EVER WANT TO HURT ME.
AND FOR ALL THAT'S HAPPENED SINCE THAT DAY...

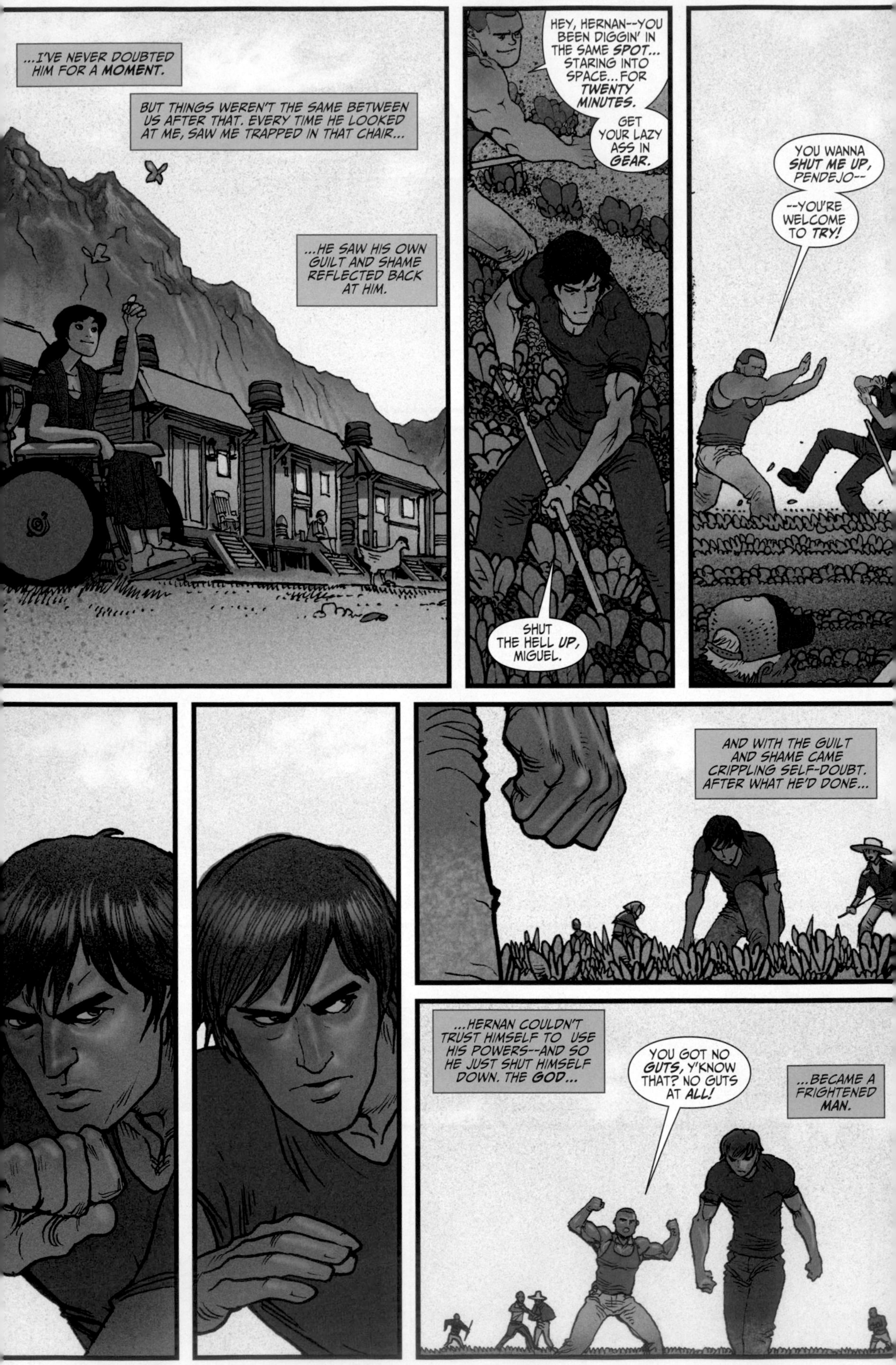
...I'VE NEVER DOUBTED HIM FOR A MOMENT.
BUT THINGS WEREN'T THE SAME BETWEEN US AFTER THAT. EVERY TIME HE LOOKED AT ME, SAW ME TRAPPED IN THAT CHAIR...
...HE SAW HIS OWN GUILT AND SHAME REFLECTED BACK AT HIM.
HEY, HERNAN--YOU BEEN DIGGIN' IN THE SAME SPOT... STARING INTO SPACE...FOR TWENTY MINUTES.
GET YOUR LAZY ASS IN GEAR.
SHUT THE HELL UP, MIGUEL.
YOU WANNA SHUT ME UP, PENDEJO--
--YOU'RE WELCOME TO TRY!
AND WITH THE GUILT AND SHAME CAME CRIPPLING SELF-DOUBT. AFTER WHAT HE'D DONE...
...HERNAN COULDN'T TRUST HIMSELF TO USE HIS POWERS--AND SO HE JUST SHUT HIMSELF DOWN. THE GOD...
YOU GOT NO GUTS, Y'KNOW THAT? NO GUTS AT ALL!
...BECAME A FRIGHTENED MAN.

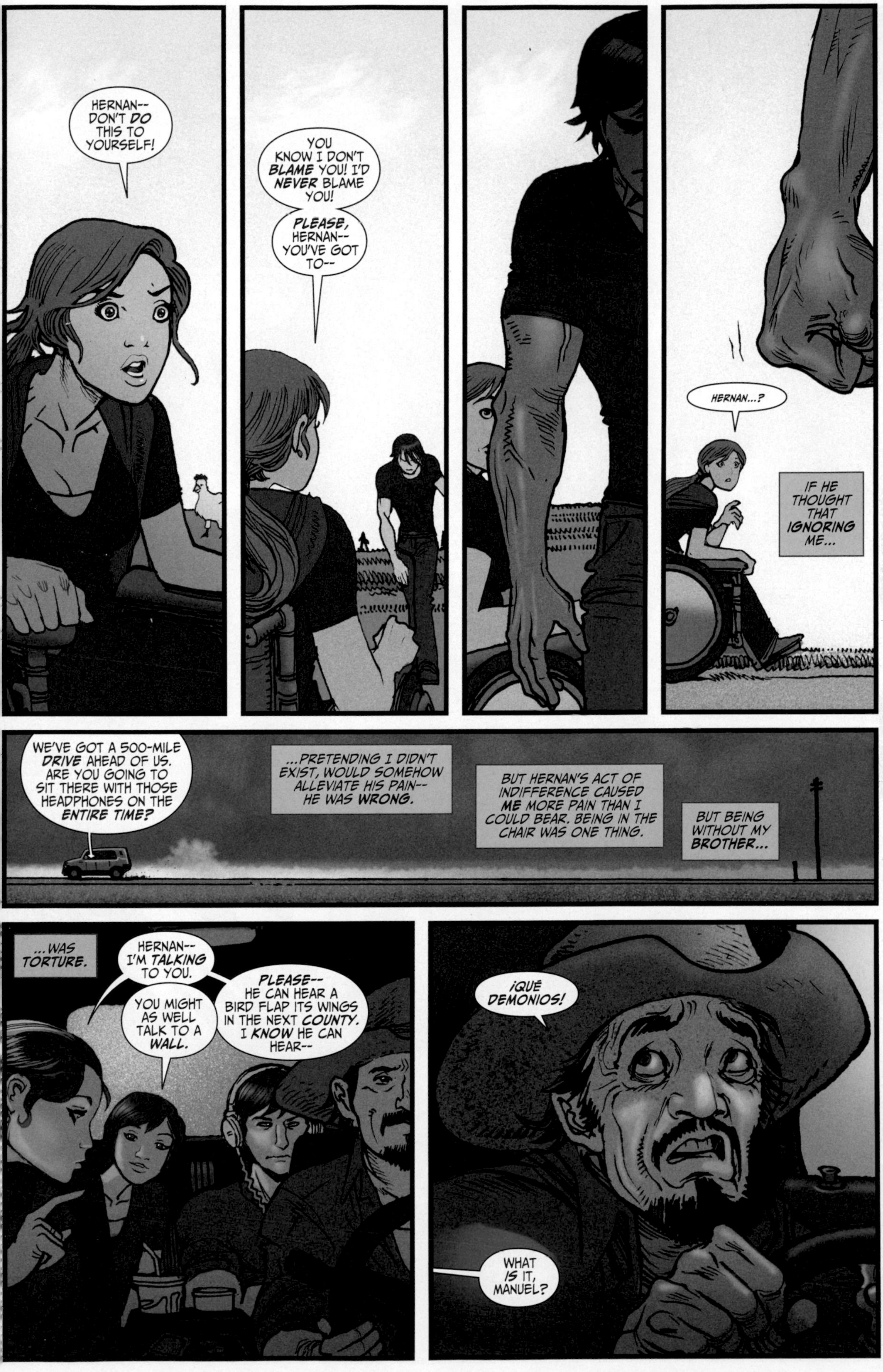
HERNAN-- DON'T DO THIS TO YOURSELF!
YOU KNOW I DON'T BLAME YOU! I'D NEVER BLAME YOU!
PLEASE, HERNAN-- YOU'VE GOT TO--
HERNAN...?
IF HE THOUGHT THAT IGNORING ME...
WE'VE GOT A 500-MILE DRIVE AHEAD OF US. ARE YOU GOING TO SIT THERE WITH THOSE HEADPHONES ON THE ENTIRE TIME?
...PRETENDING I DIDN'T EXIST, WOULD SOMEHOW ALLEVIATE HIS PAIN-- HE WAS WRONG.
BUT HERNAN'S ACT OF INDIFFERENCE CAUSED ME MORE PAIN THAN I COULD BEAR. BEING IN THE CHAIR WAS ONE THING.
BUT BEING WITHOUT MY BROTHER...
...WAS TORTURE.
HERNAN-- I'M TALKING TO YOU.
YOU MIGHT AS WELL TALK TO A WALL.
PLEASE-- HE CAN HEAR A BIRD FLAP ITS WINGS IN THE NEXT COUNTY. I KNOW HE CAN HEAR--
¡QUÉ DEMONIOS!
WHAT IS IT, MANUEL?

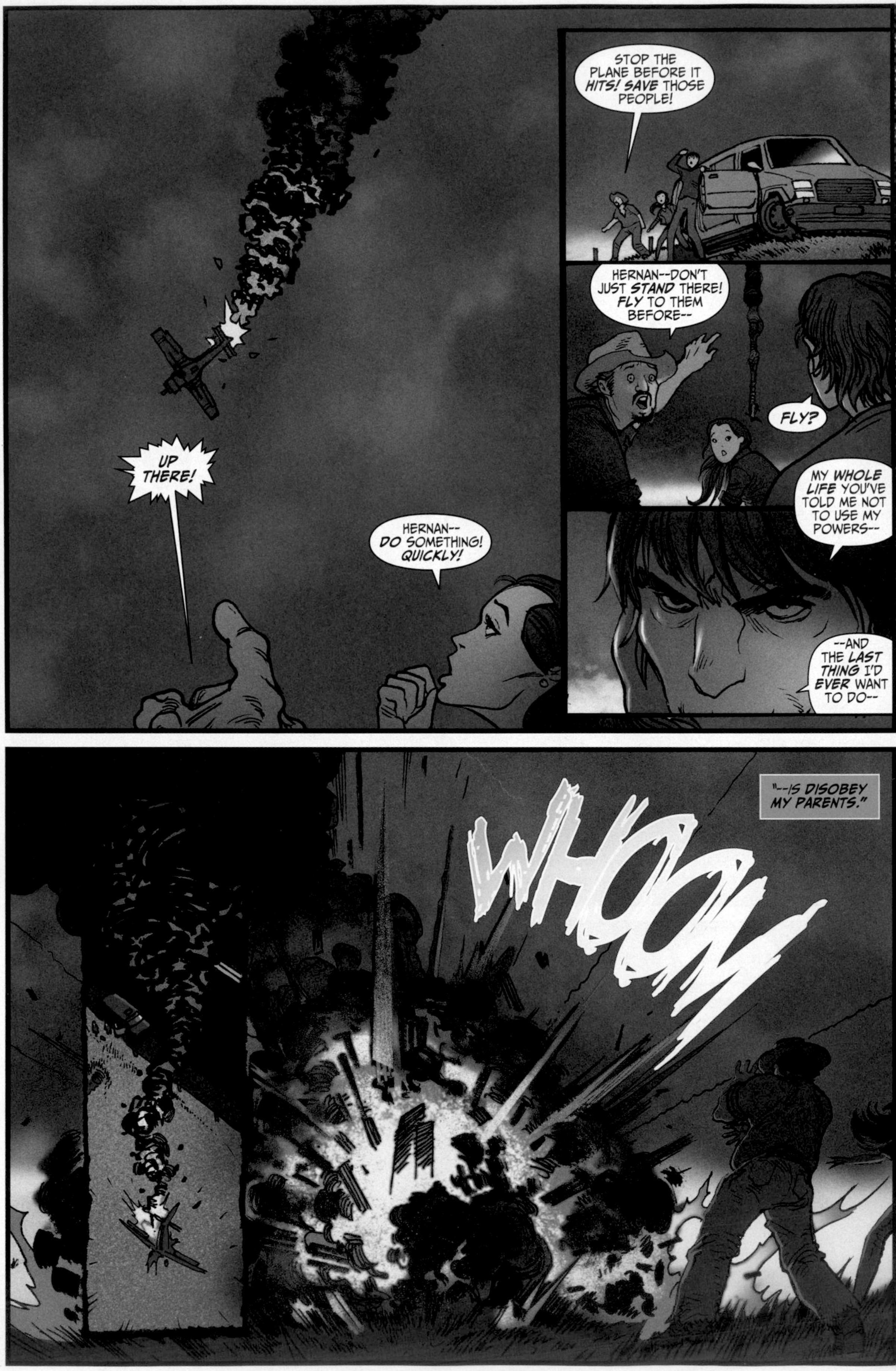
STOP THE PLANE BEFORE IT HITS! SAVE THOSE PEOPLE!
UP THERE!
HERNAN-- DO SOMETHING! QUICKLY!
HERNAN--DON'T JUST STAND THERE! FLY TO THEM BEFORE--
FLY?
MY WHOLE LIFE YOU'VE TOLD ME NOT TO USE MY POWERS--
--AND THE LAST THING I'D EVER WANT TO DO--
"--IS DISOBEY MY PARENTS."
WHOOM

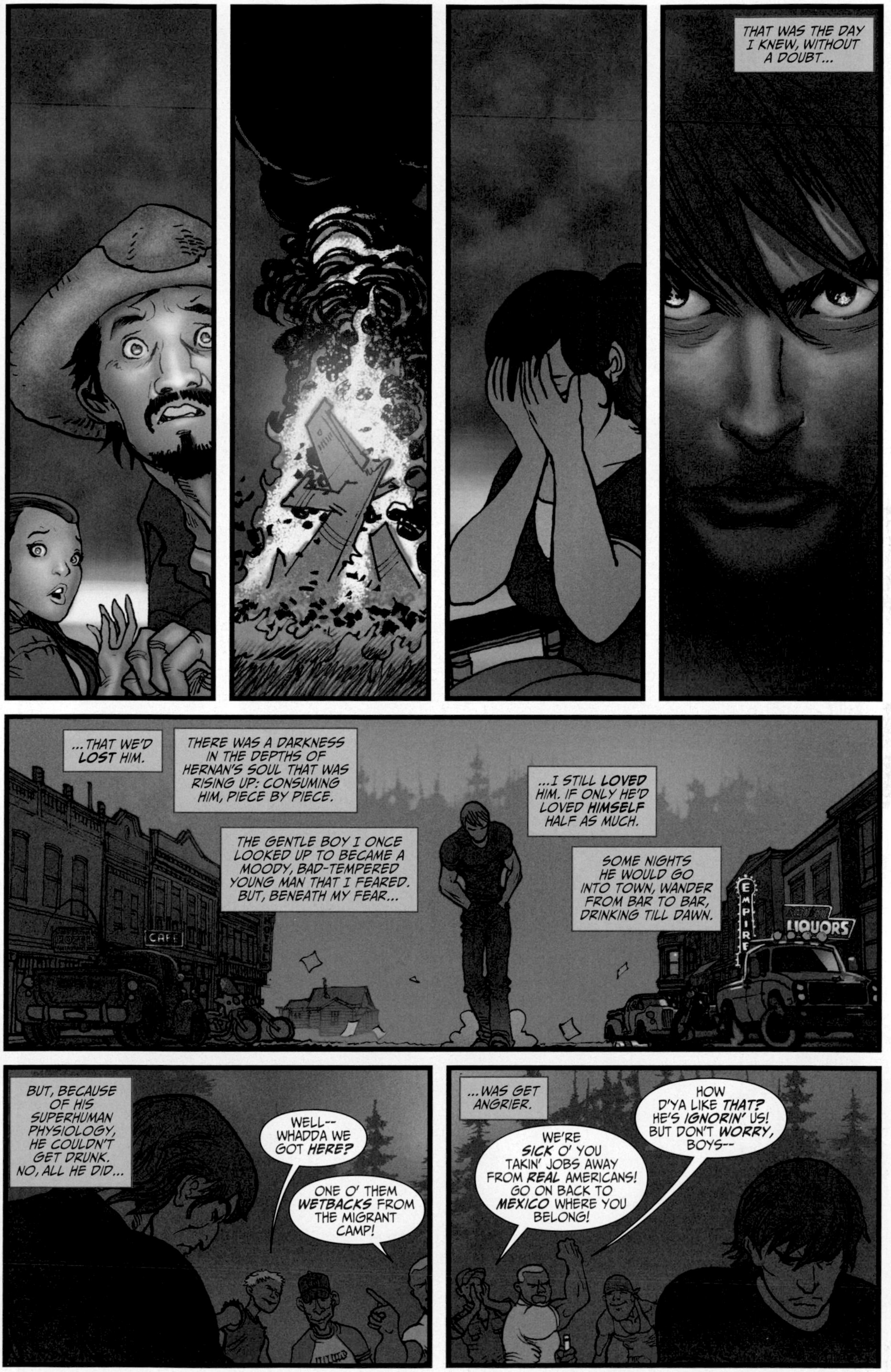

THAT WAS THE DAY I KNEW, WITHOUT A DOUBT...
...THAT WE'D LOST HIM.
THERE WAS A DARKNESS IN THE DEPTHS OF HERNAN'S SOUL THAT WAS RISING UP: CONSUMING HIM, PIECE BY PIECE.
THE GENTLE BOY I ONCE LOOKED UP TO BECAME A MOODY, BAD-TEMPERED YOUNG MAN THAT I FEARED. BUT, BENEATH MY FEAR...
...I STILL LOVED HIM. IF ONLY HE'D LOVED HIMSELF HALF AS MUCH.
SOME NIGHTS HE WOULD GO INTO TOWN, WANDER FROM BAR TO BAR, DRINKING TILL DAWN.
CAFE
EMPIRE
LIQUORS
BUT, BECAUSE OF HIS SUPERHUMAN PHYSIOLOGY, HE COULDN'T GET DRUNK. NO, ALL HE DID...
WELL-- WHADDA WE GOT HERE?
ONE O' THEM WETBACKS FROM THE MIGRANT CAMP!
...WAS GET ANGRIER.
WE'RE SICK O' YOU TAKIN' JOBS AWAY FROM REAL AMERICANS! GO ON BACK TO MEXICO WHERE YOU BELONG!
HOW D'YA LIKE THAT? HE'S IGNORIN' US! BUT DON'T WORRY, BOYS--

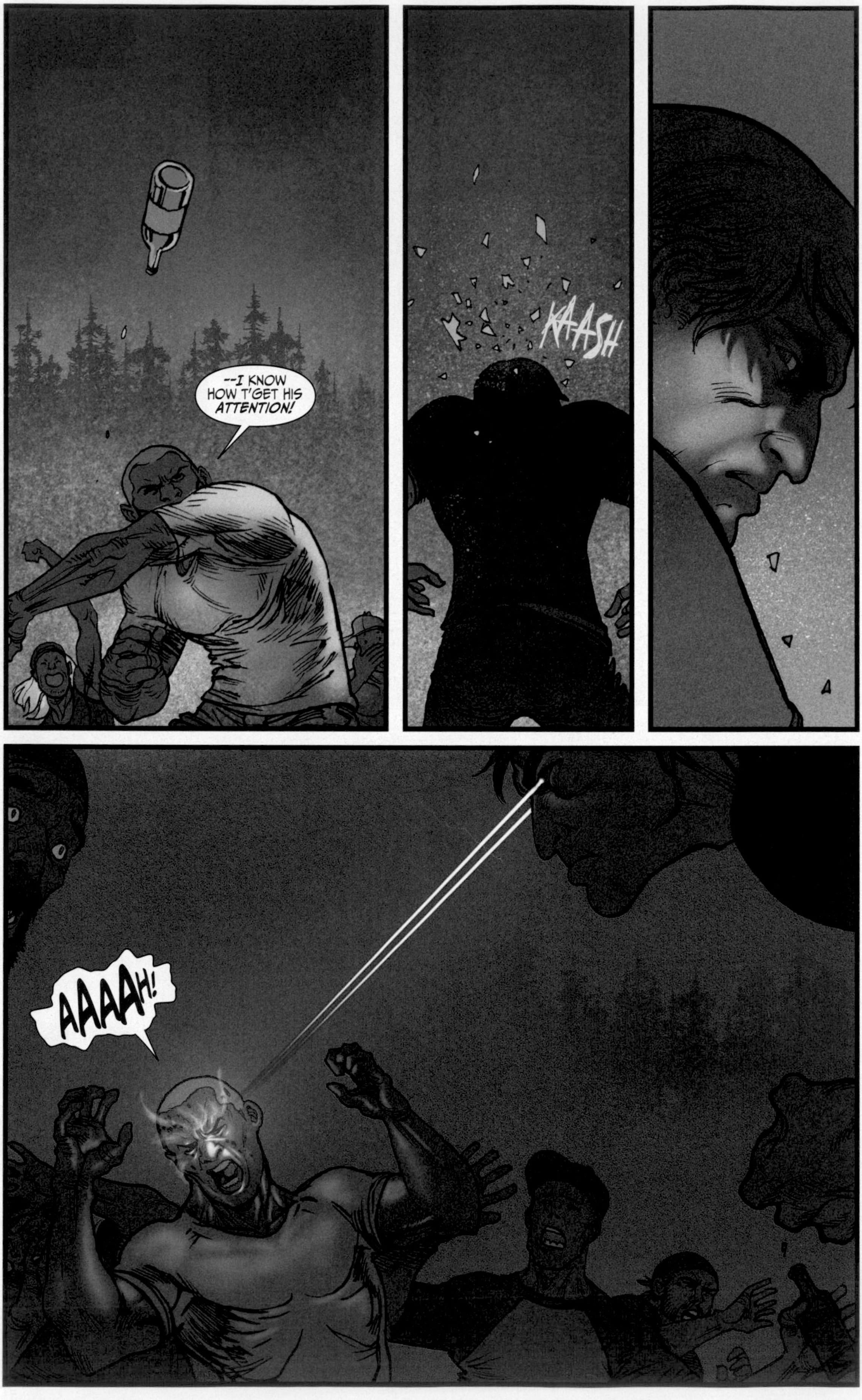
--I KNOW HOW T'GET HIS ATTENTION!
KAASH
AAAAH!

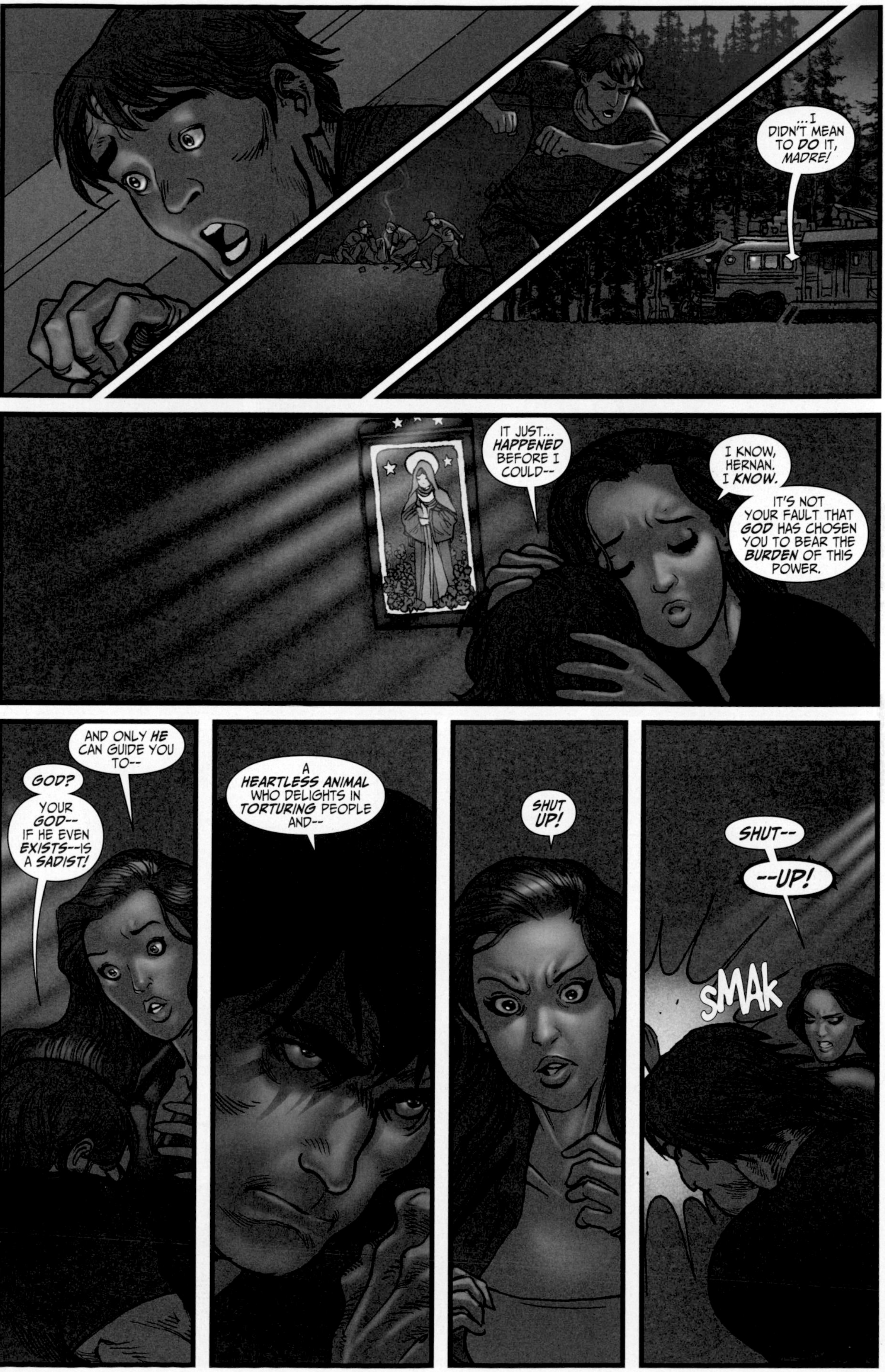

...I DIDN'T MEAN TO DO IT, MADRE!
IT JUST... HAPPENED BEFORE I COULD--
I KNOW, HERNAN. I KNOW.
IT'S NOT YOUR FAULT THAT GOD HAS CHOSEN YOU TO BEAR THE BURDEN OF THIS POWER.
AND ONLY HE CAN GUIDE YOU TO--
GOD?
YOUR GOD-- IF HE EVEN EXISTS--IS A SADIST!
A HEARTLESS ANIMAL WHO DELIGHTS IN TORTURING PEOPLE AND--
SHUT UP!
SHUT--
--UP!
SMAK

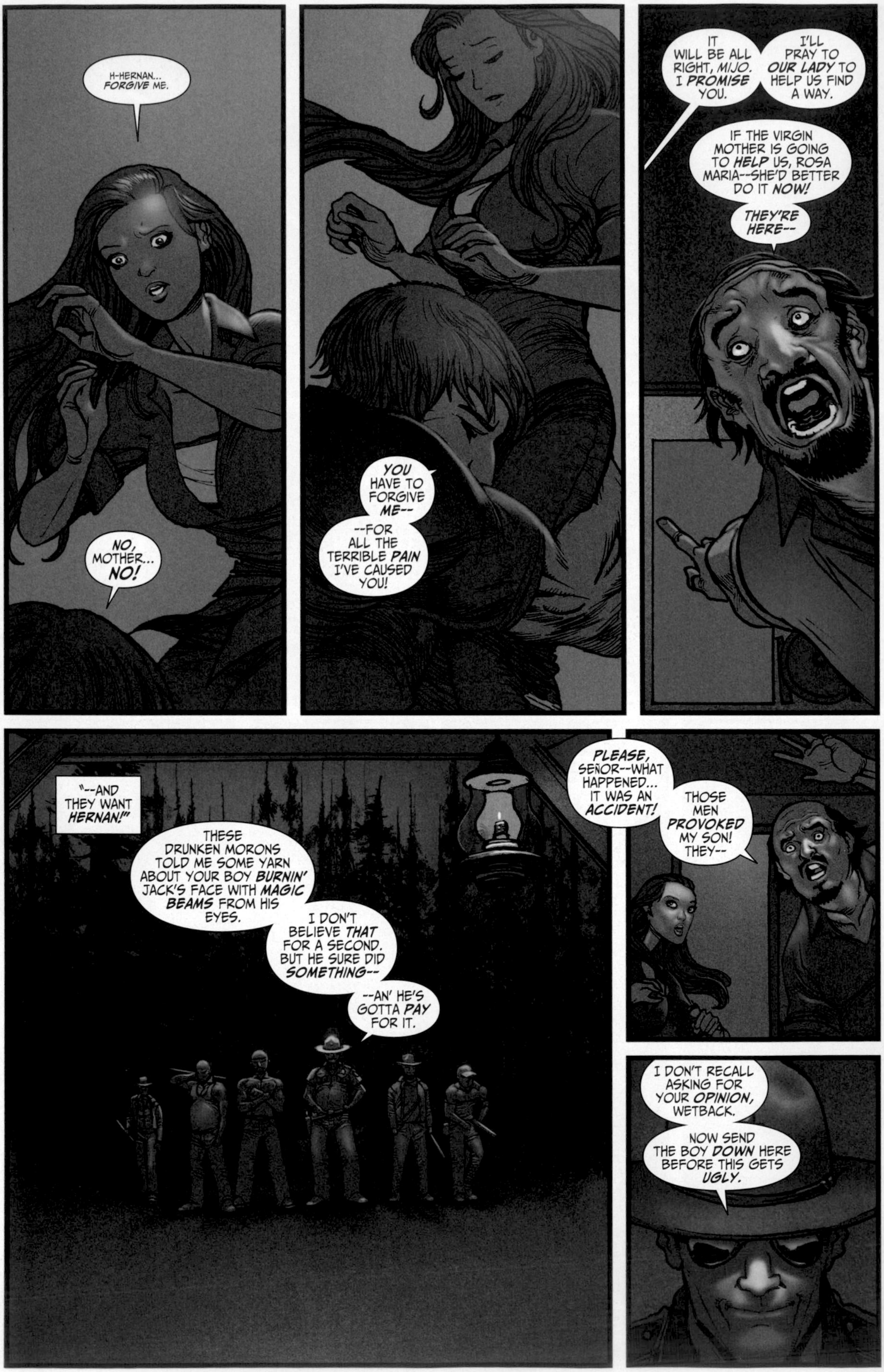
H-HERNAN... FORGIVE ME.
NO, MOTHER... NO!
YOU HAVE TO FORGIVE ME--
--FOR ALL THE TERRIBLE PAIN I'VE CAUSED YOU!
IT WILL BE ALL RIGHT, MIJO. I PROMISE YOU.
I'LL PRAY TO OUR LADY TO HELP US FIND A WAY.
IF THE VIRGIN MOTHER IS GOING TO HELP US, ROSA MARIA--SHE'D BETTER DO IT NOW!
THEY'RE HERE--
"--AND THEY WANT HERNAN!"
THESE DRUNKEN MORONS TOLD ME SOME YARN ABOUT YOUR BOY BURNIN' JACK'S FACE WITH MAGIC BEAMS FROM HIS EYES.
I DON'T BELIEVE THAT FOR A SECOND. BUT HE SURE DID SOMETHING--
--AN' HE'S GOTTA PAY FOR IT.
PLEASE, SEÑOR--WHAT HAPPENED... IT WAS AN ACCIDENT!
THOSE MEN PROVOKED MY SON! THEY--
I DON'T RECALL ASKING FOR YOUR OPINION, WETBACK.
NOW SEND THE BOY DOWN HERE BEFORE THIS GETS UGLY.

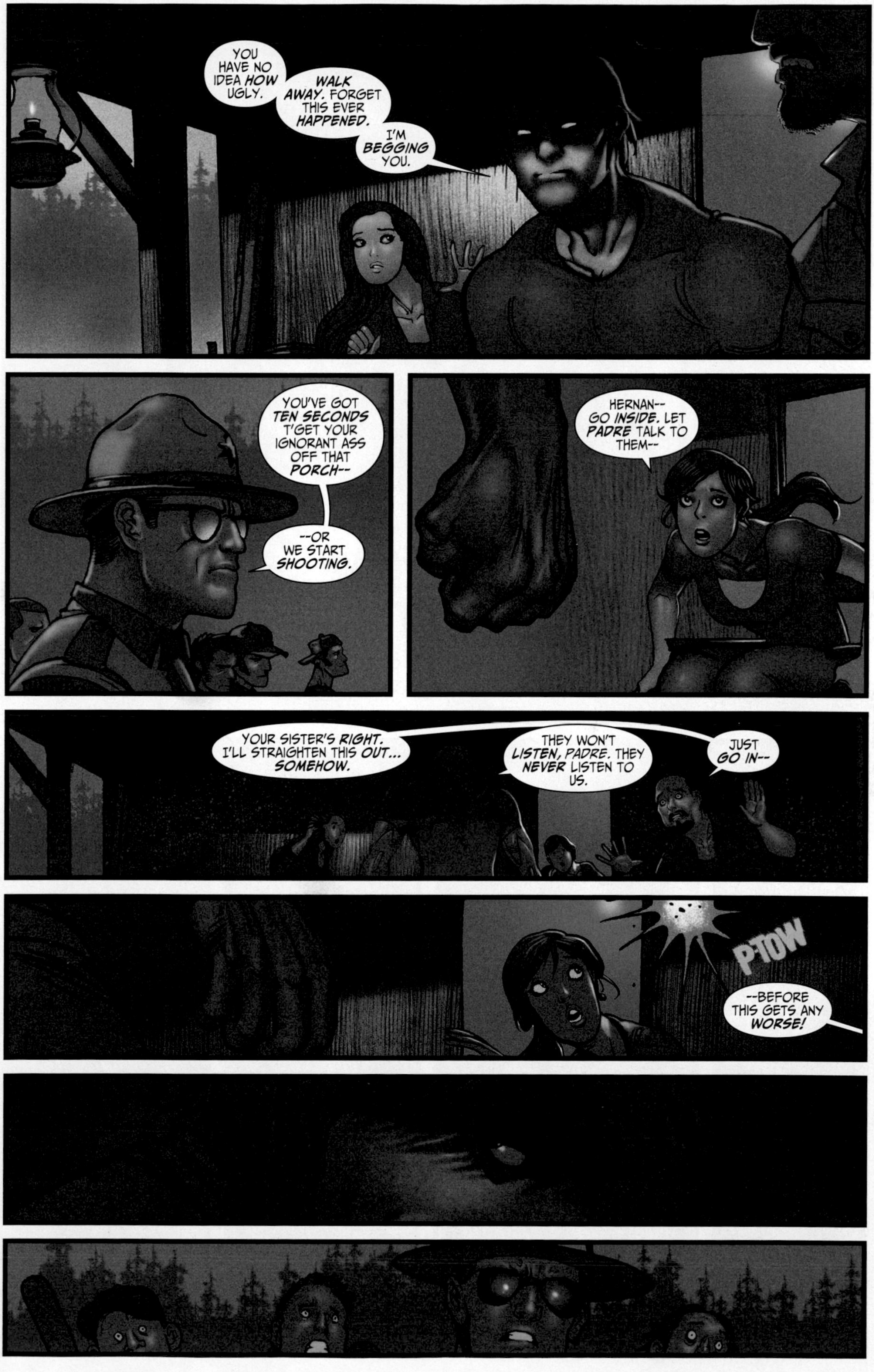

YOU HAVE NO IDEA HOW UGLY.
WALK AWAY. FORGET THIS EVER HAPPENED.
I'M BEGGING YOU.
YOU'VE GOT TEN SECONDS T'GET YOUR IGNORANT ASS OFF THAT PORCH--
--OR WE START SHOOTING.
HERNAN-- GO INSIDE. LET PADRE TALK TO THEM--
YOUR SISTER'S RIGHT. I'LL STRAIGHTEN THIS OUT... SOMEHOW.
THEY WON'T LISTEN, PADRE. THEY NEVER LISTEN TO US.
JUST GO IN--
P-TOW
--BEFORE THIS GETS ANY WORSE!

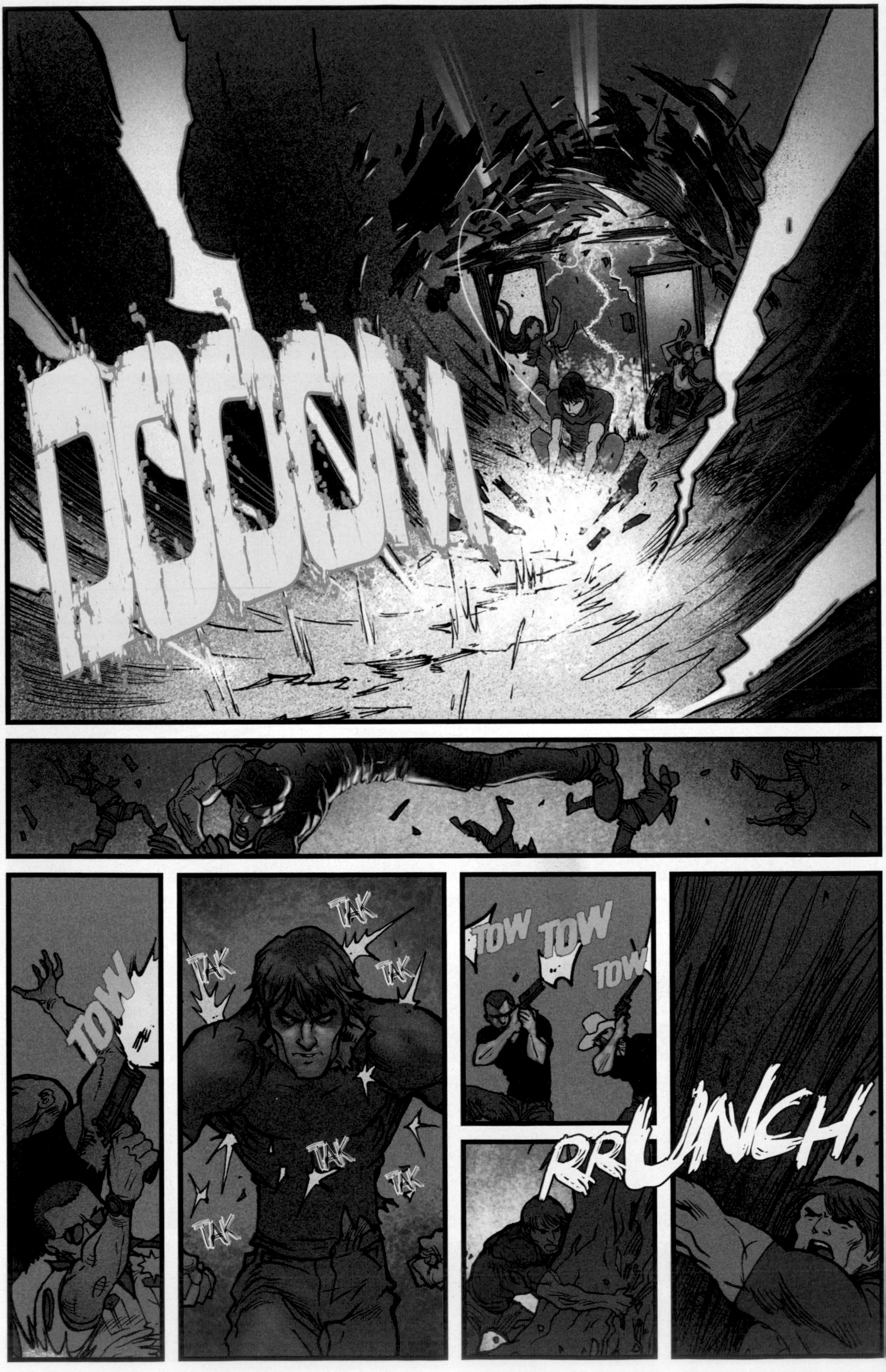
DOOOM
TOW
TAK
TAK
TAK
TAK
TAK
TAK
TOW
TOW
TOW
RRUNCH

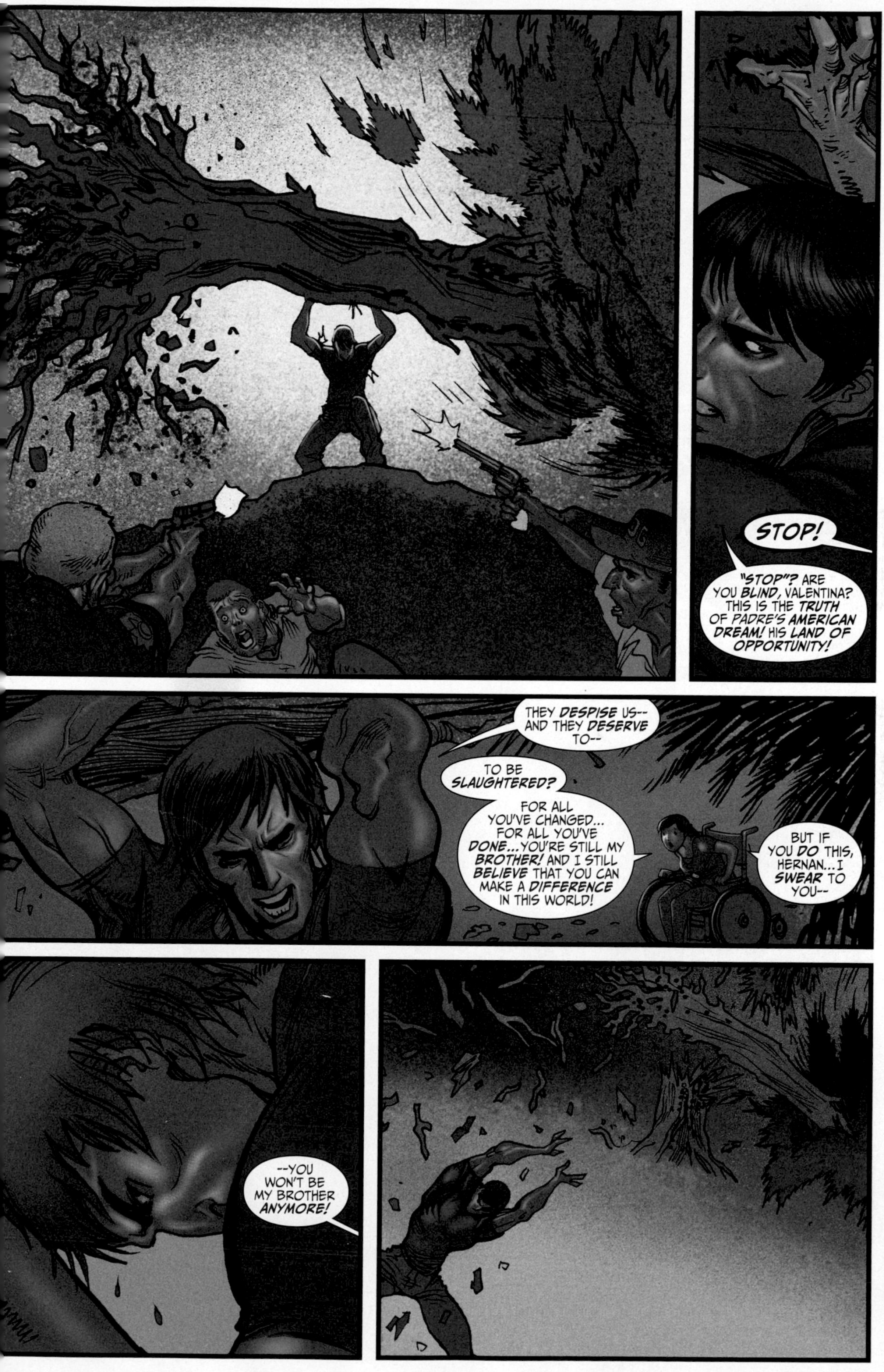
STOP!
"STOP"? ARE YOU BLIND, VALENTINA? THIS IS THE TRUTH OF PADRE'S AMERICAN DREAM! HIS LAND OF OPPORTUNITY!
THEY DESPISE US-- AND THEY DESERVE TO--
TO BE SLAUGHTERED?
FOR ALL YOU'VE CHANGED... FOR ALL YOU'VE DONE...YOU'RE STILL MY BROTHER! AND I STILL BELIEVE THAT YOU CAN MAKE A DIFFERENCE IN THIS WORLD!
BUT IF YOU DO THIS, HERNAN...I SWEAR TO YOU--
--YOU WON'T BE MY BROTHER ANYMORE!

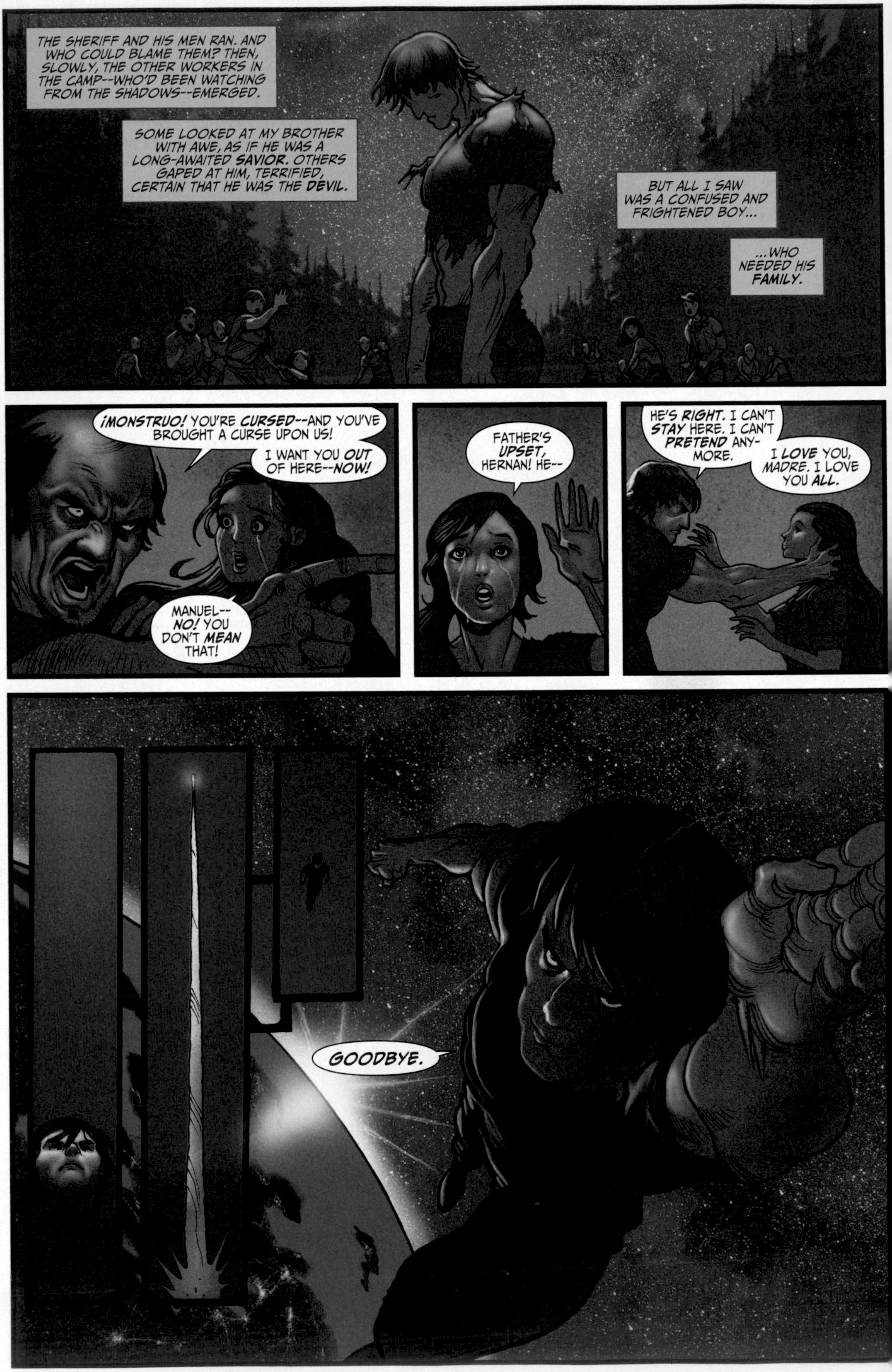
THE SHERIFF AND HIS MEN RAN. AND WHO COULD BLAME THEM? THEN, SLOWLY, THE OTHER WORKERS IN THE CAMP--WHO'D BEEN WATCHING FROM THE SHADOWS--EMERGED.
SOME LOOKED AT MY BROTHER WITH AWE, AS IF HE WAS A LONG-AWAITED SAVIOR. OTHERS GAPED AT HIM, TERRIFIED, CERTAIN THAT HE WAS THE DEVIL.
BUT ALL I SAW WAS A CONFUSED AND FRIGHTENED BOY...
...WHO NEEDED HIS FAMILY.
¡MONSTRUO! YOU'RE CURSED--AND YOU'VE BROUGHT A CURSE UPON US!
I WANT YOU OUT OF HERE--NOW!
MANUEL--NO! YOU DON'T MEAN THAT!
FATHER'S UPSET, HERNAN! HE--
HE'S RIGHT. I CAN'T STAY HERE. I CAN'T PRETEND ANYMORE.
I LOVE YOU, MADRE. I LOVE YOU ALL.
GOODBYE.

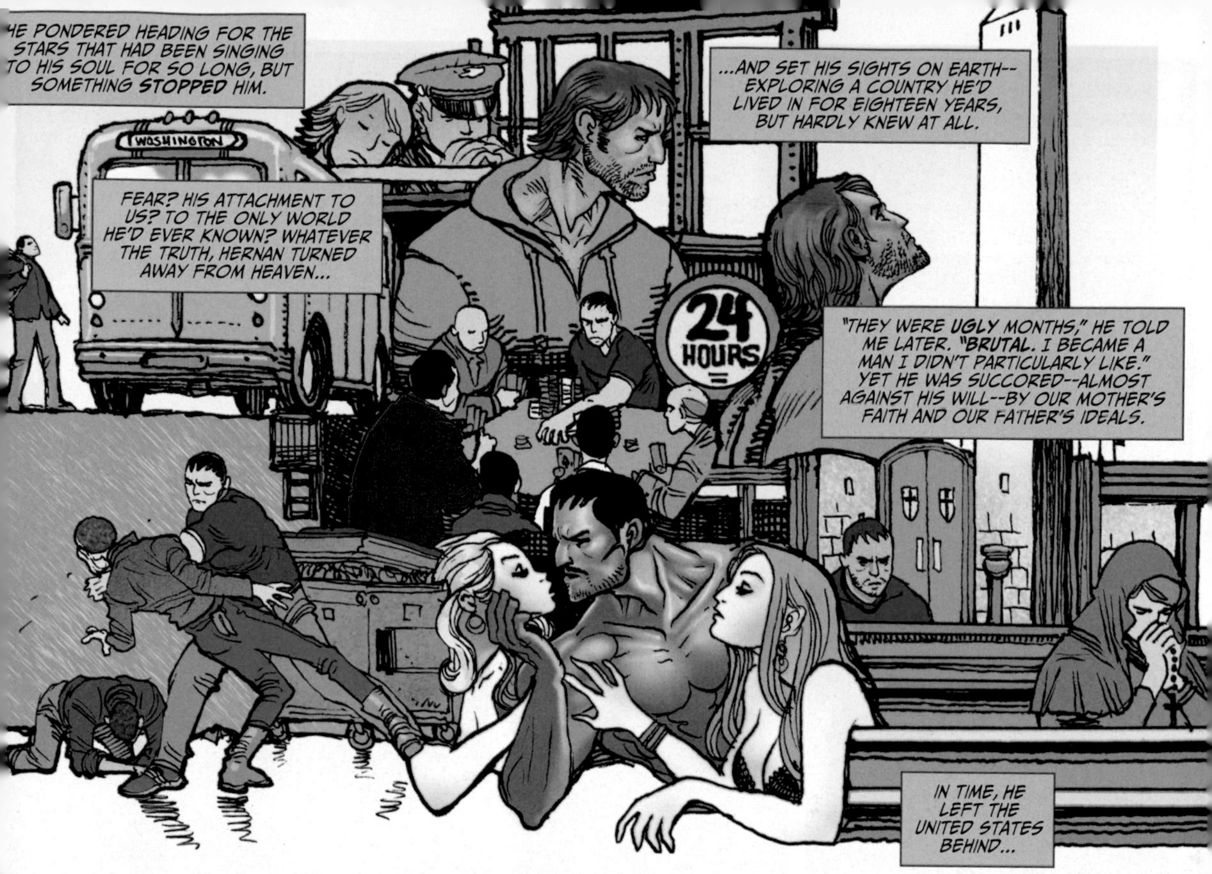
HE PONDERED HEADING FOR THE STARS THAT HAD BEEN SINGING TO HIS SOUL FOR SO LONG, BUT SOMETHING STOPPED HIM.
...AND SET HIS SIGHTS ON EARTH--EXPLORING A COUNTRY HE'D LIVED IN FOR EIGHTEEN YEARS, BUT HARDLY KNEW AT ALL.
FEAR? HIS ATTACHMENT TO US? TO THE ONLY WORLD HE'D EVER KNOWN? WHATEVER THE TRUTH, HERNAN TURNED AWAY FROM HEAVEN...
WASHINGTON
24 HOURS
"THEY WERE UGLY MONTHS," HE TOLD ME LATER. "BRUTAL. I BECAME A MAN I DIDN'T PARTICULARLY LIKE." YET HE WAS SUCCORED--ALMOST AGAINST HIS WILL--BY OUR MOTHER'S FAITH AND OUR FATHER'S IDEALS.
IN TIME, HE LEFT THE UNITED STATES BEHIND...

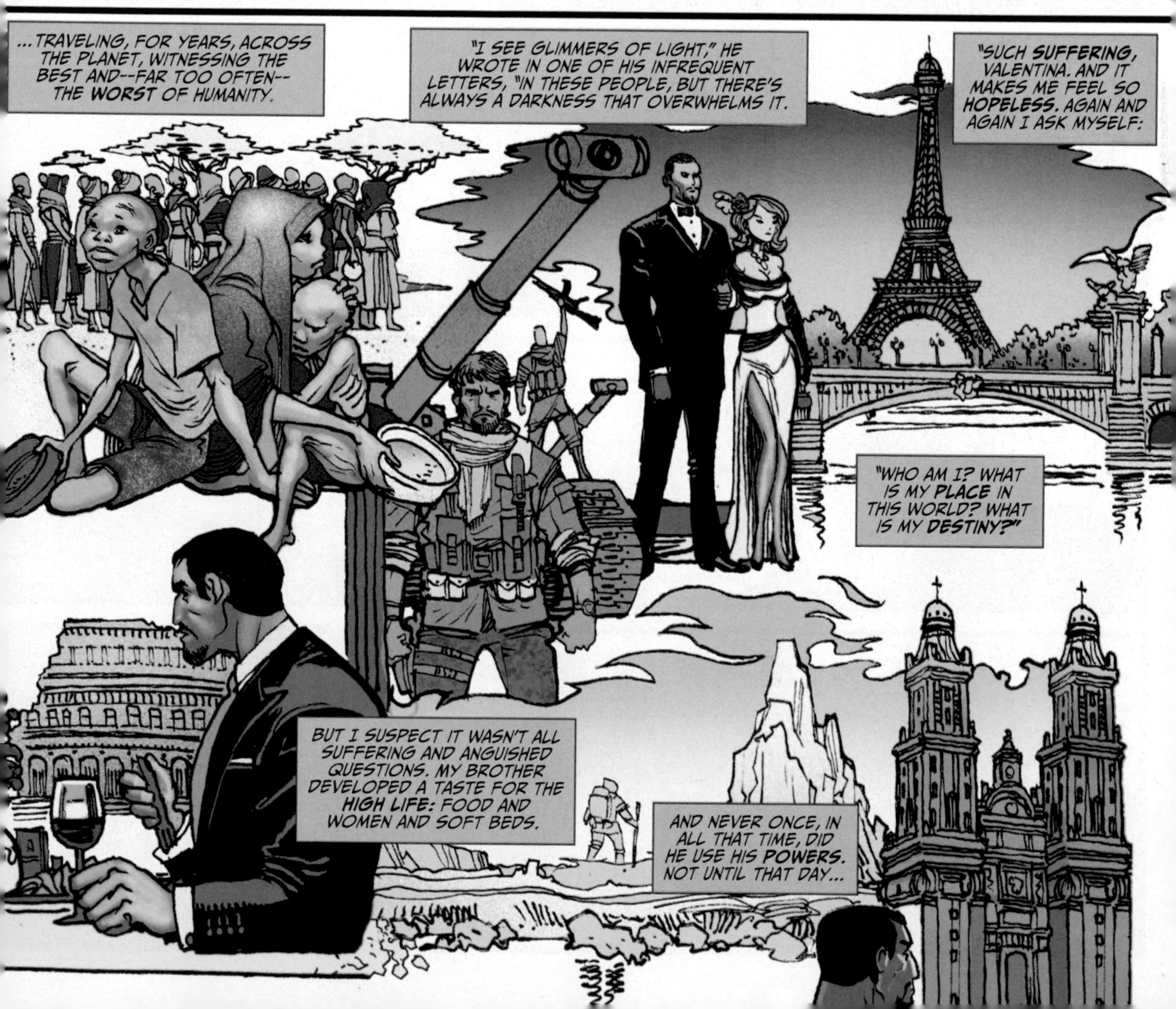
...TRAVELING, FOR YEARS, ACROSS THE PLANET, WITNESSING THE BEST AND--FAR TOO OFTEN--THE WORST OF HUMANITY.
"I SEE GLIMMERS OF LIGHT," HE WROTE IN ONE OF HIS INFREQUENT LETTERS, "IN THESE PEOPLE, BUT THERE'S ALWAYS A DARKNESS THAT OVERWHELMS IT.
"SUCH SUFFERING, VALENTINA. AND IT MAKES ME FEEL SO HOPELESS. AGAIN AND AGAIN I ASK MYSELF:
"WHO AM I? WHAT IS MY PLACE IN THIS WORLD? WHAT IS MY DESTINY?"
BUT I SUSPECT IT WASN'T ALL SUFFERING AND ANGUISHED QUESTIONS. MY BROTHER DEVELOPED A TASTE FOR THE HIGH LIFE: FOOD AND WOMEN AND SOFT BEDS.
AND NEVER ONCE, IN ALL THAT TIME, DID HE USE HIS POWERS. NOT UNTIL THAT DAY...

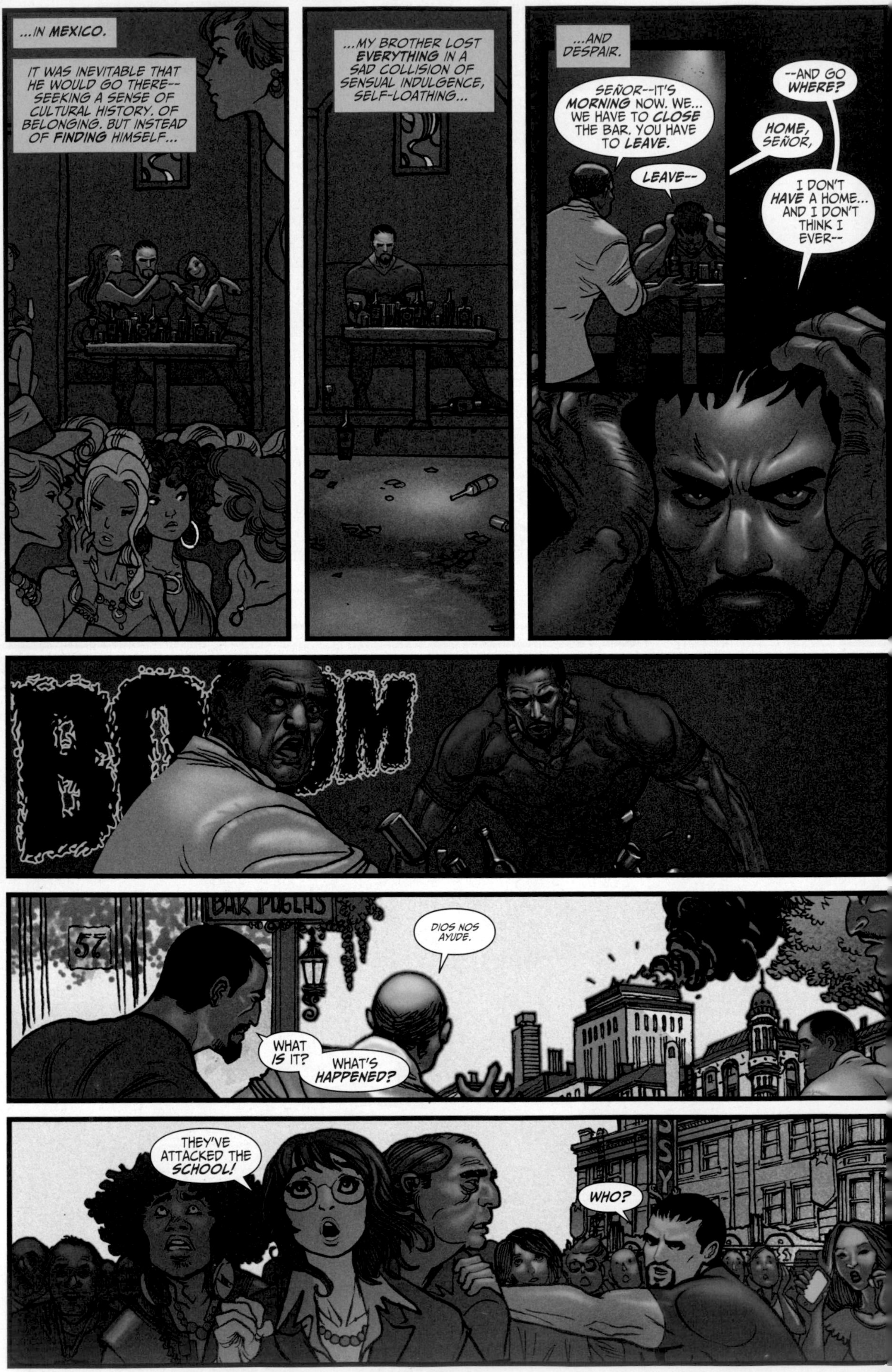
...IN MEXICO.
IT WAS INEVITABLE THAT HE WOULD GO THERE-- SEEKING A SENSE OF CULTURAL HISTORY. OF BELONGING. BUT INSTEAD OF FINDING HIMSELF...
...MY BROTHER LOST EVERYTHING IN A SAD COLLISION OF SENSUAL INDULGENCE, SELF-LOATHING...
...AND DESPAIR.
SEÑOR--IT'S MORNING NOW. WE... WE HAVE TO CLOSE THE BAR. YOU HAVE TO LEAVE.
LEAVE--
--AND GO WHERE?
HOME, SEÑOR,
I DON'T HAVE A HOME... AND I DON'T THINK I EVER--
BOOM
BAR PUGLAS
57
DIOS NOS AYUDE.
WHAT IS IT?
WHAT'S HAPPENED?
THEY'VE ATTACKED THE SCHOOL!
WHO?

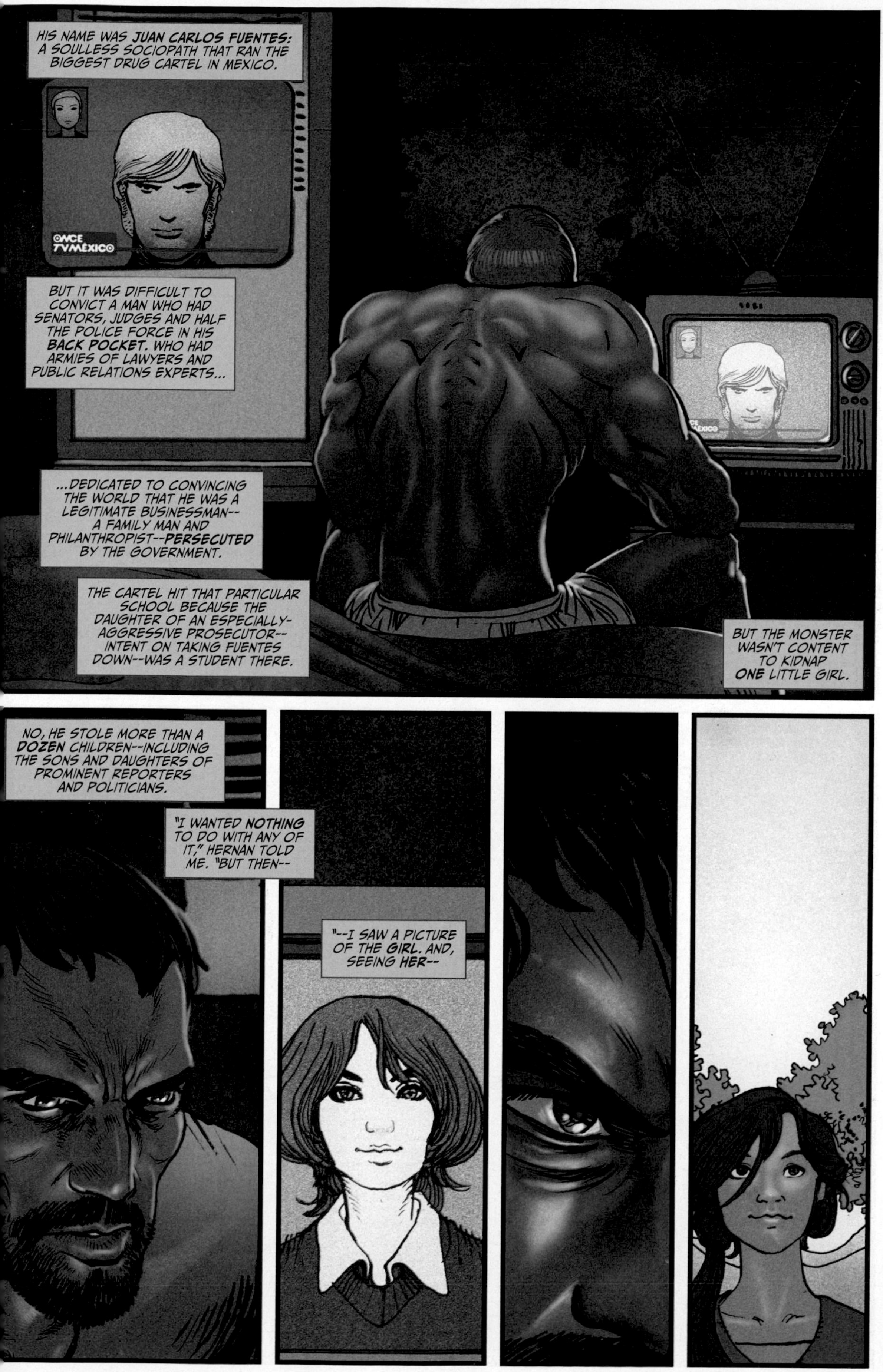
HIS NAME WAS **JUAN CARLOS FUENTES:** A SOULLESS SOCIOPATH THAT RAN THE BIGGEST DRUG CARTEL IN MEXICO.
ONCE TV MÉXICO
BUT IT WAS DIFFICULT TO CONVICT A MAN WHO HAD SENATORS, JUDGES AND HALF THE POLICE FORCE IN HIS **BACK POCKET.** WHO HAD ARMIES OF LAWYERS AND PUBLIC RELATIONS EXPERTS...
...DEDICATED TO CONVINCING THE WORLD THAT HE WAS A LEGITIMATE BUSINESSMAN-- A FAMILY MAN AND PHILANTHROPIST--**PERSECUTED** BY THE GOVERNMENT.
THE CARTEL HIT THAT PARTICULAR SCHOOL BECAUSE THE DAUGHTER OF AN ESPECIALLY-AGGRESSIVE PROSECUTOR--INTENT ON TAKING FUENTES DOWN--WAS A STUDENT THERE.
BUT THE MONSTER WASN'T CONTENT TO KIDNAP **ONE** LITTLE GIRL.
NO, HE STOLE MORE THAN A **DOZEN** CHILDREN--INCLUDING THE SONS AND DAUGHTERS OF PROMINENT REPORTERS AND POLITICIANS.
"I WANTED **NOTHING** TO DO WITH ANY OF IT," HERNAN TOLD ME. "BUT THEN--
"--I SAW A PICTURE OF THE **GIRL.** AND, SEEING **HER**--

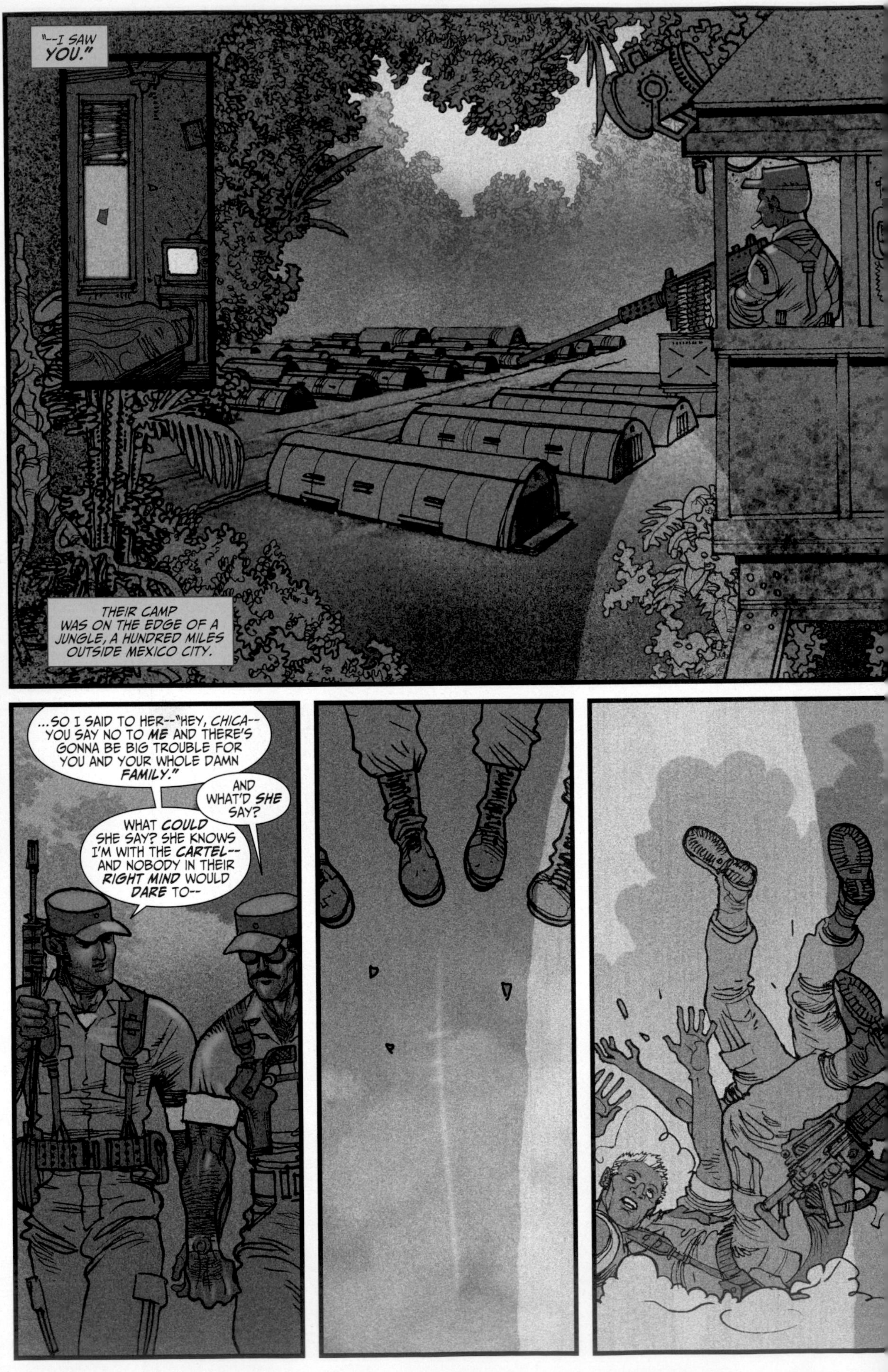
"--I SAW YOU."
THEIR CAMP WAS ON THE EDGE OF A JUNGLE, A HUNDRED MILES OUTSIDE MEXICO CITY.
...SO I SAID TO HER--"HEY, CHICA--YOU SAY NO TO ME AND THERE'S GONNA BE BIG TROUBLE FOR YOU AND YOUR WHOLE DAMN FAMILY."
AND WHAT'D SHE SAY?
WHAT COULD SHE SAY? SHE KNOWS I'M WITH THE CARTEL--AND NOBODY IN THEIR RIGHT MIND WOULD DARE TO--

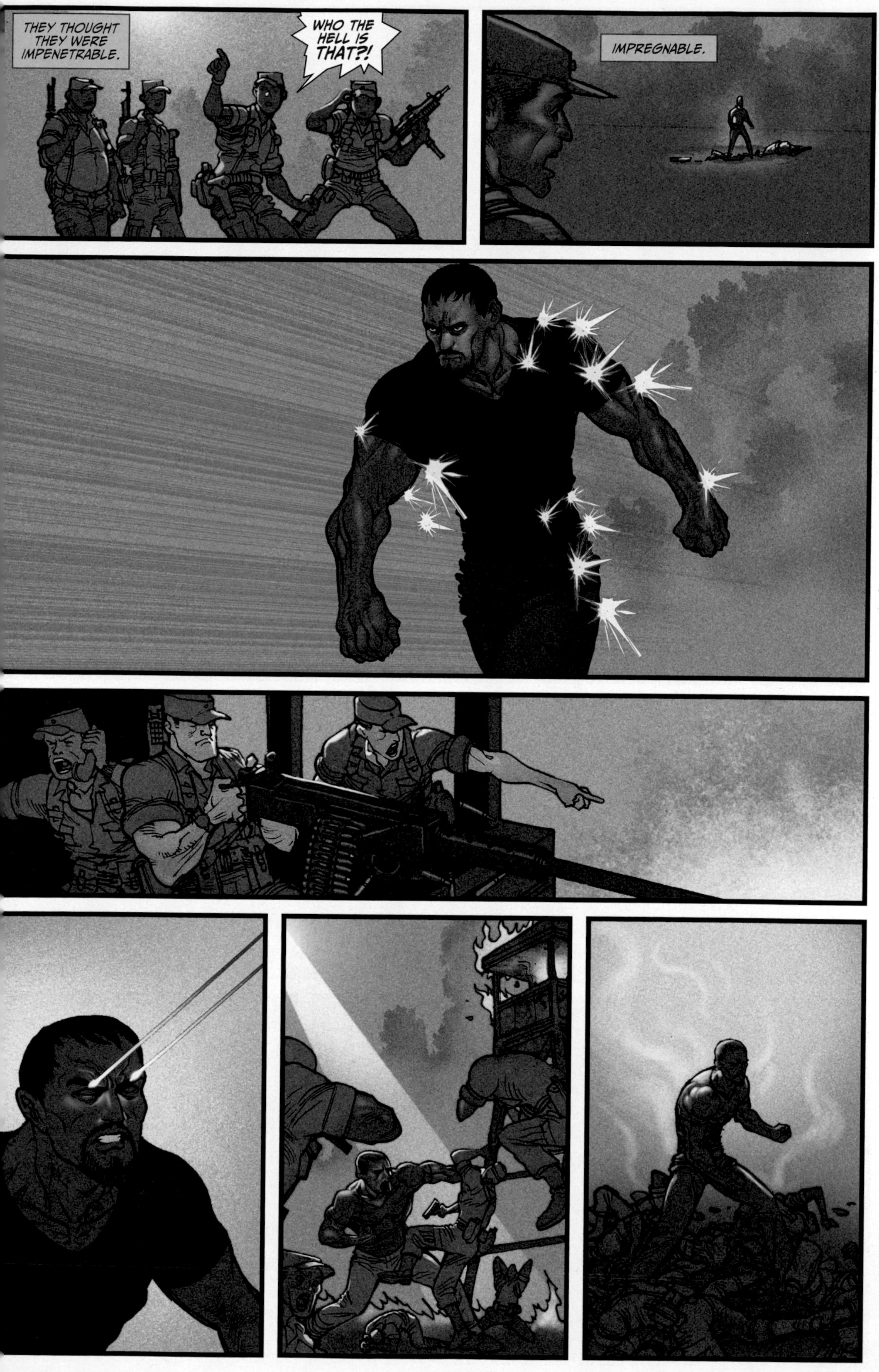
THEY THOUGHT THEY WERE IMPENETRABLE.
WHO THE HELL IS THAT?!
IMPREGNABLE.

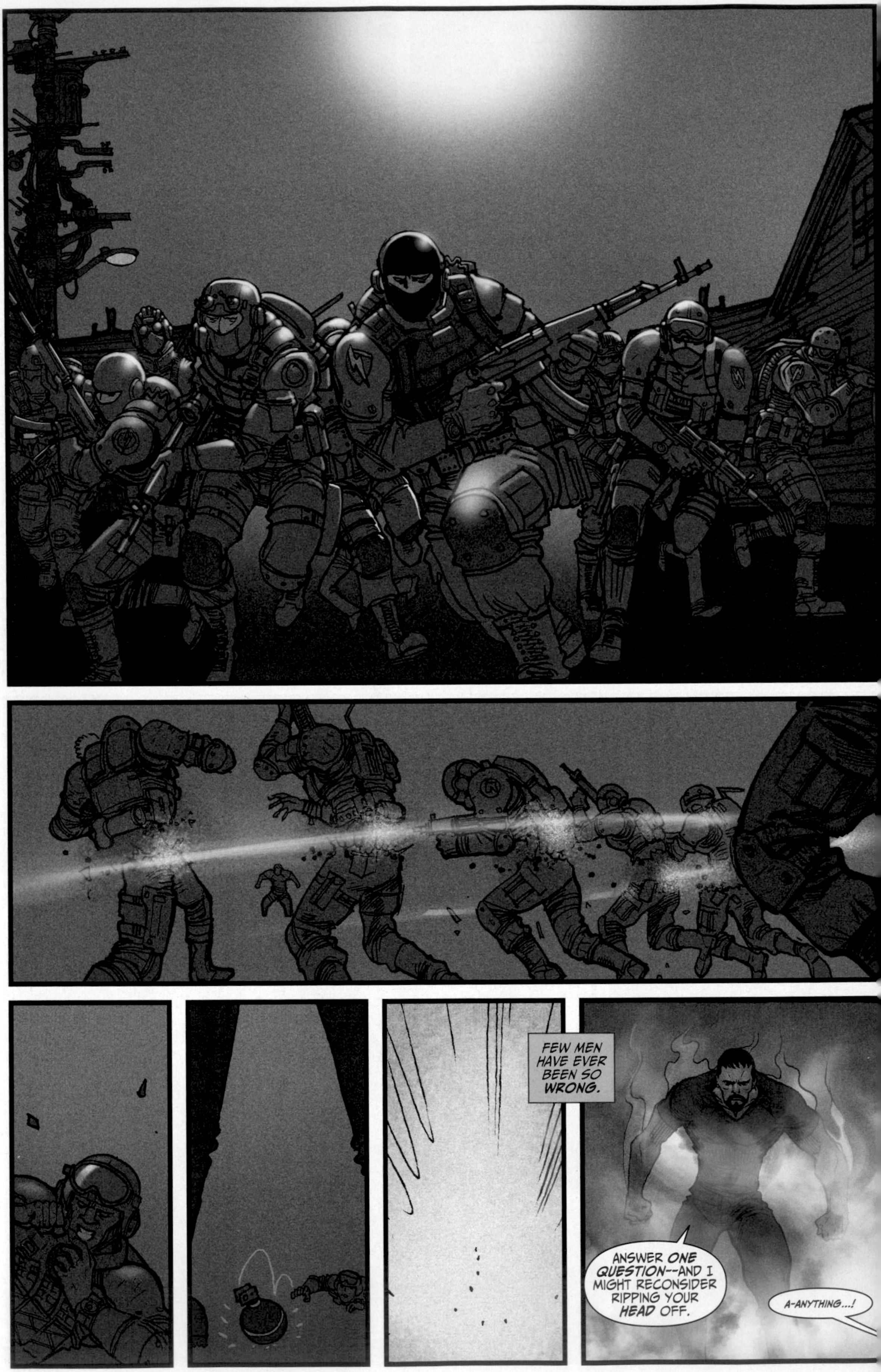
FEW MEN HAVE EVER BEEN SO WRONG.
ANSWER ONE QUESTION--AND I MIGHT RECONSIDER RIPPING YOUR HEAD OFF.
A-ANYTHING...!

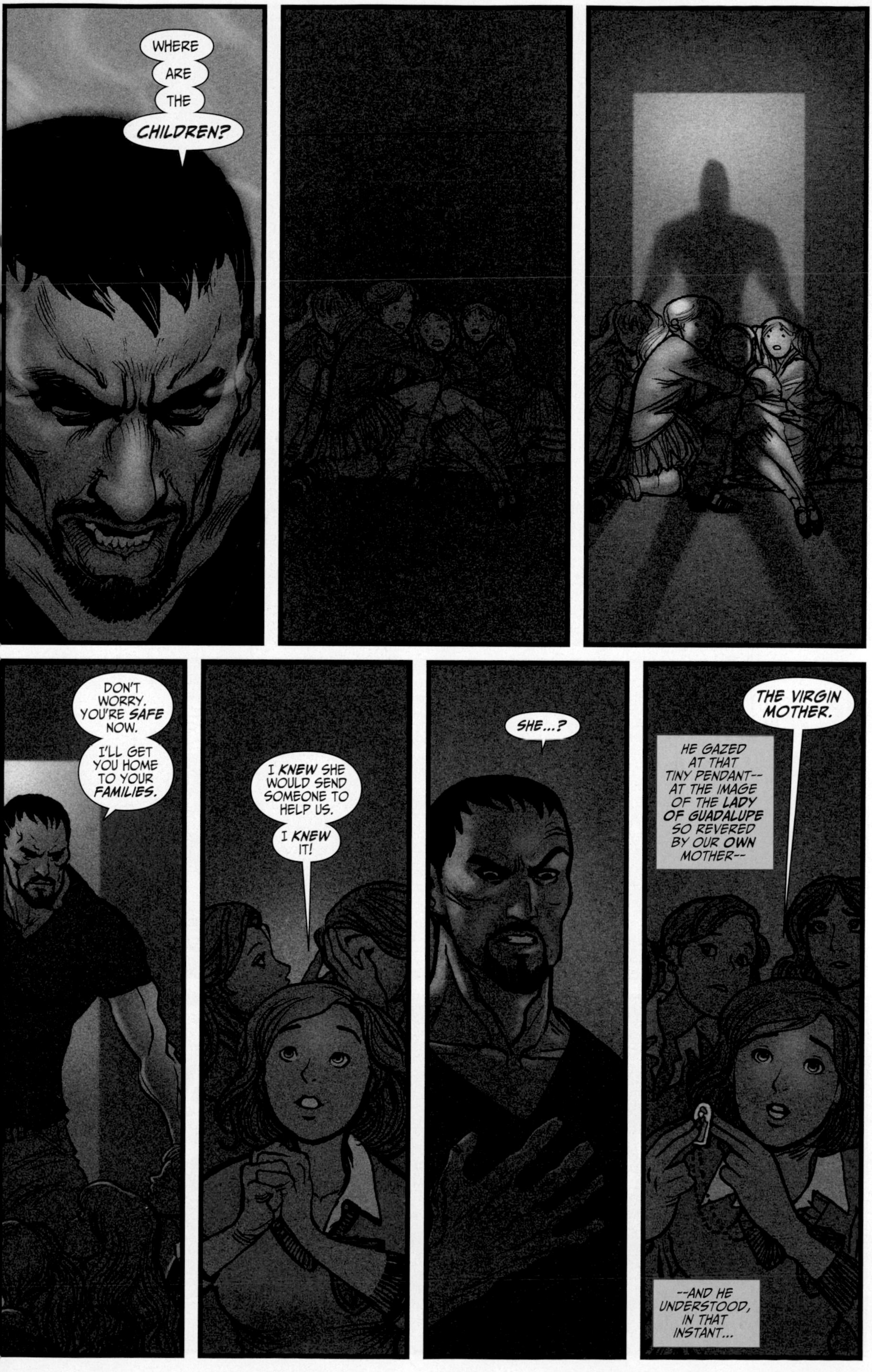
WHERE ARE THE CHILDREN?
DON'T WORRY. YOU'RE SAFE NOW.
I'LL GET YOU HOME TO YOUR FAMILIES.
I KNEW SHE WOULD SEND SOMEONE TO HELP US.
I KNEW IT!
SHE...?
THE VIRGIN MOTHER.
HE GAZED AT THAT TINY PENDANT-- AT THE IMAGE OF THE LADY OF GUADALUPE SO REVERED BY OUR OWN MOTHER--
--AND HE UNDERSTOOD, IN THAT INSTANT...

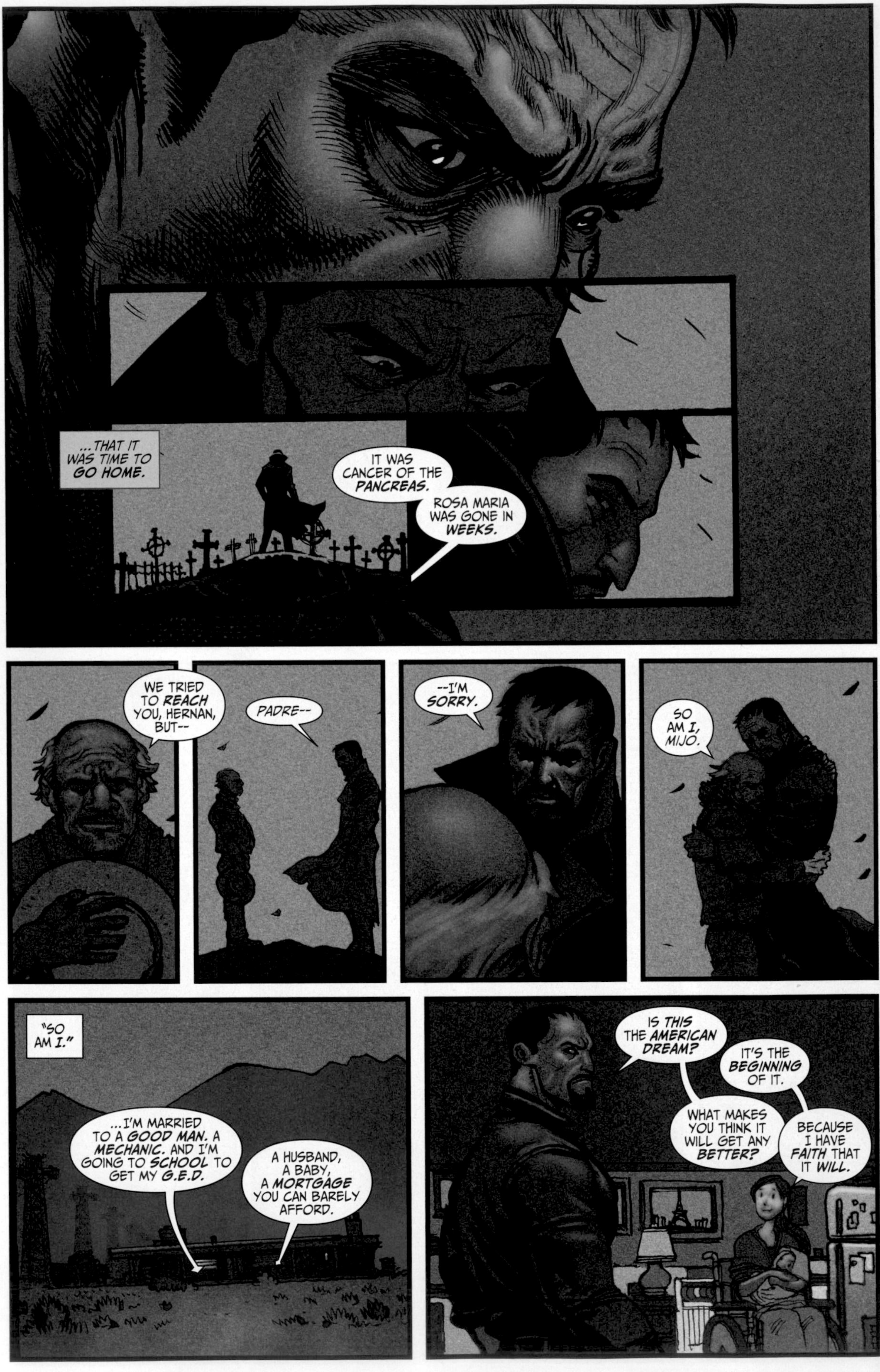

...THAT IT WAS TIME TO GO HOME.
IT WAS CANCER OF THE PANCREAS.
ROSA MARIA WAS GONE IN WEEKS.
WE TRIED TO REACH YOU, HERNAN, BUT--
PADRE--
--I'M SORRY.
SO AM I, MIJO.
"SO AM I."
...I'M MARRIED TO A GOOD MAN. A MECHANIC. AND I'M GOING TO SCHOOL TO GET MY G.E.D.
A HUSBAND, A BABY, A MORTGAGE YOU CAN BARELY AFFORD.
IS THIS THE AMERICAN DREAM?
IT'S THE BEGINNING OF IT.
WHAT MAKES YOU THINK IT WILL GET ANY BETTER?
BECAUSE I HAVE FAITH THAT IT WILL.

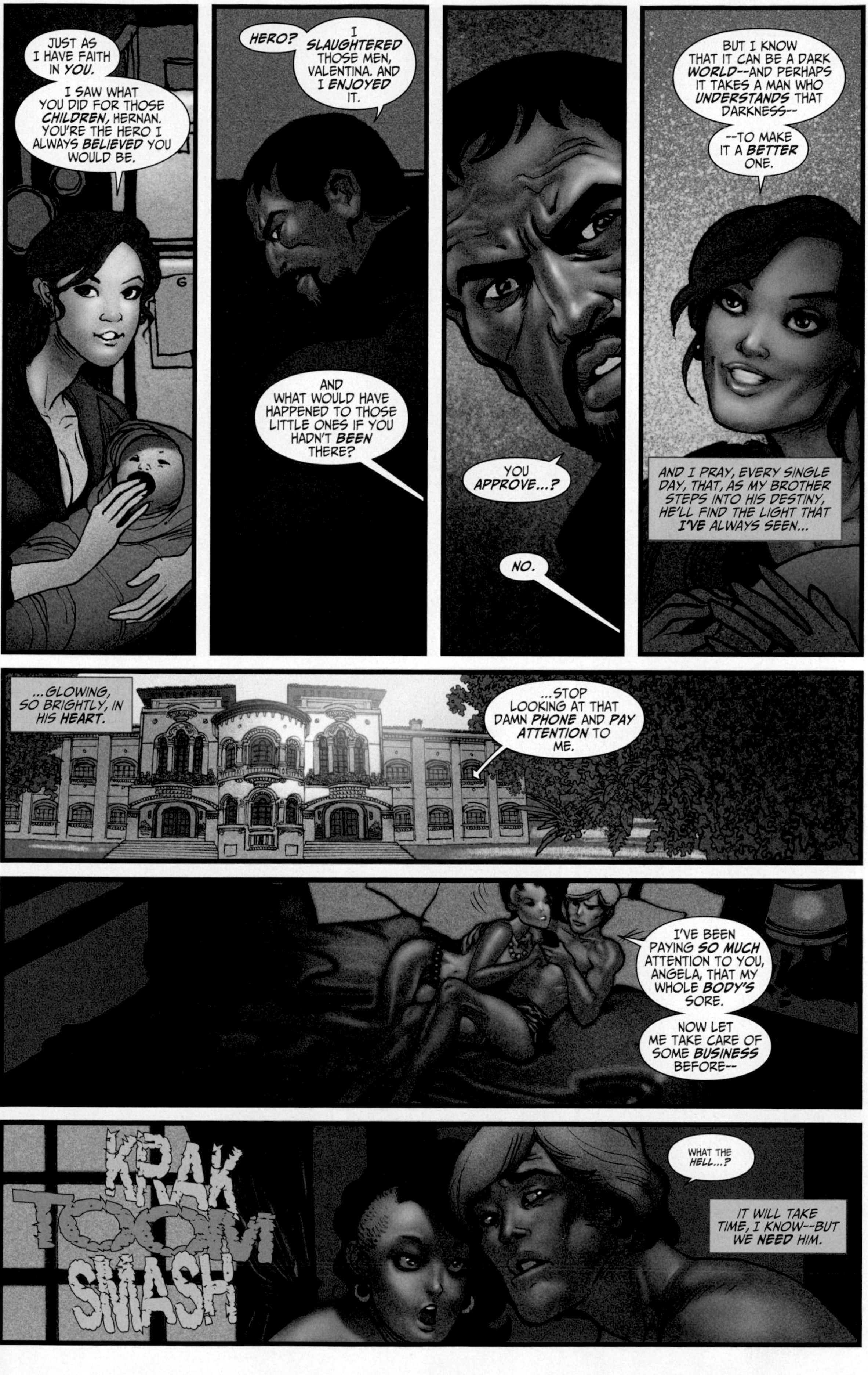
JUST AS I HAVE FAITH IN YOU.
I SAW WHAT YOU DID FOR THOSE CHILDREN, HERNAN. YOU'RE THE HERO I ALWAYS BELIEVED YOU WOULD BE.
HERO?
I SLAUGHTERED THOSE MEN, VALENTINA. AND I ENJOYED IT.
AND WHAT WOULD HAVE HAPPENED TO THOSE LITTLE ONES IF YOU HADN'T BEEN THERE?
YOU APPROVE...?
NO.
BUT I KNOW THAT IT CAN BE A DARK WORLD--AND PERHAPS IT TAKES A MAN WHO UNDERSTANDS THAT DARKNESS--
--TO MAKE IT A BETTER ONE.
AND I PRAY, EVERY SINGLE DAY, THAT, AS MY BROTHER STEPS INTO HIS DESTINY, HE'LL FIND THE LIGHT THAT I'VE ALWAYS SEEN...
...GLOWING, SO BRIGHTLY, IN HIS HEART.
...STOP LOOKING AT THAT DAMN PHONE AND PAY ATTENTION TO ME.
I'VE BEEN PAYING SO MUCH ATTENTION TO YOU, ANGELA, THAT MY WHOLE BODY'S SORE.
NOW LET ME TAKE CARE OF SOME BUSINESS BEFORE--
KRAK
TOOM
SMASH
WHAT THE HELL...?
IT WILL TAKE TIME, I KNOW--BUT WE NEED HIM.

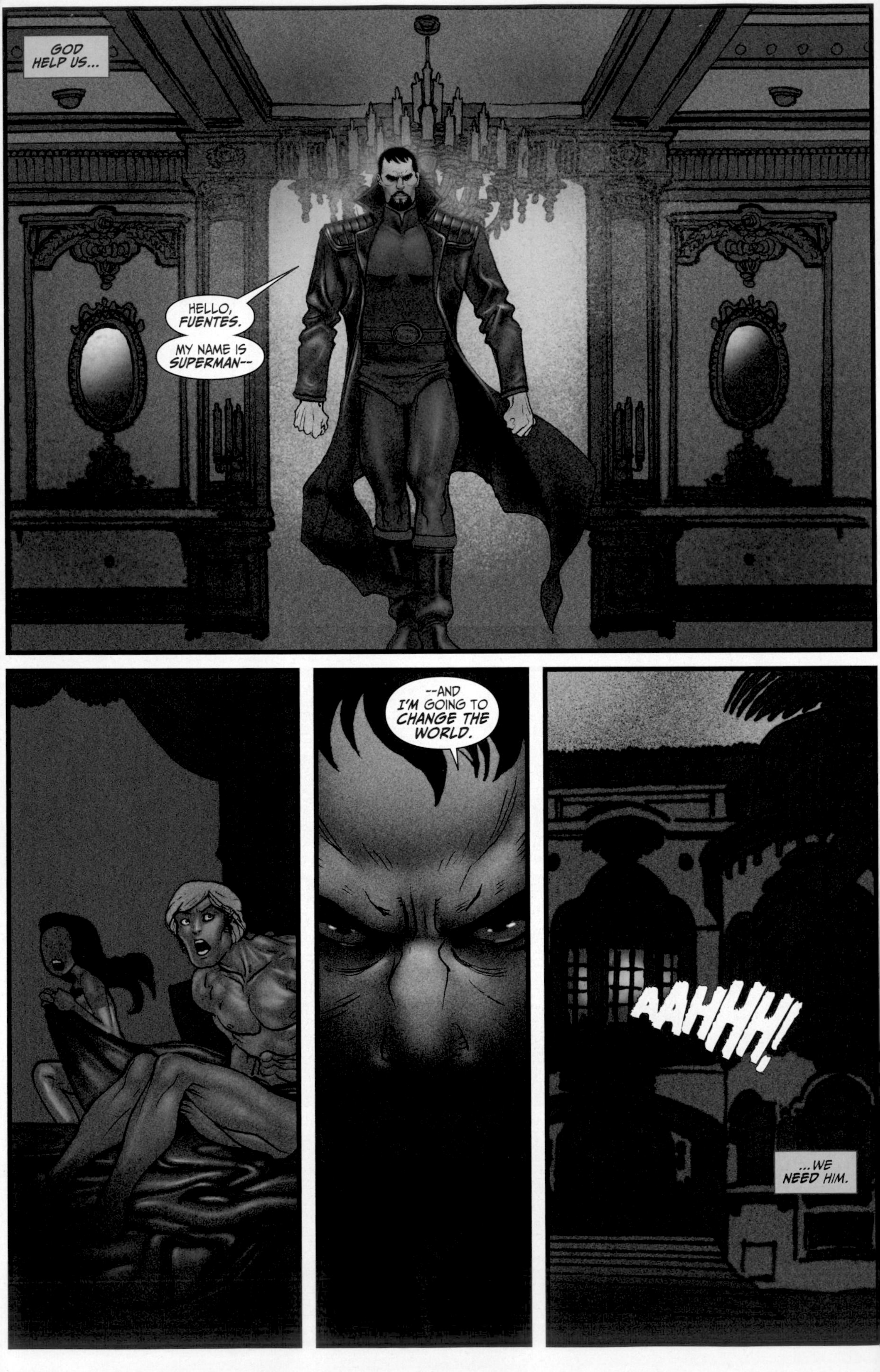
GOD HELP US...
HELLO, FUENTES.
MY NAME IS SUPERMAN--
--AND I'M GOING TO CHANGE THE WORLD.
AAHHH!
...WE NEED HIM.

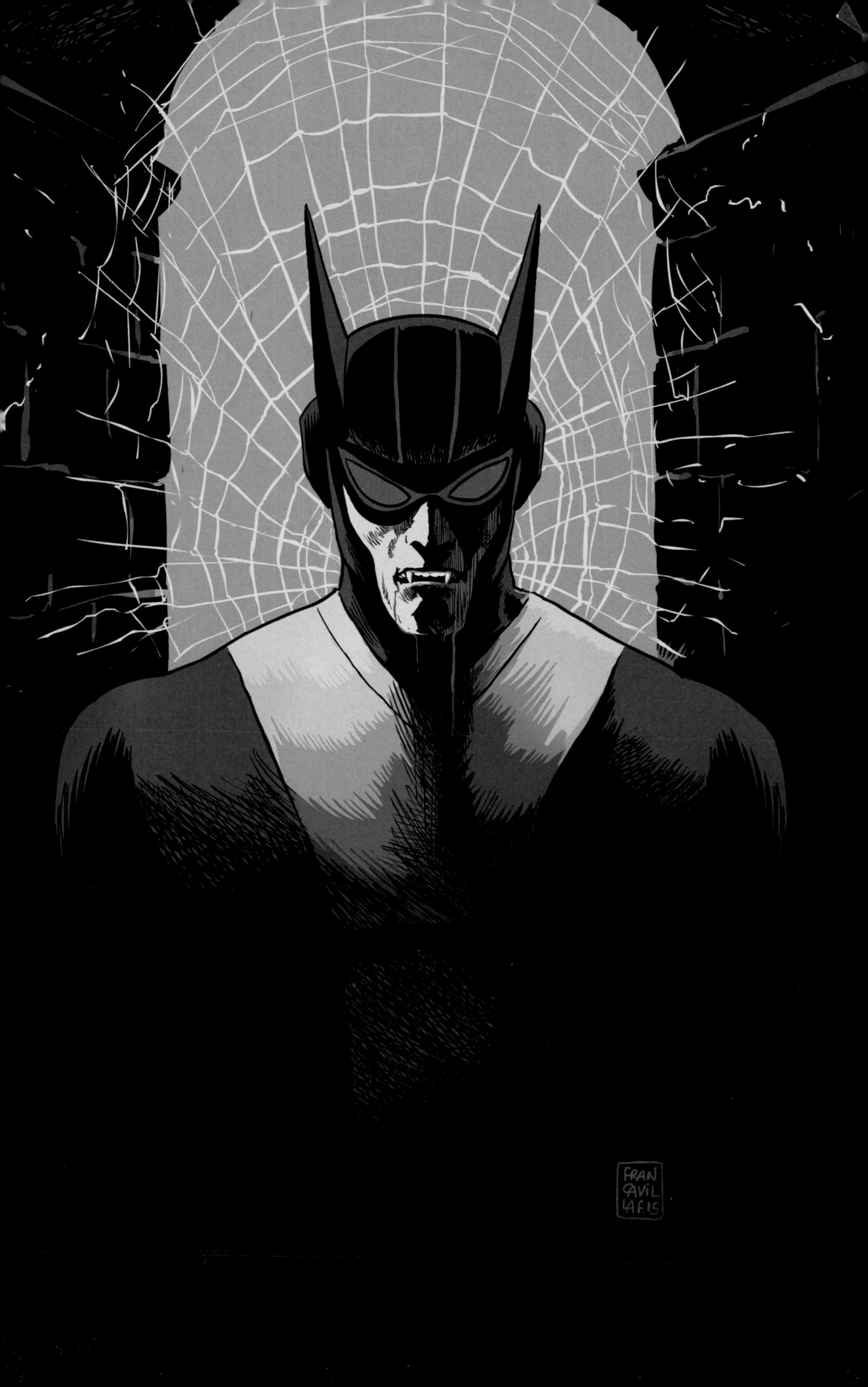
FRAN
CAVIL
LA F.15

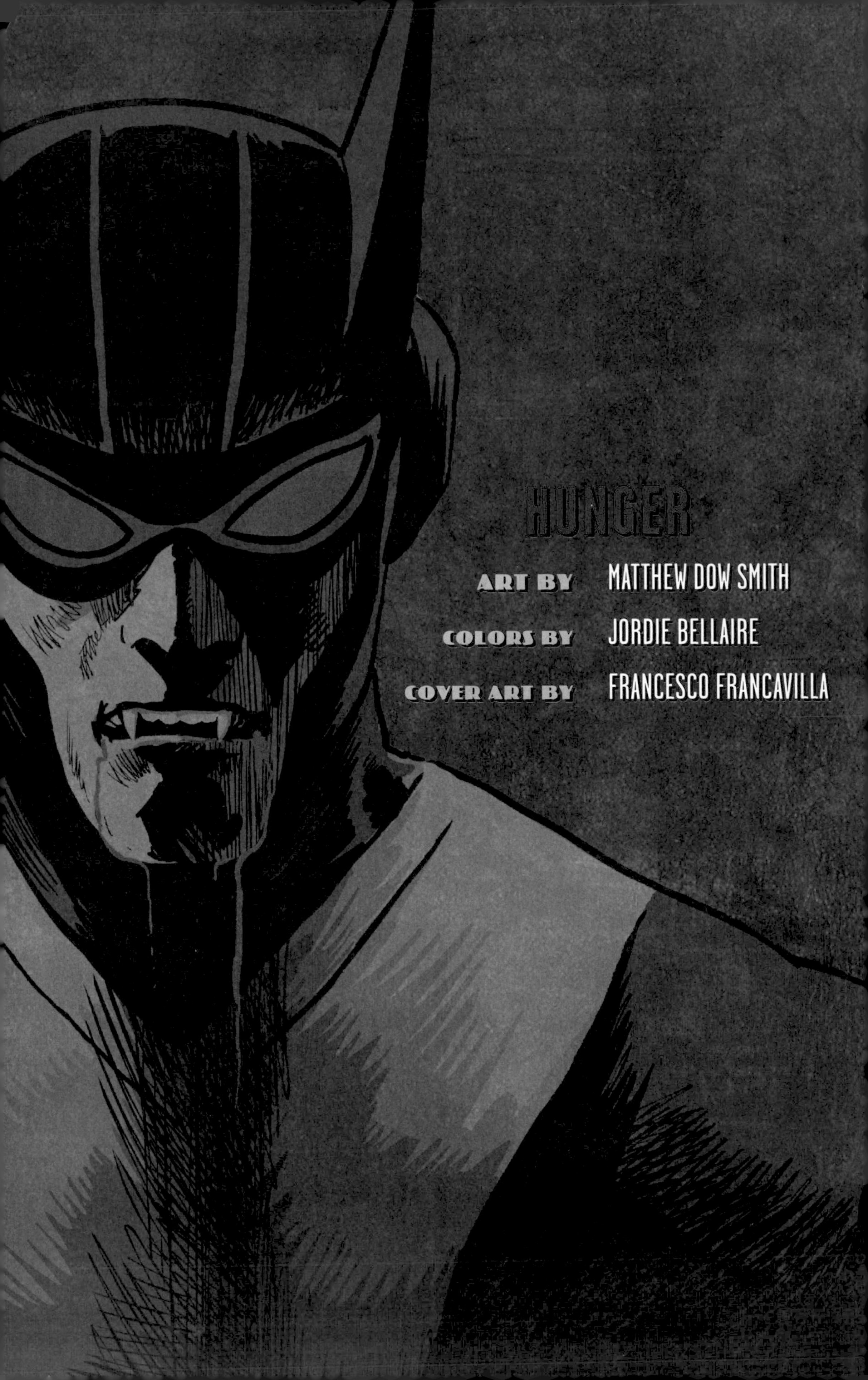

HUNGER

ART BY MATTHEW DOW SMITH

COLORS BY JORDIE BELLAIRE

COVER ART BY FRANCESCO FRANCAVILLA

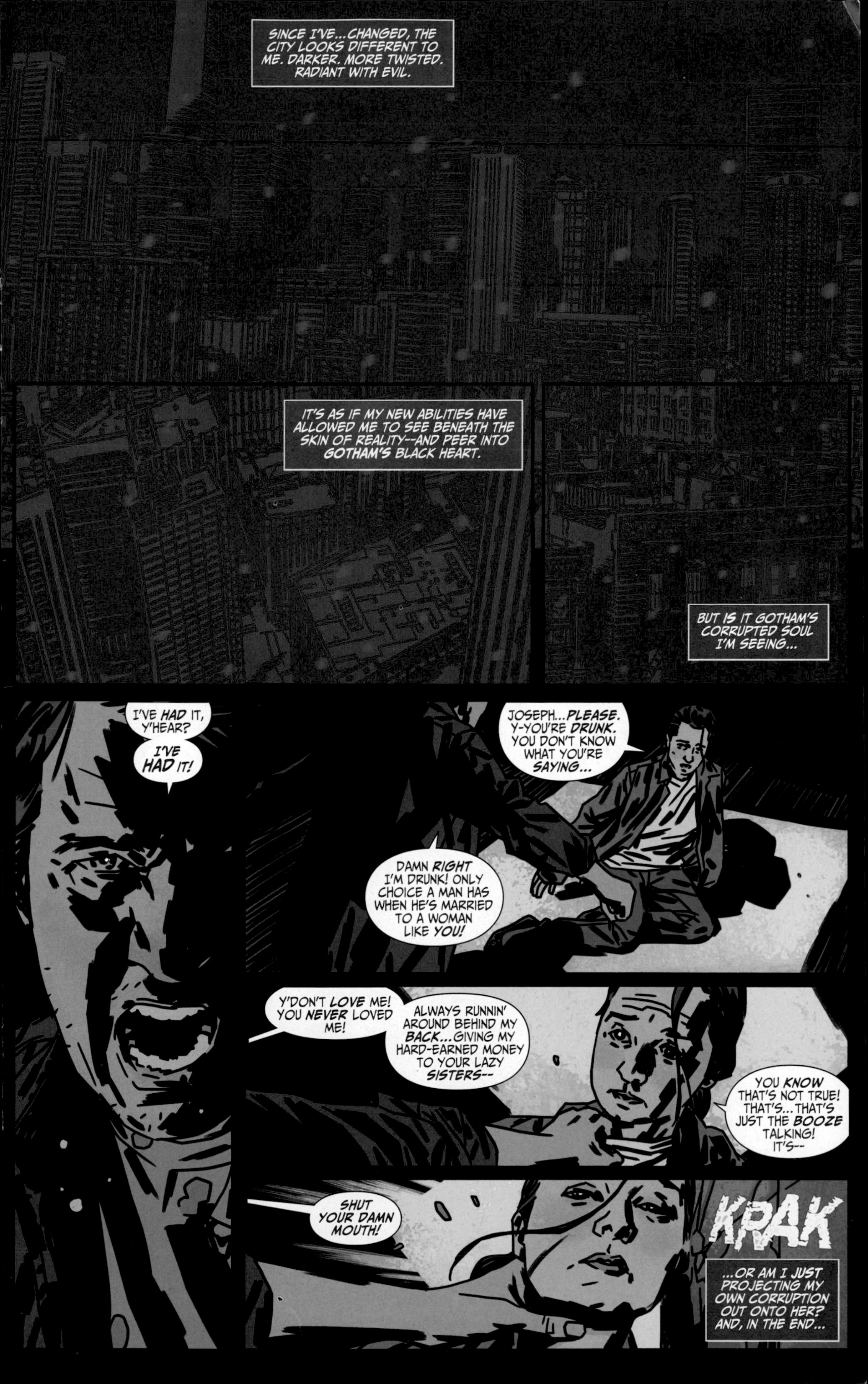
SINCE I'VE...CHANGED, THE CITY LOOKS DIFFERENT TO ME. DARKER. MORE TWISTED. RADIANT WITH EVIL.
IT'S AS IF MY NEW ABILITIES HAVE ALLOWED ME TO SEE BENEATH THE SKIN OF REALITY--AND PEER INTO GOTHAM'S BLACK HEART.
BUT IS IT GOTHAM'S CORRUPTED SOUL I'M SEEING...
I'VE HAD IT, Y'HEAR?
I'VE HAD IT!
JOSEPH...PLEASE. Y-YOU'RE DRUNK. YOU DON'T KNOW WHAT YOU'RE SAYING...
DAMN RIGHT I'M DRUNK! ONLY CHOICE A MAN HAS WHEN HE'S MARRIED TO A WOMAN LIKE YOU!
Y'DON'T LOVE ME! YOU NEVER LOVED ME!
ALWAYS RUNNIN' AROUND BEHIND MY BACK...GIVING MY HARD-EARNED MONEY TO YOUR LAZY SISTERS--
YOU KNOW THAT'S NOT TRUE! THAT'S...THAT'S JUST THE BOOZE TALKING! IT'S--
SHUT YOUR DAMN MOUTH!
KRAK
...OR AM I JUST PROJECTING MY OWN CORRUPTION OUT ONTO HER? AND, IN THE END...

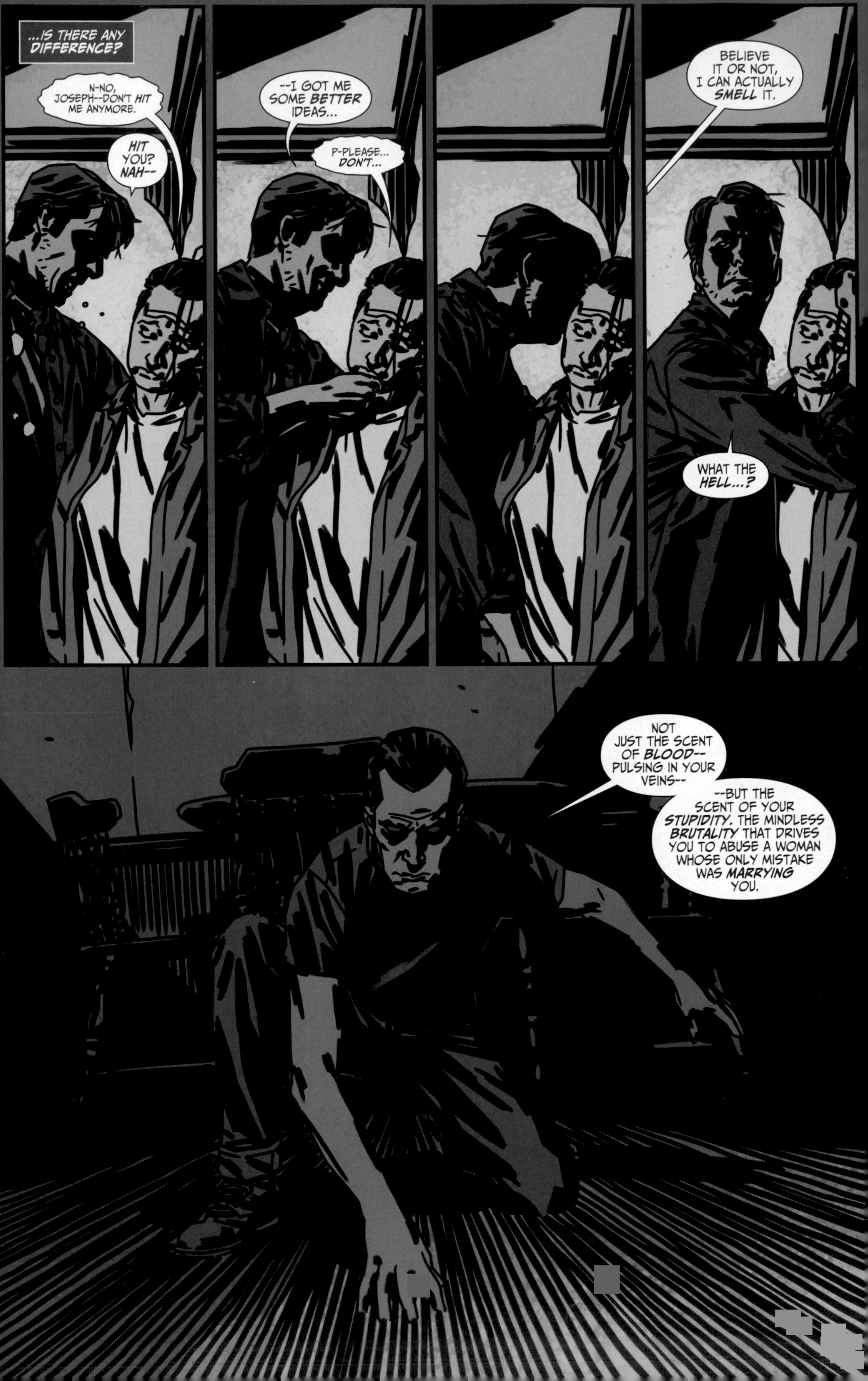
...IS THERE ANY DIFFERENCE?
N-NO, JOSEPH--DON'T HIT ME ANYMORE.
HIT YOU? NAH--
--I GOT ME SOME BETTER IDEAS...
P-PLEASE... DON'T...
BELIEVE IT OR NOT, I CAN ACTUALLY SMELL IT.
WHAT THE HELL...?
NOT JUST THE SCENT OF BLOOD-- PULSING IN YOUR VEINS--
--BUT THE SCENT OF YOUR STUPIDITY. THE MINDLESS BRUTALITY THAT DRIVES YOU TO ABUSE A WOMAN WHOSE ONLY MISTAKE WAS MARRYING YOU.

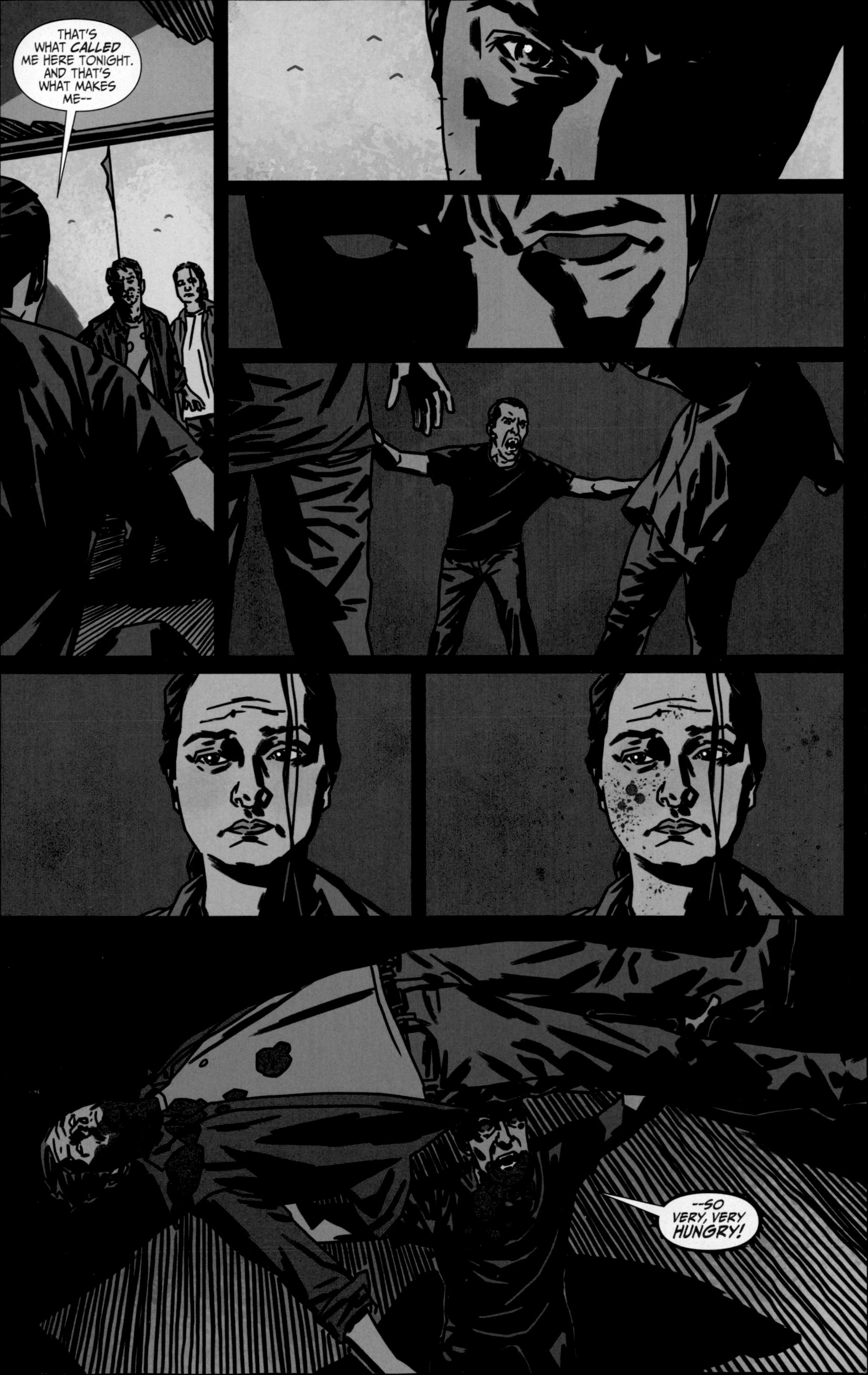
THAT'S WHAT CALLED ME HERE TONIGHT. AND THAT'S WHAT MAKES ME--
--SO VERY, VERY HUNGRY!

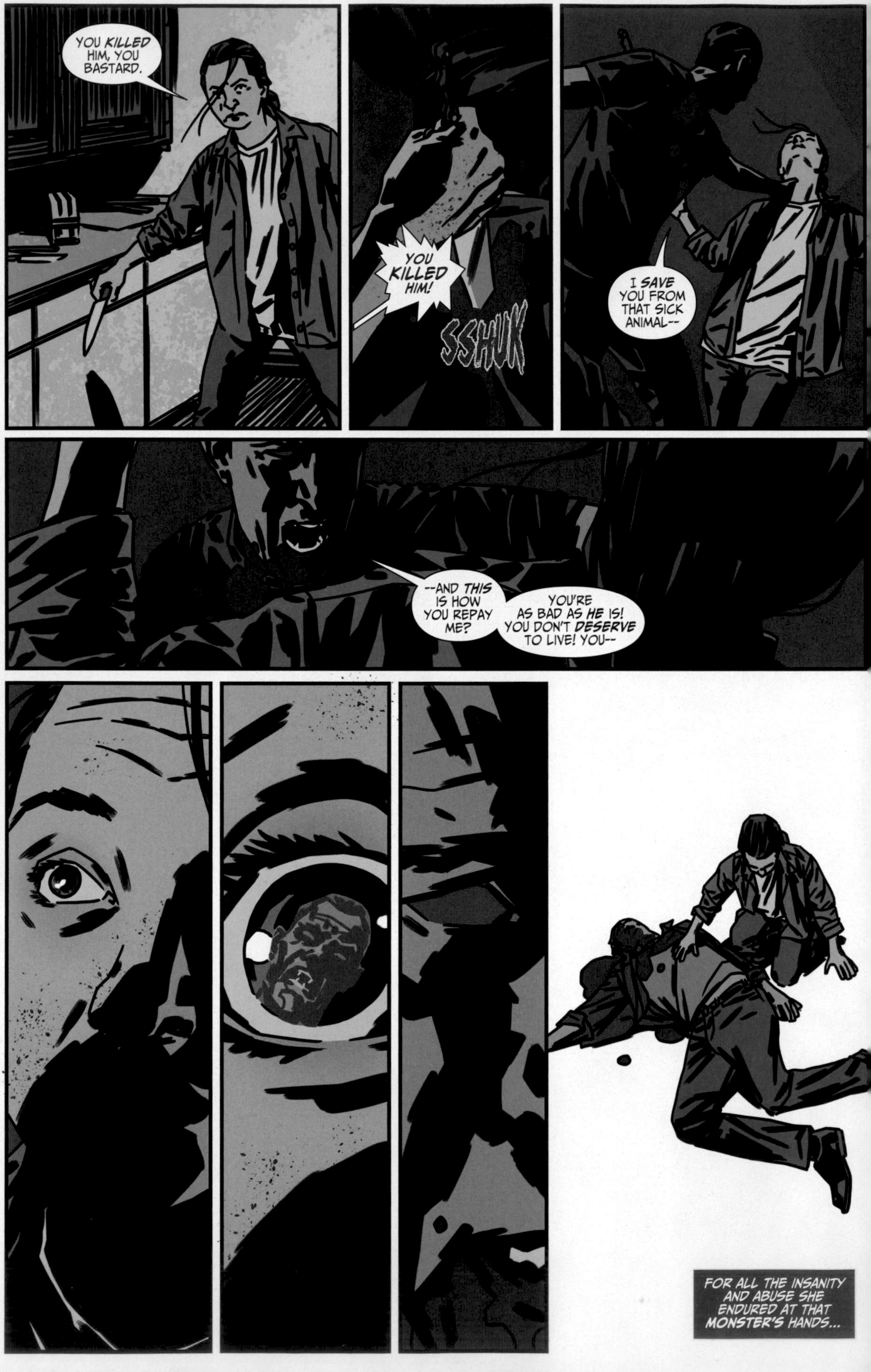
YOU KILLED HIM, YOU BASTARD.
YOU KILLED HIM!
SSHUK
I SAVE YOU FROM THAT SICK ANIMAL--
--AND THIS IS HOW YOU REPAY ME?
YOU'RE AS BAD AS HE IS! YOU DON'T DESERVE TO LIVE! YOU--
FOR ALL THE INSANITY AND ABUSE SHE ENDURED AT THAT MONSTER'S HANDS...

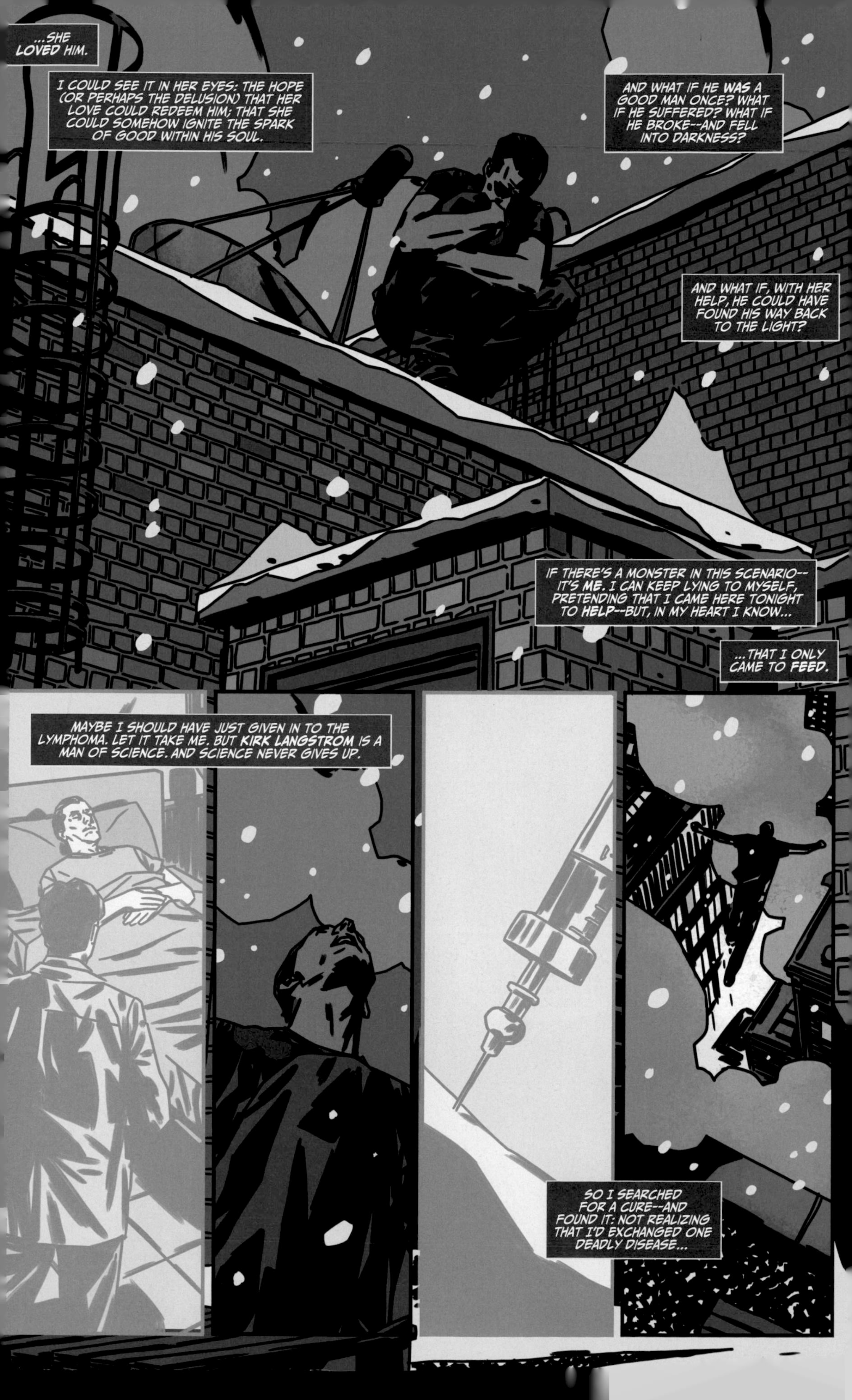
...SHE LOVED HIM.
I COULD SEE IT IN HER EYES: THE HOPE (OR PERHAPS THE DELUSION) THAT HER LOVE COULD REDEEM HIM; THAT SHE COULD SOMEHOW IGNITE THE SPARK OF GOOD WITHIN HIS SOUL.
AND WHAT IF HE WAS A GOOD MAN ONCE? WHAT IF HE SUFFERED? WHAT IF HE BROKE--AND FELL INTO DARKNESS?
AND WHAT IF, WITH HER HELP, HE COULD HAVE FOUND HIS WAY BACK TO THE LIGHT?
IF THERE'S A MONSTER IN THIS SCENARIO--IT'S ME. I CAN KEEP LYING TO MYSELF, PRETENDING THAT I CAME HERE TONIGHT TO HELP--BUT, IN MY HEART I KNOW...
...THAT I ONLY CAME TO FEED.
MAYBE I SHOULD HAVE JUST GIVEN IN TO THE LYMPHOMA. LET IT TAKE ME. BUT KIRK LANGSTROM IS A MAN OF SCIENCE. AND SCIENCE NEVER GIVES UP.
SO I SEARCHED FOR A CURE--AND FOUND IT: NOT REALIZING THAT I'D EXCHANGED ONE DEADLY DISEASE...

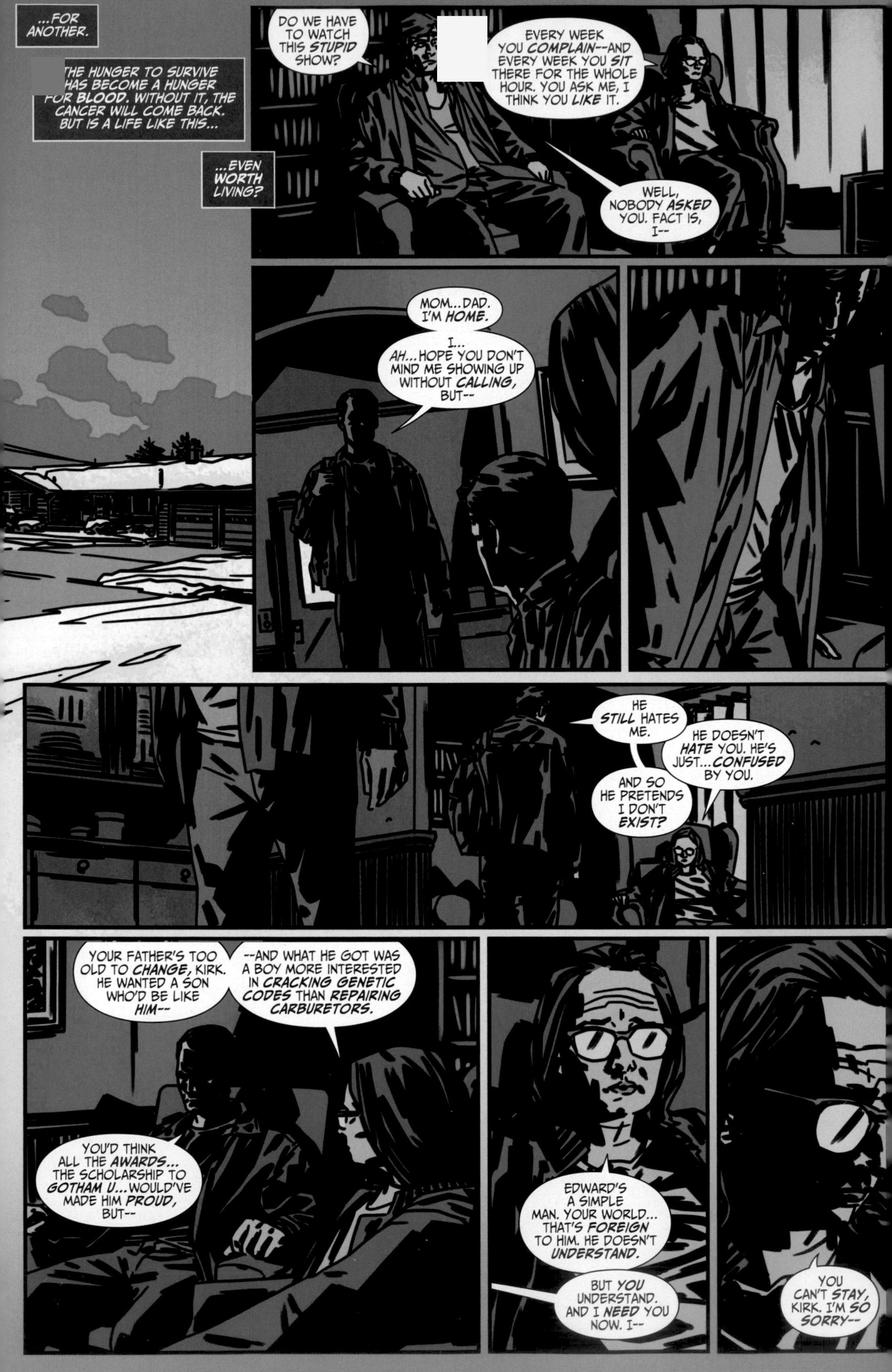
...FOR ANOTHER.
THE HUNGER TO SURVIVE HAS BECOME A HUNGER FOR BLOOD. WITHOUT IT, THE CANCER WILL COME BACK. BUT IS A LIFE LIKE THIS...
...EVEN WORTH LIVING?
DO WE HAVE TO WATCH THIS STUPID SHOW?
EVERY WEEK YOU COMPLAIN--AND EVERY WEEK YOU SIT THERE FOR THE WHOLE HOUR. YOU ASK ME, I THINK YOU LIKE IT.
WELL, NOBODY ASKED YOU. FACT IS, I--
MOM...DAD. I'M HOME.
I... AH...HOPE YOU DON'T MIND ME SHOWING UP WITHOUT CALLING, BUT--
HE STILL HATES ME.
HE DOESN'T HATE YOU. HE'S JUST...CONFUSED BY YOU.
AND SO HE PRETENDS I DON'T EXIST?
YOUR FATHER'S TOO OLD TO CHANGE, KIRK. HE WANTED A SON WHO'D BE LIKE HIM--
--AND WHAT HE GOT WAS A BOY MORE INTERESTED IN CRACKING GENETIC CODES THAN REPAIRING CARBURETORS.
YOU'D THINK ALL THE AWARDS... THE SCHOLARSHIP TO GOTHAM U...WOULD'VE MADE HIM PROUD, BUT--
EDWARD'S A SIMPLE MAN. YOUR WORLD... THAT'S FOREIGN TO HIM. HE DOESN'T UNDERSTAND.
BUT YOU UNDERSTAND. AND I NEED YOU NOW. I--
YOU CAN'T STAY, KIRK. I'M SO SORRY--

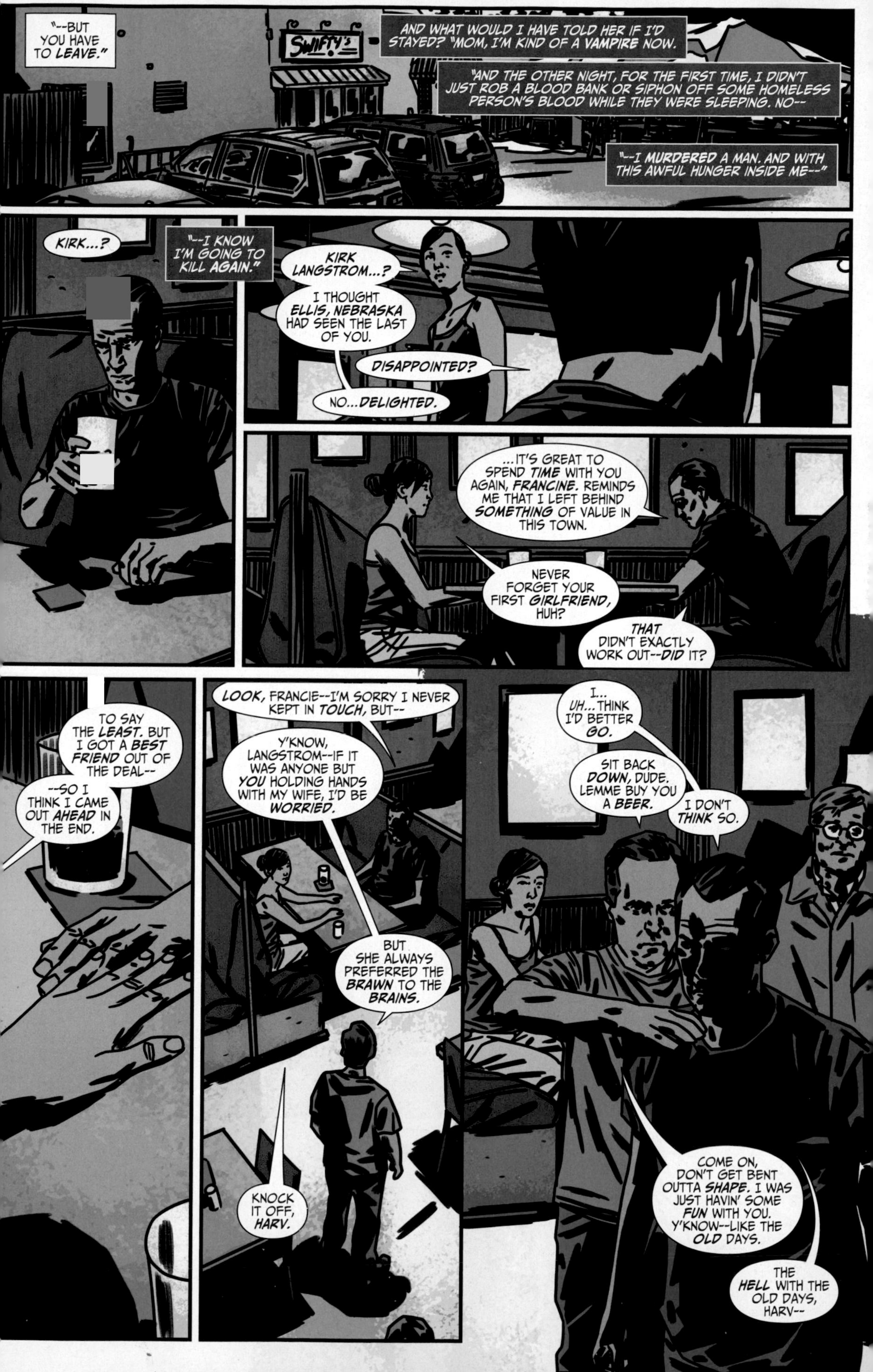
"--BUT YOU HAVE TO LEAVE."
SWIFTY'S
AND WHAT WOULD I HAVE TOLD HER IF I'D STAYED? "MOM, I'M KIND OF A VAMPIRE NOW.
"AND THE OTHER NIGHT, FOR THE FIRST TIME, I DIDN'T JUST ROB A BLOOD BANK OR SIPHON OFF SOME HOMELESS PERSON'S BLOOD WHILE THEY WERE SLEEPING. NO--
"--I MURDERED A MAN. AND WITH THIS AWFUL HUNGER INSIDE ME--"
KIRK...?
"--I KNOW I'M GOING TO KILL AGAIN."
KIRK LANGSTROM...?
I THOUGHT ELLIS, NEBRASKA HAD SEEN THE LAST OF YOU.
DISAPPOINTED?
NO...DELIGHTED.
...IT'S GREAT TO SPEND TIME WITH YOU AGAIN, FRANCINE. REMINDS ME THAT I LEFT BEHIND SOMETHING OF VALUE IN THIS TOWN.
NEVER FORGET YOUR FIRST GIRLFRIEND, HUH?
THAT DIDN'T EXACTLY WORK OUT--DID IT?
TO SAY THE LEAST. BUT I GOT A BEST FRIEND OUT OF THE DEAL--
--SO I THINK I CAME OUT AHEAD IN THE END.
LOOK, FRANCIE--I'M SORRY I NEVER KEPT IN TOUCH, BUT--
Y'KNOW, LANGSTROM--IF IT WAS ANYONE BUT YOU HOLDING HANDS WITH MY WIFE, I'D BE WORRIED.
BUT SHE ALWAYS PREFERRED THE BRAWN TO THE BRAINS.
KNOCK IT OFF, HARV.
I... UH...THINK I'D BETTER GO.
SIT BACK DOWN, DUDE. LEMME BUY YOU A BEER.
I DON'T THINK SO.
COME ON, DON'T GET BENT OUTTA SHAPE. I WAS JUST HAVIN' SOME FUN WITH YOU. Y'KNOW--LIKE THE OLD DAYS.
THE HELL WITH THE OLD DAYS, HARV--

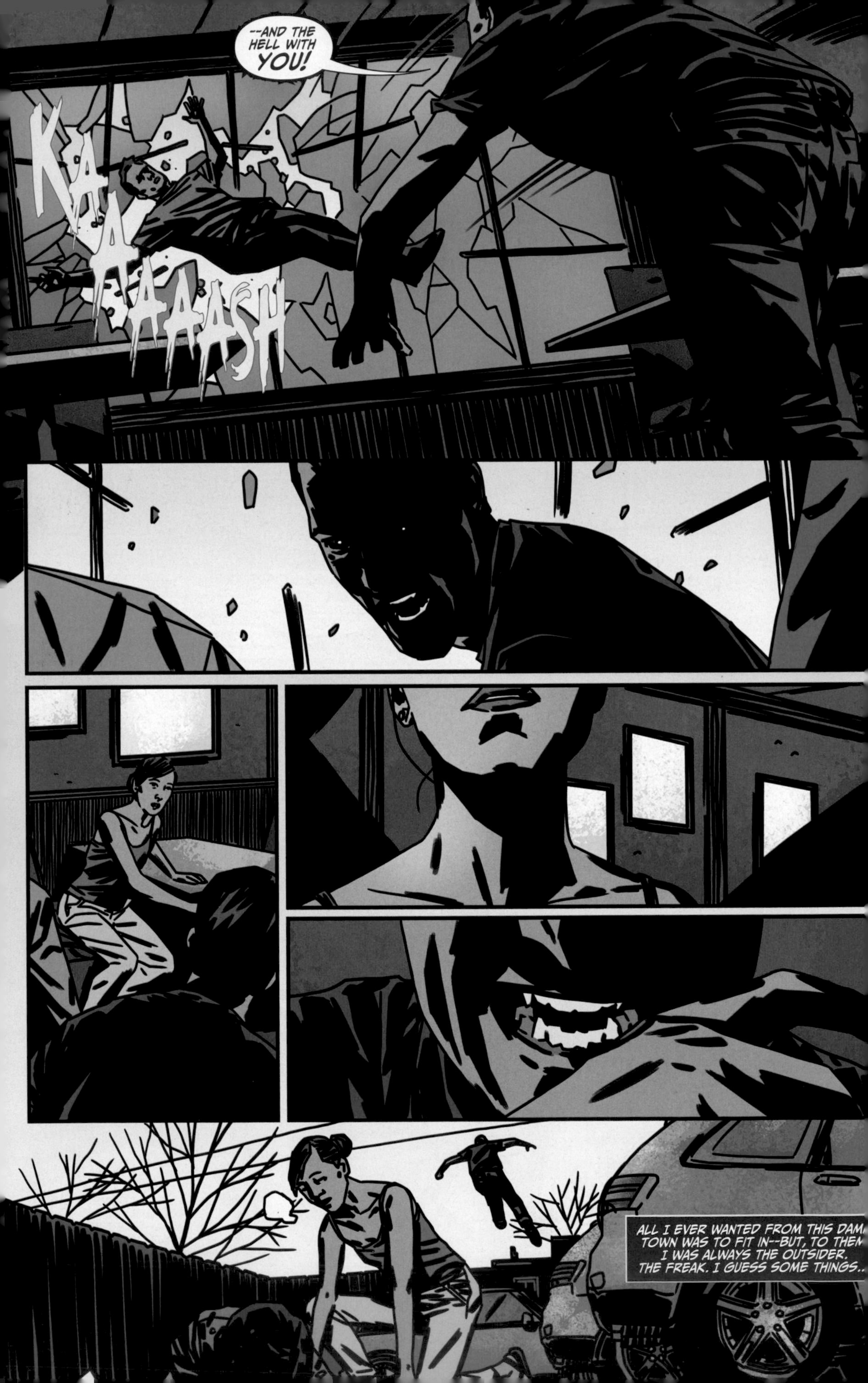
--AND THE HELL WITH YOU!
KA-A-AAASH
ALL I EVER WANTED FROM THIS DAM TOWN WAS TO FIT IN--BUT, TO THEM I WAS ALWAYS THE OUTSIDER. THE FREAK. I GUESS SOME THINGS...

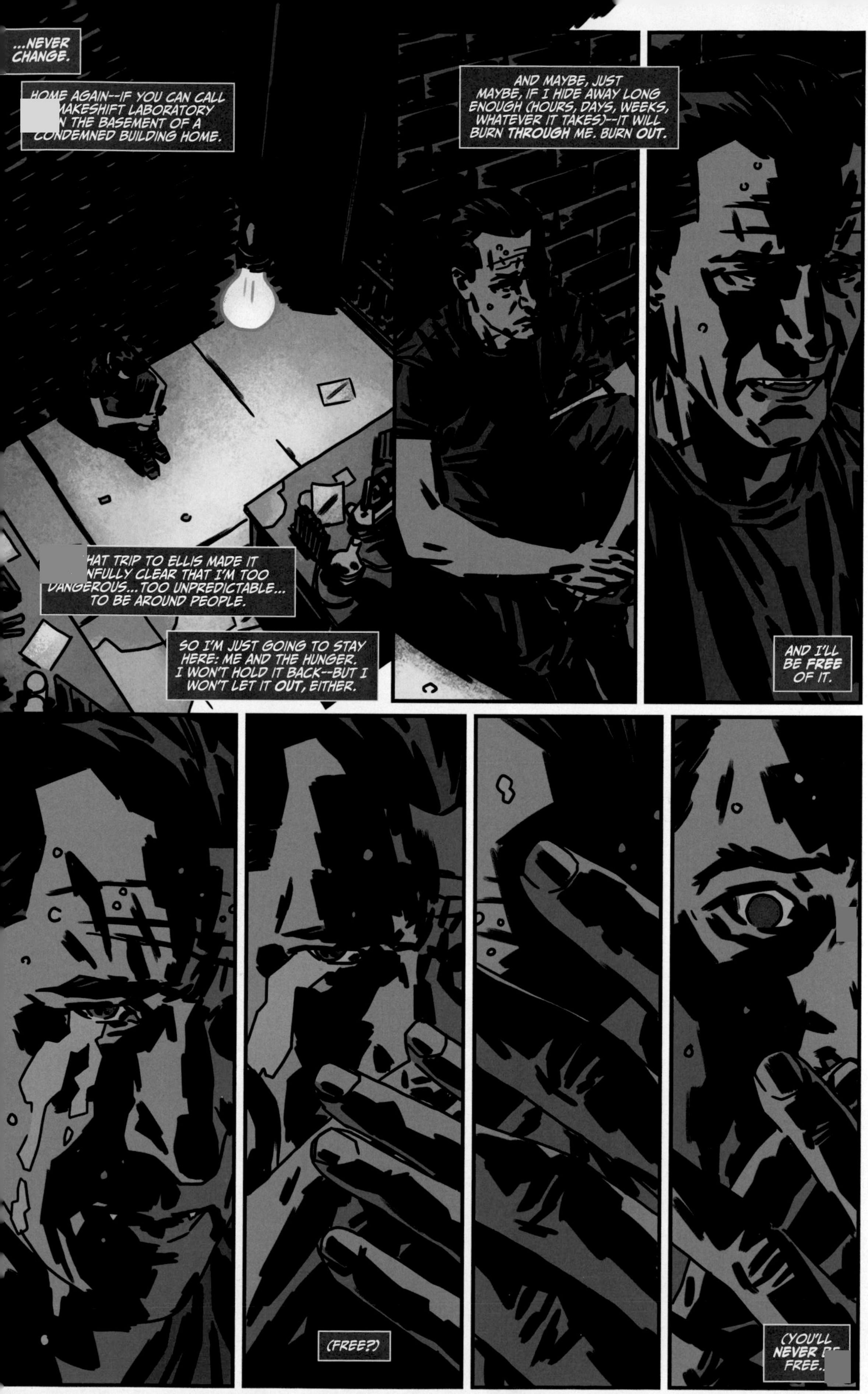

...NEVER CHANGE.
HOME AGAIN--IF YOU CAN CALL MAKESHIFT LABORATORY N THE BASEMENT OF A CONDEMNED BUILDING HOME.
HAT TRIP TO ELLIS MADE IT NFULLY CLEAR THAT I'M TOO DANGEROUS...TOO UNPREDICTABLE... TO BE AROUND PEOPLE.
SO I'M JUST GOING TO STAY HERE: ME AND THE HUNGER. I WON'T HOLD IT BACK--BUT I WON'T LET IT OUT, EITHER.
AND MAYBE, JUST MAYBE, IF I HIDE AWAY LONG ENOUGH (HOURS, DAYS, WEEKS, WHATEVER IT TAKES)--IT WILL BURN THROUGH ME. BURN OUT.
AND I'LL BE FREE OF IT.
(FREE?)
(YOU'LL NEVER FREE.

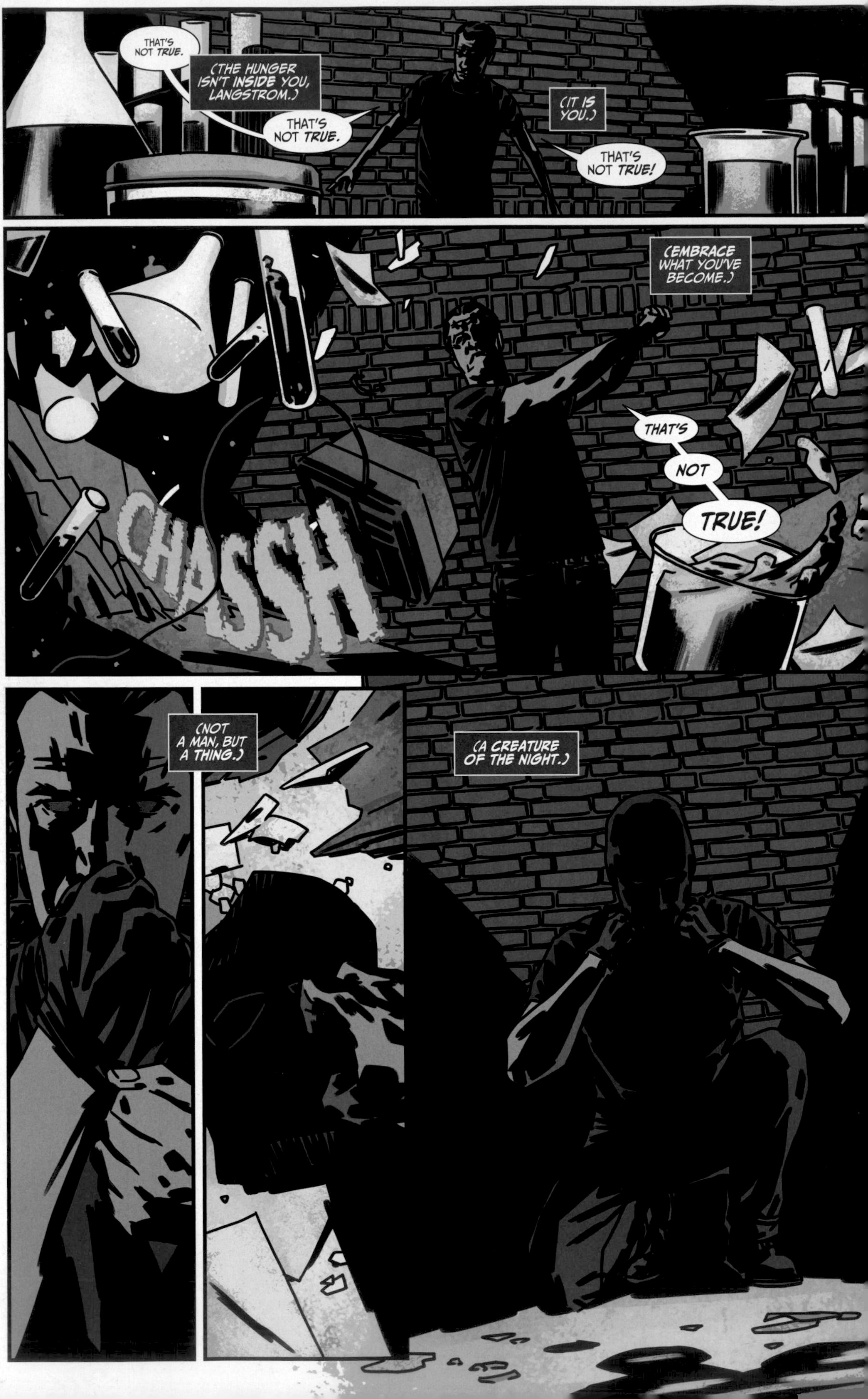
THAT'S NOT TRUE.
(THE HUNGER ISN'T INSIDE YOU, LANGSTROM.)
THAT'S NOT TRUE.
(IT IS YOU.)
THAT'S NOT TRUE!
(EMBRACE WHAT YOU'VE BECOME.)
THAT'S NOT TRUE!
CHASSH
(NOT A MAN, BUT A THING.)
(A CREATURE OF THE NIGHT.)

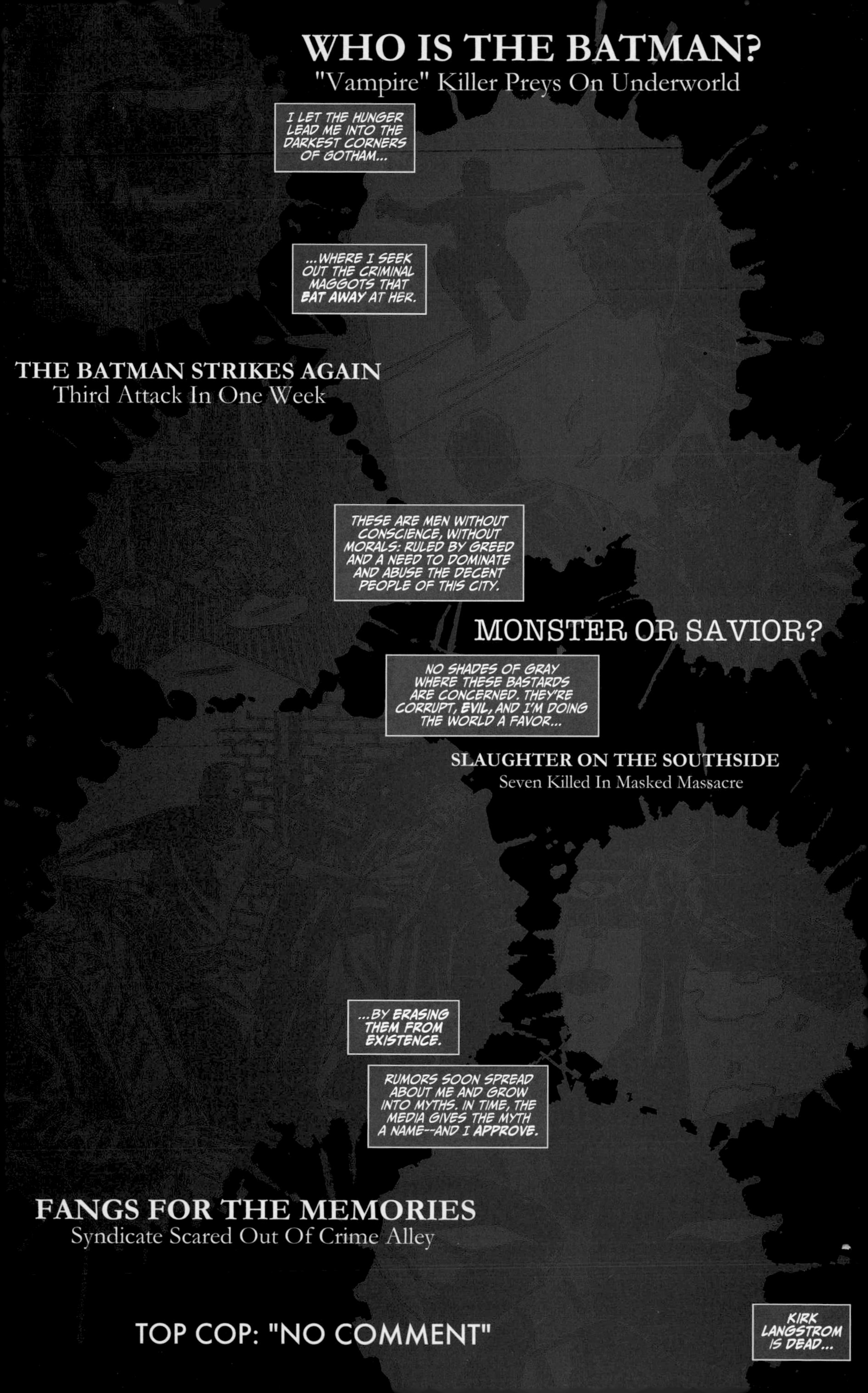

WHO IS THE BATMAN?
"Vampire" Killer Preys On Underworld

I LET THE HUNGER LEAD ME INTO THE DARKEST CORNERS OF GOTHAM...

...WHERE I SEEK OUT THE CRIMINAL MAGGOTS THAT *EAT AWAY AT HER.*

THE BATMAN STRIKES AGAIN
Third Attack In One Week

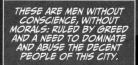

THESE ARE MEN WITHOUT CONSCIENCE, WITHOUT MORALS: RULED BY GREED AND A NEED TO DOMINATE AND ABUSE THE DECENT PEOPLE OF THIS CITY.

MONSTER OR SAVIOR?

NO SHADES OF GRAY WHERE THESE BASTARDS ARE CONCERNED. THEY'RE CORRUPT, EVIL, AND I'M DOING THE WORLD A FAVOR...

SLAUGHTER ON THE SOUTHSIDE
Seven Killed In Masked Massacre

...BY ERASING THEM FROM EXISTENCE.

RUMORS SOON SPREAD ABOUT ME AND GROW INTO MYTHS. IN TIME, THE MEDIA GIVES THE MYTH A NAME--AND I *APPROVE.*

FANGS FOR THE MEMORIES
Syndicate Scared Out Of Crime Alley

TOP COP: "NO COMMENT"

KIRK LANGSTROM IS DEAD...

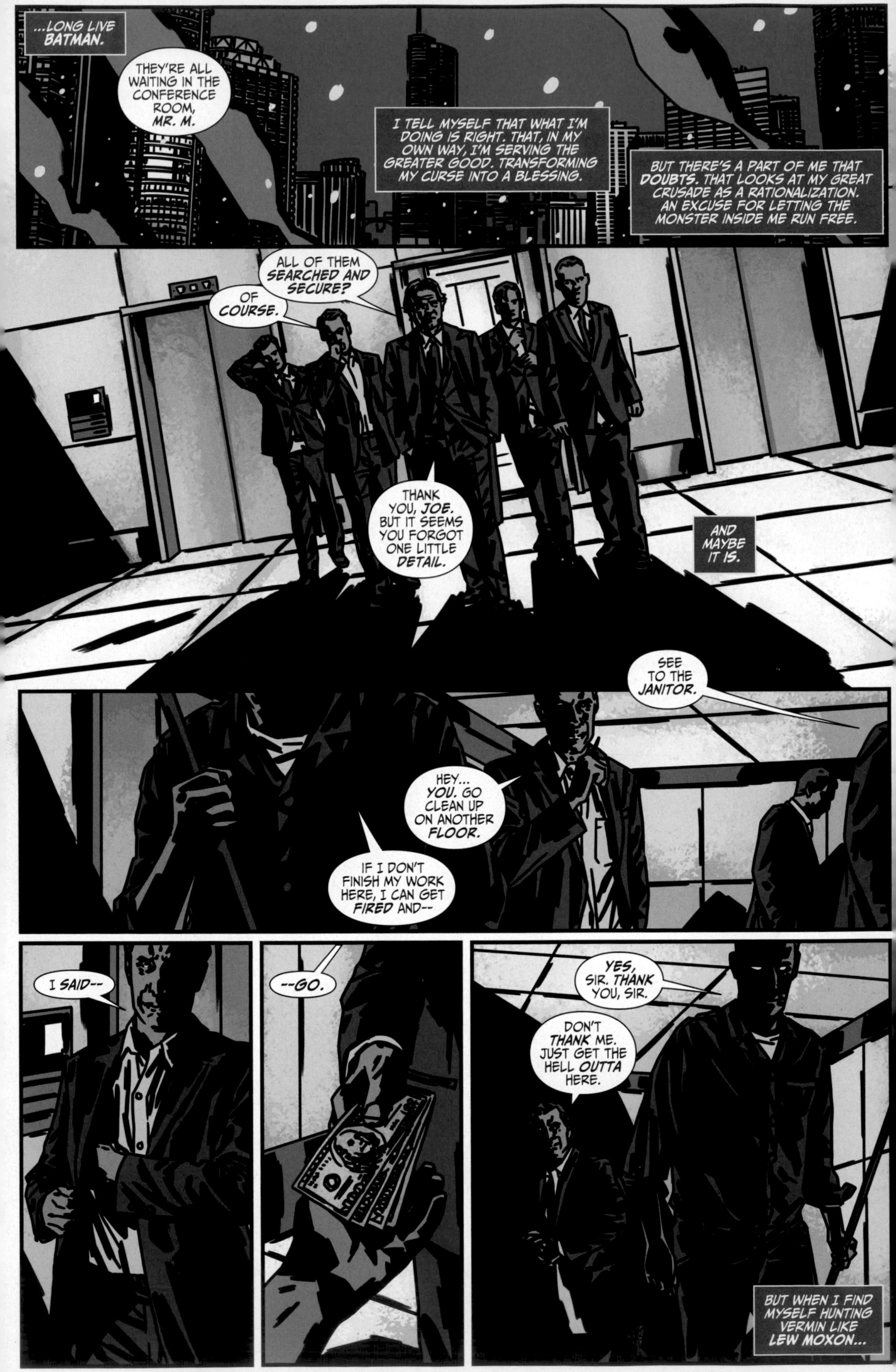
...LONG LIVE BATMAN.
THEY'RE ALL WAITING IN THE CONFERENCE ROOM, MR. M.
I TELL MYSELF THAT WHAT I'M DOING IS RIGHT. THAT, IN MY OWN WAY, I'M SERVING THE GREATER GOOD. TRANSFORMING MY CURSE INTO A BLESSING.
BUT THERE'S A PART OF ME THAT DOUBTS. THAT LOOKS AT MY GREAT CRUSADE AS A RATIONALIZATION. AN EXCUSE FOR LETTING THE MONSTER INSIDE ME RUN FREE.
ALL OF THEM SEARCHED AND SECURE?
OF COURSE.
THANK YOU, JOE. BUT IT SEEMS YOU FORGOT ONE LITTLE DETAIL.
AND MAYBE IT IS.
SEE TO THE JANITOR.
HEY... YOU. GO CLEAN UP ON ANOTHER FLOOR.
IF I DON'T FINISH MY WORK HERE, I CAN GET FIRED AND--
I SAID--
--GO.
YES, SIR. THANK YOU, SIR.
DON'T THANK ME. JUST GET THE HELL OUTTA HERE.
BUT WHEN I FIND MYSELF HUNTING VERMIN LIKE LEW MOXON...

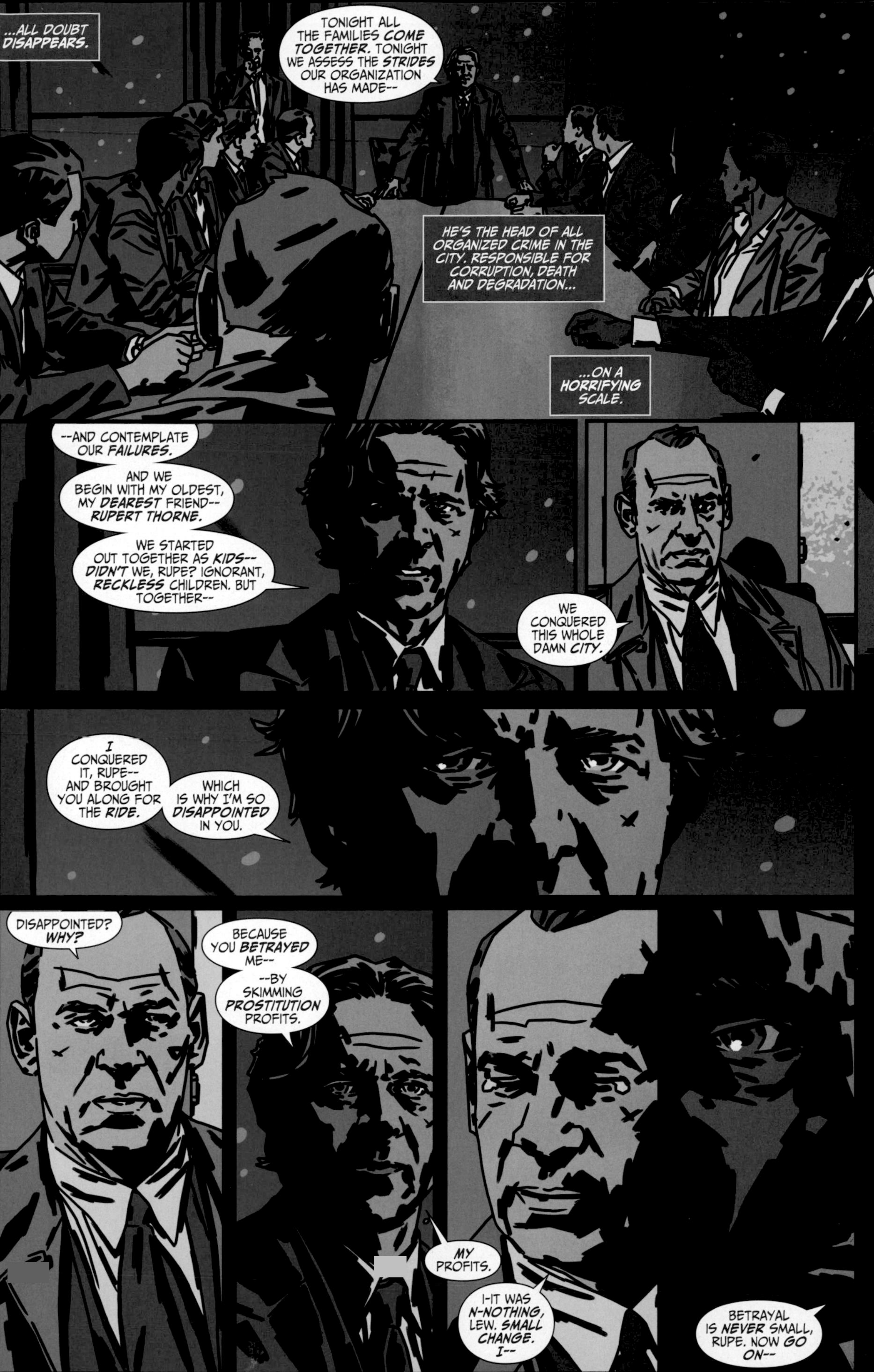
...ALL DOUBT DISAPPEARS.
TONIGHT ALL THE FAMILIES COME TOGETHER. TONIGHT WE ASSESS THE STRIDES OUR ORGANIZATION HAS MADE--
HE'S THE HEAD OF ALL ORGANIZED CRIME IN THE CITY. RESPONSIBLE FOR CORRUPTION, DEATH AND DEGRADATION...
...ON A HORRIFYING SCALE.
--AND CONTEMPLATE OUR FAILURES.
AND WE BEGIN WITH MY OLDEST, MY DEAREST FRIEND-- RUPERT THORNE.
WE STARTED OUT TOGETHER AS KIDS-- DIDN'T WE, RUPE? IGNORANT, RECKLESS CHILDREN. BUT TOGETHER--
WE CONQUERED THIS WHOLE DAMN CITY.
I CONQUERED IT, RUPE-- AND BROUGHT YOU ALONG FOR THE RIDE.
WHICH IS WHY I'M SO DISAPPOINTED IN YOU.
DISAPPOINTED? WHY?
BECAUSE YOU BETRAYED ME--
--BY SKIMMING PROSTITUTION PROFITS.
MY PROFITS.
I-IT WAS N-NOTHING, LEW. SMALL CHANGE. I--
BETRAYAL IS NEVER SMALL, RUPE. NOW GO ON--

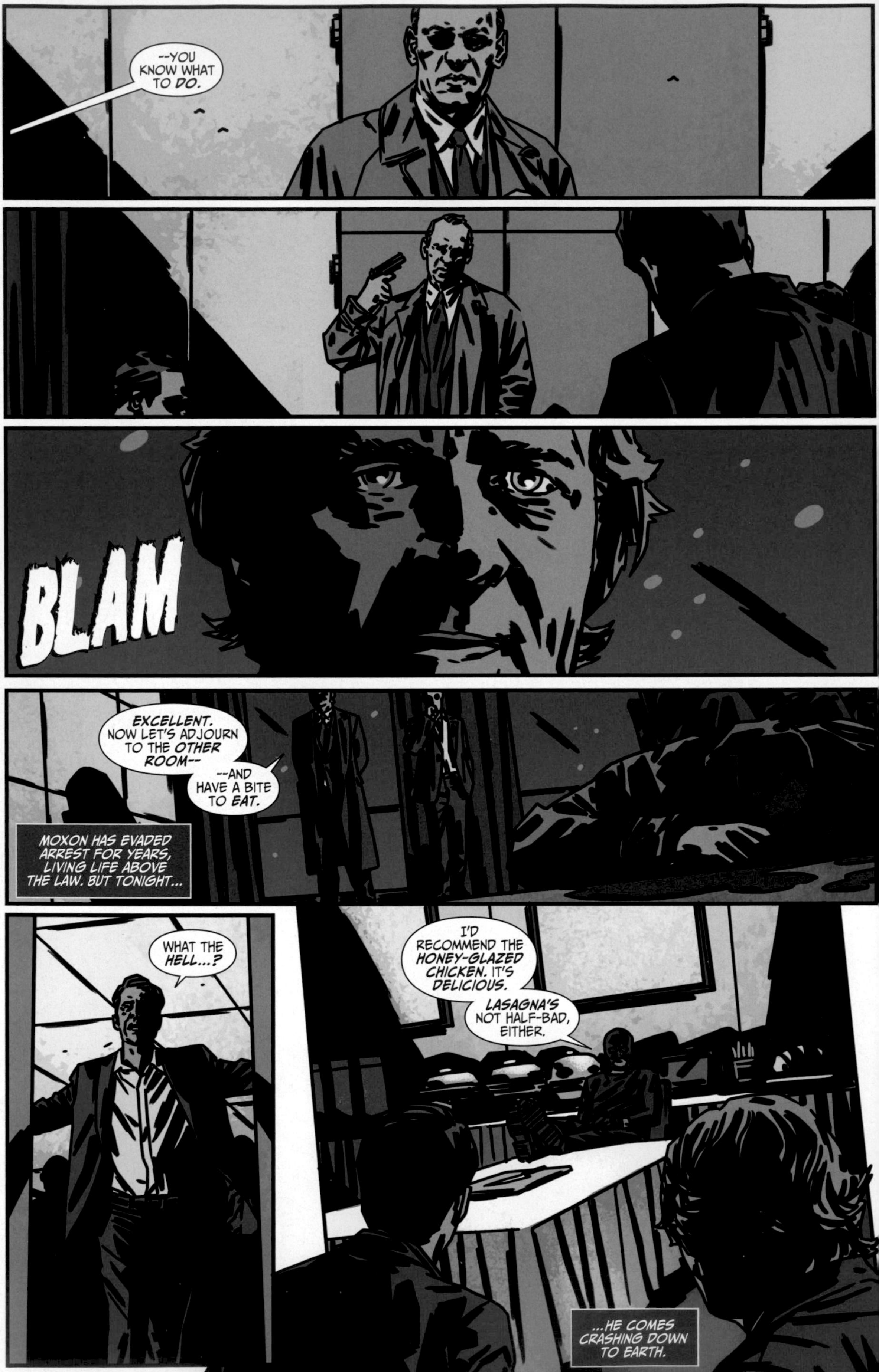
--YOU KNOW WHAT TO DO.
BLAM
EXCELLENT. NOW LET'S ADJOURN TO THE OTHER ROOM--
--AND HAVE A BITE TO EAT.
MOXON HAS EVADED ARREST FOR YEARS, LIVING LIFE ABOVE THE LAW. BUT TONIGHT...
WHAT THE HELL...?
I'D RECOMMEND THE HONEY-GLAZED CHICKEN. IT'S DELICIOUS.
LASAGNA'S NOT HALF-BAD, EITHER.
...HE COMES CRASHING DOWN TO EARTH.

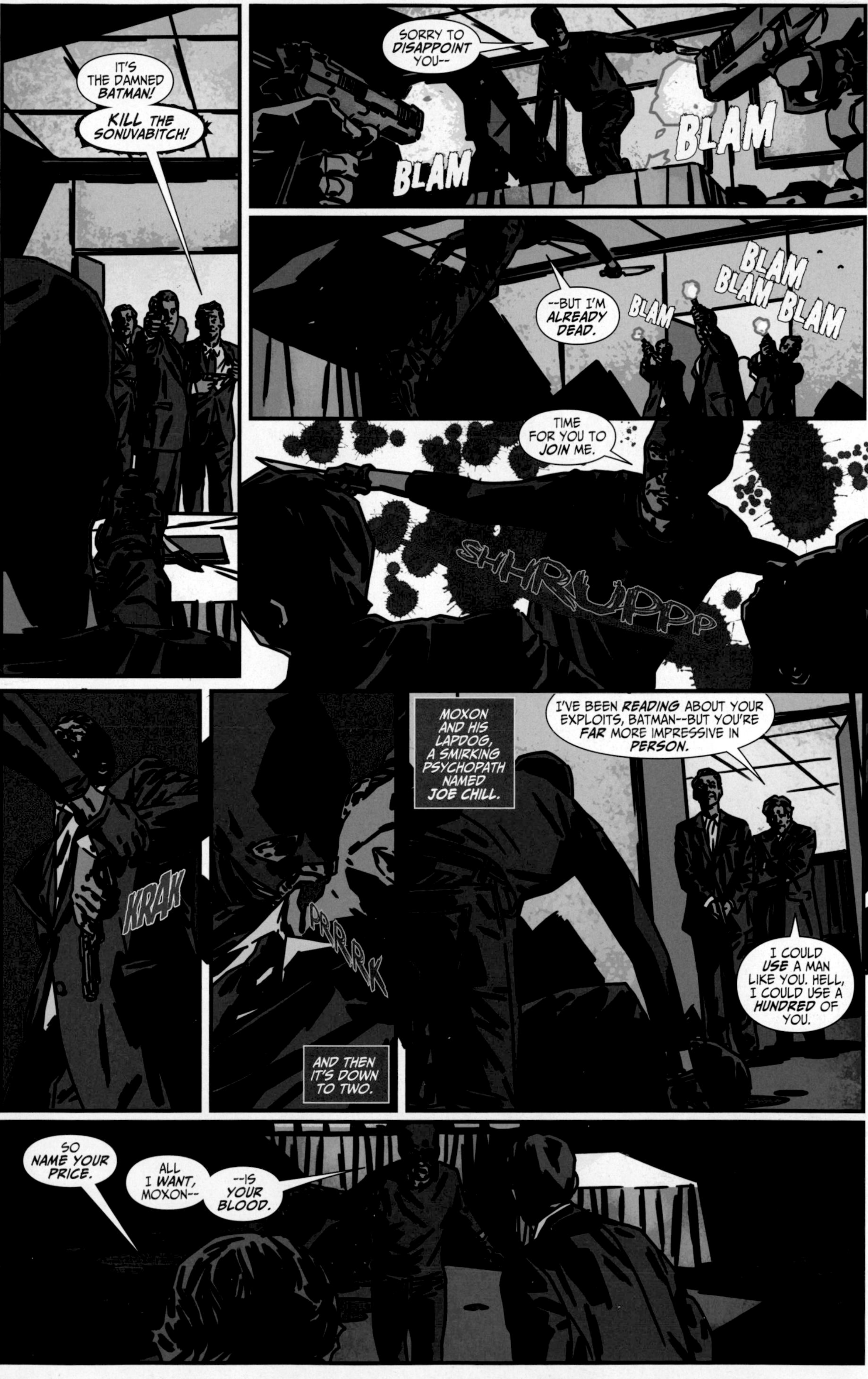
IT'S THE DAMNED BATMAN!
KILL THE SONUVABITCH!
SORRY TO DISAPPOINT YOU--
BLAM
BLAM
--BUT I'M ALREADY DEAD.
BLAM
BLAM BLAM BLAM BLAM
TIME FOR YOU TO JOIN ME.
SHHRUPPP
KRAK
PRRRK
AND THEN IT'S DOWN TO TWO.
MOXON AND HIS LAPDOG, A SMIRKING PSYCHOPATH NAMED JOE CHILL.
I'VE BEEN READING ABOUT YOUR EXPLOITS, BATMAN--BUT YOU'RE FAR MORE IMPRESSIVE IN PERSON.
I COULD USE A MAN LIKE YOU. HELL, I COULD USE A HUNDRED OF YOU.
SO NAME YOUR PRICE.
ALL I WANT, MOXON--
--IS YOUR BLOOD.

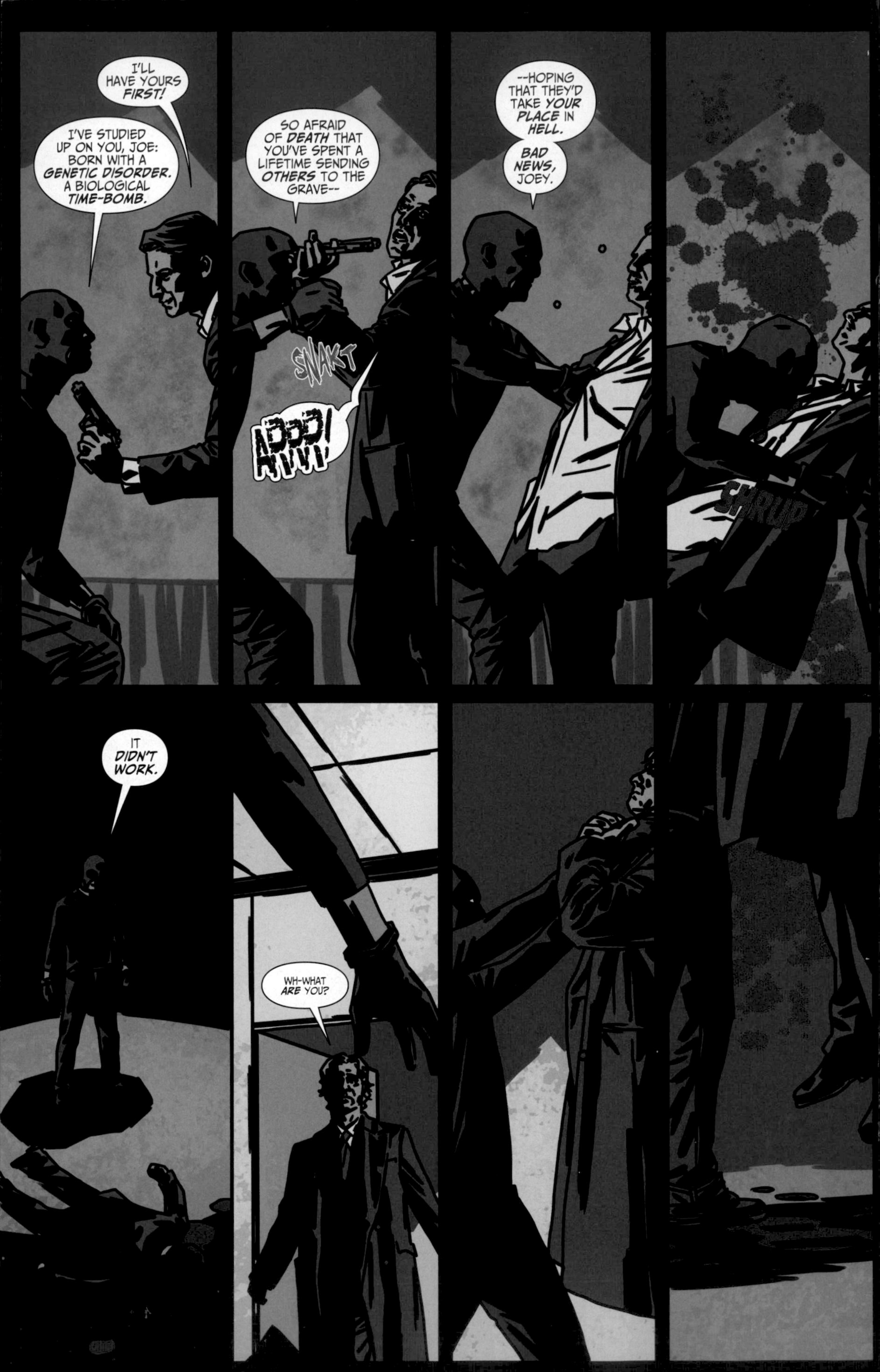
I'LL HAVE YOURS FIRST!
I'VE STUDIED UP ON YOU, JOE: BORN WITH A GENETIC DISORDER. A BIOLOGICAL TIME-BOMB.
SO AFRAID OF DEATH THAT YOU'VE SPENT A LIFETIME SENDING OTHERS TO THE GRAVE--
SNAKT
--HOPING THAT THEY'D TAKE YOUR PLACE IN HELL.
BAD NEWS, JOEY.
SHRUP
IT DIDN'T WORK.
WH-WHAT ARE YOU?

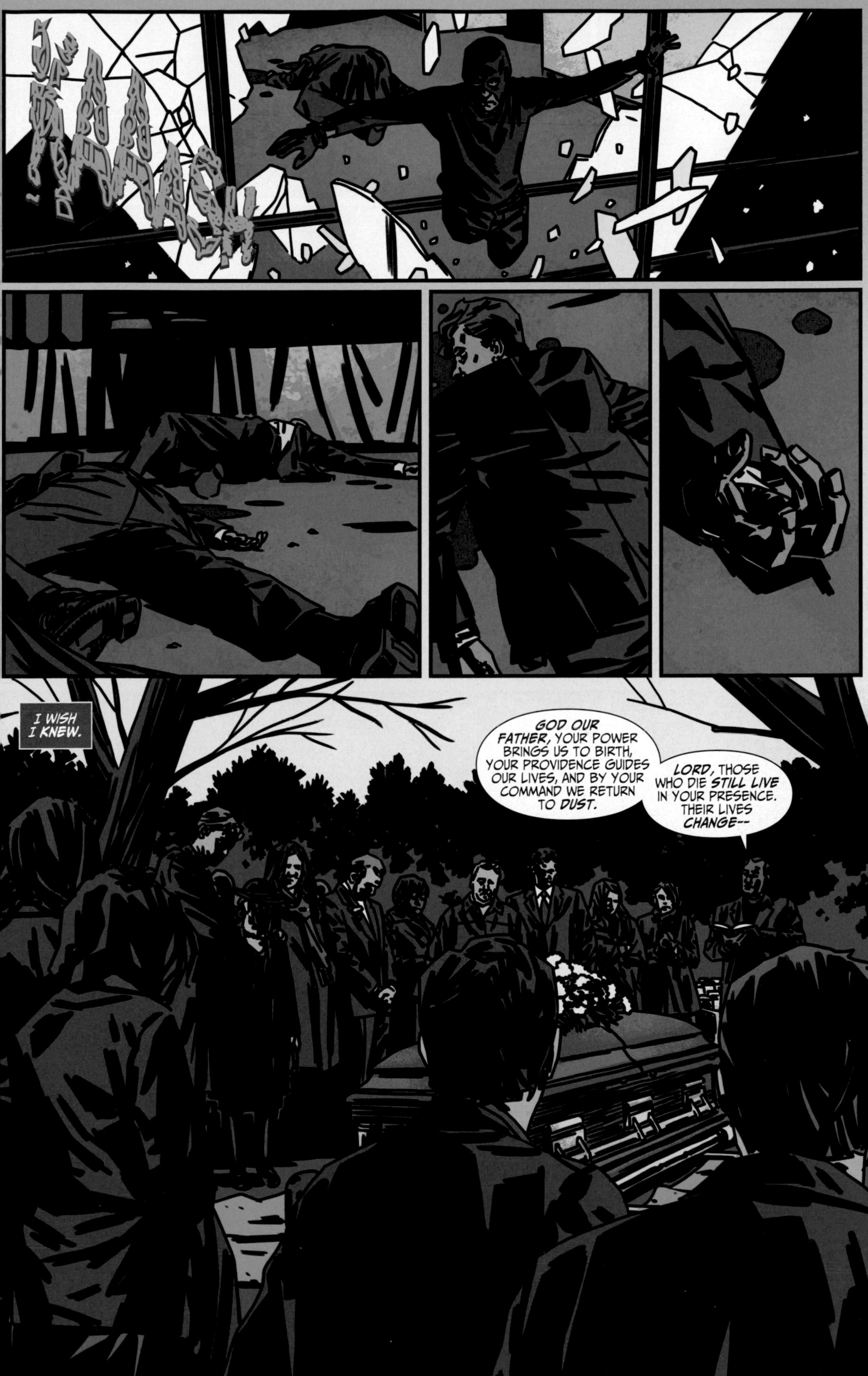
I WISH I KNEW.
GOD OUR FATHER, YOUR POWER BRINGS US TO BIRTH, YOUR PROVIDENCE GUIDES OUR LIVES, AND BY YOUR COMMAND WE RETURN TO DUST.
LORD, THOSE WHO DIE STILL LIVE IN YOUR PRESENCE. THEIR LIVES CHANGE--

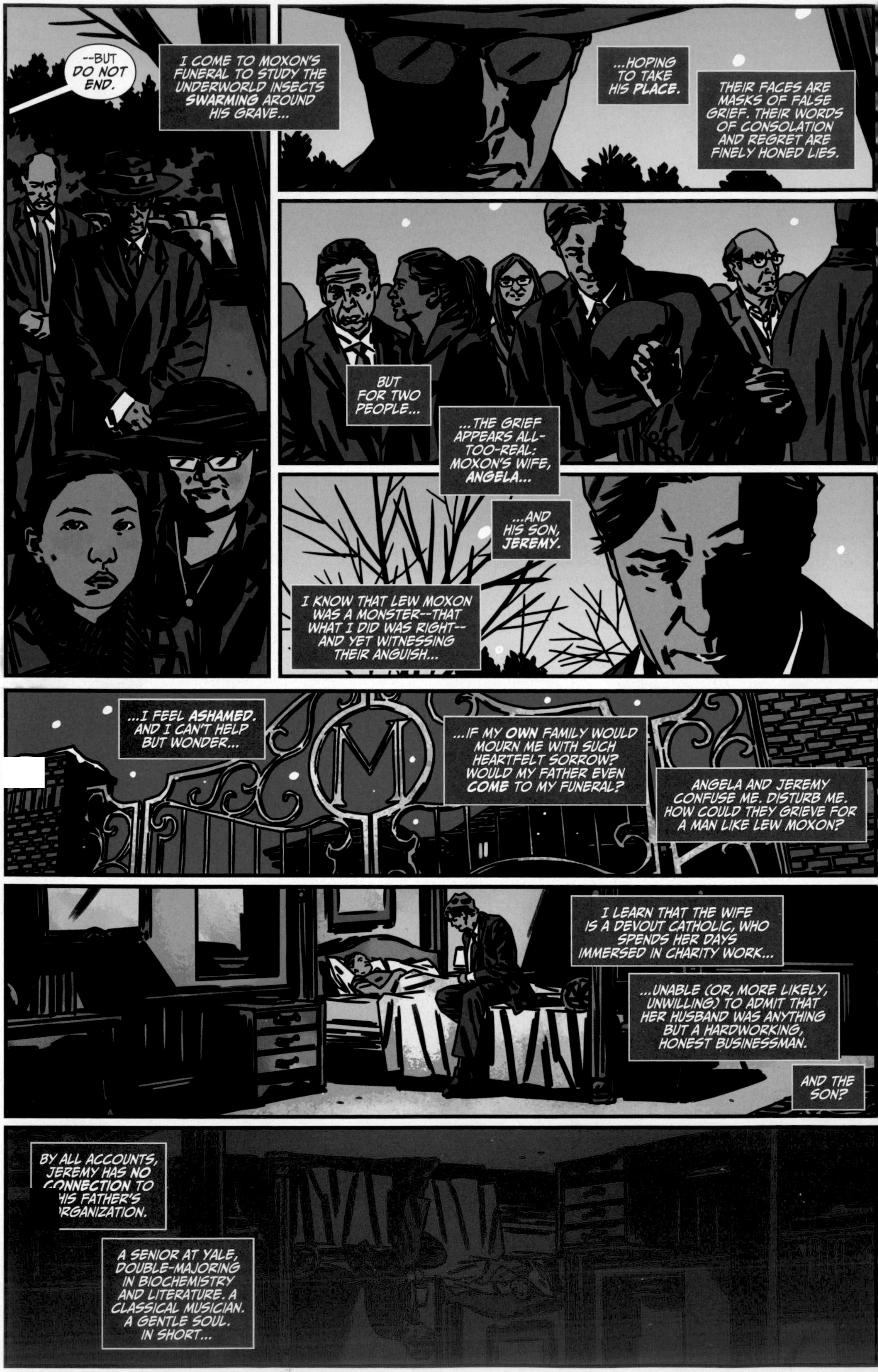
--BUT DO NOT END.
I COME TO MOXON'S FUNERAL TO STUDY THE UNDERWORLD INSECTS SWARMING AROUND HIS GRAVE...
...HOPING TO TAKE HIS PLACE.
THEIR FACES ARE MASKS OF FALSE GRIEF. THEIR WORDS OF CONSOLATION AND REGRET ARE FINELY HONED LIES.
BUT FOR TWO PEOPLE...
...THE GRIEF APPEARS ALL-TOO-REAL: MOXON'S WIFE, ANGELA...
...AND HIS SON, JEREMY.
I KNOW THAT LEW MOXON WAS A MONSTER--THAT WHAT I DID WAS RIGHT--AND YET WITNESSING THEIR ANGUISH...
...I FEEL ASHAMED. AND I CAN'T HELP BUT WONDER...
...IF MY OWN FAMILY WOULD MOURN ME WITH SUCH HEARTFELT SORROW? WOULD MY FATHER EVEN COME TO MY FUNERAL?
ANGELA AND JEREMY CONFUSE ME. DISTURB ME. HOW COULD THEY GRIEVE FOR A MAN LIKE LEW MOXON?
I LEARN THAT THE WIFE IS A DEVOUT CATHOLIC, WHO SPENDS HER DAYS IMMERSED IN CHARITY WORK...
...UNABLE (OR, MORE LIKELY, UNWILLING) TO ADMIT THAT HER HUSBAND WAS ANYTHING BUT A HARDWORKING, HONEST BUSINESSMAN.
AND THE SON?
BY ALL ACCOUNTS, JEREMY HAS NO CONNECTION TO HIS FATHER'S RGANIZATION.
A SENIOR AT YALE, DOUBLE-MAJORING IN BIOCHEMISTRY AND LITERATURE. A CLASSICAL MUSICIAN. A GENTLE SOUL. IN SHORT...

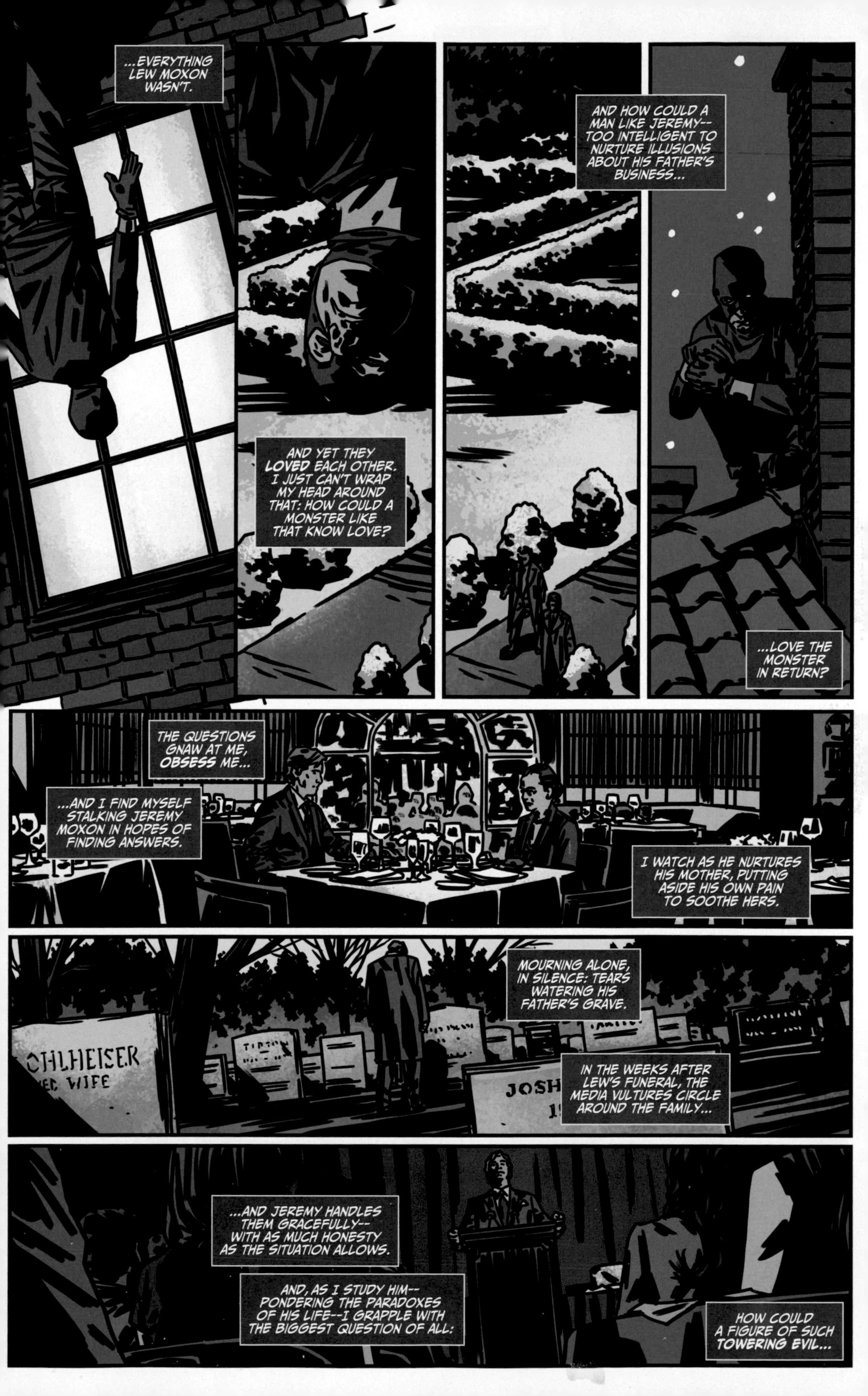
...EVERYTHING LEW MOXON WASN'T.
AND YET THEY LOVED EACH OTHER. I JUST CAN'T WRAP MY HEAD AROUND THAT: HOW COULD A MONSTER LIKE THAT KNOW LOVE?
AND HOW COULD A MAN LIKE JEREMY-- TOO INTELLIGENT TO NURTURE ILLUSIONS ABOUT HIS FATHER'S BUSINESS...
...LOVE THE MONSTER IN RETURN?
THE QUESTIONS GNAW AT ME, OBSESS ME...
...AND I FIND MYSELF STALKING JEREMY MOXON IN HOPES OF FINDING ANSWERS.
I WATCH AS HE NURTURES HIS MOTHER, PUTTING ASIDE HIS OWN PAIN TO SOOTHE HERS.
MOURNING ALONE, IN SILENCE: TEARS WATERING HIS FATHER'S GRAVE.
IN THE WEEKS AFTER LEW'S FUNERAL, THE MEDIA VULTURES CIRCLE AROUND THE FAMILY...
...AND JEREMY HANDLES THEM GRACEFULLY-- WITH AS MUCH HONESTY AS THE SITUATION ALLOWS.
AND, AS I STUDY HIM-- PONDERING THE PARADOXES OF HIS LIFE--I GRAPPLE WITH THE BIGGEST QUESTION OF ALL:
HOW COULD A FIGURE OF SUCH TOWERING EVIL...

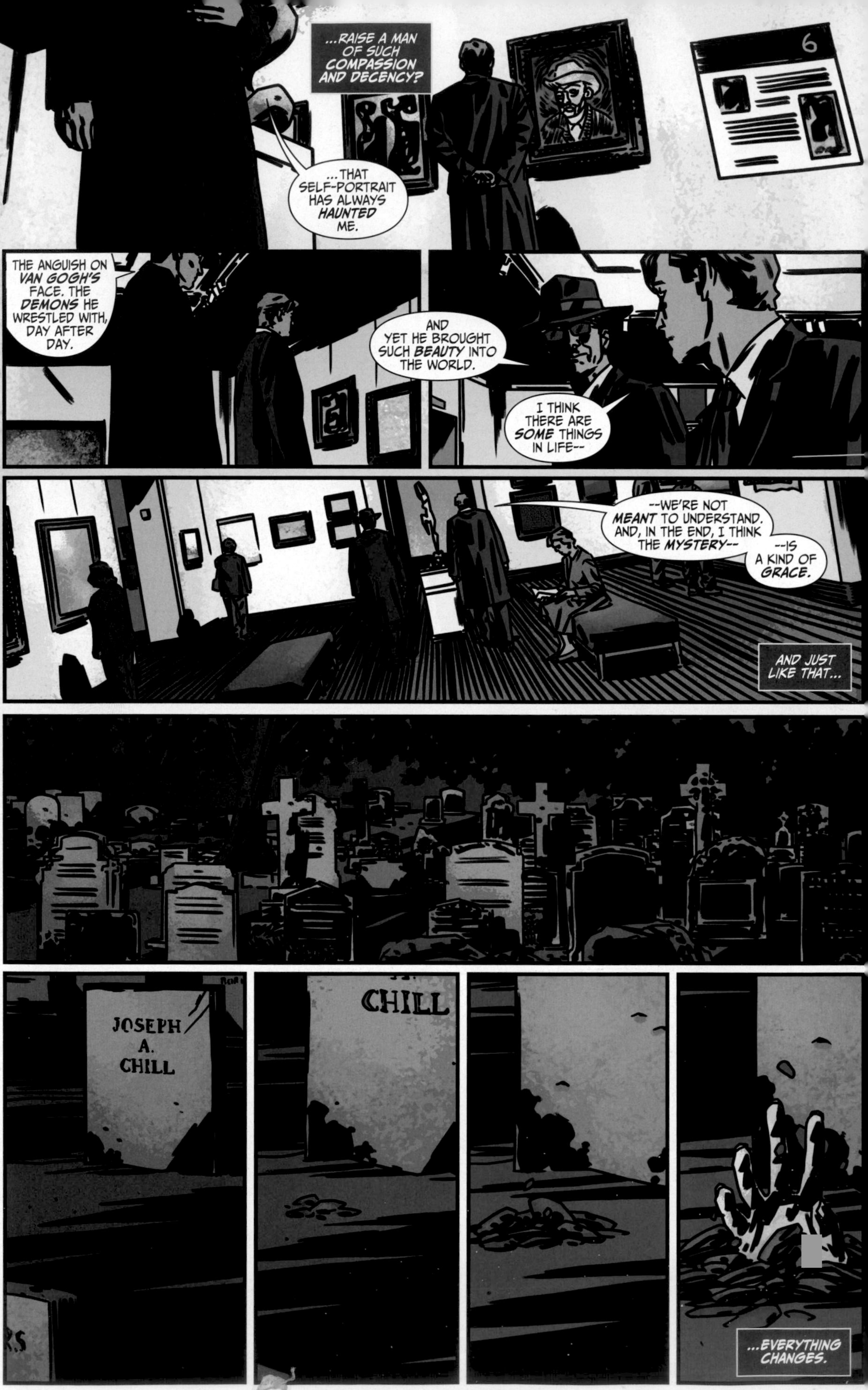
...RAISE A MAN OF SUCH COMPASSION AND DECENCY?
...THAT SELF-PORTRAIT HAS ALWAYS HAUNTED ME.
6
THE ANGUISH ON VAN GOGH'S FACE. THE DEMONS HE WRESTLED WITH, DAY AFTER DAY.
AND YET HE BROUGHT SUCH BEAUTY INTO THE WORLD.
I THINK THERE ARE SOME THINGS IN LIFE--
--WE'RE NOT MEANT TO UNDERSTAND. AND, IN THE END, I THINK THE MYSTERY--
--IS A KIND OF GRACE.
AND JUST LIKE THAT...
JOSEPH A. CHILL
CHILL
...EVERYTHING CHANGES.

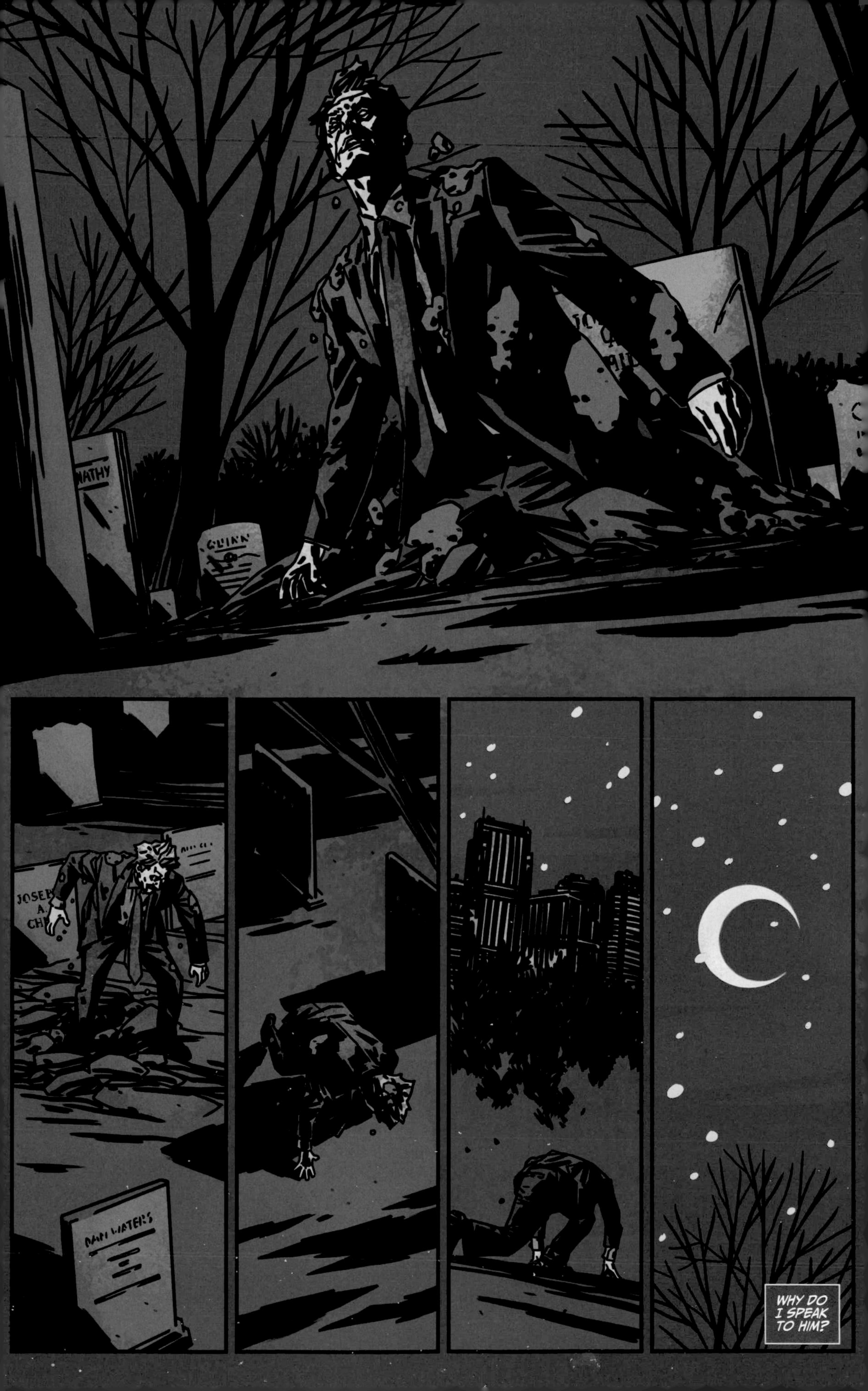
QUINN
WHY DO I SPEAK TO HIM?

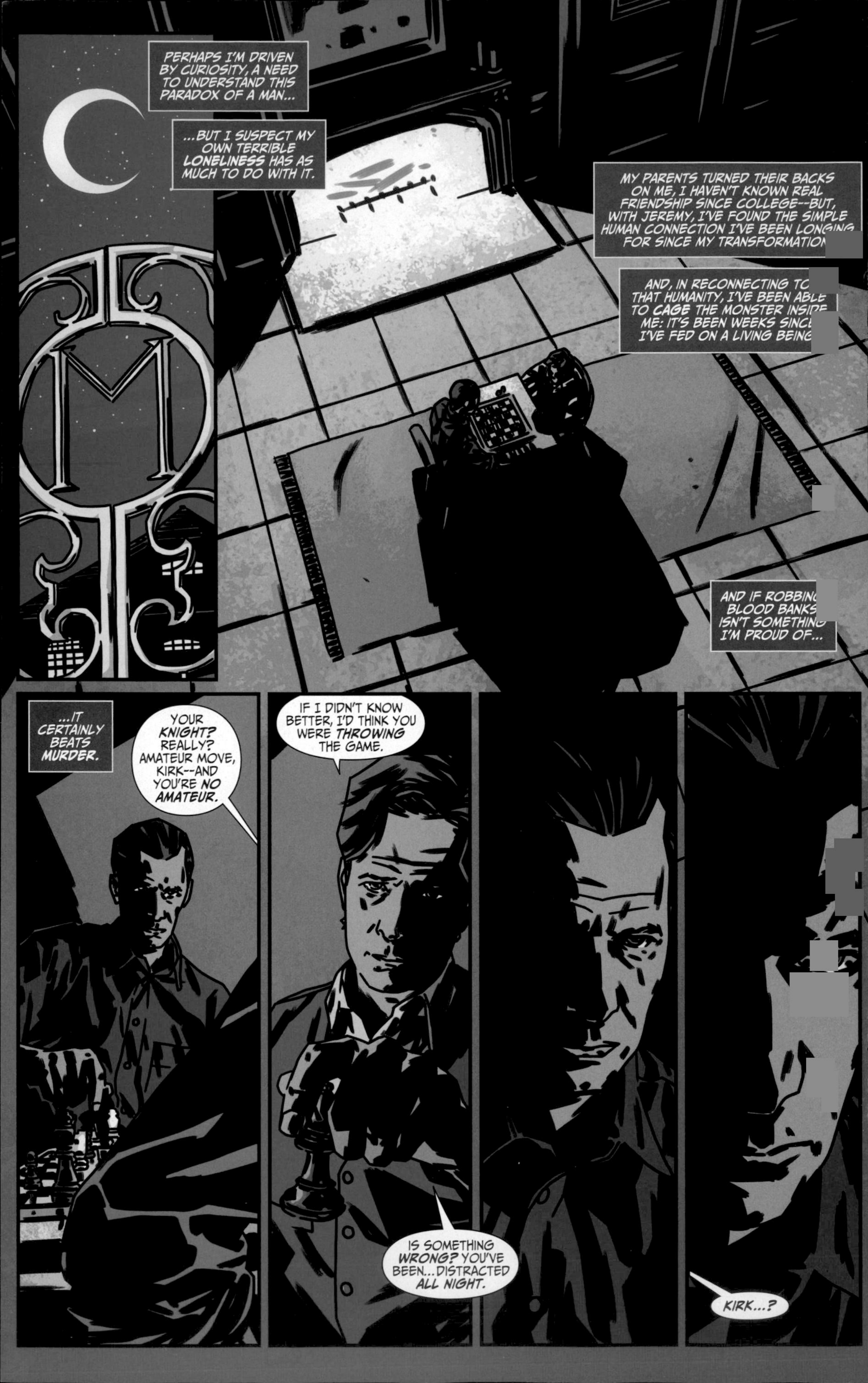
PERHAPS I'M DRIVEN BY CURIOSITY, A NEED TO UNDERSTAND THIS PARADOX OF A MAN...
...BUT I SUSPECT MY OWN TERRIBLE LONELINESS HAS AS MUCH TO DO WITH IT.
MY PARENTS TURNED THEIR BACKS ON ME, I HAVEN'T KNOWN REAL FRIENDSHIP SINCE COLLEGE--BUT, WITH JEREMY, I'VE FOUND THE SIMPLE HUMAN CONNECTION I'VE BEEN LONGING FOR SINCE MY TRANSFORMATIO
AND, IN RECONNECTING TO THAT HUMANITY, I'VE BEEN ABLE TO CAGE THE MONSTER INSIDE ME: IT'S BEEN WEEKS SINCE I'VE FED ON A LIVING BEING
AND IF ROBBING BLOOD BANKS ISN'T SOMETHING I'M PROUD OF...
...IT CERTAINLY BEATS MURDER.
YOUR KNIGHT? REALLY? AMATEUR MOVE, KIRK--AND YOU'RE NO AMATEUR.
IF I DIDN'T KNOW BETTER, I'D THINK YOU WERE THROWING THE GAME.
IS SOMETHING WRONG? YOU'VE BEEN...DISTRACTED ALL NIGHT.
KIRK...?

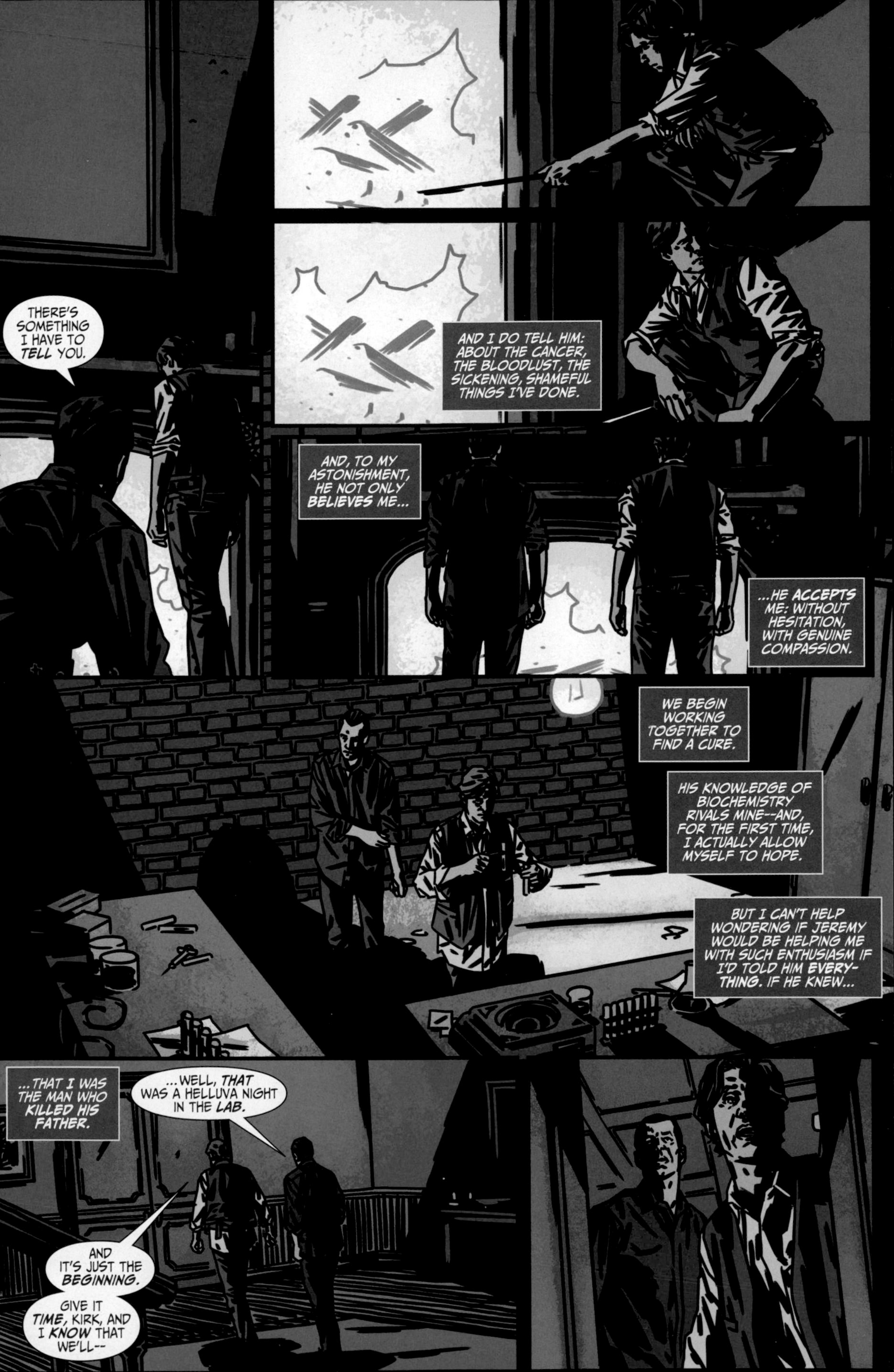

THERE'S SOMETHING I HAVE TO TELL YOU.
AND I DO TELL HIM: ABOUT THE CANCER, THE BLOODLUST, THE SICKENING, SHAMEFUL THINGS I'VE DONE.
AND, TO MY ASTONISHMENT, HE NOT ONLY BELIEVES ME...
...HE ACCEPTS ME: WITHOUT HESITATION, WITH GENUINE COMPASSION.
WE BEGIN WORKING TOGETHER TO FIND A CURE.
HIS KNOWLEDGE OF BIOCHEMISTRY RIVALS MINE--AND, FOR THE FIRST TIME, I ACTUALLY ALLOW MYSELF TO HOPE.
BUT I CAN'T HELP WONDERING IF JEREMY WOULD BE HELPING ME WITH SUCH ENTHUSIASM IF I'D TOLD HIM EVERY-THING. IF HE KNEW...
...THAT I WAS THE MAN WHO KILLED HIS FATHER.
...WELL, THAT WAS A HELLUVA NIGHT IN THE LAB.
AND IT'S JUST THE BEGINNING.
GIVE IT TIME, KIRK, AND I KNOW THAT WE'LL--

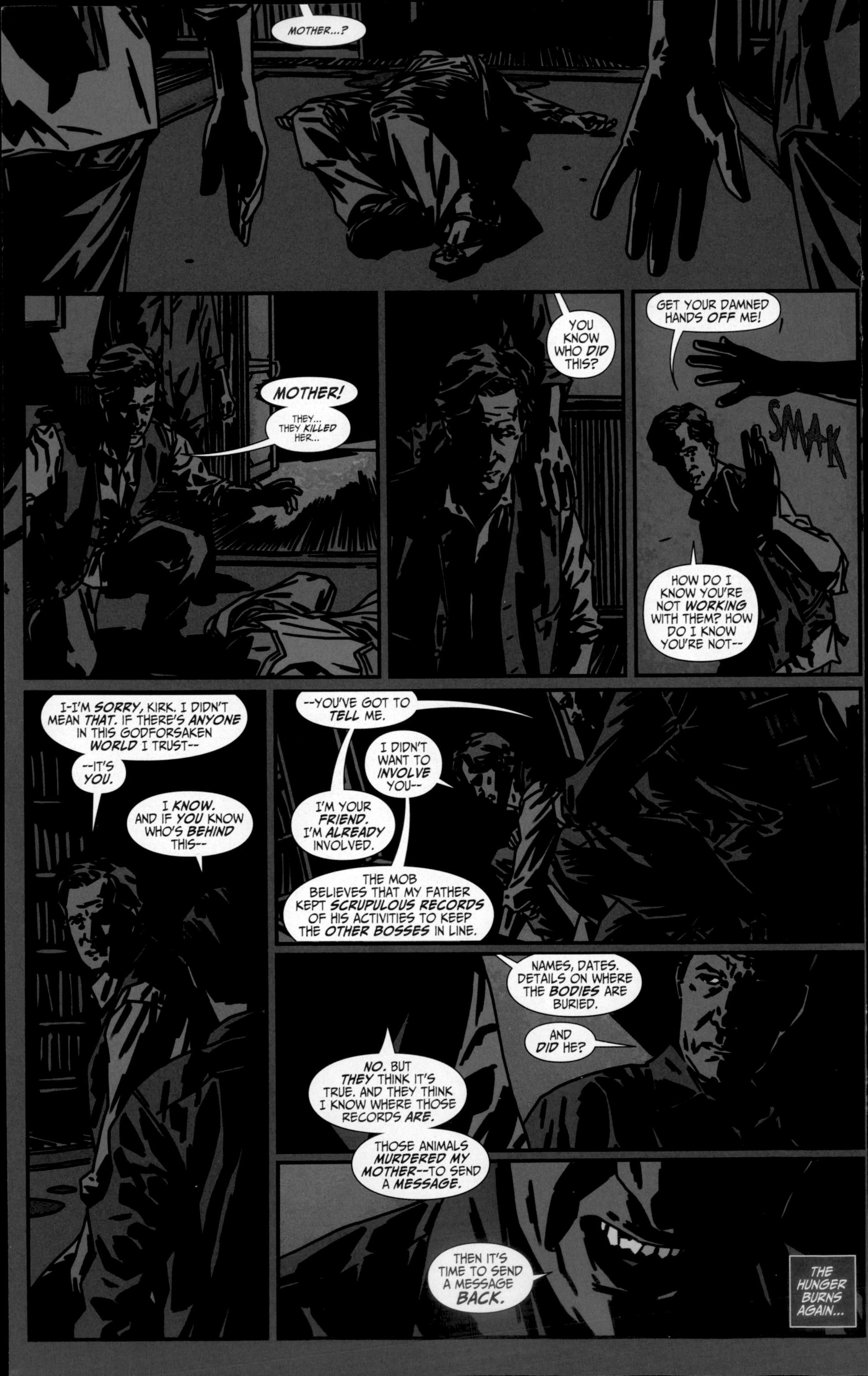
MOTHER...?
MOTHER!
THEY... THEY KILLED HER...
YOU KNOW WHO DID THIS?
GET YOUR DAMNED HANDS OFF ME!
SMAK
HOW DO I KNOW YOU'RE NOT WORKING WITH THEM? HOW DO I KNOW YOU'RE NOT--
I-I'M SORRY, KIRK. I DIDN'T MEAN THAT. IF THERE'S ANYONE IN THIS GODFORSAKEN WORLD I TRUST--
--IT'S YOU.
I KNOW. AND IF YOU KNOW WHO'S BEHIND THIS--
--YOU'VE GOT TO TELL ME.
I DIDN'T WANT TO INVOLVE YOU--
I'M YOUR FRIEND. I'M ALREADY INVOLVED.
THE MOB BELIEVES THAT MY FATHER KEPT SCRUPULOUS RECORDS OF HIS ACTIVITIES TO KEEP THE OTHER BOSSES IN LINE.
NAMES, DATES. DETAILS ON WHERE THE BODIES ARE BURIED.
AND DID HE?
NO. BUT THEY THINK IT'S TRUE. AND THEY THINK I KNOW WHERE THOSE RECORDS ARE.
THOSE ANIMALS MURDERED MY MOTHER--TO SEND A MESSAGE.
THEN IT'S TIME TO SEND A MESSAGE BACK.
THE HUNGER BURNS AGAIN...

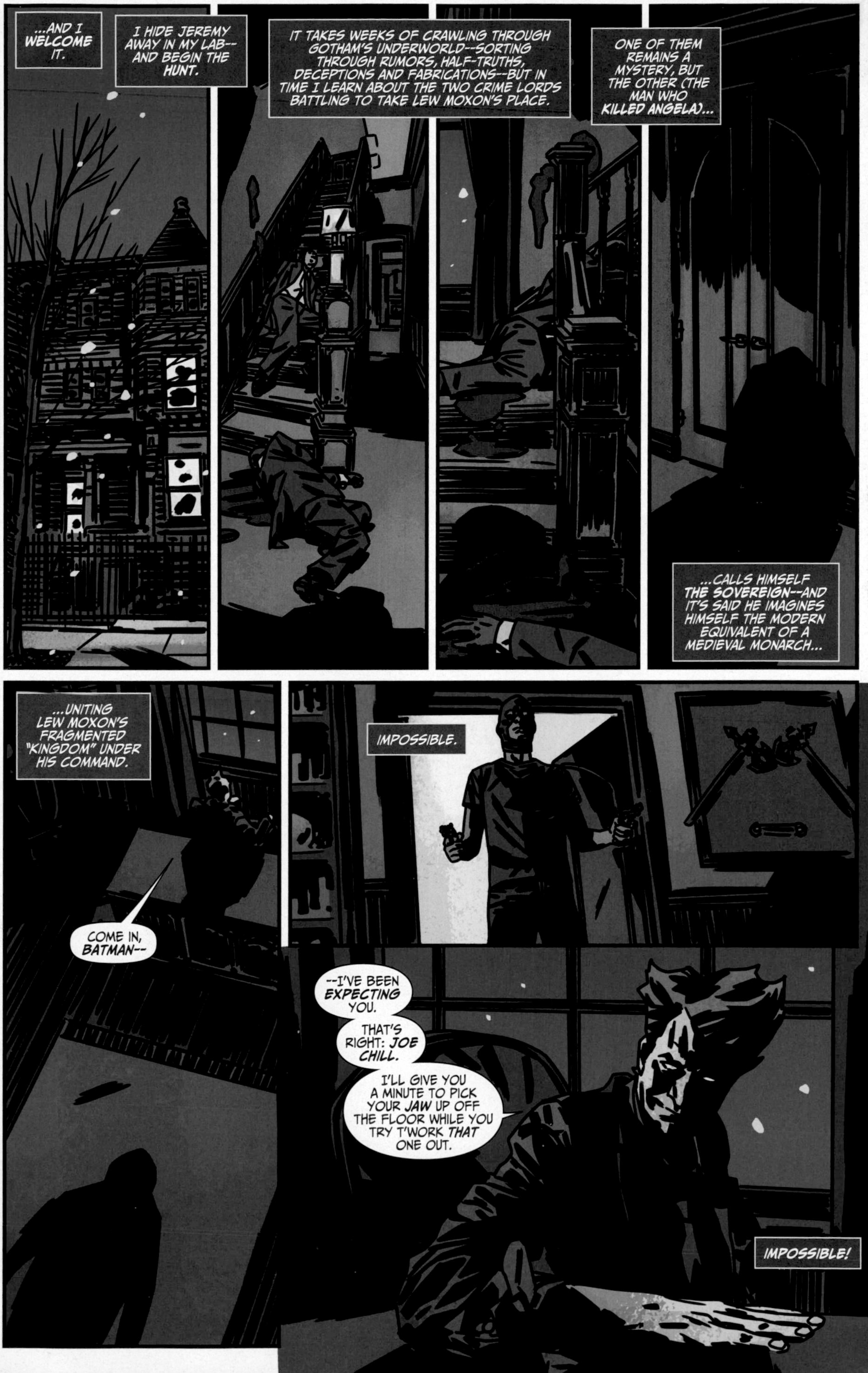

...AND I WELCOME IT.
I HIDE JEREMY AWAY IN MY LAB-- AND BEGIN THE HUNT.
IT TAKES WEEKS OF CRAWLING THROUGH GOTHAM'S UNDERWORLD--SORTING THROUGH RUMORS, HALF-TRUTHS, DECEPTIONS AND FABRICATIONS--BUT IN TIME I LEARN ABOUT THE TWO CRIME LORDS BATTLING TO TAKE LEW MOXON'S PLACE.
ONE OF THEM REMAINS A MYSTERY, BUT THE OTHER (THE MAN WHO KILLED ANGELA)...
...CALLS HIMSELF THE SOVEREIGN--AND IT'S SAID HE IMAGINES HIMSELF THE MODERN EQUIVALENT OF A MEDIEVAL MONARCH...
...UNITING LEW MOXON'S FRAGMENTED "KINGDOM" UNDER HIS COMMAND.
IMPOSSIBLE.
COME IN, BATMAN--
--I'VE BEEN EXPECTING YOU.
THAT'S RIGHT: JOE CHILL.
I'LL GIVE YOU A MINUTE TO PICK YOUR JAW UP OFF THE FLOOR WHILE YOU TRY T'WORK THAT ONE OUT.
IMPOSSIBLE!

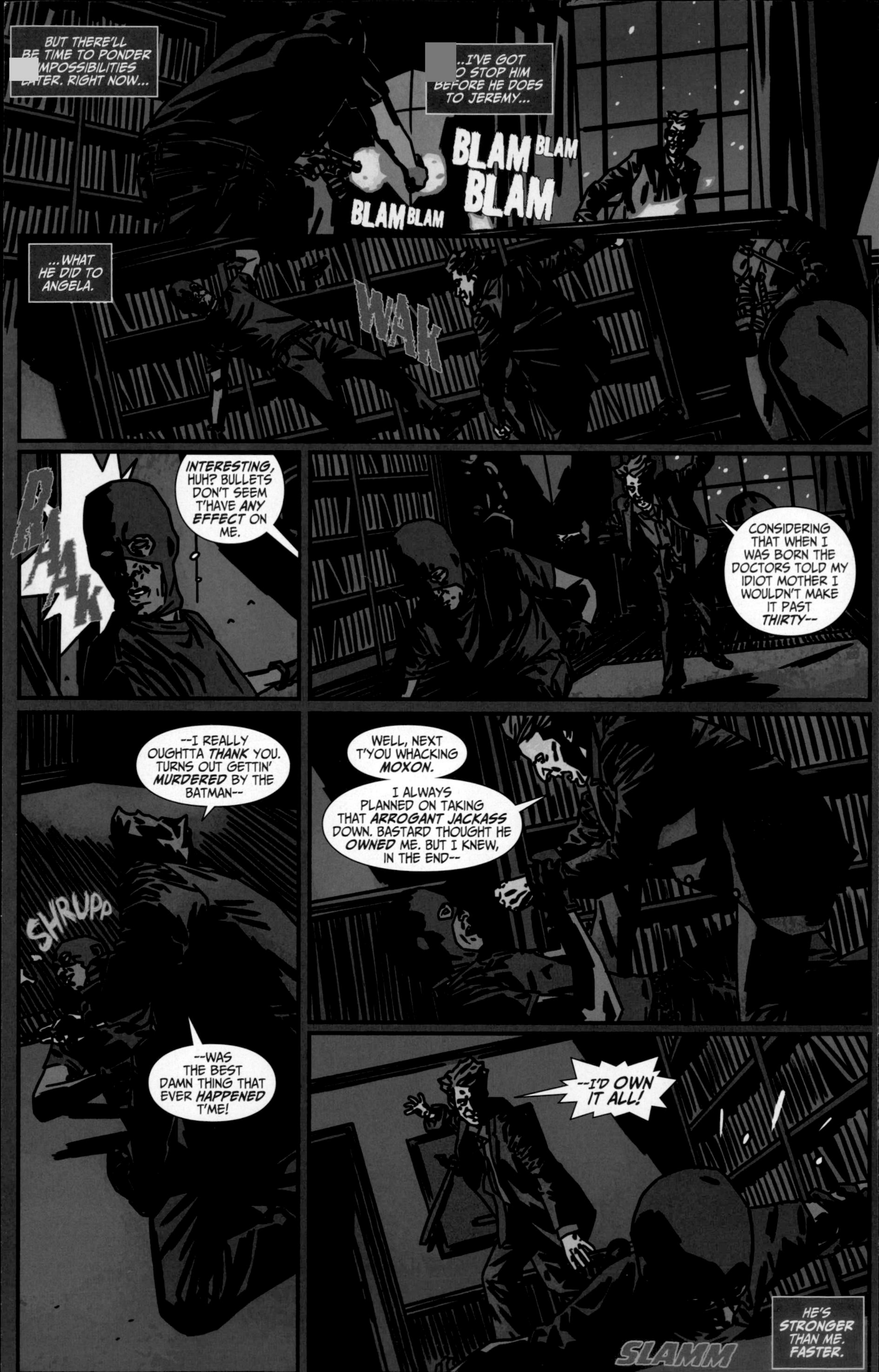
BUT THERE'LL BE TIME TO PONDER IMPOSSIBILITIES LATER. RIGHT NOW...
...I'VE GOT TO STOP HIM BEFORE HE DOES TO JEREMY...
BLAM BLAM BLAM
BLAM BLAM
...WHAT HE DID TO ANGELA.
WAK
RAAK
INTERESTING, HUH? BULLETS DON'T SEEM T'HAVE ANY EFFECT ON ME.
CONSIDERING THAT WHEN I WAS BORN THE DOCTORS TOLD MY IDIOT MOTHER I WOULDN'T MAKE IT PAST THIRTY--
--I REALLY OUGHTTA THANK YOU. TURNS OUT GETTIN' MURDERED BY THE BATMAN--
SHRUPP
--WAS THE BEST DAMN THING THAT EVER HAPPENED T'ME!
WELL, NEXT T'YOU WHACKING MOXON.
I ALWAYS PLANNED ON TAKING THAT ARROGANT JACKASS DOWN. BASTARD THOUGHT HE OWNED ME. BUT I KNEW, IN THE END--
--I'D OWN IT ALL!
HE'S STRONGER THAN ME. FASTER.
SLAMM

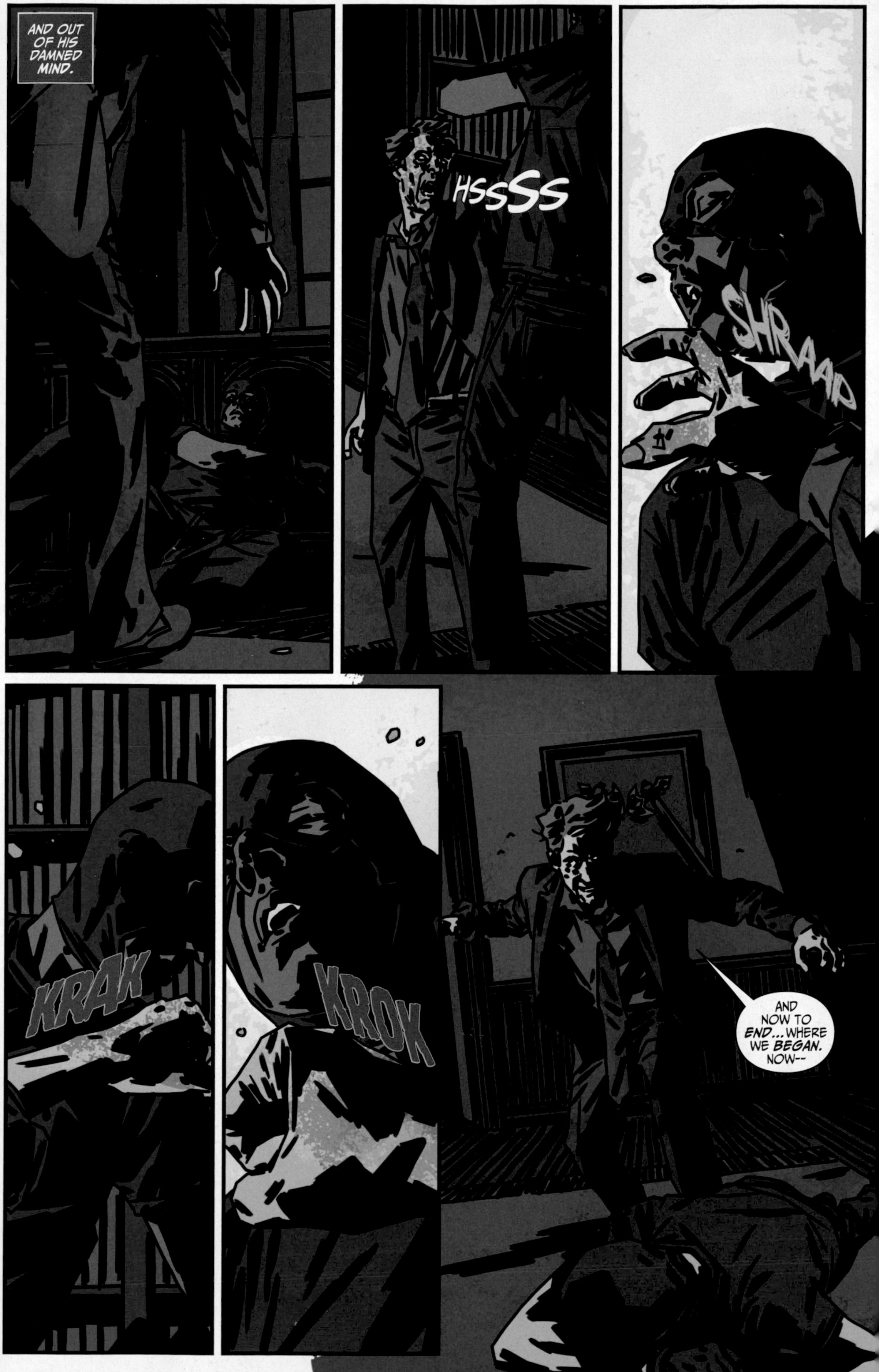
AND OUT OF HIS DAMNED MIND.
HSSSSS
SHRAAAP
KRAK
KROK
AND NOW TO END... WHERE WE BEGAN. NOW--

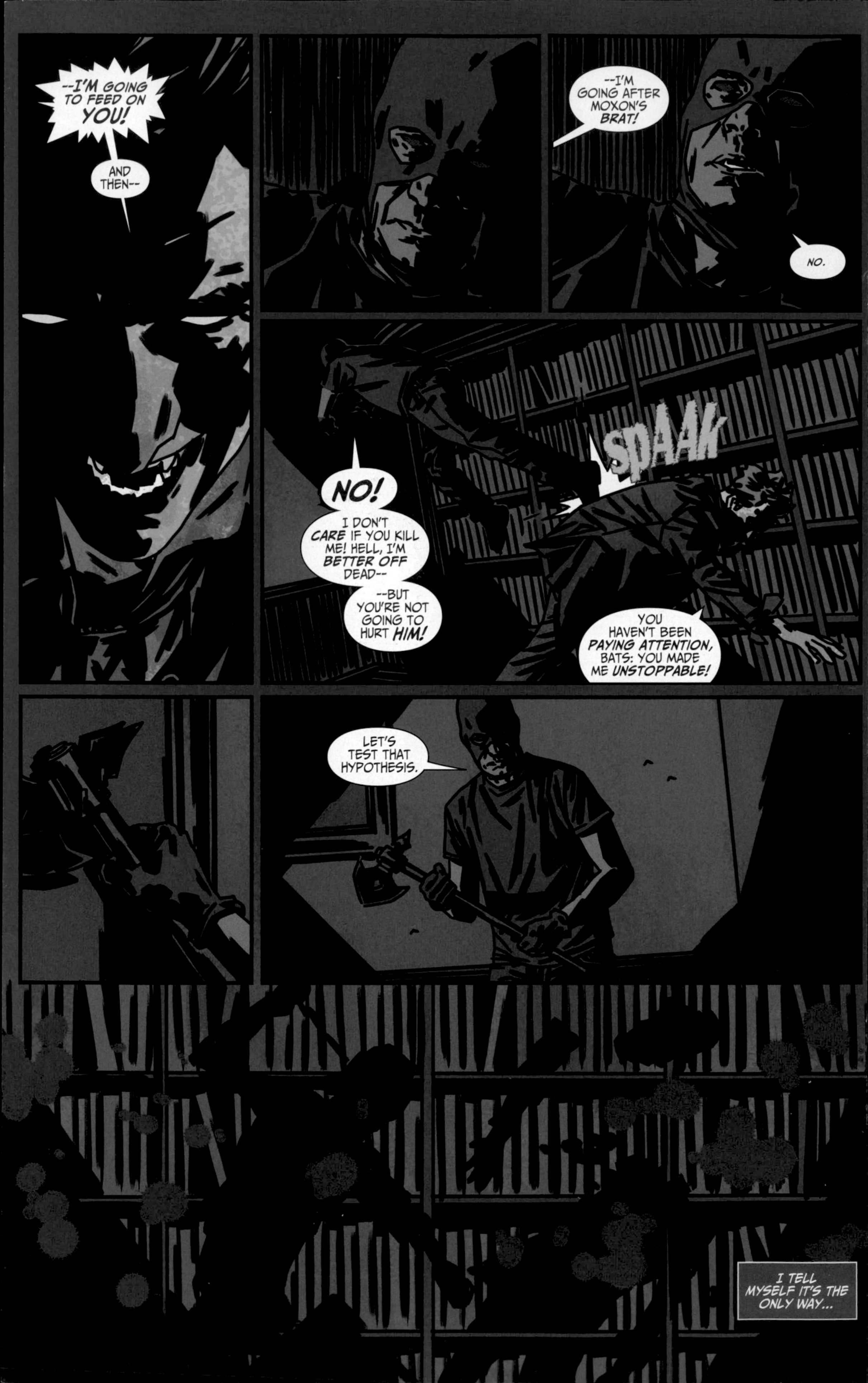
--I'M GOING TO FEED ON YOU!
AND THEN--
--I'M GOING AFTER MOXON'S BRAT!
NO.
SPAAK
NO!
I DON'T CARE IF YOU KILL ME! HELL, I'M BETTER OFF DEAD--
--BUT YOU'RE NOT GOING TO HURT HIM!
YOU HAVEN'T BEEN PAYING ATTENTION, BATS: YOU MADE ME UNSTOPPABLE!
LET'S TEST THAT HYPOTHESIS.
I TELL MYSELF IT'S THE ONLY WAY...

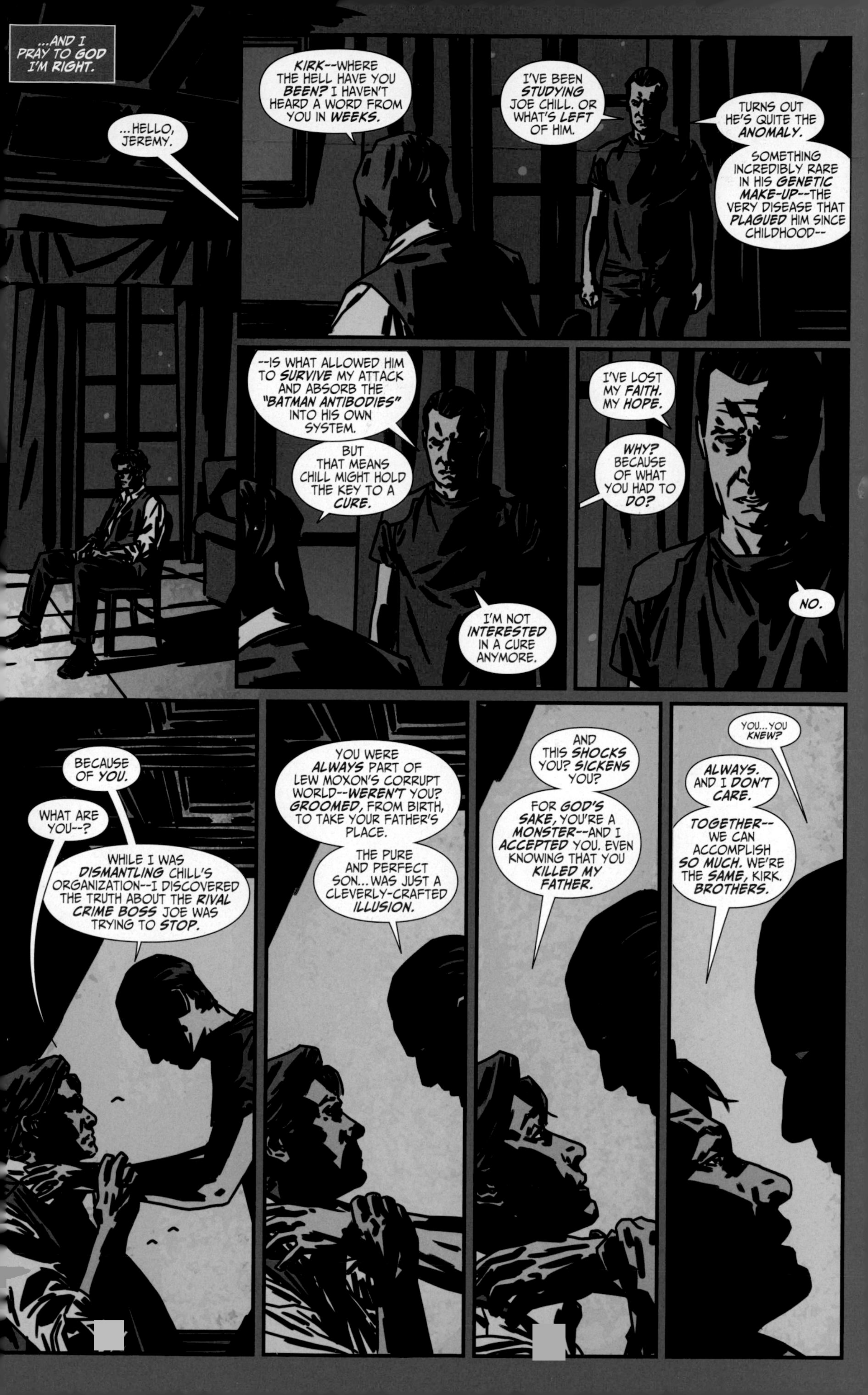
...AND I PRAY TO GOD I'M RIGHT.
...HELLO, JEREMY.
KIRK--WHERE THE HELL HAVE YOU BEEN? I HAVEN'T HEARD A WORD FROM YOU IN WEEKS.
I'VE BEEN STUDYING JOE CHILL. OR WHAT'S LEFT OF HIM.
TURNS OUT HE'S QUITE THE ANOMALY.
SOMETHING INCREDIBLY RARE IN HIS GENETIC MAKE-UP--THE VERY DISEASE THAT PLAGUED HIM SINCE CHILDHOOD--
--IS WHAT ALLOWED HIM TO SURVIVE MY ATTACK AND ABSORB THE "BATMAN ANTIBODIES" INTO HIS OWN SYSTEM.
BUT THAT MEANS CHILL MIGHT HOLD THE KEY TO A CURE.
I'M NOT INTERESTED IN A CURE ANYMORE.
I'VE LOST MY FAITH. MY HOPE.
WHY? BECAUSE OF WHAT YOU HAD TO DO?
NO.
BECAUSE OF YOU.
WHAT ARE YOU--?
WHILE I WAS DISMANTLING CHILL'S ORGANIZATION--I DISCOVERED THE TRUTH ABOUT THE RIVAL CRIME BOSS JOE WAS TRYING TO STOP.
YOU WERE ALWAYS PART OF LEW MOXON'S CORRUPT WORLD--WEREN'T YOU? GROOMED, FROM BIRTH, TO TAKE YOUR FATHER'S PLACE.
THE PURE AND PERFECT SON...WAS JUST A CLEVERLY-CRAFTED ILLUSION.
AND THIS SHOCKS YOU? SICKENS YOU?
FOR GOD'S SAKE, YOU'RE A MONSTER--AND I ACCEPTED YOU. EVEN KNOWING THAT YOU KILLED MY FATHER.
YOU...YOU KNEW?
ALWAYS. AND I DON'T CARE.
TOGETHER--WE CAN ACCOMPLISH SO MUCH. WE'RE THE SAME, KIRK. BROTHERS.

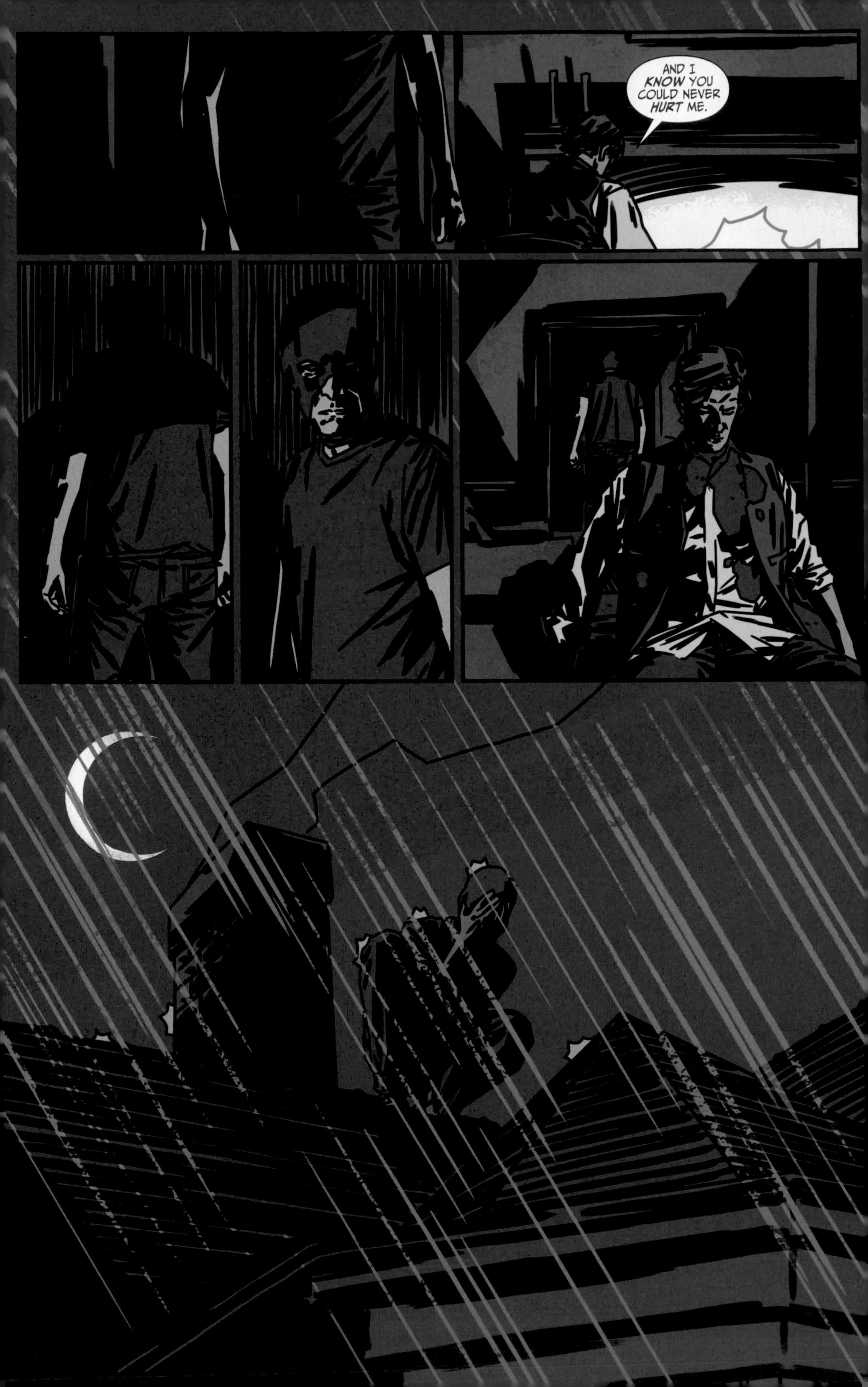
AND I KNOW YOU COULD NEVER HURT ME.

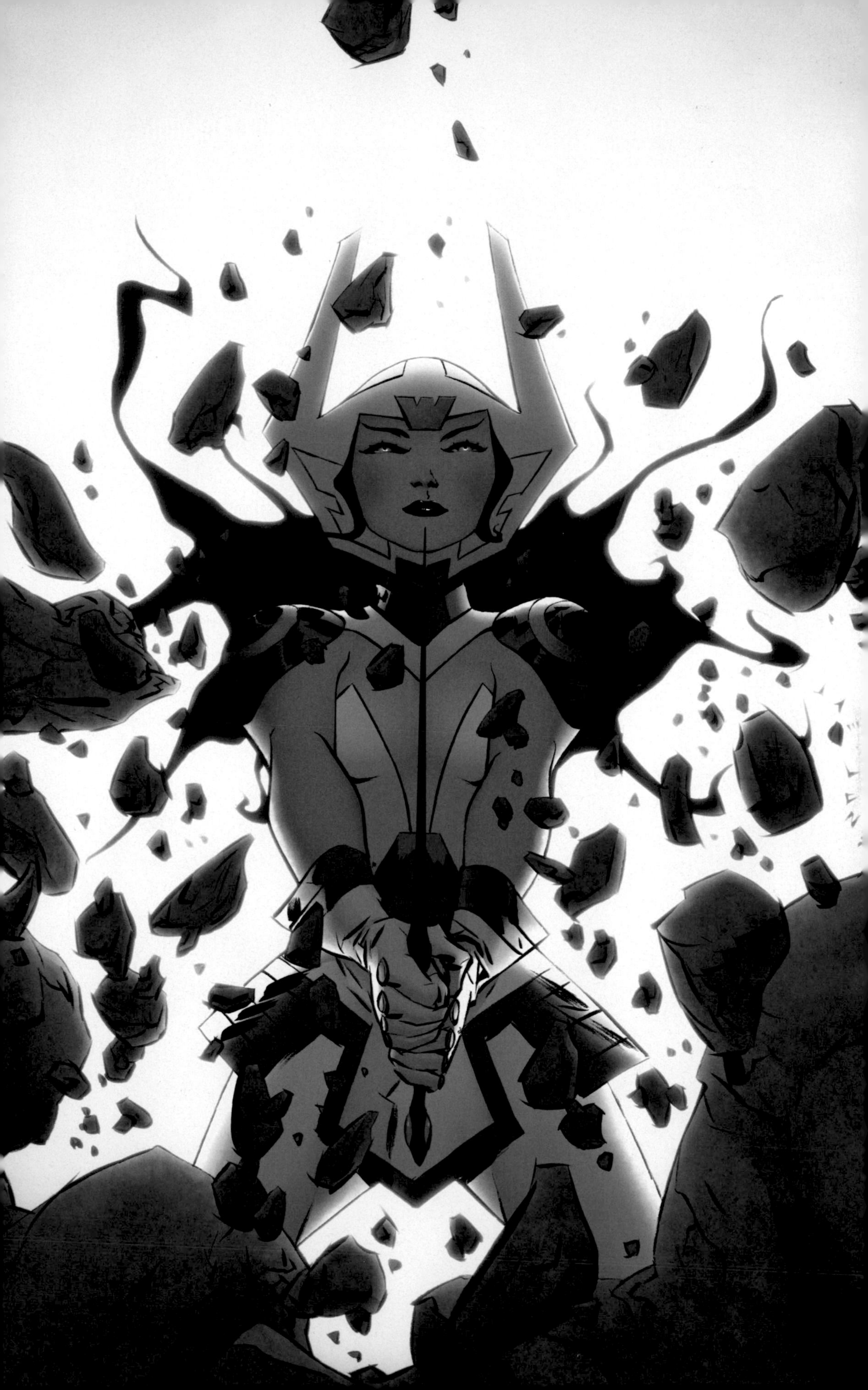

THE DREAM

PENCILS BY RICK LEONARDI

INKS BY DAN GREEN

COLORS BY ALLEN PASSALAQUA

COVER ART BY JAE LEE AND JUNE CHUNG

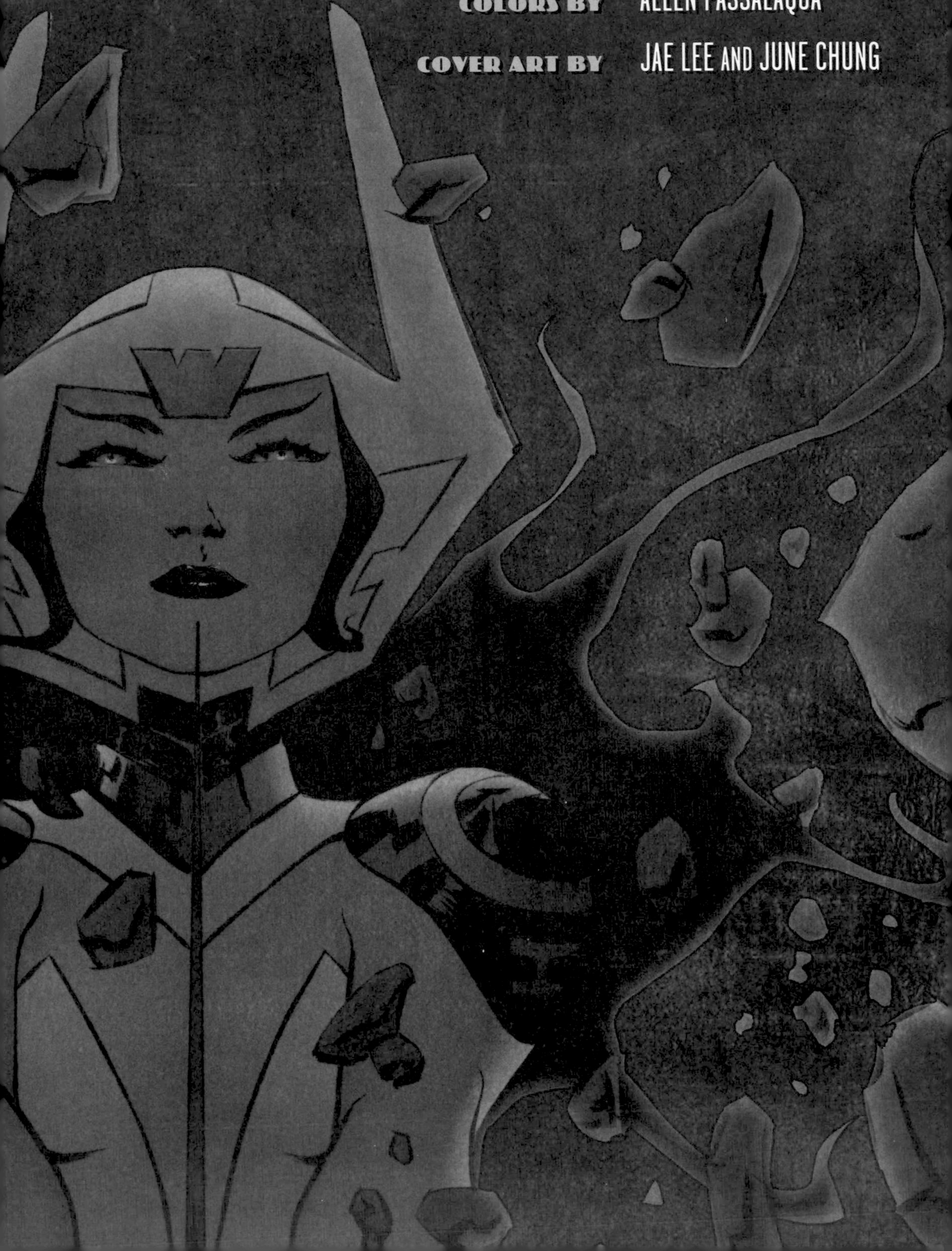

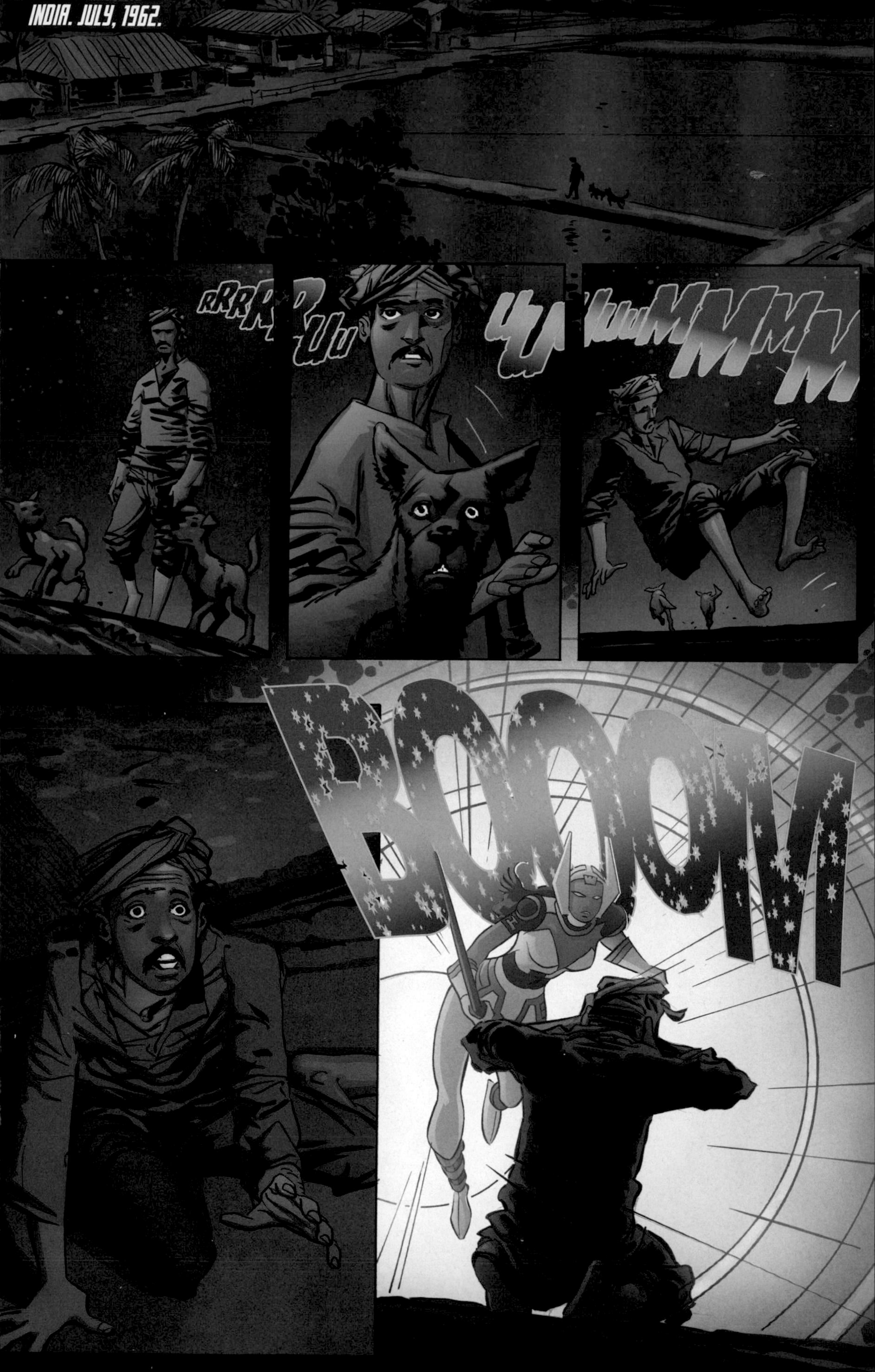
INDIA. JULY, 1962.
RRRRRUUUUUUMMMMMM
BOOOM

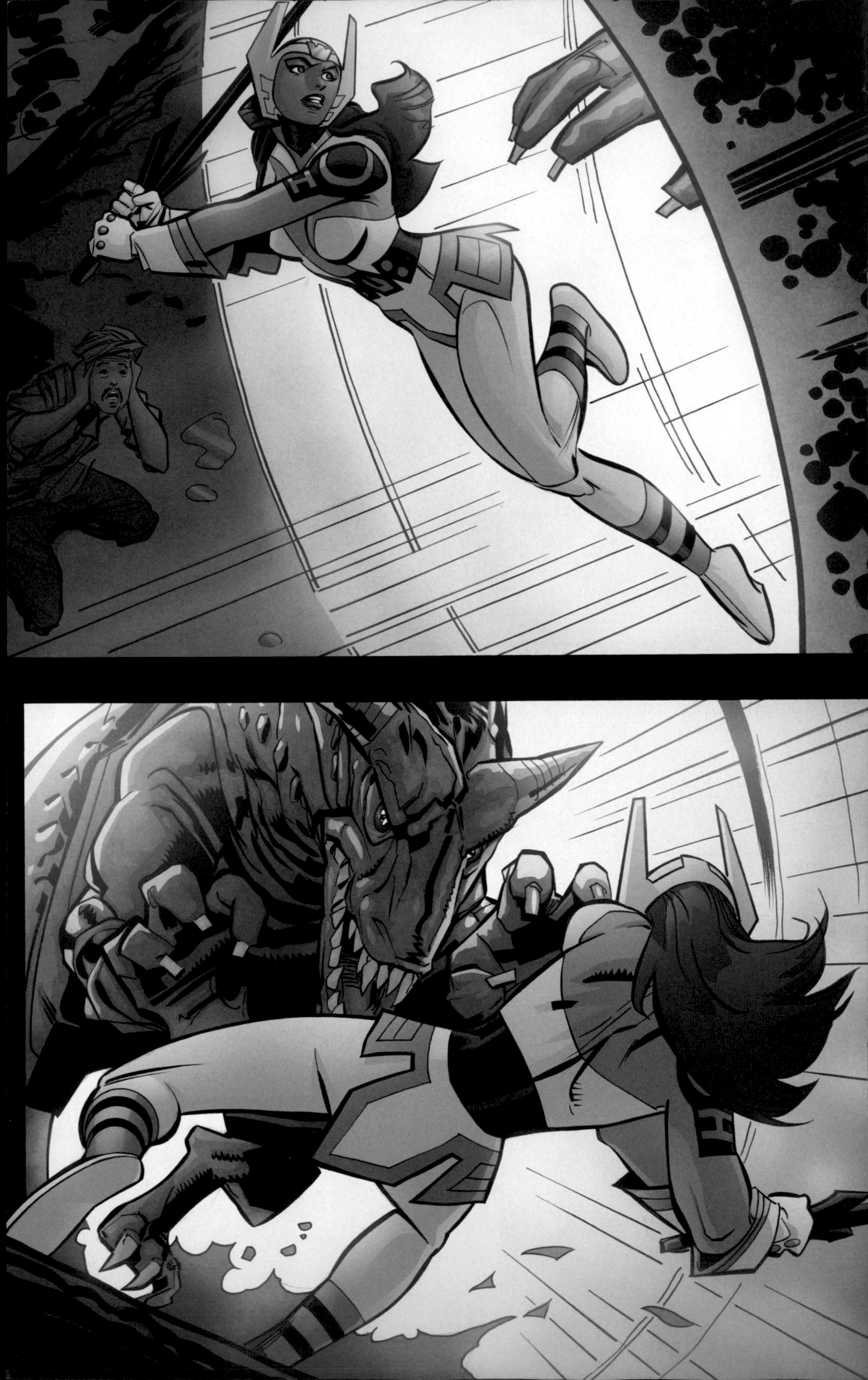

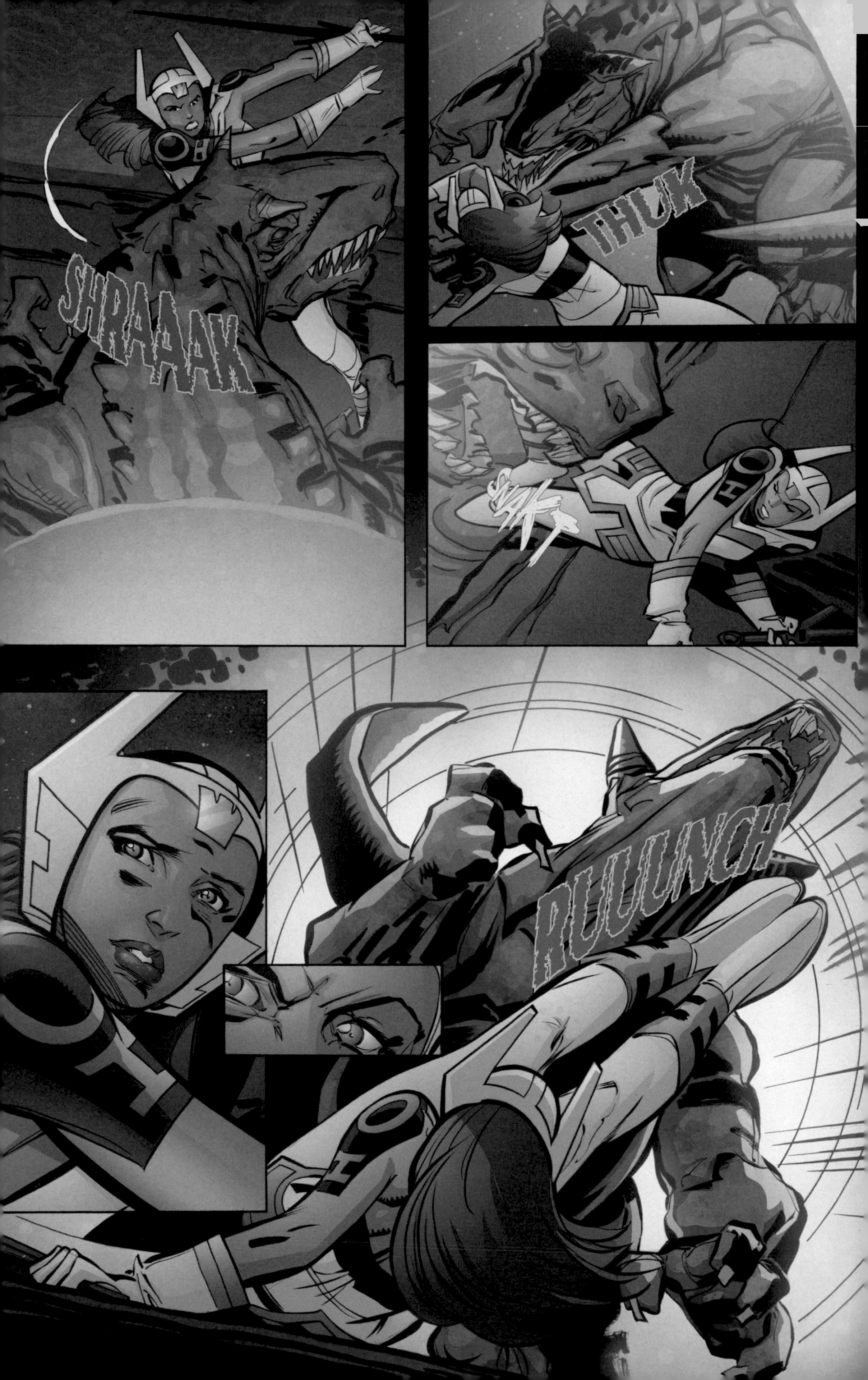
SHRAAAK
THUK
SNAKT
RUUUNCH

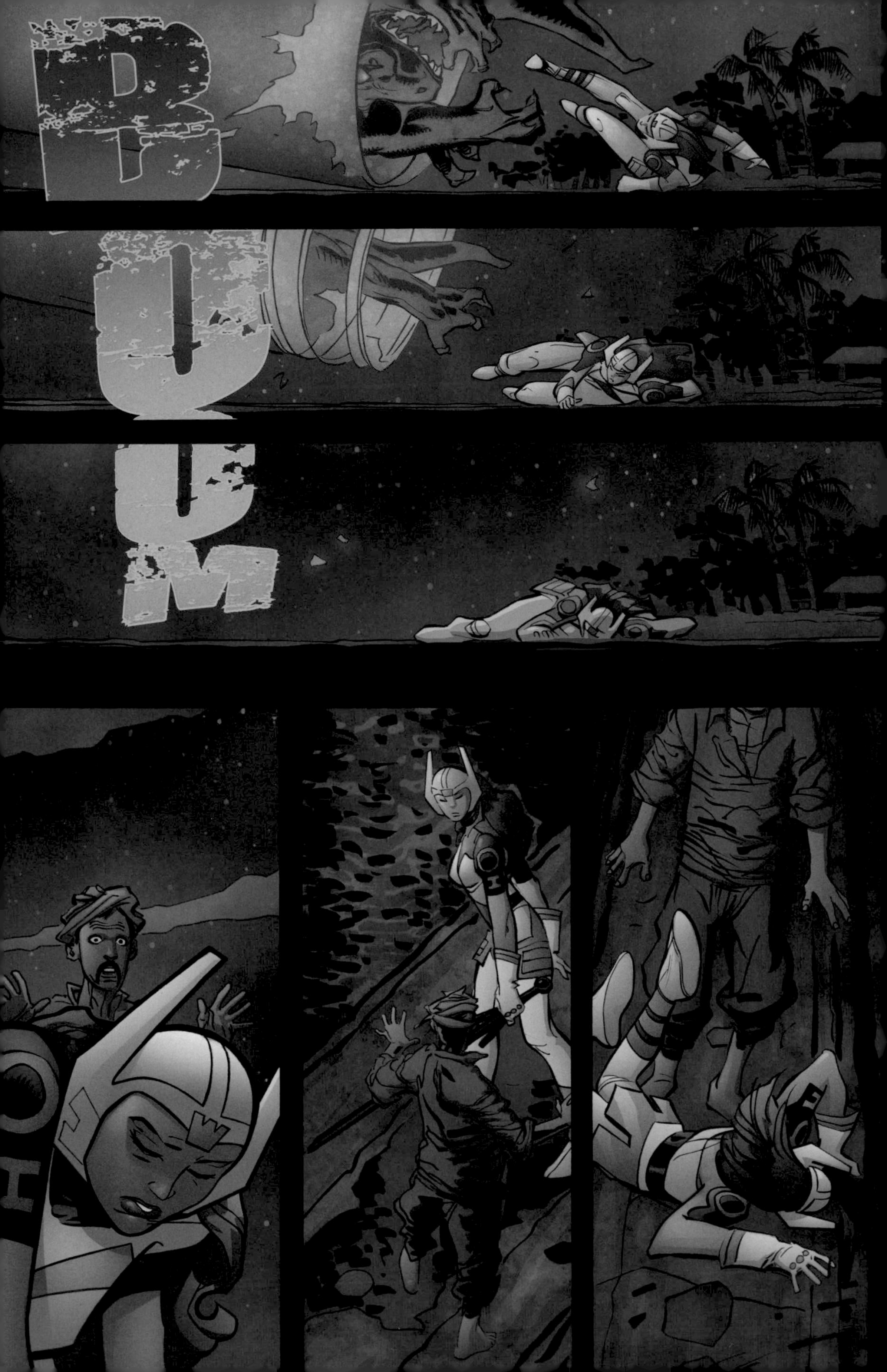
BRUUM

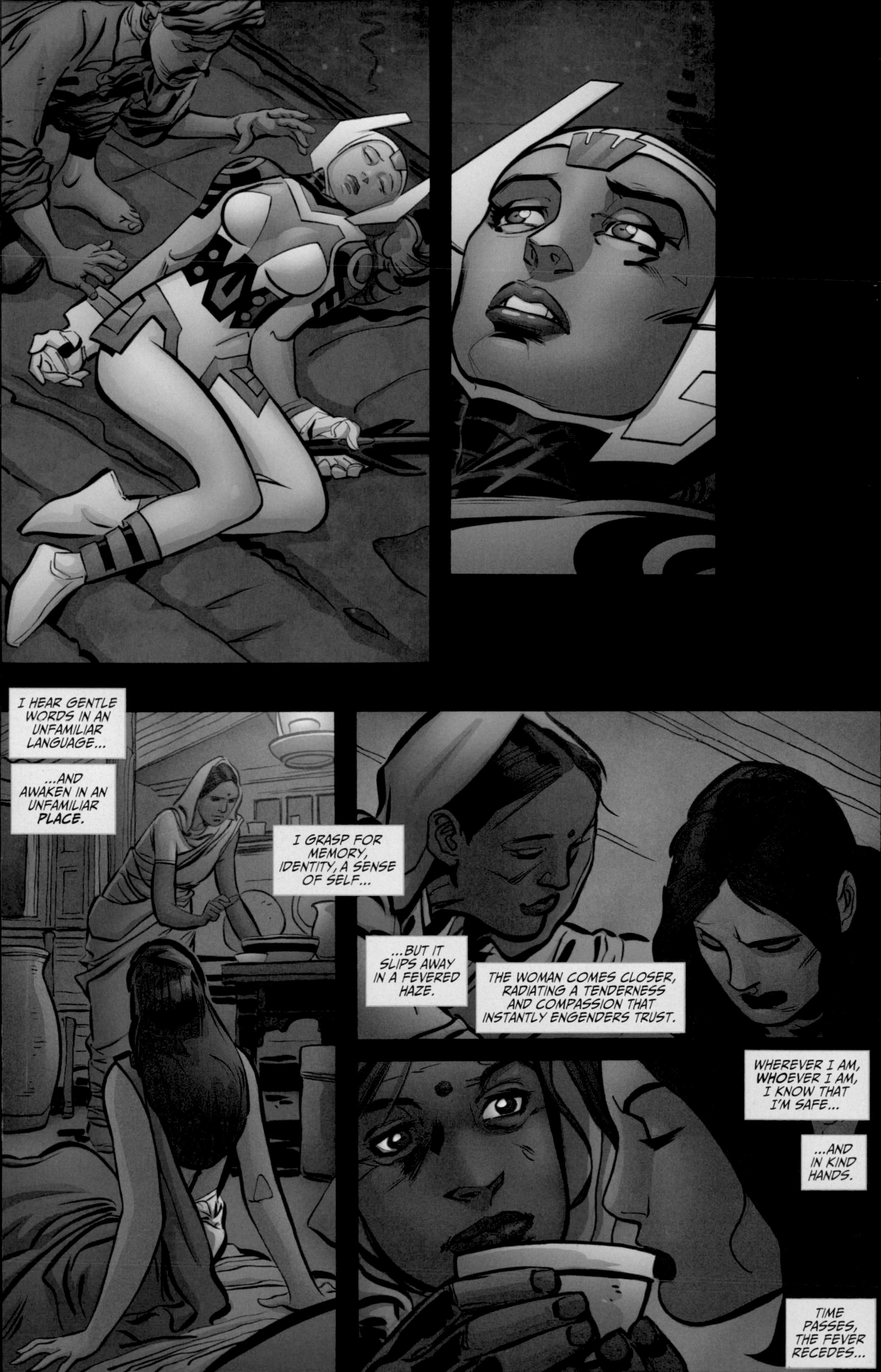
I HEAR GENTLE WORDS IN AN UNFAMILIAR LANGUAGE...
...AND AWAKEN IN AN UNFAMILIAR PLACE.
I GRASP FOR MEMORY, IDENTITY, A SENSE OF SELF...
...BUT IT SLIPS AWAY IN A FEVERED HAZE.
THE WOMAN COMES CLOSER, RADIATING A TENDERNESS AND COMPASSION THAT INSTANTLY ENGENDERS TRUST.
WHEREVER I AM, WHOEVER I AM, I KNOW THAT I'M SAFE...
...AND IN KIND HANDS.
TIME PASSES, THE FEVER RECEDES...

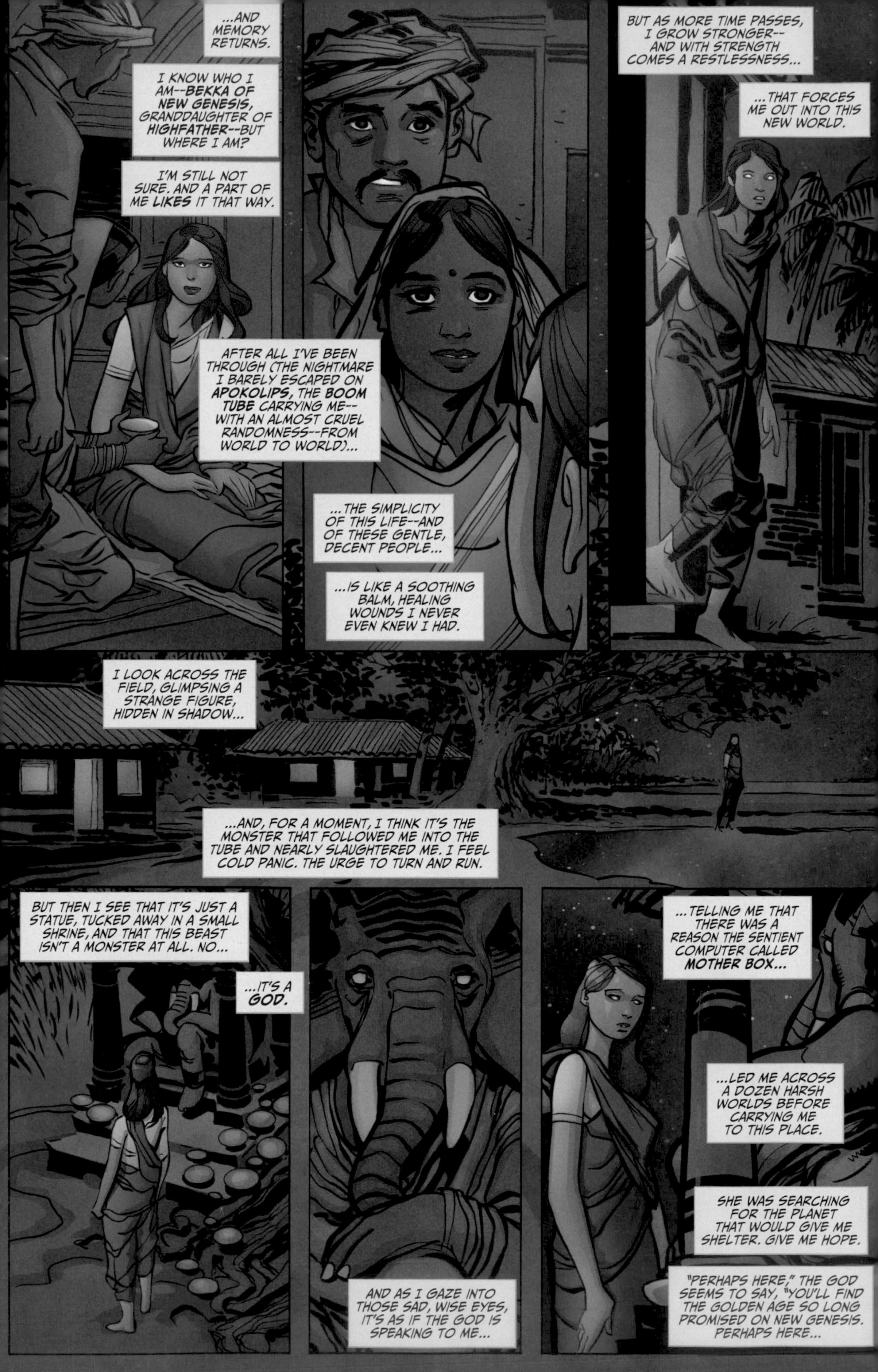
...AND MEMORY RETURNS.
I KNOW WHO I AM--BEKKA OF NEW GENESIS, GRANDDAUGHTER OF HIGHFATHER--BUT WHERE I AM?
I'M STILL NOT SURE. AND A PART OF ME LIKES IT THAT WAY.
AFTER ALL I'VE BEEN THROUGH (THE NIGHTMARE I BARELY ESCAPED ON APOKOLIPS, THE BOOM TUBE CARRYING ME--WITH AN ALMOST CRUEL RANDOMNESS--FROM WORLD TO WORLD)...
...THE SIMPLICITY OF THIS LIFE--AND OF THESE GENTLE, DECENT PEOPLE...
...IS LIKE A SOOTHING BALM, HEALING WOUNDS I NEVER EVEN KNEW I HAD.
BUT AS MORE TIME PASSES, I GROW STRONGER--AND WITH STRENGTH COMES A RESTLESSNESS...
...THAT FORCES ME OUT INTO THIS NEW WORLD.
I LOOK ACROSS THE FIELD, GLIMPSING A STRANGE FIGURE, HIDDEN IN SHADOW...
...AND, FOR A MOMENT, I THINK IT'S THE MONSTER THAT FOLLOWED ME INTO THE TUBE AND NEARLY SLAUGHTERED ME. I FEEL COLD PANIC. THE URGE TO TURN AND RUN.
BUT THEN I SEE THAT IT'S JUST A STATUE, TUCKED AWAY IN A SMALL SHRINE, AND THAT THIS BEAST ISN'T A MONSTER AT ALL. NO...
...IT'S A GOD.
AND AS I GAZE INTO THOSE SAD, WISE EYES, IT'S AS IF THE GOD IS SPEAKING TO ME...
...TELLING ME THAT THERE WAS A REASON THE SENTIENT COMPUTER CALLED MOTHER BOX...
...LED ME ACROSS A DOZEN HARSH WORLDS BEFORE CARRYING ME TO THIS PLACE.
SHE WAS SEARCHING FOR THE PLANET THAT WOULD GIVE ME SHELTER. GIVE ME HOPE.
"PERHAPS HERE," THE GOD SEEMS TO SAY, "YOU'LL FIND THE GOLDEN AGE SO LONG PROMISED ON NEW GENESIS. PERHAPS HERE...

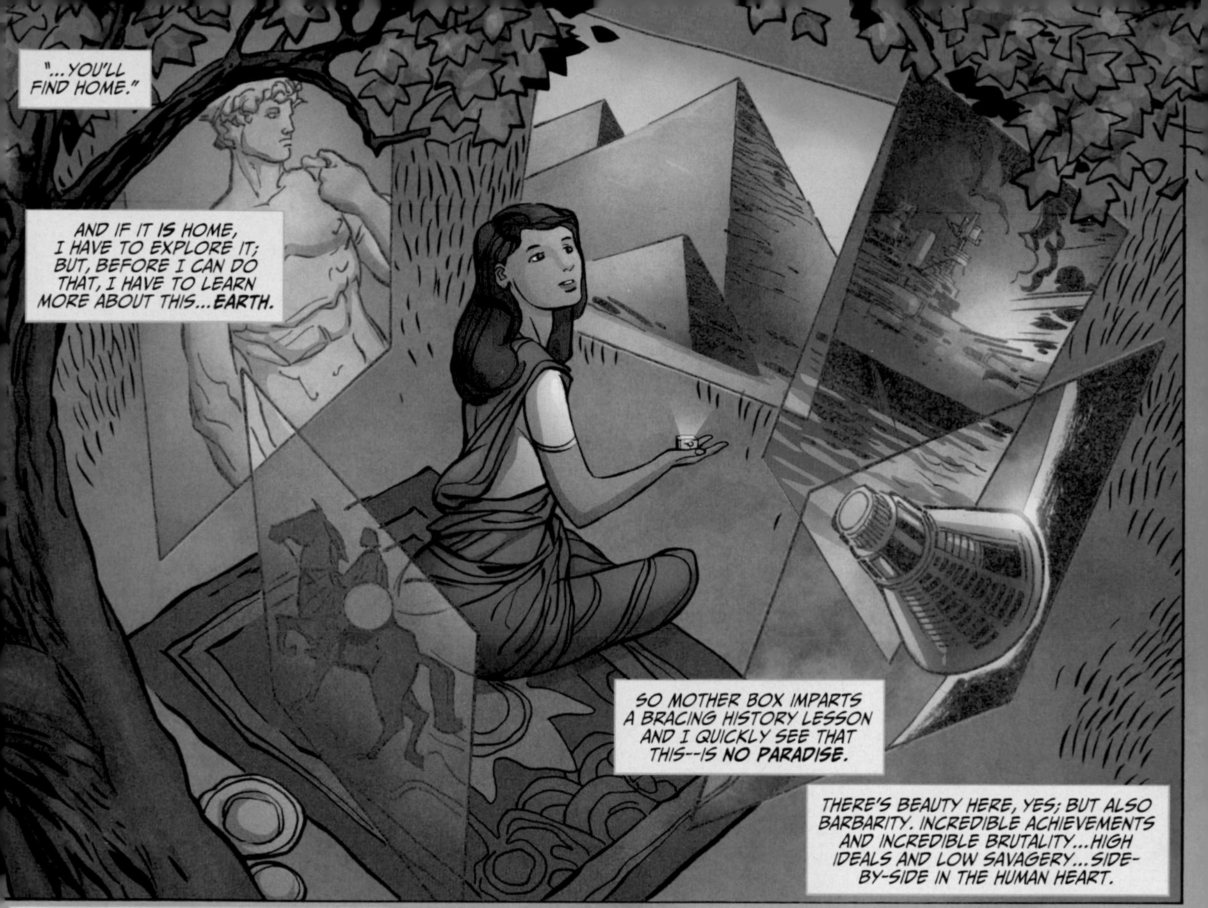
"...YOU'LL FIND HOME."
AND IF IT **IS** HOME, I HAVE TO EXPLORE IT; BUT, BEFORE I CAN DO THAT, I HAVE TO LEARN MORE ABOUT THIS... **EARTH.**
SO MOTHER BOX IMPARTS A BRACING HISTORY LESSON AND I QUICKLY SEE THAT THIS--IS **NO PARADISE.**
THERE'S BEAUTY HERE, YES; BUT ALSO BARBARITY. INCREDIBLE ACHIEVEMENTS AND INCREDIBLE BRUTALITY...HIGH IDEALS AND LOW SAVAGERY...SIDE-BY-SIDE IN THE HUMAN HEART.

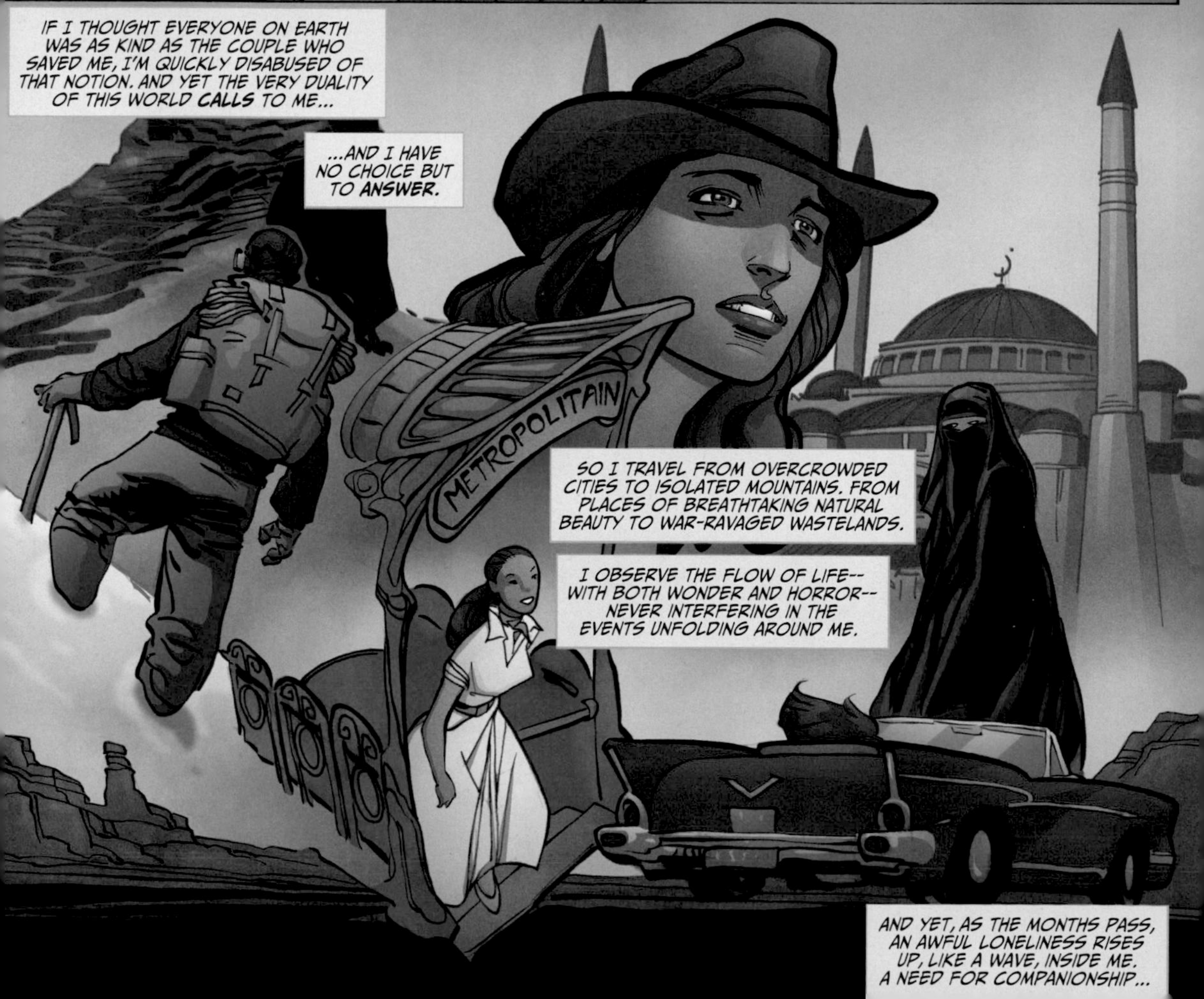
IF I THOUGHT EVERYONE ON EARTH WAS AS KIND AS THE COUPLE WHO SAVED ME, I'M QUICKLY DISABUSED OF THAT NOTION. AND YET THE VERY DUALITY OF THIS WORLD **CALLS** TO ME...
...AND I HAVE NO CHOICE BUT TO **ANSWER.**
METROPOLITAIN
SO I TRAVEL FROM OVERCROWDED CITIES TO ISOLATED MOUNTAINS. FROM PLACES OF BREATHTAKING NATURAL BEAUTY TO WAR-RAVAGED WASTELANDS.
I OBSERVE THE FLOW OF LIFE-- WITH BOTH WONDER AND HORROR-- NEVER INTERFERING IN THE EVENTS UNFOLDING AROUND ME.
AND YET, AS THE MONTHS PASS, AN AWFUL LONELINESS RISES UP, LIKE A WAVE, INSIDE ME. A NEED FOR COMPANIONSHIP...

...AND SOMETHING MORE.

THE CHARACTERISTICS OF THESE NEW MISSILE SITES INDICATE TWO DISTINCT TYPES OF INSTALLATIONS. SEVERAL OF THEM INCLUDE MEDIUM RANGE BALLISTIC MISSILES--

--CAPABLE OF CARRYING A NUCLEAR WARHEAD FOR A DISTANCE OF MORE THAN ONE THOUSAND NAUTICAL MILES.

EACH OF THESE MISSILES, IN SHORT, IS CAPABLE OF STRIKING WASHINGTON, D.C., THE PANAMA CANAL, CAPE CANAVERAL, MEXICO CITY--

--OR ANY OTHER CITY IN THE SOUTHEASTERN PART OF THE UNITED STATES, IN CENTRAL AMERICA, OR IN THE CARIBBEAN AREA.

TRANSLATION: "KISS YOUR ASS GOODBYE, KIDS. HERE COMES ARMAGEDDON."

ANY HOSTILE MOVE ANYWHERE IN THE WORLD AGAINST THE SAFETY AND FREEDOM OF PEOPLES TO WHOM WE ARE COMMITTED...WILL BE MET BY WHATEVER ACTION IS NEEDED.

NORTHERN CALIFORNIA. OCTOBER, 1962.

I OUGHTTA TAKE OUT KENNEDY AND KHRUSHCHEV. BUT THEY'D ONLY BE REPLACED BY TWO MORE WAR-MONGERING BUFFOONS.

TAKE 'EM OUT? LADY-- YOU'RE DRUNK.

TOTALLY. BUT IF WE'RE GOING TO DIE TONIGHT--

--LET'S NOT DO IT ALONE.

A NIGHT OF SOULLESS PASSION DIDN'T FORESTALL ARMAGEDDON, BUT KENNEDY DID.

HE SURPRISED ME. PROVED HE HAD THE COURAGE TO MAKE NOT JUST WAR, BUT PEACE.

A YEAR LATER HE WAS DEAD. SO MUCH FOR THE PEACEMAKERS.

AND YET, THAT BRAVE AND RECKLESS MAN'S MURDER REMINDED ME OF THE DEAD I LEFT BEHIND--AND FILLED ME WITH AN ILLOGICAL HOPE.

PERHAPS, I MUSED, IT'S TIME FOR ME TO GET MORE DIRECTLY INVOLVED...

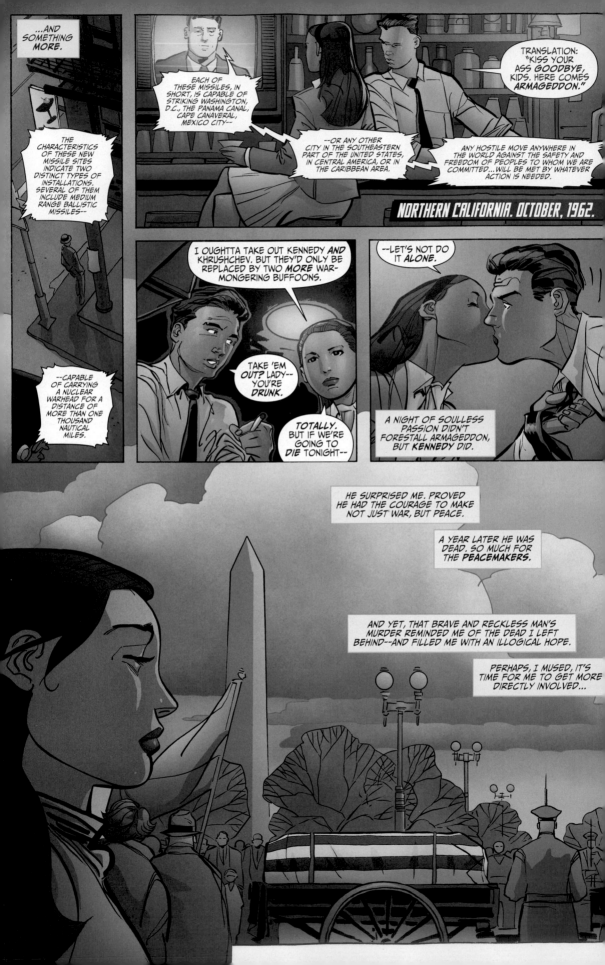

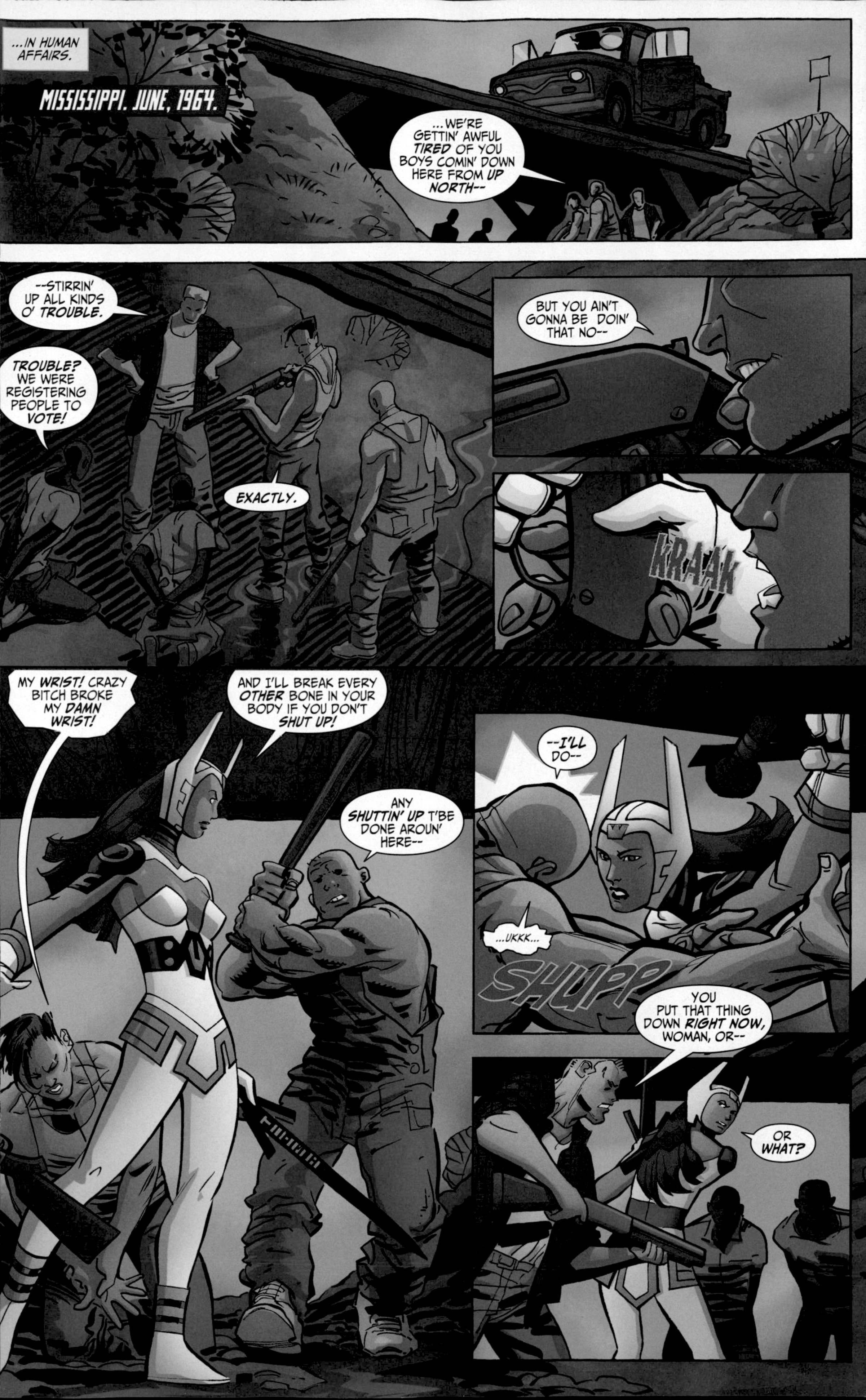
...IN HUMAN AFFAIRS.
MISSISSIPPI. JUNE, 1964.
...WE'RE GETTIN' AWFUL TIRED OF YOU BOYS COMIN' DOWN HERE FROM UP NORTH--
--STIRRIN' UP ALL KINDS O' TROUBLE.
TROUBLE? WE WERE REGISTERING PEOPLE TO VOTE!
EXACTLY.
BUT YOU AIN'T GONNA BE DOIN' THAT NO--
KRAAK
MY WRIST! CRAZY BITCH BROKE MY DAMN WRIST!
AND I'LL BREAK EVERY OTHER BONE IN YOUR BODY IF YOU DON'T SHUT UP!
ANY SHUTTIN' UP T'BE DONE AROUN' HERE--
--I'LL DO--
...UKKK...
SHUPP
YOU PUT THAT THING DOWN RIGHT NOW, WOMAN, OR--
OR WHAT?

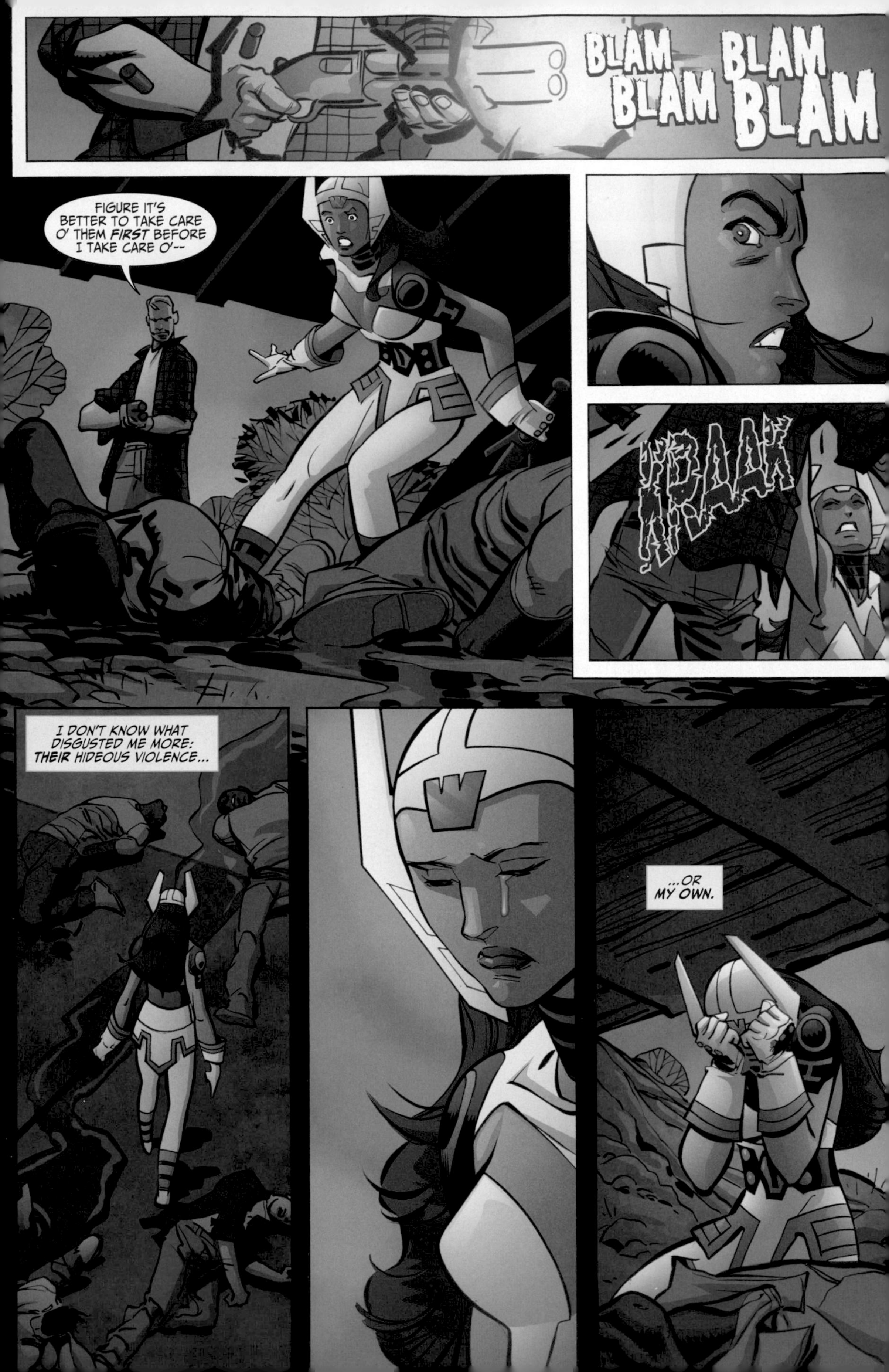
BLAM BLAM BLAM BLAM
FIGURE IT'S BETTER TO TAKE CARE O' THEM *FIRST* BEFORE I TAKE CARE O'--
KRAAK
I DON'T KNOW WHAT DISGUSTED ME MORE: **THEIR** HIDEOUS VIOLENCE...
...OR MY OWN.

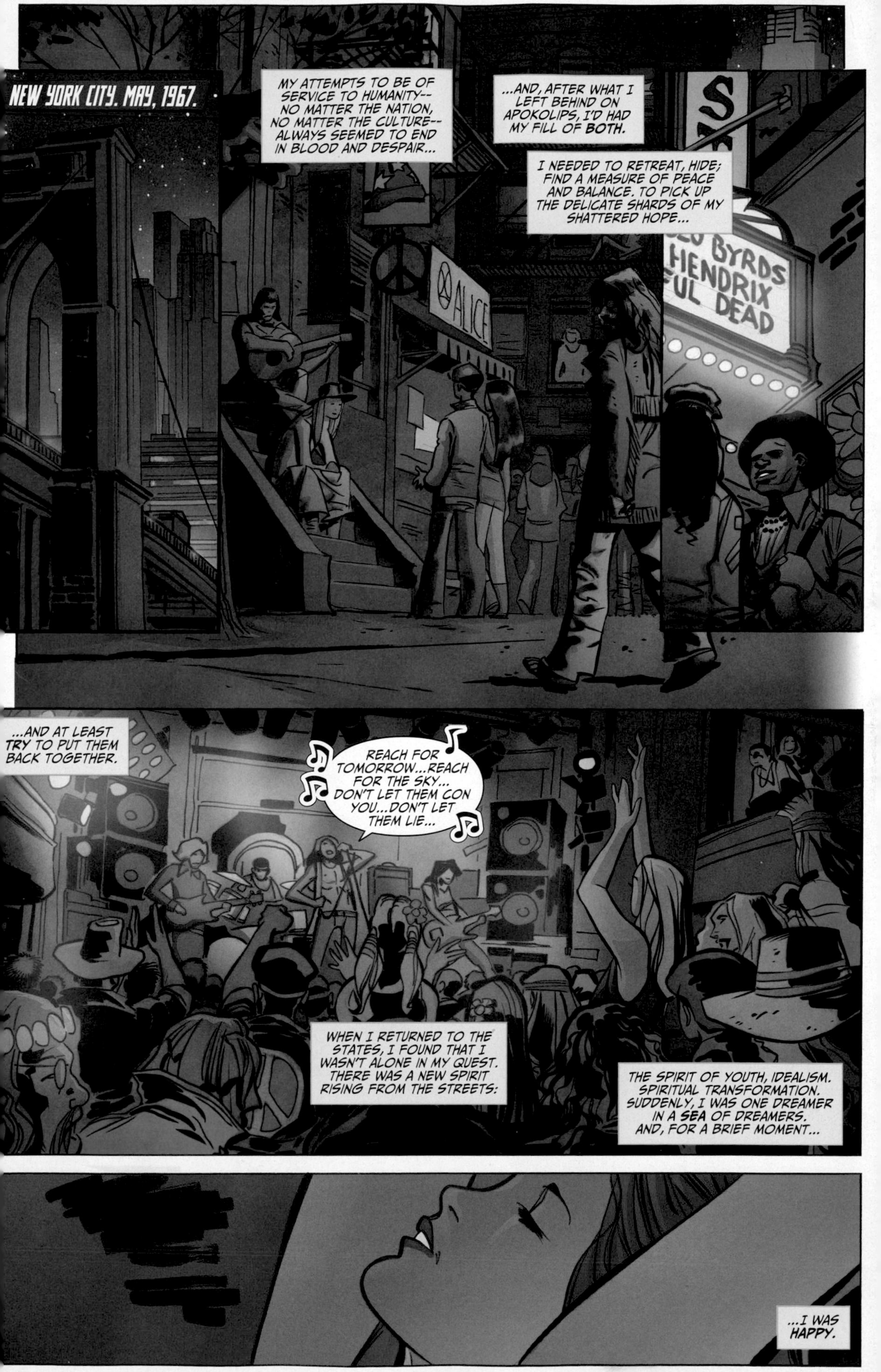
NEW YORK CITY. MAY, 1967.
MY ATTEMPTS TO BE OF SERVICE TO HUMANITY-- NO MATTER THE NATION, NO MATTER THE CULTURE-- ALWAYS SEEMED TO END IN BLOOD AND DESPAIR...
...AND, AFTER WHAT I LEFT BEHIND ON APOKOLIPS, I'D HAD MY FILL OF BOTH.
I NEEDED TO RETREAT, HIDE; FIND A MEASURE OF PEACE AND BALANCE. TO PICK UP THE DELICATE SHARDS OF MY SHATTERED HOPE...
ALICE
BYRDS
HENDRIX
FUL DEAD
...AND AT LEAST TRY TO PUT THEM BACK TOGETHER.
REACH FOR TOMORROW...REACH FOR THE SKY... DON'T LET THEM CON YOU...DON'T LET THEM LIE...
WHEN I RETURNED TO THE STATES, I FOUND THAT I WASN'T ALONE IN MY QUEST. THERE WAS A NEW SPIRIT RISING FROM THE STREETS:
THE SPIRIT OF YOUTH, IDEALISM. SPIRITUAL TRANSFORMATION. SUDDENLY, I WAS ONE DREAMER IN A SEA OF DREAMERS. AND, FOR A BRIEF MOMENT...
...I WAS HAPPY.

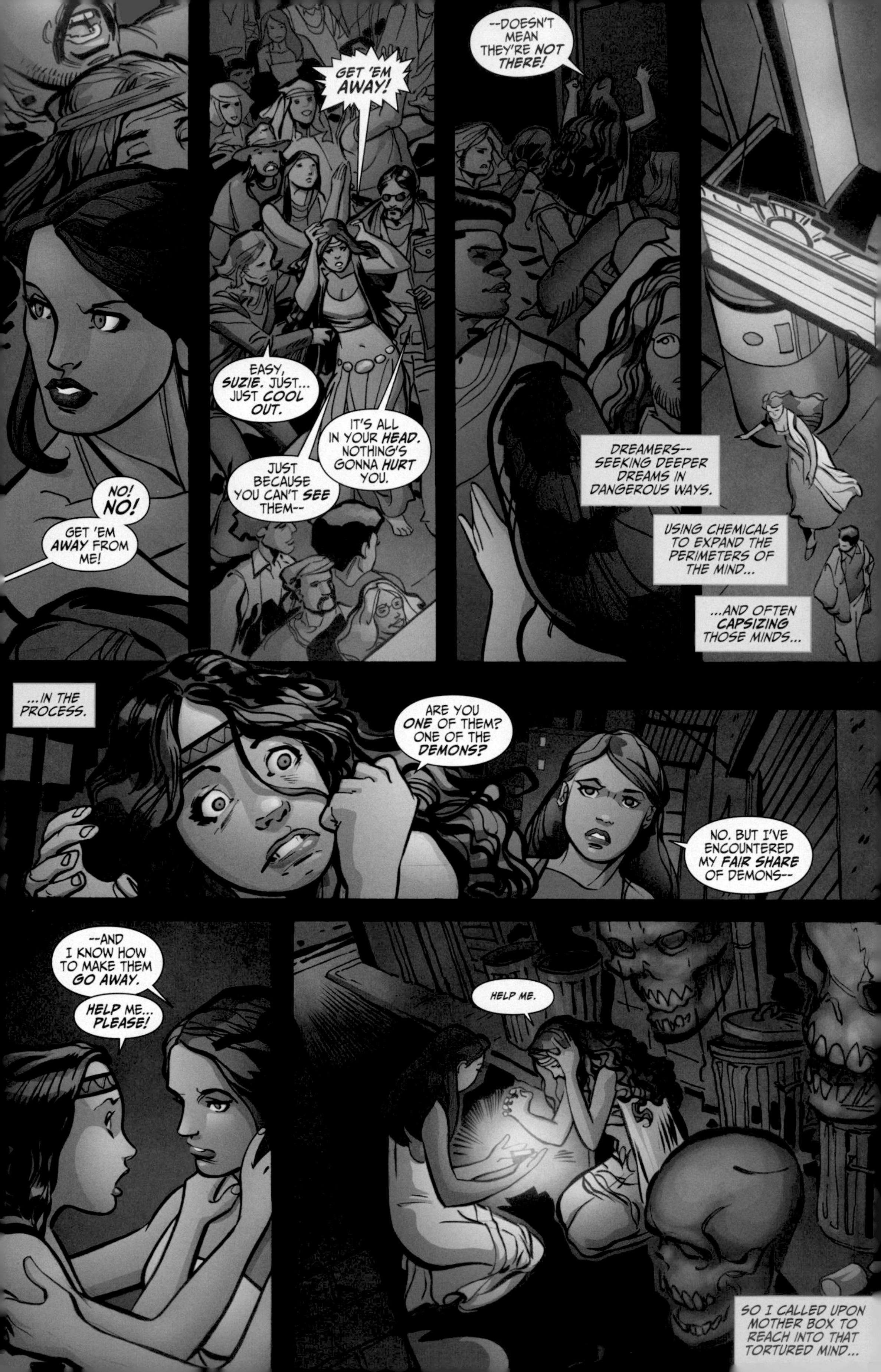

NO! NO!
GET 'EM AWAY FROM ME!
GET 'EM AWAY!
EASY, SUZIE. JUST... JUST COOL OUT.
IT'S ALL IN YOUR HEAD. NOTHING'S GONNA HURT YOU.
JUST BECAUSE YOU CAN'T SEE THEM--
--DOESN'T MEAN THEY'RE NOT THERE!
DREAMERS-- SEEKING DEEPER DREAMS IN DANGEROUS WAYS.
USING CHEMICALS TO EXPAND THE PERIMETERS OF THE MIND...
...AND OFTEN CAPSIZING THOSE MINDS...
...IN THE PROCESS.
ARE YOU ONE OF THEM? ONE OF THE DEMONS?
NO. BUT I'VE ENCOUNTERED MY FAIR SHARE OF DEMONS--
--AND I KNOW HOW TO MAKE THEM GO AWAY.
HELP ME... PLEASE!
HELP ME.
SO I CALLED UPON MOTHER BOX TO REACH INTO THAT TORTURED MIND...

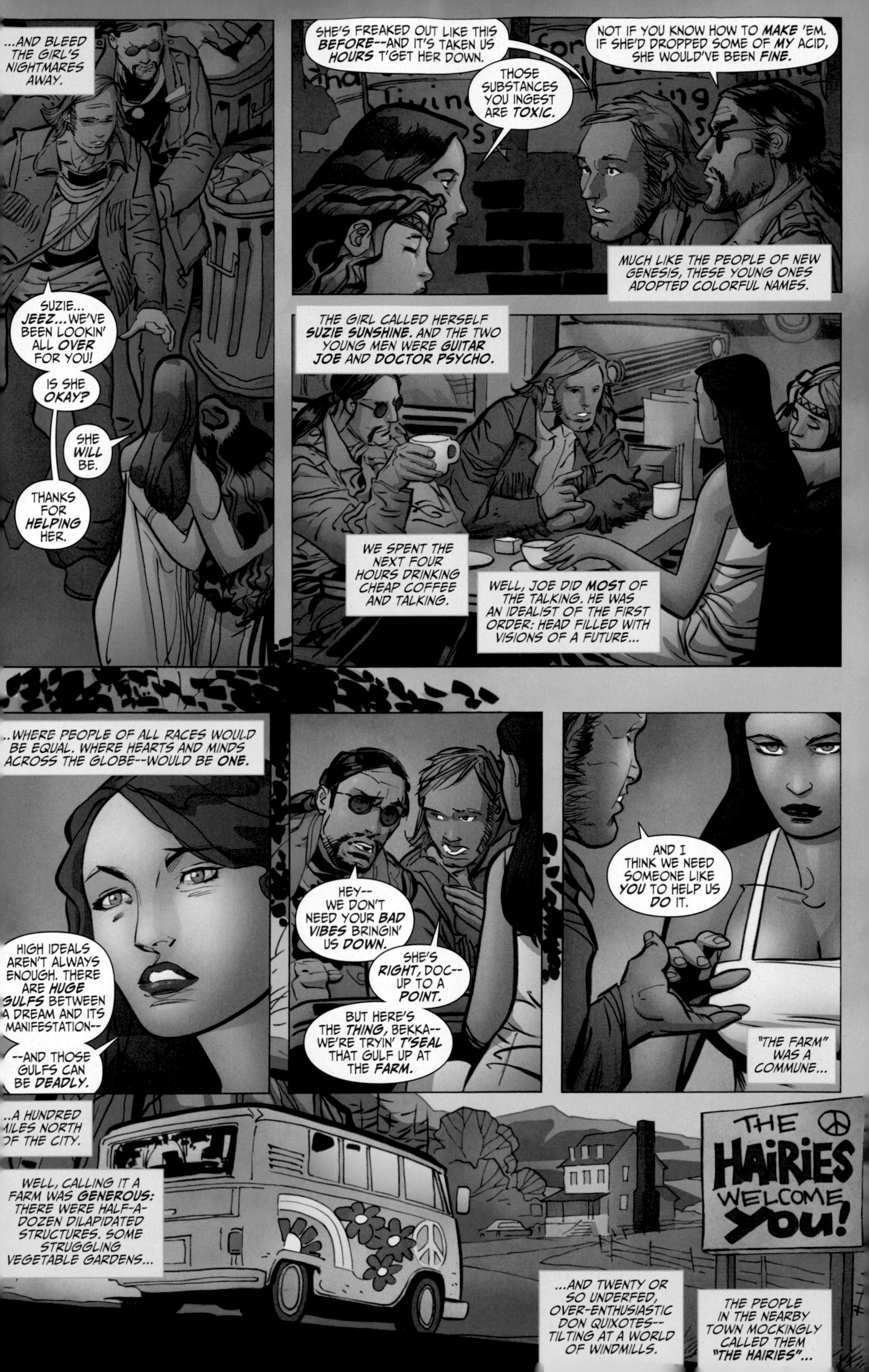
...AND BLEED THE GIRL'S NIGHTMARES AWAY.
SUZIE... JEEZ... WE'VE BEEN LOOKIN' ALL OVER FOR YOU!
IS SHE OKAY?
SHE WILL BE.
THANKS FOR HELPING HER.
SHE'S FREAKED OUT LIKE THIS BEFORE--AND IT'S TAKEN US HOURS T'GET HER DOWN.
NOT IF YOU KNOW HOW TO MAKE 'EM. IF SHE'D DROPPED SOME OF MY ACID, SHE WOULD'VE BEEN FINE.
THOSE SUBSTANCES YOU INGEST ARE TOXIC.
MUCH LIKE THE PEOPLE OF NEW GENESIS, THESE YOUNG ONES ADOPTED COLORFUL NAMES.
THE GIRL CALLED HERSELF SUZIE SUNSHINE. AND THE TWO YOUNG MEN WERE GUITAR JOE AND DOCTOR PSYCHO.
WE SPENT THE NEXT FOUR HOURS DRINKING CHEAP COFFEE AND TALKING.
WELL, JOE DID MOST OF THE TALKING. HE WAS AN IDEALIST OF THE FIRST ORDER: HEAD FILLED WITH VISIONS OF A FUTURE...
...WHERE PEOPLE OF ALL RACES WOULD BE EQUAL. WHERE HEARTS AND MINDS ACROSS THE GLOBE--WOULD BE ONE.
HIGH IDEALS AREN'T ALWAYS ENOUGH. THERE ARE HUGE GULFS BETWEEN A DREAM AND ITS MANIFESTATION--
--AND THOSE GULFS CAN BE DEADLY.
HEY-- WE DON'T NEED YOUR BAD VIBES BRINGIN' US DOWN.
SHE'S RIGHT, DOC-- UP TO A POINT.
BUT HERE'S THE THING, BEKKA-- WE'RE TRYIN' T'SEAL THAT GULF UP AT THE FARM.
AND I THINK WE NEED SOMEONE LIKE YOU TO HELP US DO IT.
"THE FARM" WAS A COMMUNE...
...A HUNDRED MILES NORTH OF THE CITY.
WELL, CALLING IT A FARM WAS GENEROUS: THERE WERE HALF-A-DOZEN DILAPIDATED STRUCTURES. SOME STRUGGLING VEGETABLE GARDENS...
THE HAIRIES WELCOME YOU!
...AND TWENTY OR SO UNDERFED, OVER-ENTHUSIASTIC DON QUIXOTES--TILTING AT A WORLD OF WINDMILLS.
THE PEOPLE IN THE NEARBY TOWN MOCKINGLY CALLED THEM "THE HAIRIES"...

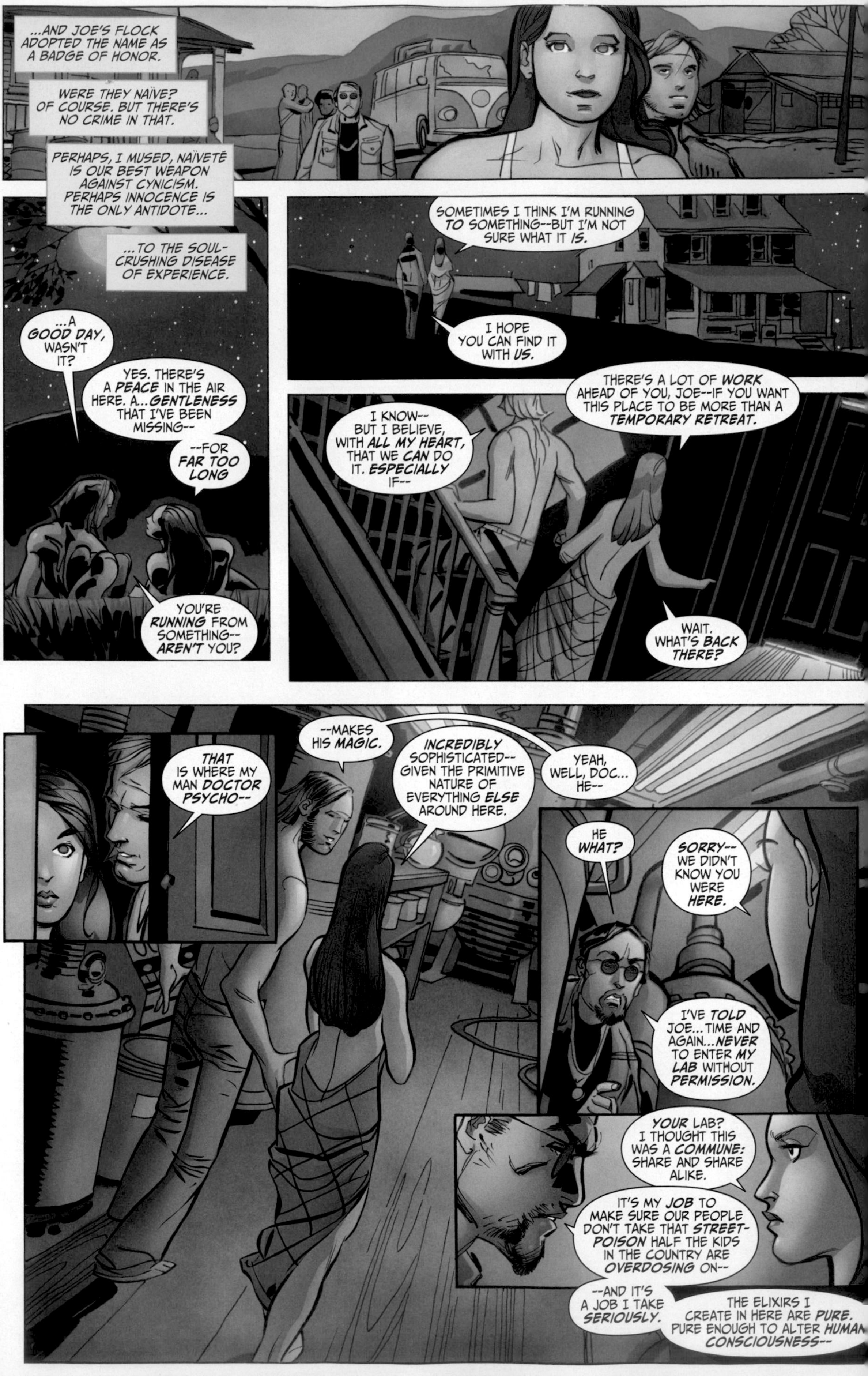
...AND JOE'S FLOCK ADOPTED THE NAME AS A BADGE OF HONOR.
WERE THEY NAÏVE? OF COURSE. BUT THERE'S NO CRIME IN THAT.
PERHAPS, I MUSED, NAÏVETÉ IS OUR BEST WEAPON AGAINST CYNICISM. PERHAPS INNOCENCE IS THE ONLY ANTIDOTE...
...TO THE SOUL-CRUSHING DISEASE OF EXPERIENCE.
...A GOOD DAY, WASN'T IT?
YES. THERE'S A PEACE IN THE AIR HERE. A...GENTLENESS THAT I'VE BEEN MISSING--
--FOR FAR TOO LONG
YOU'RE RUNNING FROM SOMETHING--AREN'T YOU?
SOMETIMES I THINK I'M RUNNING TO SOMETHING--BUT I'M NOT SURE WHAT IT IS.
I HOPE YOU CAN FIND IT WITH US.
THERE'S A LOT OF WORK AHEAD OF YOU, JOE--IF YOU WANT THIS PLACE TO BE MORE THAN A TEMPORARY RETREAT.
I KNOW-- BUT I BELIEVE, WITH ALL MY HEART, THAT WE CAN DO IT. ESPECIALLY IF--
WAIT. WHAT'S BACK THERE?
THAT IS WHERE MY MAN DOCTOR PSYCHO--
--MAKES HIS MAGIC.
INCREDIBLY SOPHISTICATED--GIVEN THE PRIMITIVE NATURE OF EVERYTHING ELSE AROUND HERE.
YEAH, WELL, DOC... HE--
HE WHAT?
SORRY--WE DIDN'T KNOW YOU WERE HERE.
I'VE TOLD JOE...TIME AND AGAIN...NEVER TO ENTER MY LAB WITHOUT PERMISSION.
YOUR LAB? I THOUGHT THIS WAS A COMMUNE: SHARE AND SHARE ALIKE.
IT'S MY JOB TO MAKE SURE OUR PEOPLE DON'T TAKE THAT STREET-POISON HALF THE KIDS IN THE COUNTRY ARE OVERDOSING ON--
--AND IT'S A JOB I TAKE SERIOUSLY.
THE ELIXIRS I CREATE IN HERE ARE PURE. PURE ENOUGH TO ALTER HUMAN CONSCIOUSNESS--

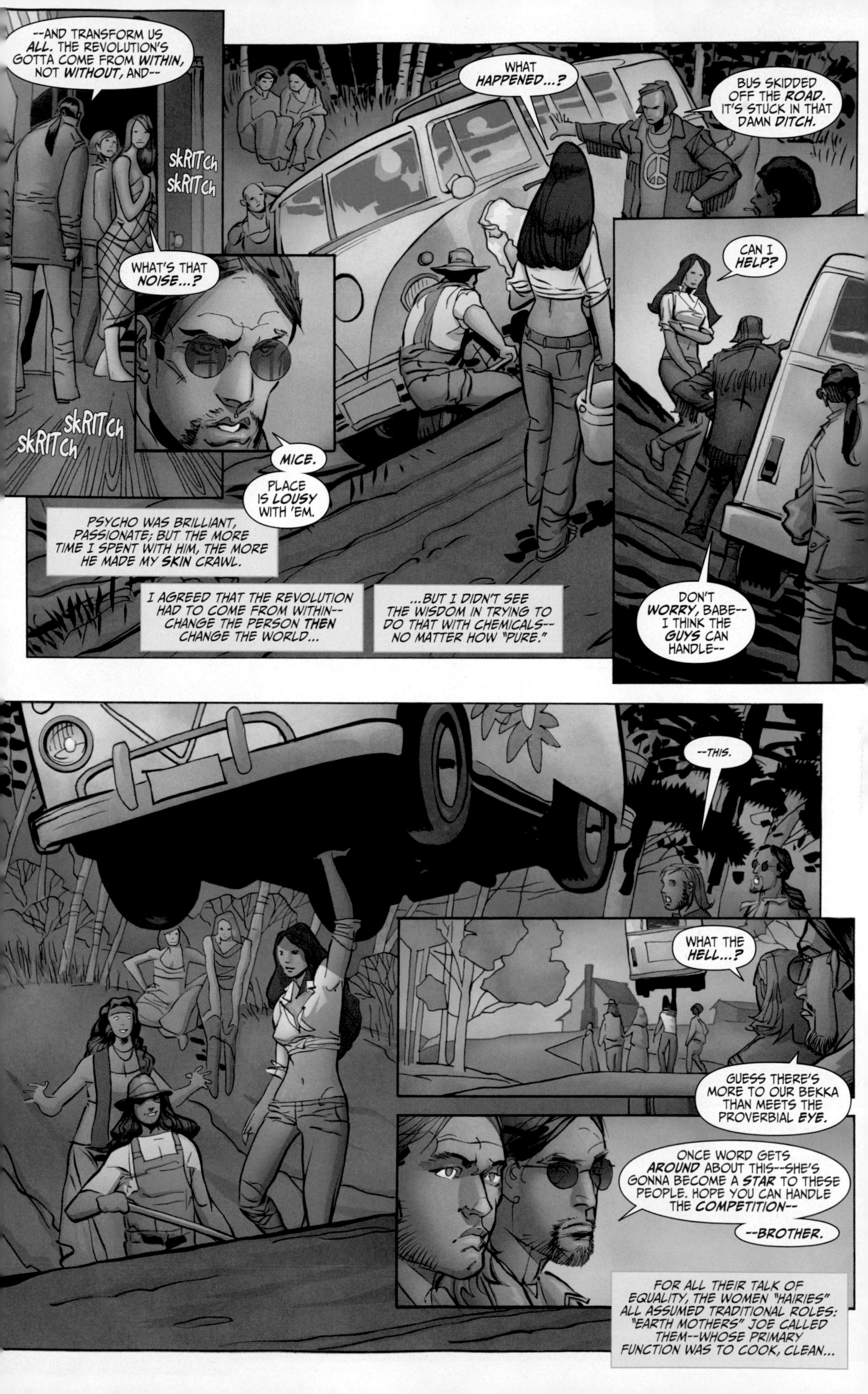
--AND TRANSFORM US ALL. THE REVOLUTION'S GOTTA COME FROM WITHIN, NOT WITHOUT, AND--
sKRITCh sKRITCh
WHAT'S THAT NOISE...?
sKRITCh sKRITCh
MICE.
PLACE IS LOUSY WITH 'EM.
PSYCHO WAS BRILLIANT, PASSIONATE; BUT THE MORE TIME I SPENT WITH HIM, THE MORE HE MADE MY SKIN CRAWL.
WHAT HAPPENED...?
BUS SKIDDED OFF THE ROAD. IT'S STUCK IN THAT DAMN DITCH.
I AGREED THAT THE REVOLUTION HAD TO COME FROM WITHIN-- CHANGE THE PERSON THEN CHANGE THE WORLD...
...BUT I DIDN'T SEE THE WISDOM IN TRYING TO DO THAT WITH CHEMICALS-- NO MATTER HOW "PURE."
CAN I HELP?
DON'T WORRY, BABE-- I THINK THE GUYS CAN HANDLE--
--THIS.
WHAT THE HELL...?
GUESS THERE'S MORE TO OUR BEKKA THAN MEETS THE PROVERBIAL EYE.
ONCE WORD GETS AROUND ABOUT THIS--SHE'S GONNA BECOME A STAR TO THESE PEOPLE. HOPE YOU CAN HANDLE THE COMPETITION--
--BROTHER.
FOR ALL THEIR TALK OF EQUALITY, THE WOMEN "HAIRIES" ALL ASSUMED TRADITIONAL ROLES: "EARTH MOTHERS" JOE CALLED THEM--WHOSE PRIMARY FUNCTION WAS TO COOK, CLEAN...

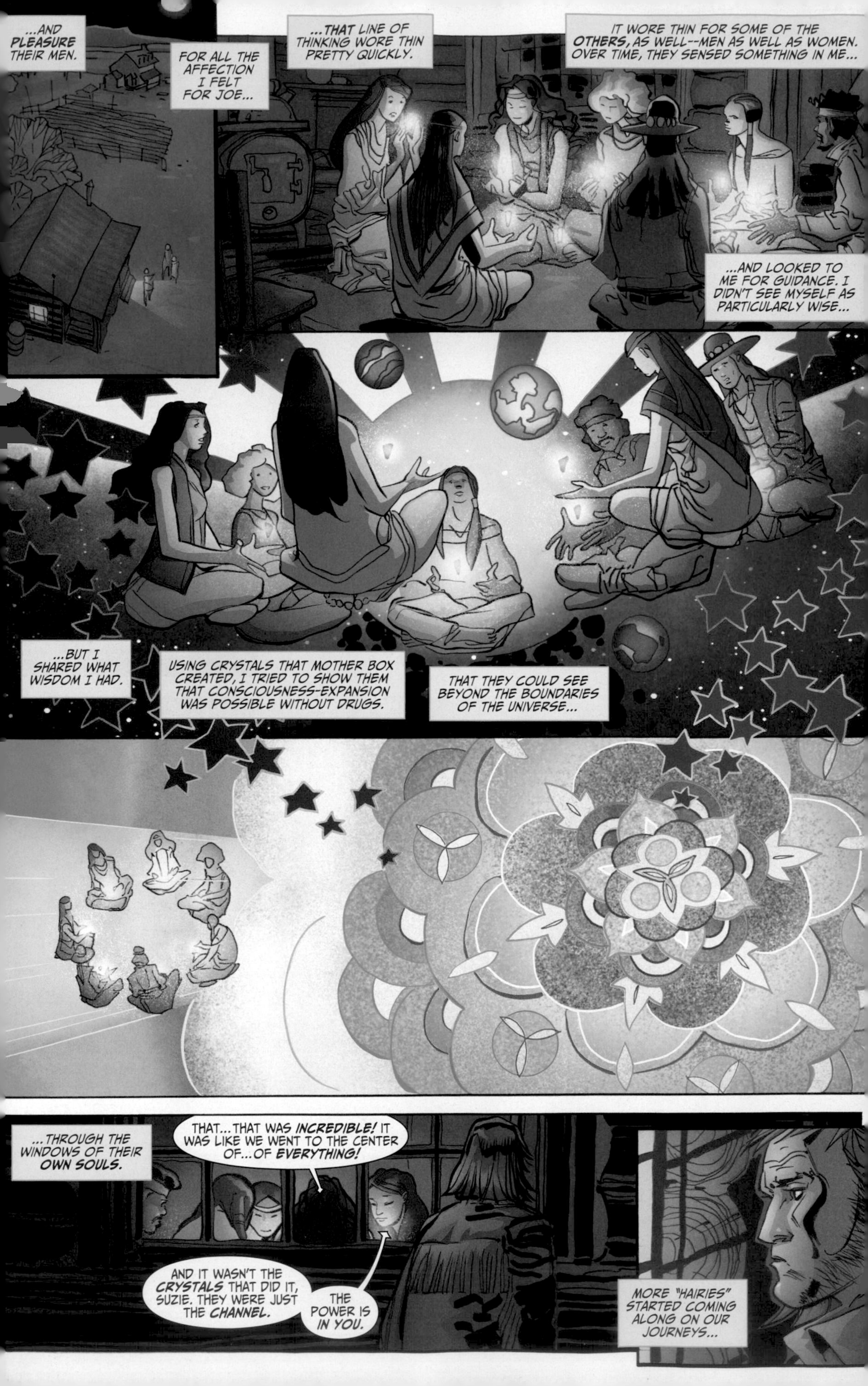
...AND PLEASURE THEIR MEN.
FOR ALL THE AFFECTION I FELT FOR JOE...
...THAT LINE OF THINKING WORE THIN PRETTY QUICKLY.
IT WORE THIN FOR SOME OF THE OTHERS, AS WELL--MEN AS WELL AS WOMEN. OVER TIME, THEY SENSED SOMETHING IN ME...
...AND LOOKED TO ME FOR GUIDANCE. I DIDN'T SEE MYSELF AS PARTICULARLY WISE...
...BUT I SHARED WHAT WISDOM I HAD.
USING CRYSTALS THAT MOTHER BOX CREATED, I TRIED TO SHOW THEM THAT CONSCIOUSNESS-EXPANSION WAS POSSIBLE WITHOUT DRUGS.
THAT THEY COULD SEE BEYOND THE BOUNDARIES OF THE UNIVERSE...
...THROUGH THE WINDOWS OF THEIR OWN SOULS.
THAT...THAT WAS INCREDIBLE! IT WAS LIKE WE WENT TO THE CENTER OF...OF EVERYTHING!
AND IT WASN'T THE CRYSTALS THAT DID IT, SUZIE. THEY WERE JUST THE CHANNEL.
THE POWER IS IN YOU.
MORE "HAIRIES" STARTED COMING ALONG ON OUR JOURNEYS...

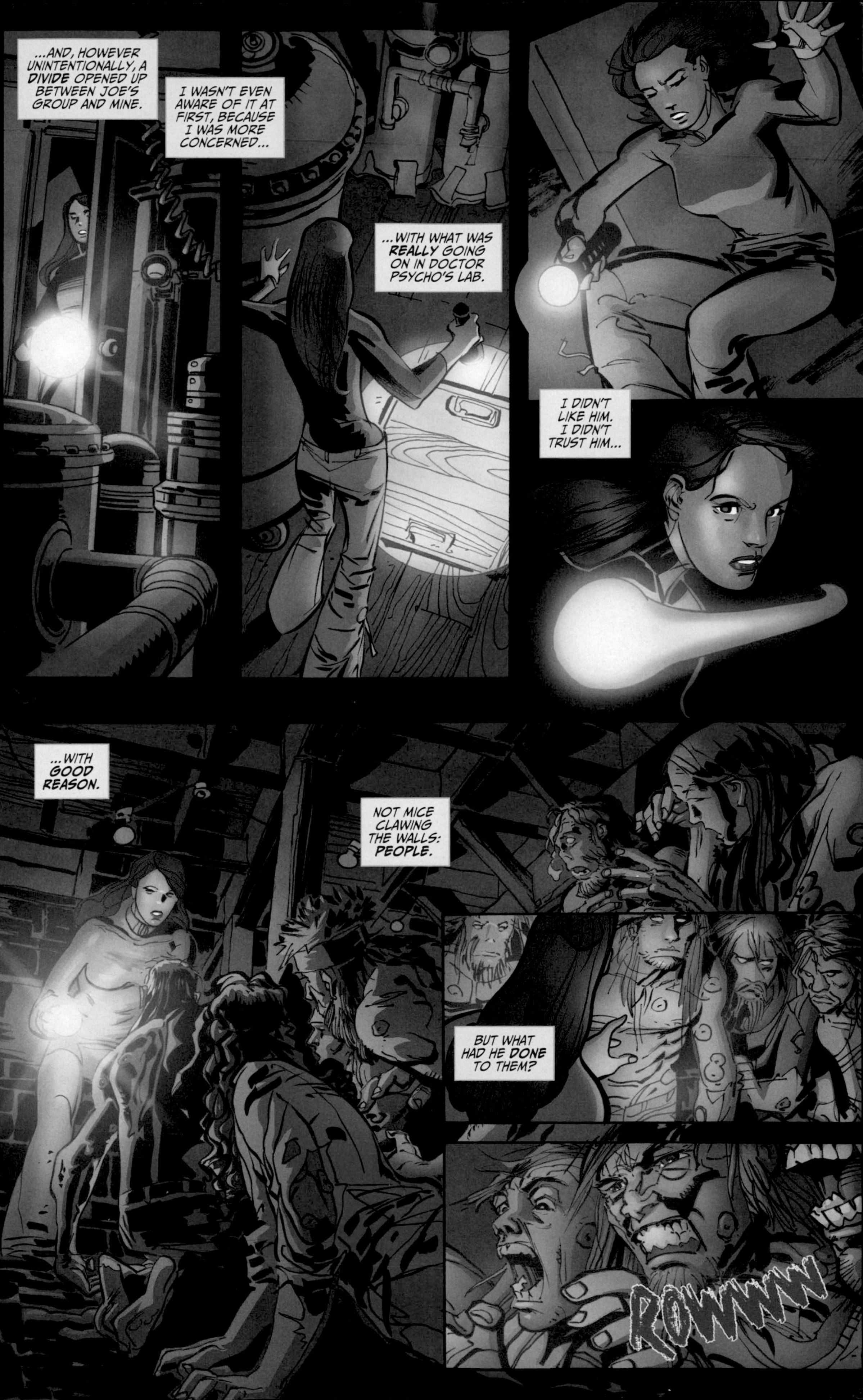
...AND, HOWEVER UNINTENTIONALLY, A DIVIDE OPENED UP BETWEEN JOE'S GROUP AND MINE.
I WASN'T EVEN AWARE OF IT AT FIRST, BECAUSE I WAS MORE CONCERNED...
...WITH WHAT WAS REALLY GOING ON IN DOCTOR PSYCHO'S LAB.
I DIDN'T LIKE HIM. I DIDN'T TRUST HIM...
...WITH GOOD REASON.
NOT MICE CLAWING THE WALLS: PEOPLE.
BUT WHAT HAD HE DONE TO THEM?
ROWWWN

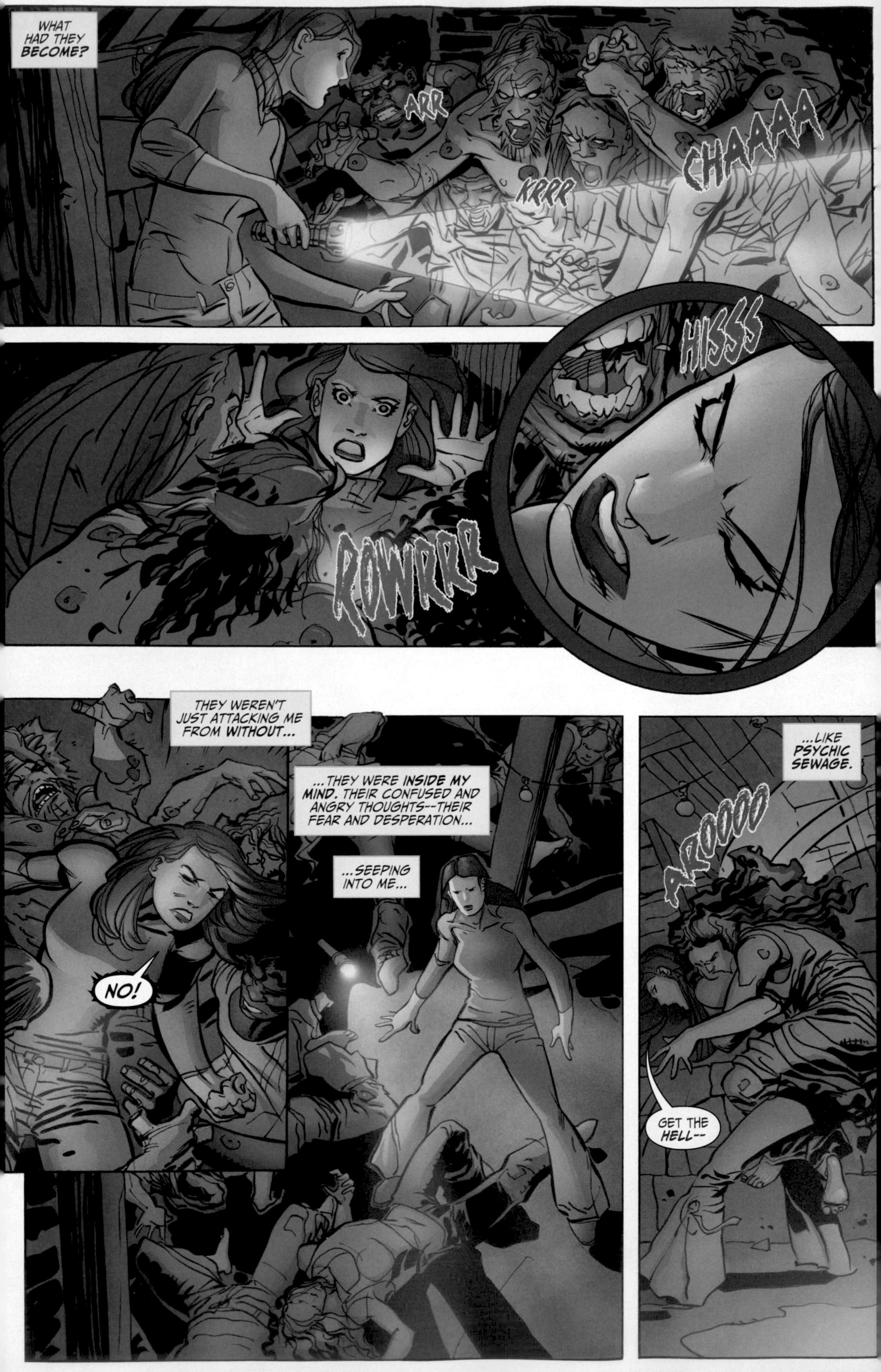
WHAT HAD THEY BECOME?
ARR
KRRR
CHAAAA
HISSS
ROWRRR
THEY WEREN'T JUST ATTACKING ME FROM WITHOUT...
NO!
...THEY WERE INSIDE MY MIND. THEIR CONFUSED AND ANGRY THOUGHTS--THEIR FEAR AND DESPERATION...
...SEEPING INTO ME...
...LIKE PSYCHIC SEWAGE.
AROOOO
GET THE HELL--

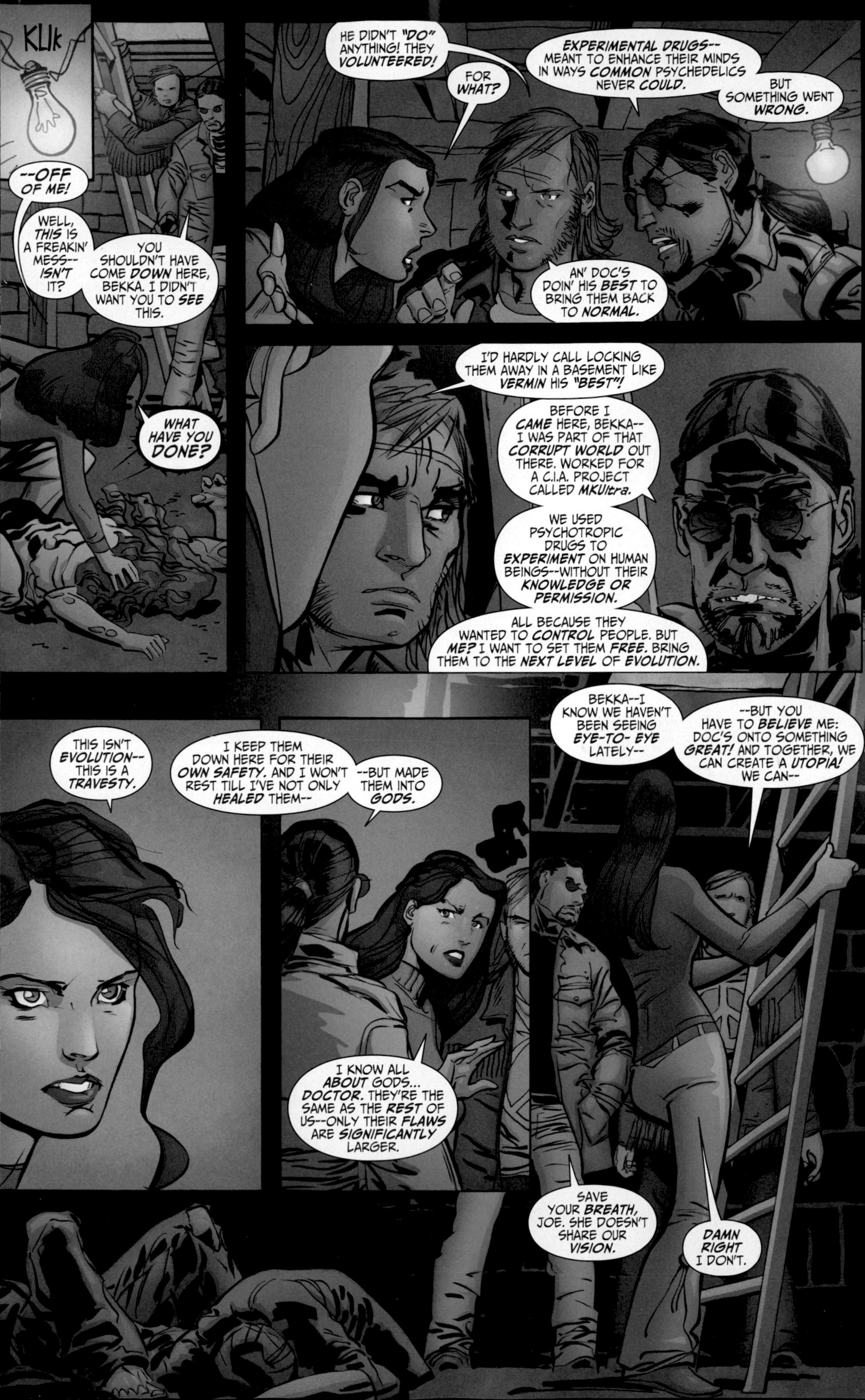
KLIK
--OFF OF ME!
WELL, THIS IS A FREAKIN' MESS-- ISN'T IT?
YOU SHOULDN'T HAVE COME DOWN HERE, BEKKA. I DIDN'T WANT YOU TO SEE THIS.
WHAT HAVE YOU DONE?
HE DIDN'T "DO" ANYTHING! THEY VOLUNTEERED!
FOR WHAT?
EXPERIMENTAL DRUGS-- MEANT TO ENHANCE THEIR MINDS IN WAYS COMMON PSYCHEDELICS NEVER COULD.
BUT SOMETHING WENT WRONG.
AN' DOC'S DOIN' HIS BEST TO BRING THEM BACK TO NORMAL.
I'D HARDLY CALL LOCKING THEM AWAY IN A BASEMENT LIKE VERMIN HIS "BEST"!
BEFORE I CAME HERE, BEKKA-- I WAS PART OF THAT CORRUPT WORLD OUT THERE. WORKED FOR A C.I.A. PROJECT CALLED MKUltra.
WE USED PSYCHOTROPIC DRUGS TO EXPERIMENT ON HUMAN BEINGS--WITHOUT THEIR KNOWLEDGE OR PERMISSION.
ALL BECAUSE THEY WANTED TO CONTROL PEOPLE. BUT ME? I WANT TO SET THEM FREE. BRING THEM TO THE NEXT LEVEL OF EVOLUTION.
THIS ISN'T EVOLUTION-- THIS IS A TRAVESTY.
I KEEP THEM DOWN HERE FOR THEIR OWN SAFETY. AND I WON'T REST TILL I'VE NOT ONLY HEALED THEM--
--BUT MADE THEM INTO GODS.
I KNOW ALL ABOUT GODS... DOCTOR. THEY'RE THE SAME AS THE REST OF US--ONLY THEIR FLAWS ARE SIGNIFICANTLY LARGER.
BEKKA--I KNOW WE HAVEN'T BEEN SEEING EYE-TO- EYE LATELY--
--BUT YOU HAVE TO BELIEVE ME: DOC'S ONTO SOMETHING GREAT! AND TOGETHER, WE CAN CREATE A UTOPIA! WE CAN--
SAVE YOUR BREATH, JOE. SHE DOESN'T SHARE OUR VISION.
DAMN RIGHT I DON'T.

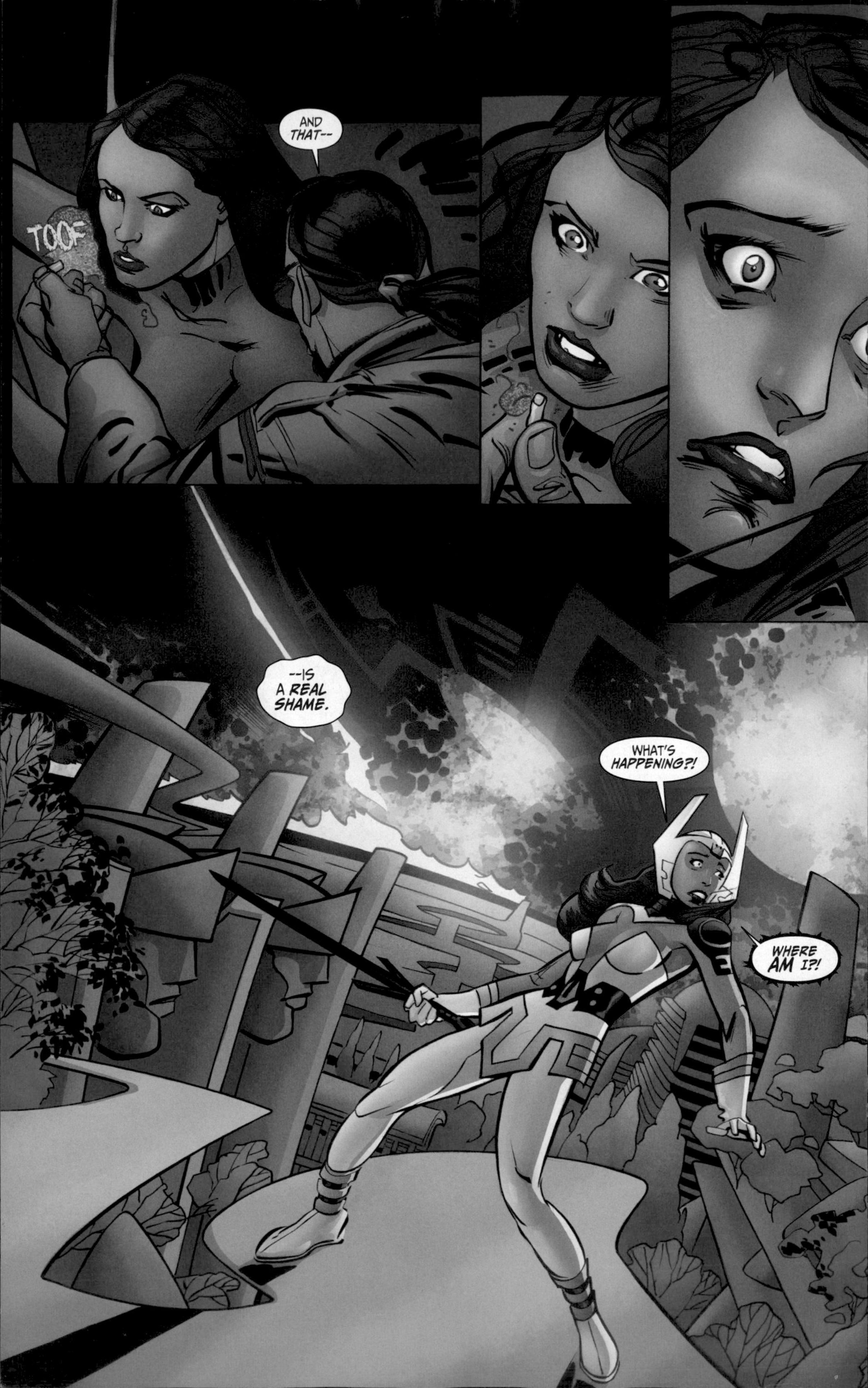

AND THAT--
TOOF
--IS A REAL SHAME.
WHAT'S HAPPENING?!
WHERE AM I?!

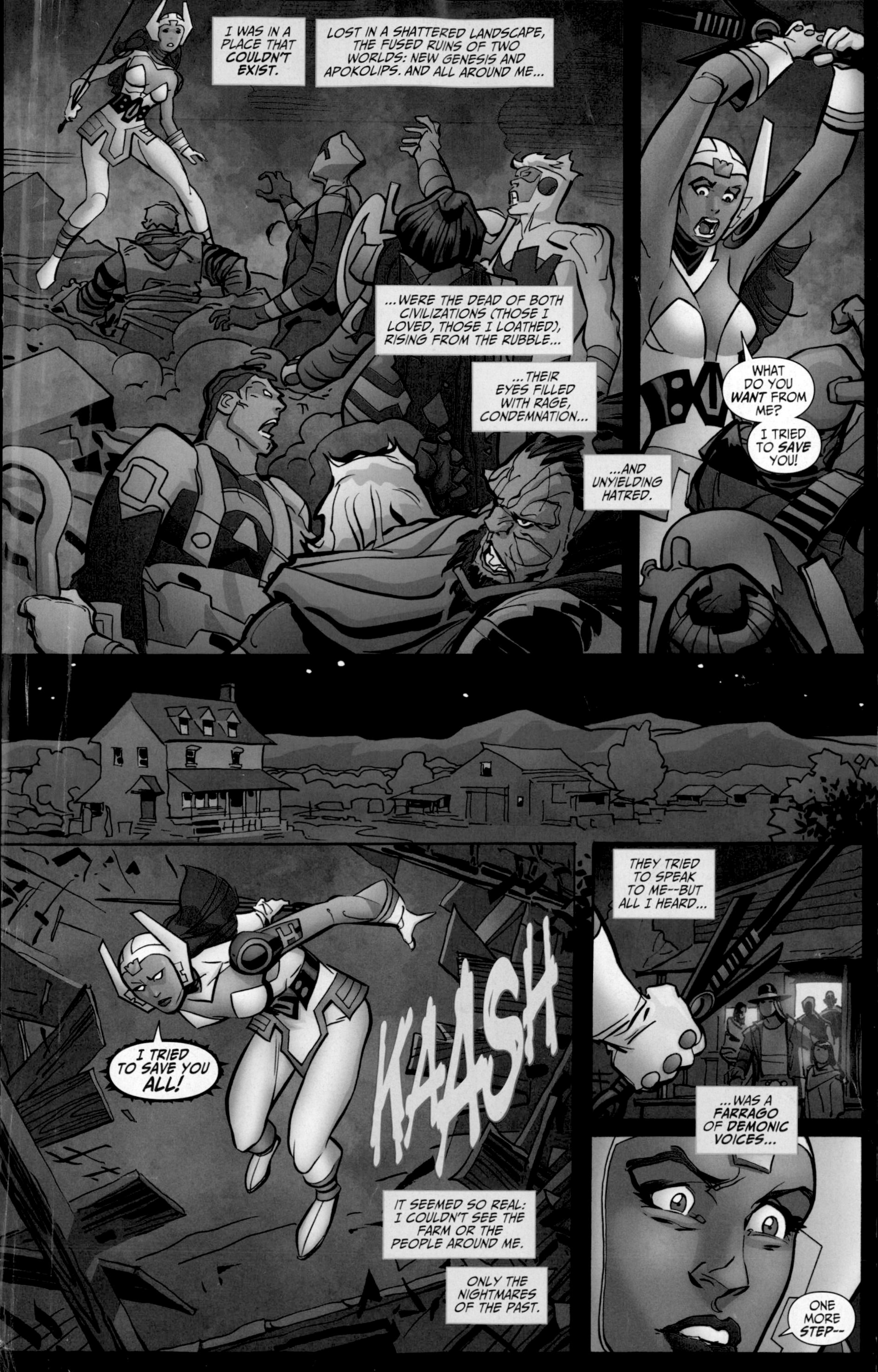
I WAS IN A PLACE THAT COULDN'T EXIST.
LOST IN A SHATTERED LANDSCAPE, THE FUSED RUINS OF TWO WORLDS: NEW GENESIS AND APOKOLIPS. AND ALL AROUND ME...
...WERE THE DEAD OF BOTH CIVILIZATIONS (THOSE I LOVED, THOSE I LOATHED), RISING FROM THE RUBBLE...
...THEIR EYES FILLED WITH RAGE, CONDEMNATION...
...AND UNYIELDING HATRED.
WHAT DO YOU WANT FROM ME?
I TRIED TO SAVE YOU!
I TRIED TO SAVE YOU ALL!
KAASH
IT SEEMED SO REAL: I COULDN'T SEE THE FARM OR THE PEOPLE AROUND ME.
ONLY THE NIGHTMARES OF THE PAST.
THEY TRIED TO SPEAK TO ME--BUT ALL I HEARD...
...WAS A FARRAGO OF DEMONIC VOICES...
ONE MORE STEP--

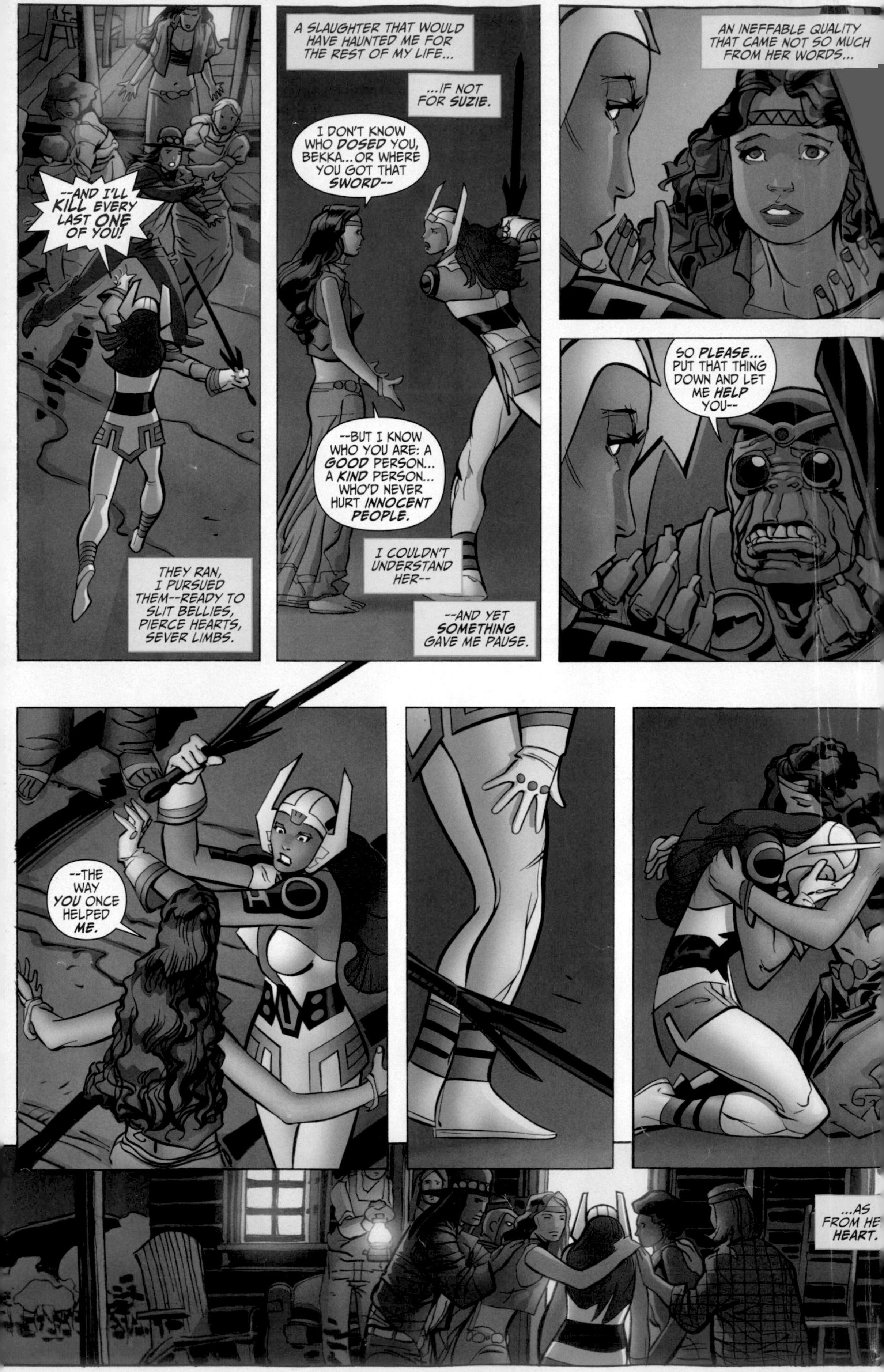
--AND I'LL KILL EVERY LAST ONE OF YOU!
THEY RAN, I PURSUED THEM--READY TO SLIT BELLIES, PIERCE HEARTS, SEVER LIMBS.
A SLAUGHTER THAT WOULD HAVE HAUNTED ME FOR THE REST OF MY LIFE...
...IF NOT FOR SUZIE.
I DON'T KNOW WHO DOSED YOU, BEKKA...OR WHERE YOU GOT THAT SWORD--
--BUT I KNOW WHO YOU ARE: A GOOD PERSON... A KIND PERSON... WHO'D NEVER HURT INNOCENT PEOPLE.
I COULDN'T UNDERSTAND HER--
--AND YET SOMETHING GAVE ME PAUSE.
AN INEFFABLE QUALITY THAT CAME NOT SO MUCH FROM HER WORDS...
SO PLEASE... PUT THAT THING DOWN AND LET ME HELP YOU--
--THE WAY YOU ONCE HELPED ME.
...AS FROM HE HEART.

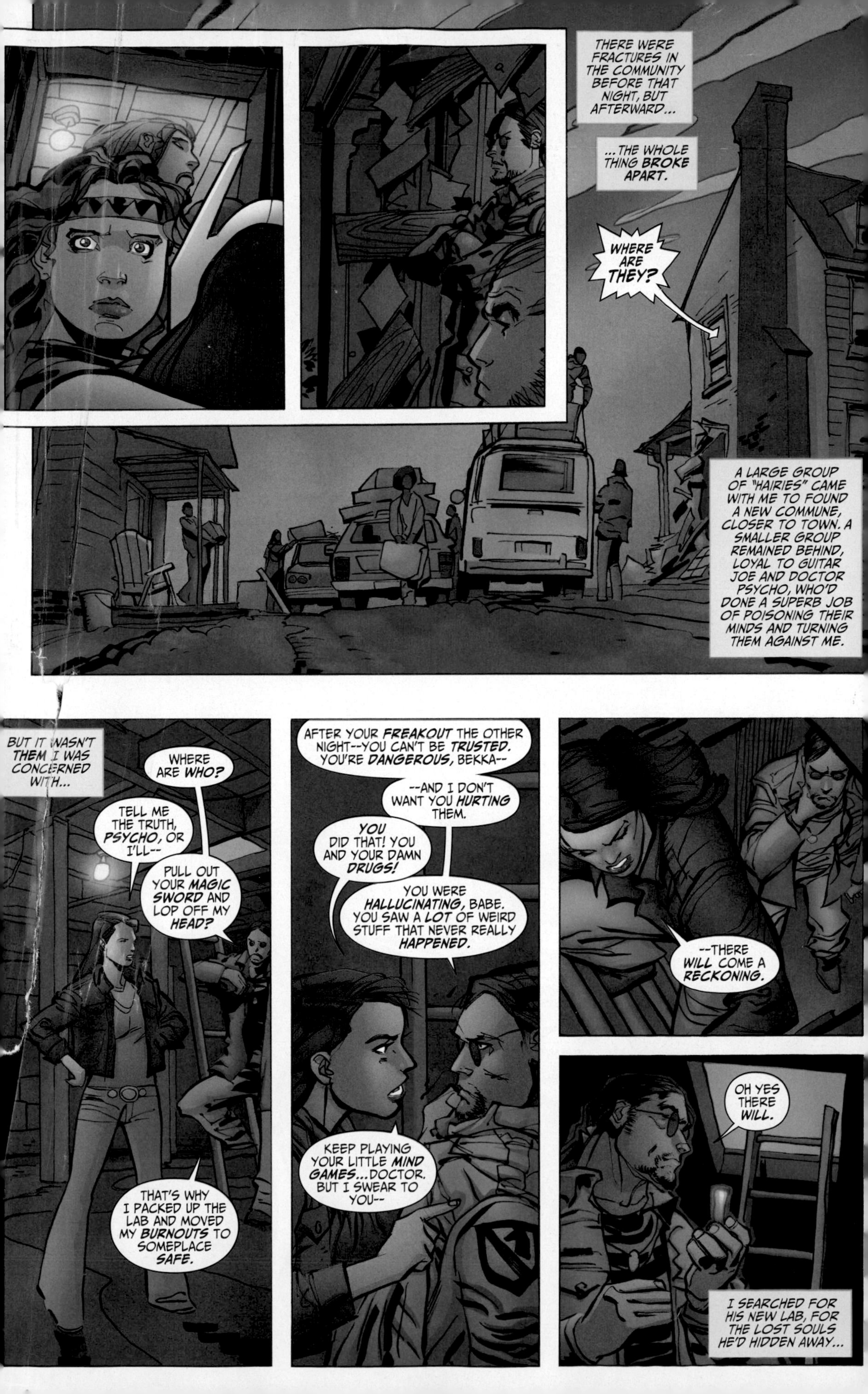
THERE WERE FRACTURES IN THE COMMUNITY BEFORE THAT NIGHT, BUT AFTERWARD...
...THE WHOLE THING BROKE APART.
WHERE ARE THEY?
A LARGE GROUP OF "HAIRIES" CAME WITH ME TO FOUND A NEW COMMUNE, CLOSER TO TOWN. A SMALLER GROUP REMAINED BEHIND, LOYAL TO GUITAR JOE AND DOCTOR PSYCHO, WHO'D DONE A SUPERB JOB OF POISONING THEIR MINDS AND TURNING THEM AGAINST ME.
BUT IT WASN'T THEM I WAS CONCERNED WITH...
WHERE ARE WHO?
TELL ME THE TRUTH, PSYCHO, OR I'LL--
PULL OUT YOUR MAGIC SWORD AND LOP OFF MY HEAD?
THAT'S WHY I PACKED UP THE LAB AND MOVED MY BURNOUTS TO SOMEPLACE SAFE.
AFTER YOUR FREAKOUT THE OTHER NIGHT--YOU CAN'T BE TRUSTED. YOU'RE DANGEROUS, BEKKA--
--AND I DON'T WANT YOU HURTING THEM.
YOU DID THAT! YOU AND YOUR DAMN DRUGS!
YOU WERE HALLUCINATING, BABE. YOU SAW A LOT OF WEIRD STUFF THAT NEVER REALLY HAPPENED.
KEEP PLAYING YOUR LITTLE MIND GAMES...DOCTOR. BUT I SWEAR TO YOU--
--THERE WILL COME A RECKONING.
OH YES THERE WILL.
I SEARCHED FOR HIS NEW LAB, FOR THE LOST SOULS HE'D HIDDEN AWAY...

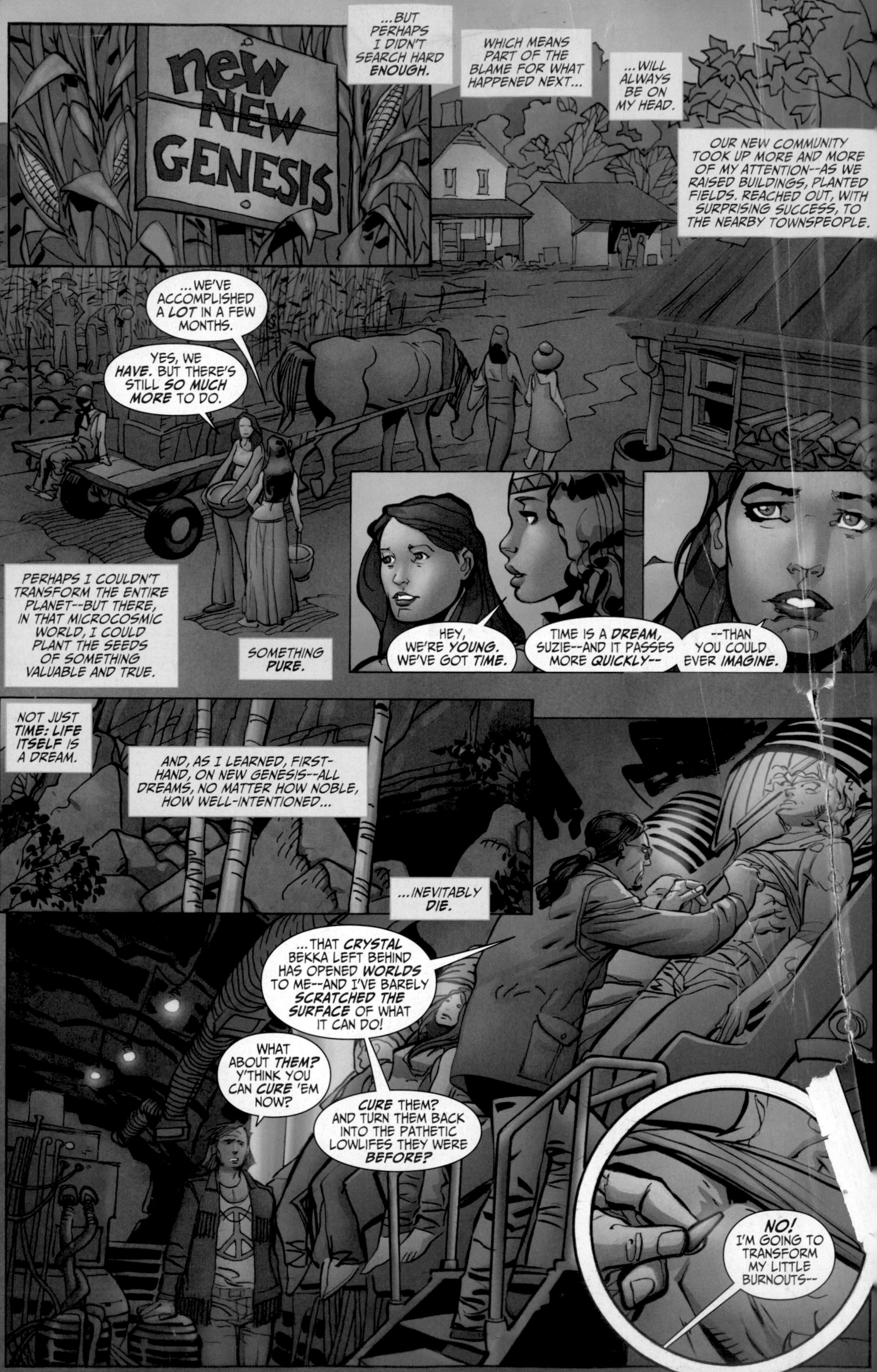

new
NEW
GENESIS
...BUT PERHAPS I DIDN'T SEARCH HARD ENOUGH.
WHICH MEANS PART OF THE BLAME FOR WHAT HAPPENED NEXT...
...WILL ALWAYS BE ON MY HEAD.
OUR NEW COMMUNITY TOOK UP MORE AND MORE OF MY ATTENTION--AS WE RAISED BUILDINGS, PLANTED FIELDS. REACHED OUT, WITH SURPRISING SUCCESS, TO THE NEARBY TOWNSPEOPLE.
...WE'VE ACCOMPLISHED A LOT IN A FEW MONTHS.
YES, WE HAVE. BUT THERE'S STILL SO MUCH MORE TO DO.
PERHAPS I COULDN'T TRANSFORM THE ENTIRE PLANET--BUT THERE, IN THAT MICROCOSMIC WORLD, I COULD PLANT THE SEEDS OF SOMETHING VALUABLE AND TRUE.
SOMETHING PURE.
HEY, WE'RE YOUNG. WE'VE GOT TIME.
TIME IS A DREAM, SUZIE--AND IT PASSES MORE QUICKLY--
--THAN YOU COULD EVER IMAGINE.
NOT JUST TIME: LIFE ITSELF IS A DREAM.
AND, AS I LEARNED, FIRST-HAND, ON NEW GENESIS--ALL DREAMS, NO MATTER HOW NOBLE, HOW WELL-INTENTIONED...
...INEVITABLY DIE.
...THAT CRYSTAL BEKKA LEFT BEHIND HAS OPENED WORLDS TO ME--AND I'VE BARELY SCRATCHED THE SURFACE OF WHAT IT CAN DO!
WHAT ABOUT THEM? Y'THINK YOU CAN CURE 'EM NOW?
CURE THEM? AND TURN THEM BACK INTO THE PATHETIC LOWLIFES THEY WERE BEFORE?
NO! I'M GOING TO TRANSFORM MY LITTLE BURNOUTS--

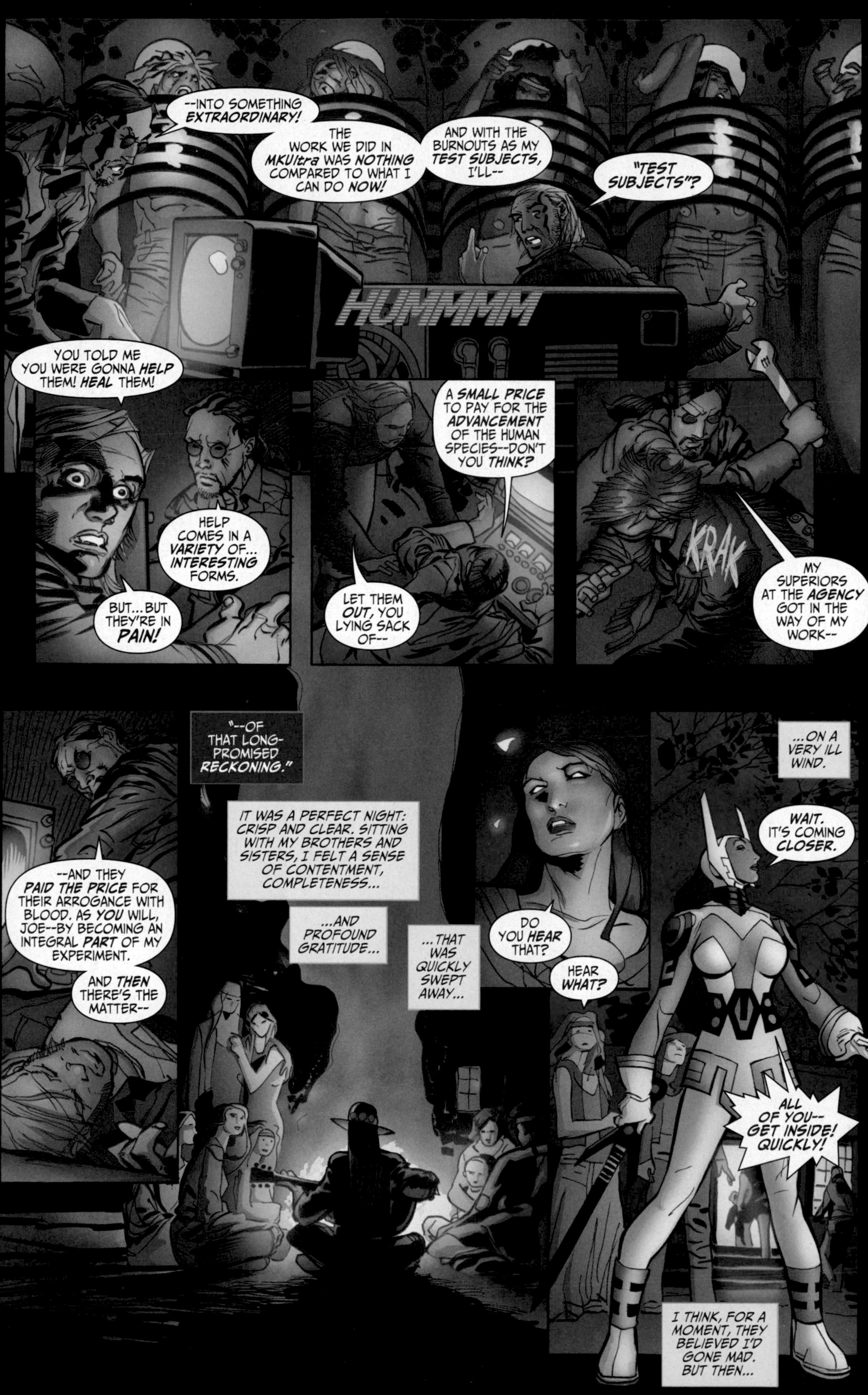

--INTO SOMETHING EXTRAORDINARY!
THE WORK WE DID IN MKUltra WAS NOTHING COMPARED TO WHAT I CAN DO NOW!
AND WITH THE BURNOUTS AS MY TEST SUBJECTS, I'LL--
"TEST SUBJECTS"?
HUMMMM
YOU TOLD ME YOU WERE GONNA HELP THEM! HEAL THEM!
HELP COMES IN A VARIETY OF... INTERESTING FORMS.
BUT... BUT THEY'RE IN PAIN!
A SMALL PRICE TO PAY FOR THE ADVANCEMENT OF THE HUMAN SPECIES--DON'T YOU THINK?
LET THEM OUT, YOU LYING SACK OF--
KRAK
MY SUPERIORS AT THE AGENCY GOT IN THE WAY OF MY WORK--
--AND THEY PAID THE PRICE FOR THEIR ARROGANCE WITH BLOOD. AS YOU WILL, JOE--BY BECOMING AN INTEGRAL PART OF MY EXPERIMENT.
AND THEN THERE'S THE MATTER--
"--OF THAT LONG-PROMISED RECKONING."
IT WAS A PERFECT NIGHT: CRISP AND CLEAR. SITTING WITH MY BROTHERS AND SISTERS, I FELT A SENSE OF CONTENTMENT, COMPLETENESS...
...AND PROFOUND GRATITUDE...
...THAT WAS QUICKLY SWEPT AWAY...
...ON A VERY ILL WIND.
DO YOU HEAR THAT?
HEAR WHAT?
WAIT. IT'S COMING CLOSER.
ALL OF YOU-- GET INSIDE! QUICKLY!
I THINK, FOR A MOMENT, THEY BELIEVED I'D GONE MAD. BUT THEN...

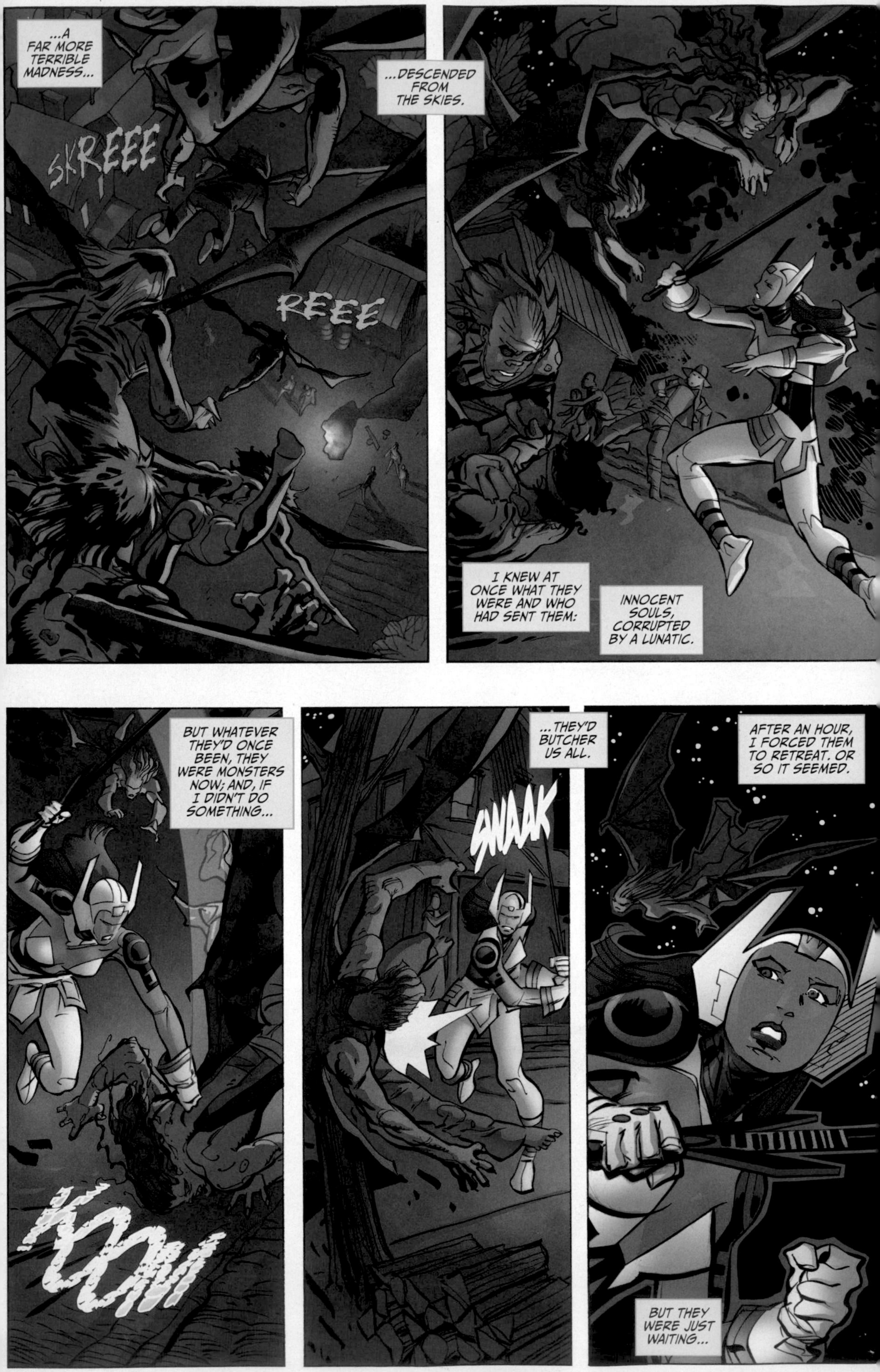
...A FAR MORE TERRIBLE MADNESS...
SKREEE
REEE
...DESCENDED FROM THE SKIES.
I KNEW AT ONCE WHAT THEY WERE AND WHO HAD SENT THEM:
INNOCENT SOULS, CORRUPTED BY A LUNATIC.
BUT WHATEVER THEY'D ONCE BEEN, THEY WERE MONSTERS NOW; AND, IF I DIDN'T DO SOMETHING...
KOOM
...THEY'D BUTCHER US ALL.
SNAAK
AFTER AN HOUR, I FORCED THEM TO RETREAT. OR SO IT SEEMED.
BUT THEY WERE JUST WAITING...

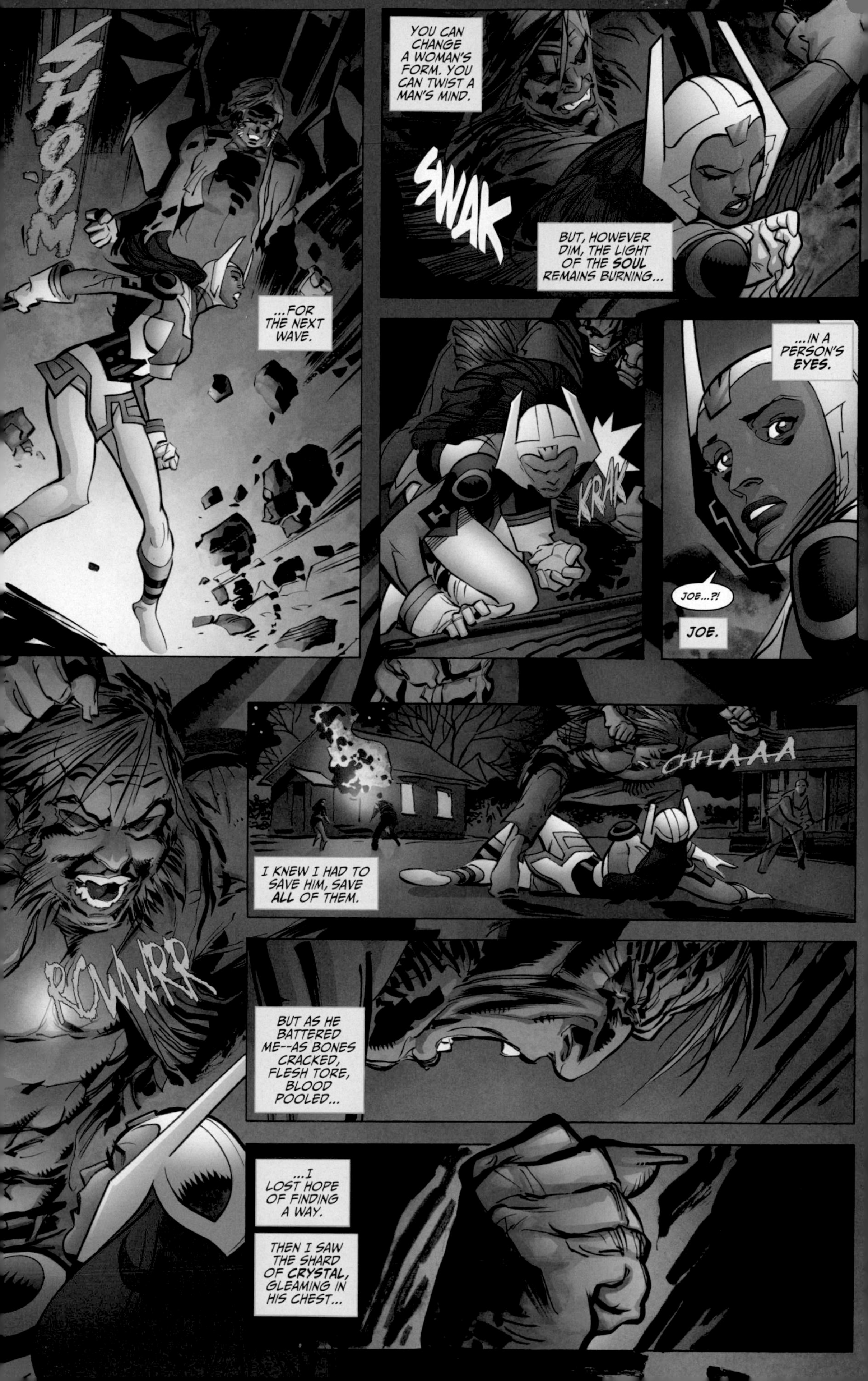
SHOOOM
...FOR THE NEXT WAVE.
YOU CAN CHANGE A WOMAN'S FORM. YOU CAN TWIST A MAN'S MIND.
SWAK
BUT, HOWEVER DIM, THE LIGHT OF THE SOUL REMAINS BURNING...
KRAK
...IN A PERSON'S EYES.
JOE...?!
JOE.
CHHAAAA
I KNEW I HAD TO SAVE HIM, SAVE ALL OF THEM.
ROWRR
BUT AS HE BATTERED ME--AS BONES CRACKED, FLESH TORE, BLOOD POOLED...
...I LOST HOPE OF FINDING A WAY.
THEN I SAW THE SHARD OF CRYSTAL, GLEAMING IN HIS CHEST...

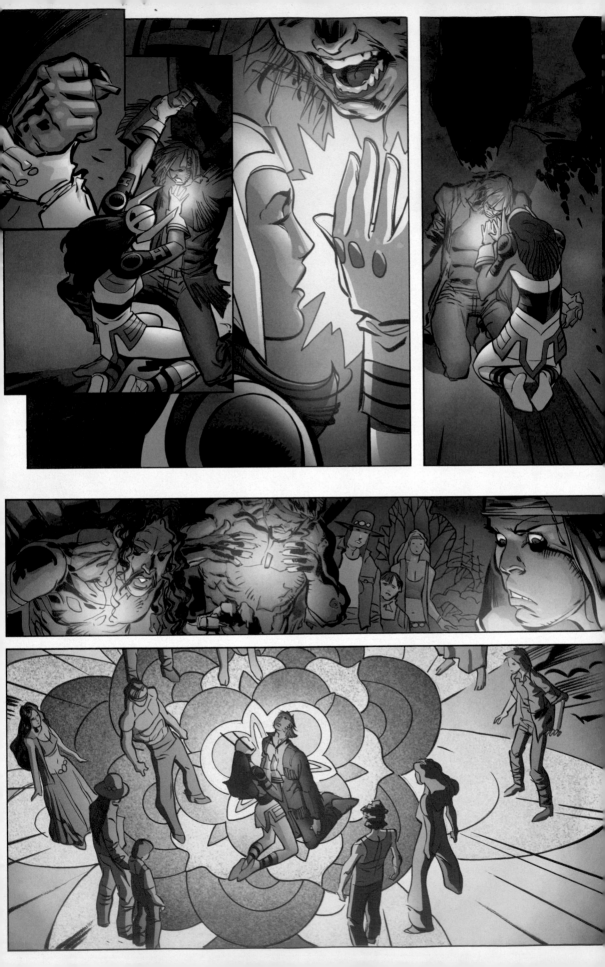

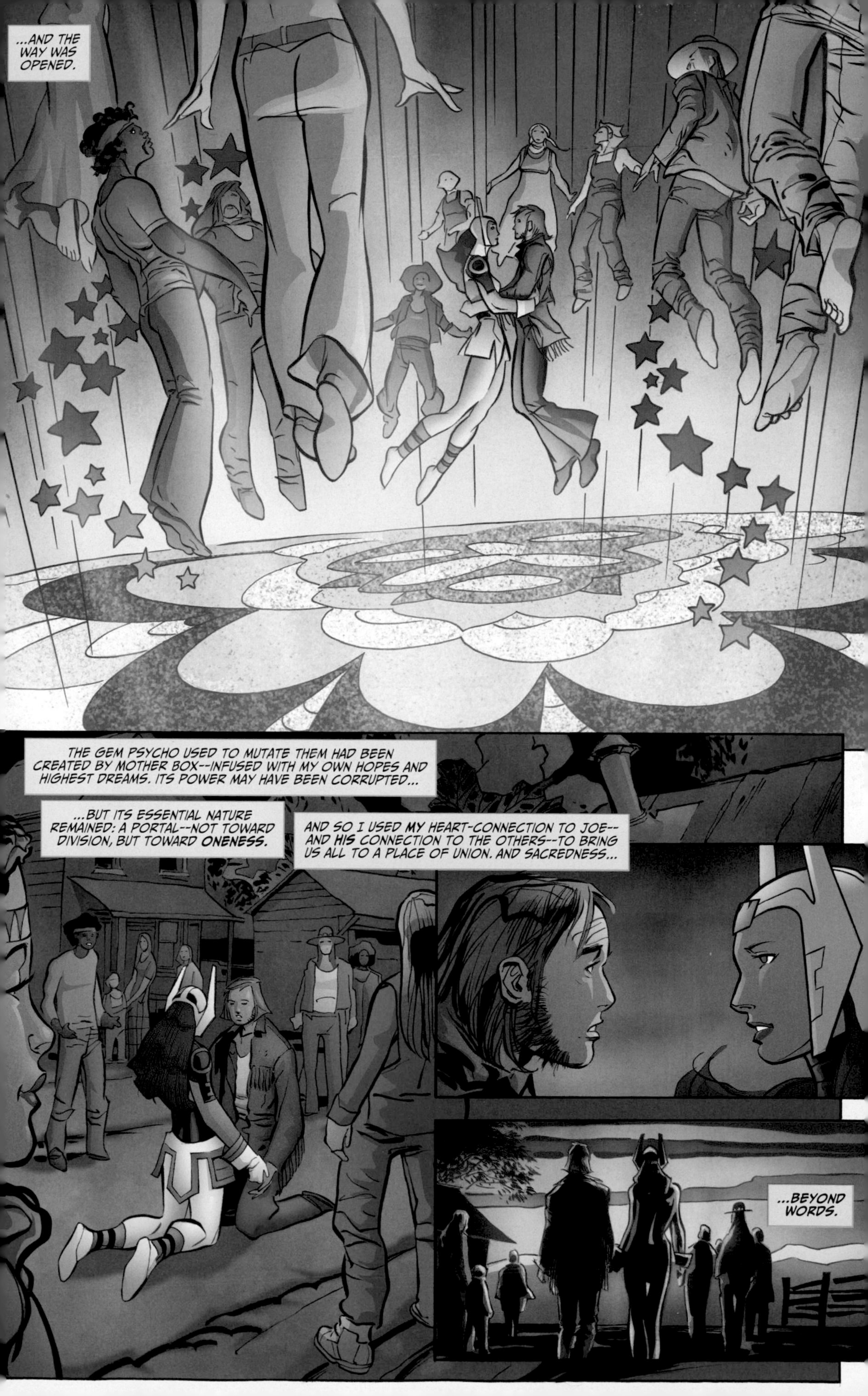
...AND THE WAY WAS OPENED.
THE GEM PSYCHO USED TO MUTATE THEM HAD BEEN CREATED BY MOTHER BOX--INFUSED WITH MY OWN HOPES AND HIGHEST DREAMS. ITS POWER MAY HAVE BEEN CORRUPTED...
...BUT ITS ESSENTIAL NATURE REMAINED: A PORTAL--NOT TOWARD DIVISION, BUT TOWARD ONENESS.
AND SO I USED MY HEART-CONNECTION TO JOE--AND HIS CONNECTION TO THE OTHERS--TO BRING US ALL TO A PLACE OF UNION. AND SACREDNESS...
...BEYOND WORDS.

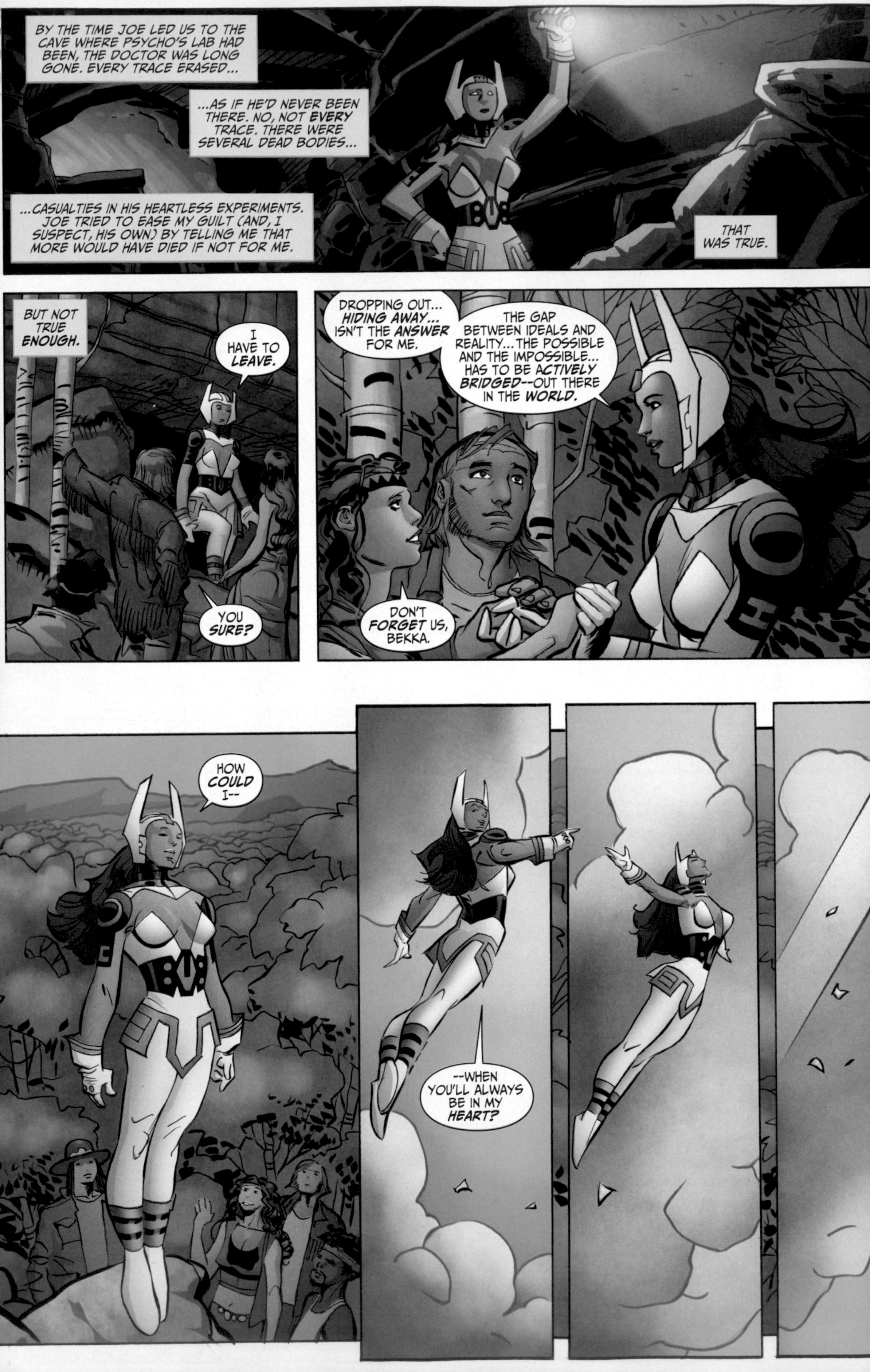
BY THE TIME JOE LED US TO THE CAVE WHERE PSYCHO'S LAB HAD BEEN, THE DOCTOR WAS LONG GONE. EVERY TRACE ERASED...
...AS IF HE'D NEVER BEEN THERE. NO, NOT EVERY TRACE. THERE WERE SEVERAL DEAD BODIES...
...CASUALTIES IN HIS HEARTLESS EXPERIMENTS. JOE TRIED TO EASE MY GUILT (AND, I SUSPECT, HIS OWN) BY TELLING ME THAT MORE WOULD HAVE DIED IF NOT FOR ME.
THAT WAS TRUE.
BUT NOT TRUE ENOUGH.
I HAVE TO LEAVE.
YOU SURE?
DROPPING OUT... HIDING AWAY... ISN'T THE ANSWER FOR ME.
THE GAP BETWEEN IDEALS AND REALITY...THE POSSIBLE AND THE IMPOSSIBLE... HAS TO BE ACTIVELY BRIDGED--OUT THERE IN THE WORLD.
DON'T FORGET US, BEKKA.
HOW COULD I--
--WHEN YOU'LL ALWAYS BE IN MY HEART?

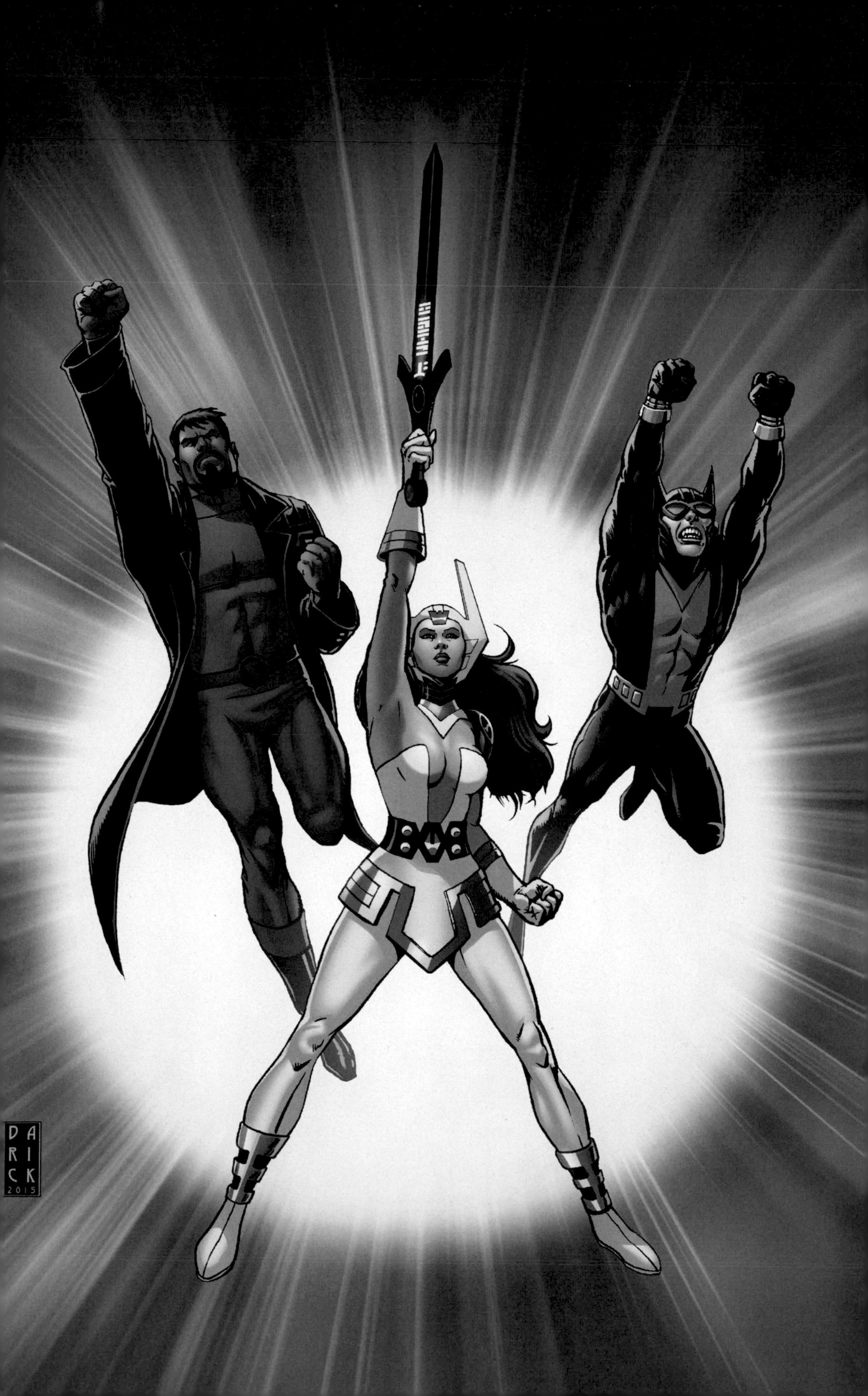
DARICK 2015

GENESIS PART 1

ART BY THONY SILAS

COLORS BY TONY AVIÑA

COVER ART BY DARICK ROBERTSON AND DIEGO RODRIGUEZ

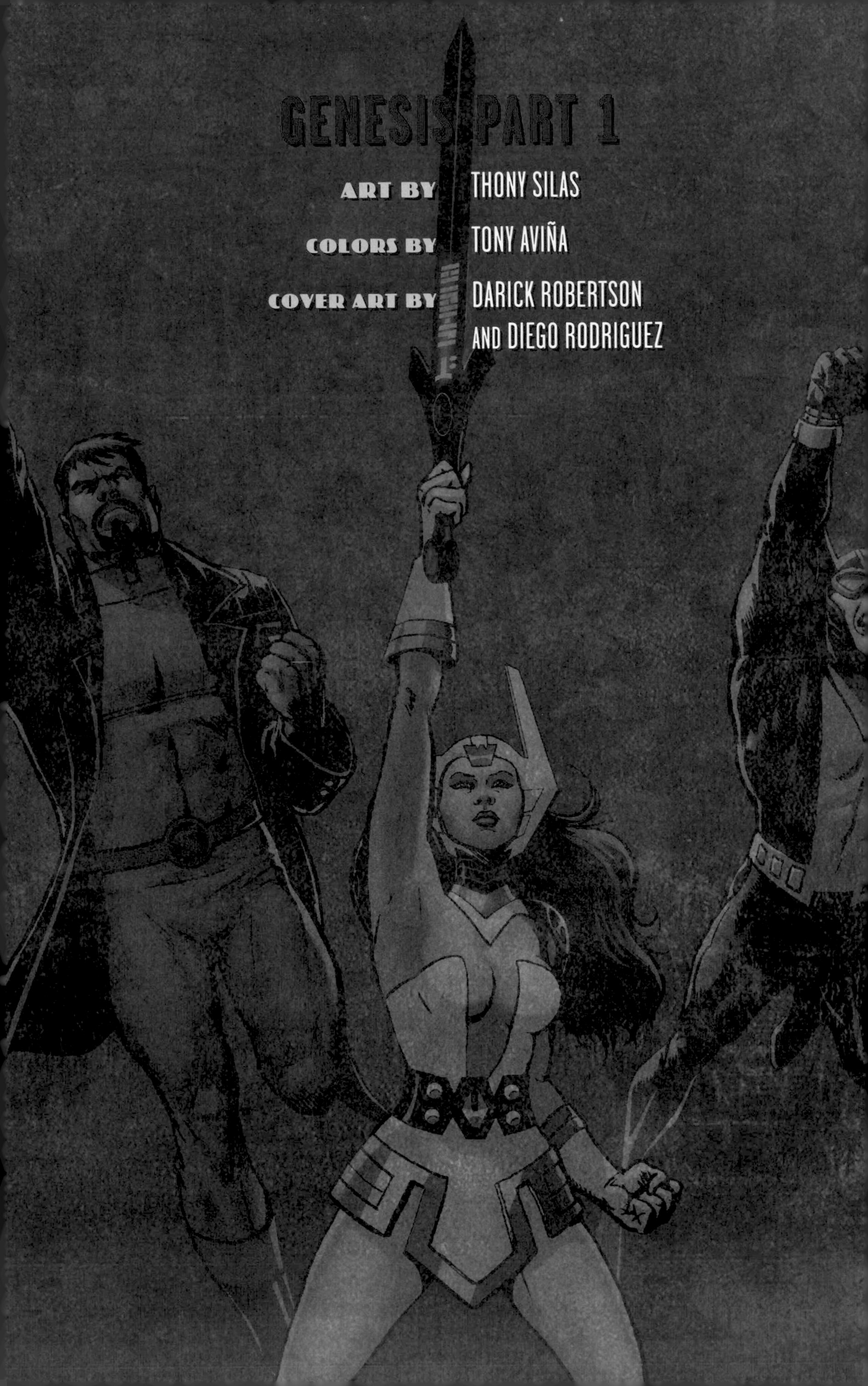

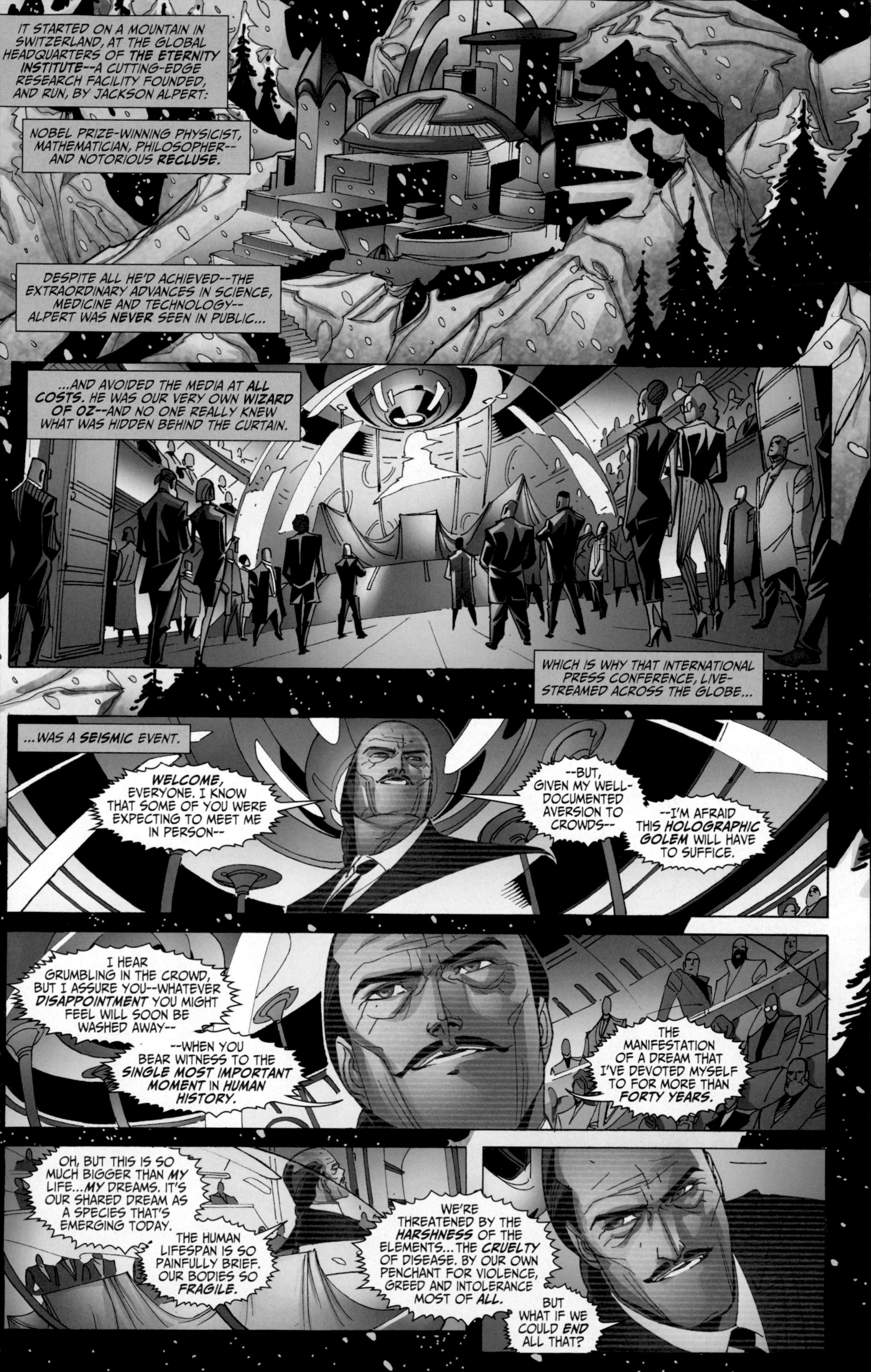

IT STARTED ON A MOUNTAIN IN SWITZERLAND, AT THE GLOBAL HEADQUARTERS OF THE ETERNITY INSTITUTE--A CUTTING-EDGE RESEARCH FACILITY FOUNDED, AND RUN, BY JACKSON ALPERT:
NOBEL PRIZE-WINNING PHYSICIST, MATHEMATICIAN, PHILOSOPHER--AND NOTORIOUS RECLUSE.
DESPITE ALL HE'D ACHIEVED--THE EXTRAORDINARY ADVANCES IN SCIENCE, MEDICINE AND TECHNOLOGY--ALPERT WAS NEVER SEEN IN PUBLIC...
...AND AVOIDED THE MEDIA AT ALL COSTS. HE WAS OUR VERY OWN WIZARD OF OZ--AND NO ONE REALLY KNEW WHAT WAS HIDDEN BEHIND THE CURTAIN.
WHICH IS WHY THAT INTERNATIONAL PRESS CONFERENCE, LIVE-STREAMED ACROSS THE GLOBE...
...WAS A SEISMIC EVENT.
WELCOME, EVERYONE. I KNOW THAT SOME OF YOU WERE EXPECTING TO MEET ME IN PERSON--
--BUT, GIVEN MY WELL-DOCUMENTED AVERSION TO CROWDS--
--I'M AFRAID THIS HOLOGRAPHIC GOLEM WILL HAVE TO SUFFICE.
I HEAR GRUMBLING IN THE CROWD, BUT I ASSURE YOU--WHATEVER DISAPPOINTMENT YOU MIGHT FEEL WILL SOON BE WASHED AWAY--
--WHEN YOU BEAR WITNESS TO THE SINGLE MOST IMPORTANT MOMENT IN HUMAN HISTORY.
THE MANIFESTATION OF A DREAM THAT I'VE DEVOTED MYSELF TO FOR MORE THAN FORTY YEARS.
OH, BUT THIS IS SO MUCH BIGGER THAN MY LIFE...MY DREAMS. IT'S OUR SHARED DREAM AS A SPECIES THAT'S EMERGING TODAY.
THE HUMAN LIFESPAN IS SO PAINFULLY BRIEF. OUR BODIES SO FRAGILE.
WE'RE THREATENED BY THE HARSHNESS OF THE ELEMENTS... THE CRUELTY OF DISEASE. BY OUR OWN PENCHANT FOR VIOLENCE, GREED AND INTOLERANCE MOST OF ALL.
BUT WHAT IF WE COULD END ALL THAT?

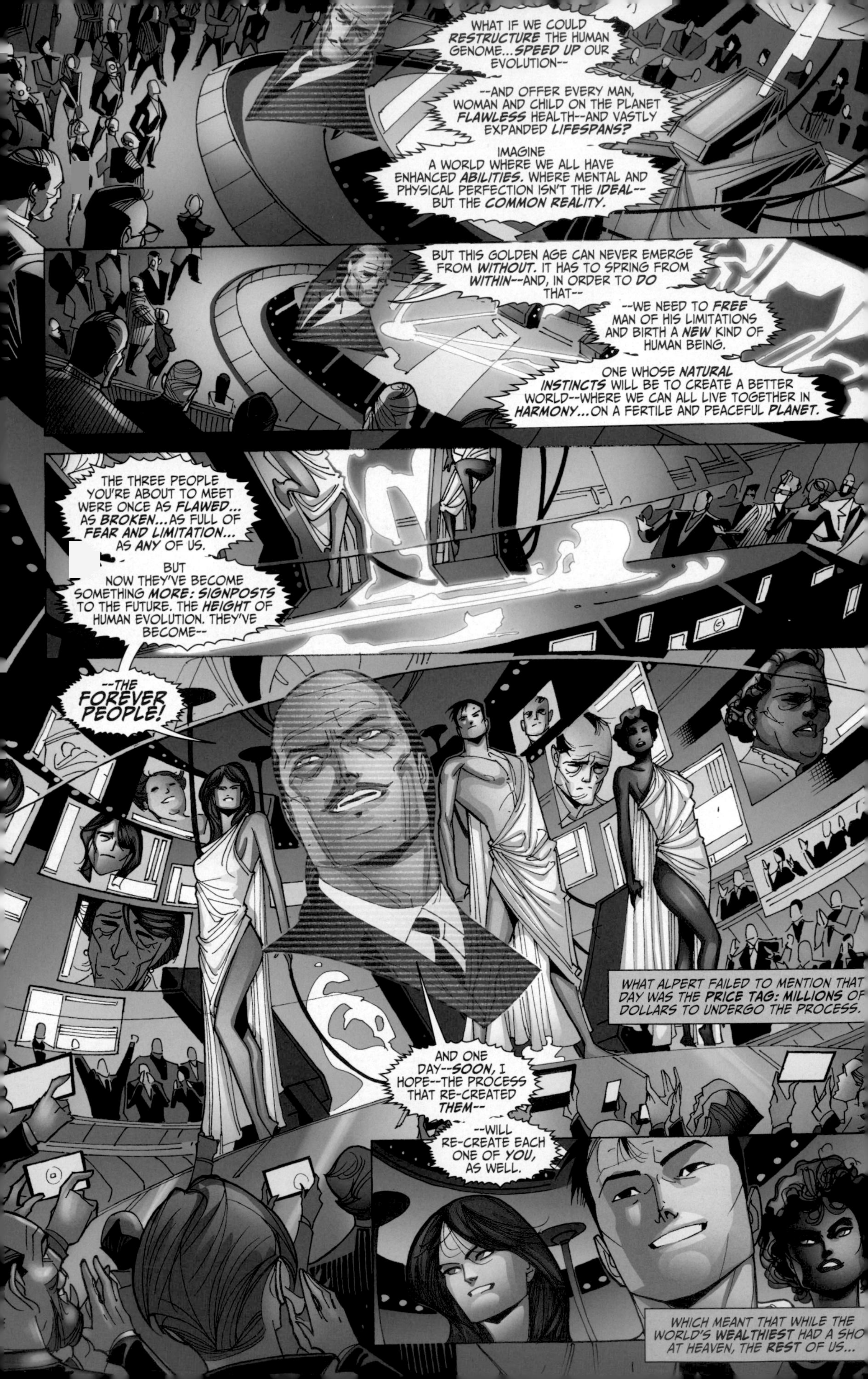
WHAT IF WE COULD RESTRUCTURE THE HUMAN GENOME...SPEED UP OUR EVOLUTION--
--AND OFFER EVERY MAN, WOMAN AND CHILD ON THE PLANET FLAWLESS HEALTH--AND VASTLY EXPANDED LIFESPANS?
IMAGINE A WORLD WHERE WE ALL HAVE ENHANCED ABILITIES. WHERE MENTAL AND PHYSICAL PERFECTION ISN'T THE IDEAL--BUT THE COMMON REALITY.
BUT THIS GOLDEN AGE CAN NEVER EMERGE FROM WITHOUT. IT HAS TO SPRING FROM WITHIN--AND, IN ORDER TO DO THAT--
--WE NEED TO FREE MAN OF HIS LIMITATIONS AND BIRTH A NEW KIND OF HUMAN BEING.
ONE WHOSE NATURAL INSTINCTS WILL BE TO CREATE A BETTER WORLD--WHERE WE CAN ALL LIVE TOGETHER IN HARMONY...ON A FERTILE AND PEACEFUL PLANET.
THE THREE PEOPLE YOU'RE ABOUT TO MEET WERE ONCE AS FLAWED... AS BROKEN...AS FULL OF FEAR AND LIMITATION... AS ANY OF US.
BUT NOW THEY'VE BECOME SOMETHING MORE: SIGNPOSTS TO THE FUTURE. THE HEIGHT OF HUMAN EVOLUTION. THEY'VE BECOME--
--THE FOREVER PEOPLE!
WHAT ALPERT FAILED TO MENTION THAT DAY WAS THE PRICE TAG: MILLIONS OF DOLLARS TO UNDERGO THE PROCESS.
AND ONE DAY--SOON, I HOPE--THE PROCESS THAT RE-CREATED THEM--
--WILL RE-CREATE EACH ONE OF YOU, AS WELL.
WHICH MEANT THAT WHILE THE WORLD'S WEALTHIEST HAD A SHOT AT HEAVEN, THE REST OF US...

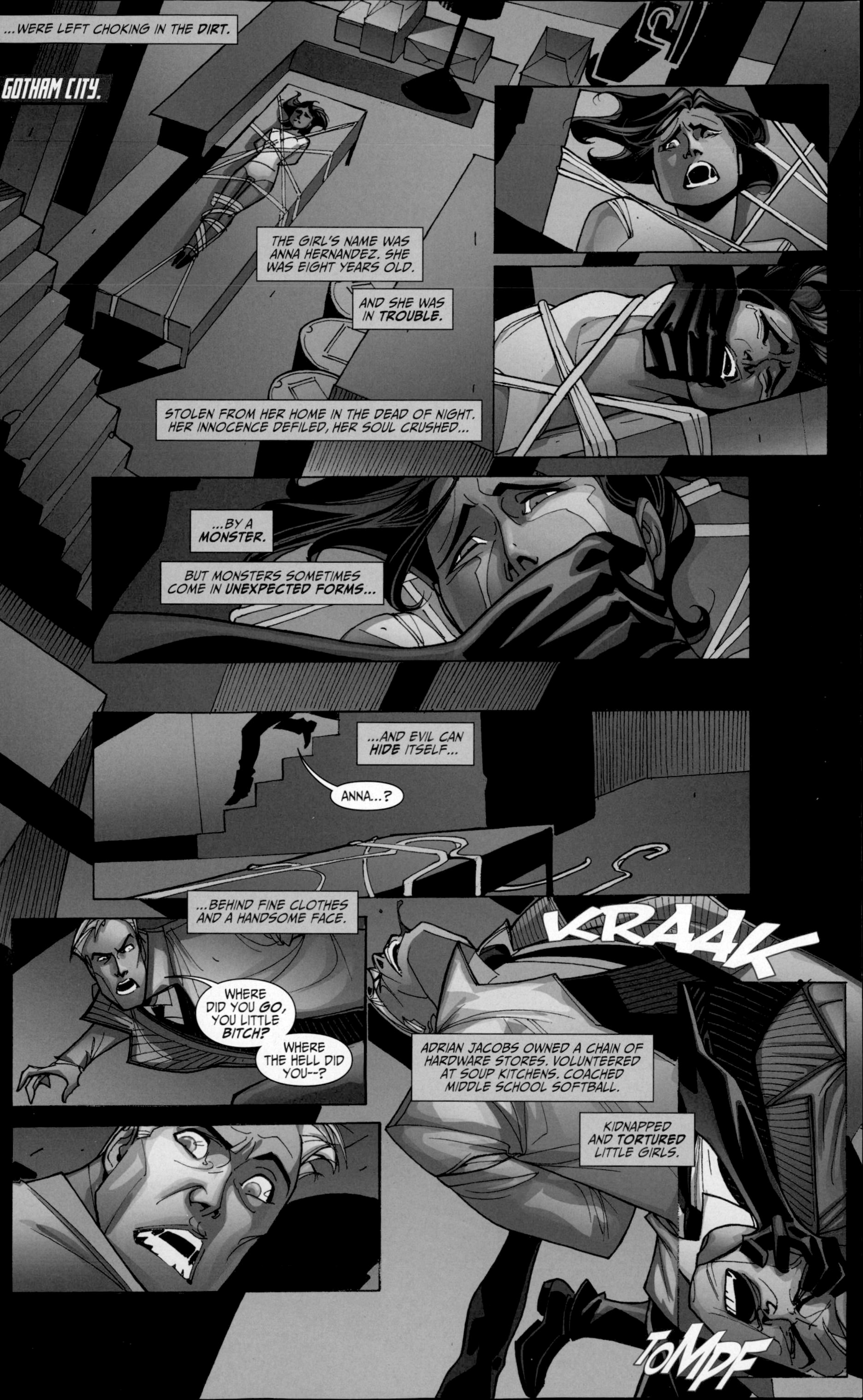

...WERE LEFT CHOKING IN THE DIRT.
GOTHAM CITY.
THE GIRL'S NAME WAS ANNA HERNANDEZ. SHE WAS EIGHT YEARS OLD.
AND SHE WAS IN TROUBLE.
STOLEN FROM HER HOME IN THE DEAD OF NIGHT. HER INNOCENCE DEFILED, HER SOUL CRUSHED...
...BY A MONSTER.
BUT MONSTERS SOMETIMES COME IN UNEXPECTED FORMS...
...AND EVIL CAN HIDE ITSELF...
ANNA...?
...BEHIND FINE CLOTHES AND A HANDSOME FACE.
WHERE DID YOU GO, YOU LITTLE BITCH?
WHERE THE HELL DID YOU--?
KRAAK
ADRIAN JACOBS OWNED A CHAIN OF HARDWARE STORES. VOLUNTEERED AT SOUP KITCHENS. COACHED MIDDLE SCHOOL SOFTBALL.
KIDNAPPED AND TORTURED LITTLE GIRLS.
TOMPF

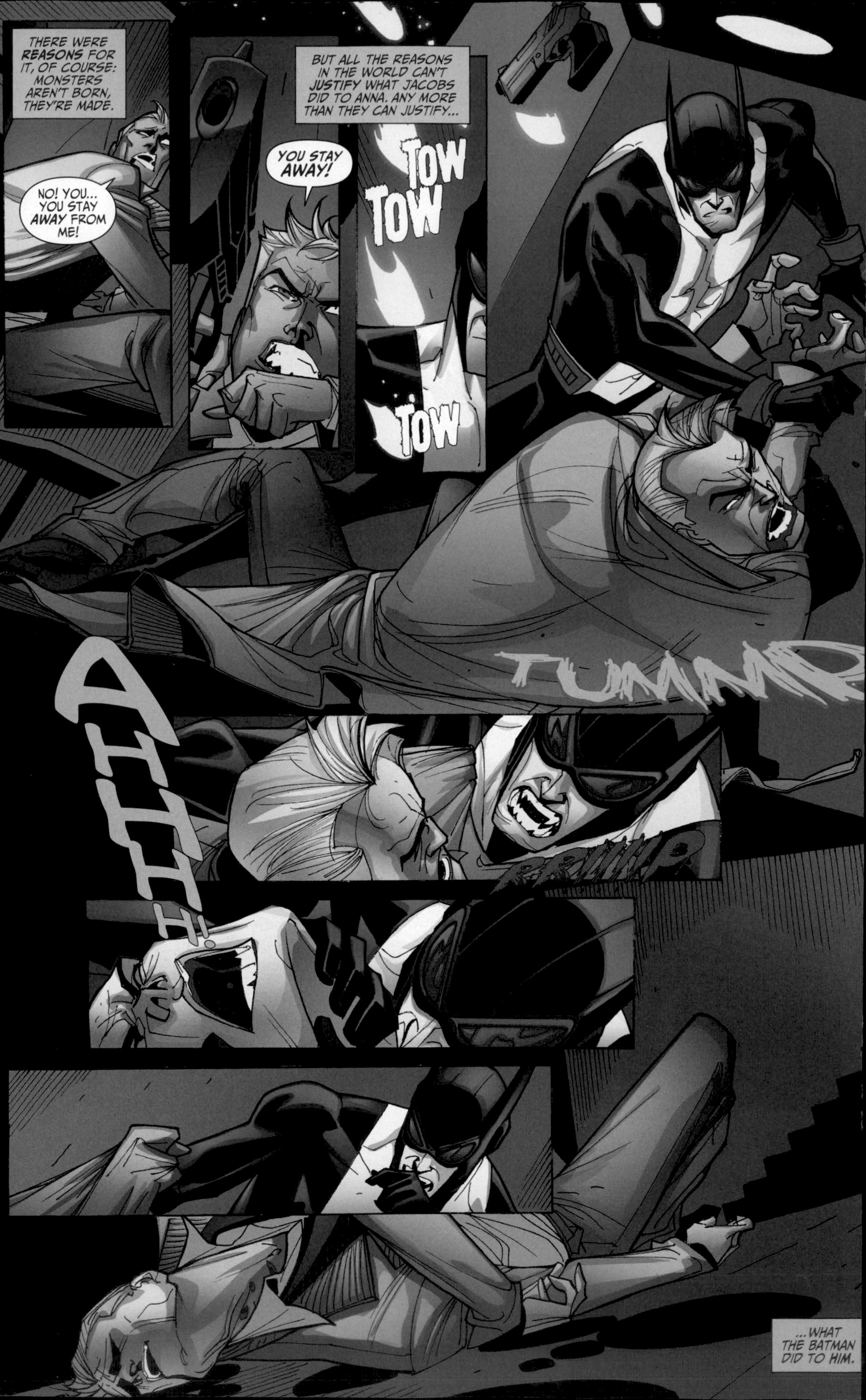
THERE WERE REASONS FOR IT, OF COURSE: MONSTERS AREN'T BORN, THEY'RE MADE.
NO! YOU... YOU STAY AWAY FROM ME!
BUT ALL THE REASONS IN THE WORLD CAN'T JUSTIFY WHAT JACOBS DID TO ANNA. ANY MORE THAN THEY CAN JUSTIFY...
YOU STAY AWAY!
TOW
TOW
TOW
TUMMP
AHHH!
...WHAT THE BATMAN DID TO HIM.

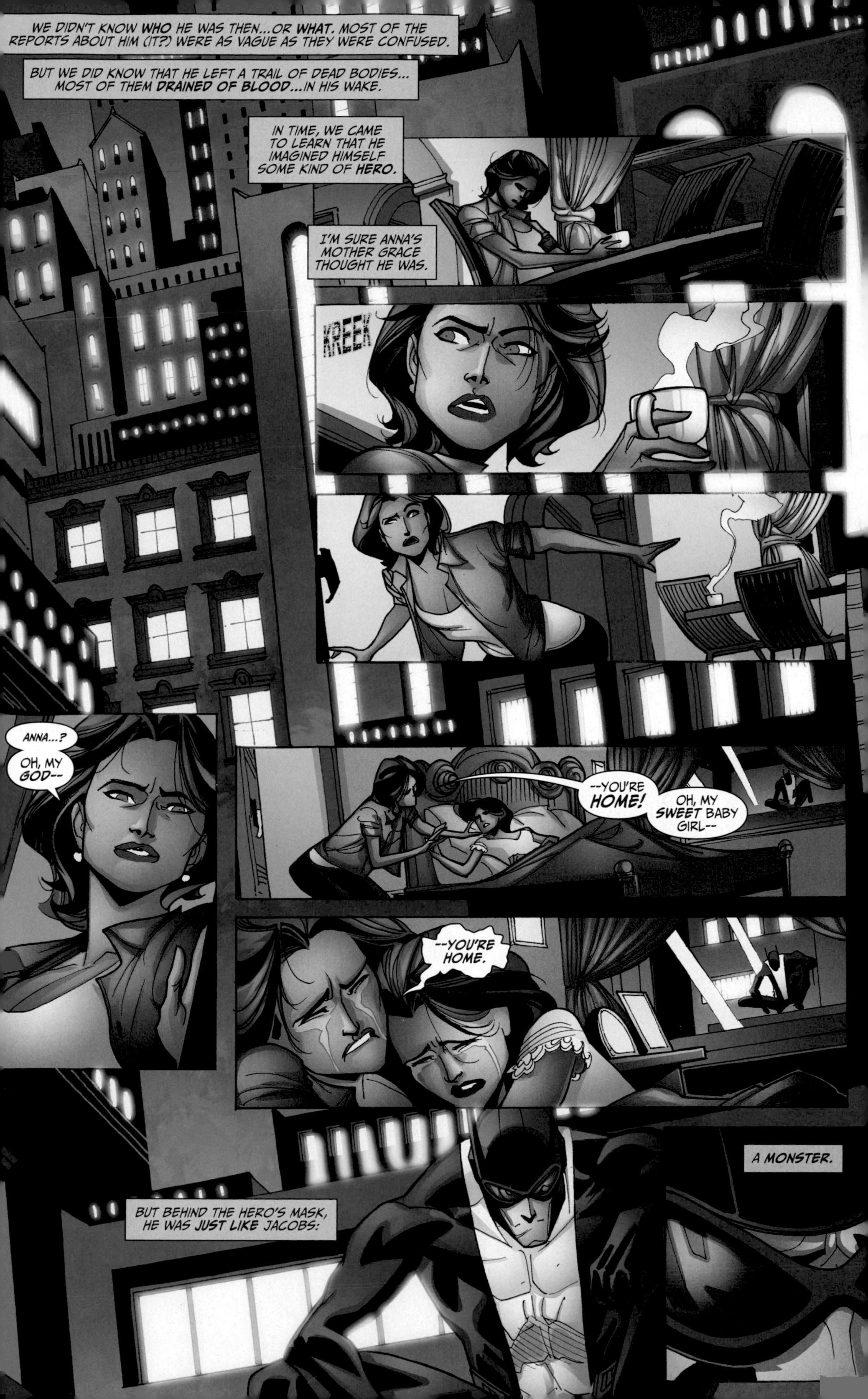
WE DIDN'T KNOW WHO HE WAS THEN...OR WHAT. MOST OF THE REPORTS ABOUT HIM (IT?) WERE AS VAGUE AS THEY WERE CONFUSED.
BUT WE DID KNOW THAT HE LEFT A TRAIL OF DEAD BODIES... MOST OF THEM DRAINED OF BLOOD...IN HIS WAKE.
IN TIME, WE CAME TO LEARN THAT HE IMAGINED HIMSELF SOME KIND OF HERO.
I'M SURE ANNA'S MOTHER GRACE THOUGHT HE WAS.
KREEK
ANNA...?
OH, MY GOD--
--YOU'RE HOME!
OH, MY SWEET BABY GIRL--
--YOU'RE HOME.
BUT BEHIND THE HERO'S MASK, HE WAS JUST LIKE JACOBS:
A MONSTER.

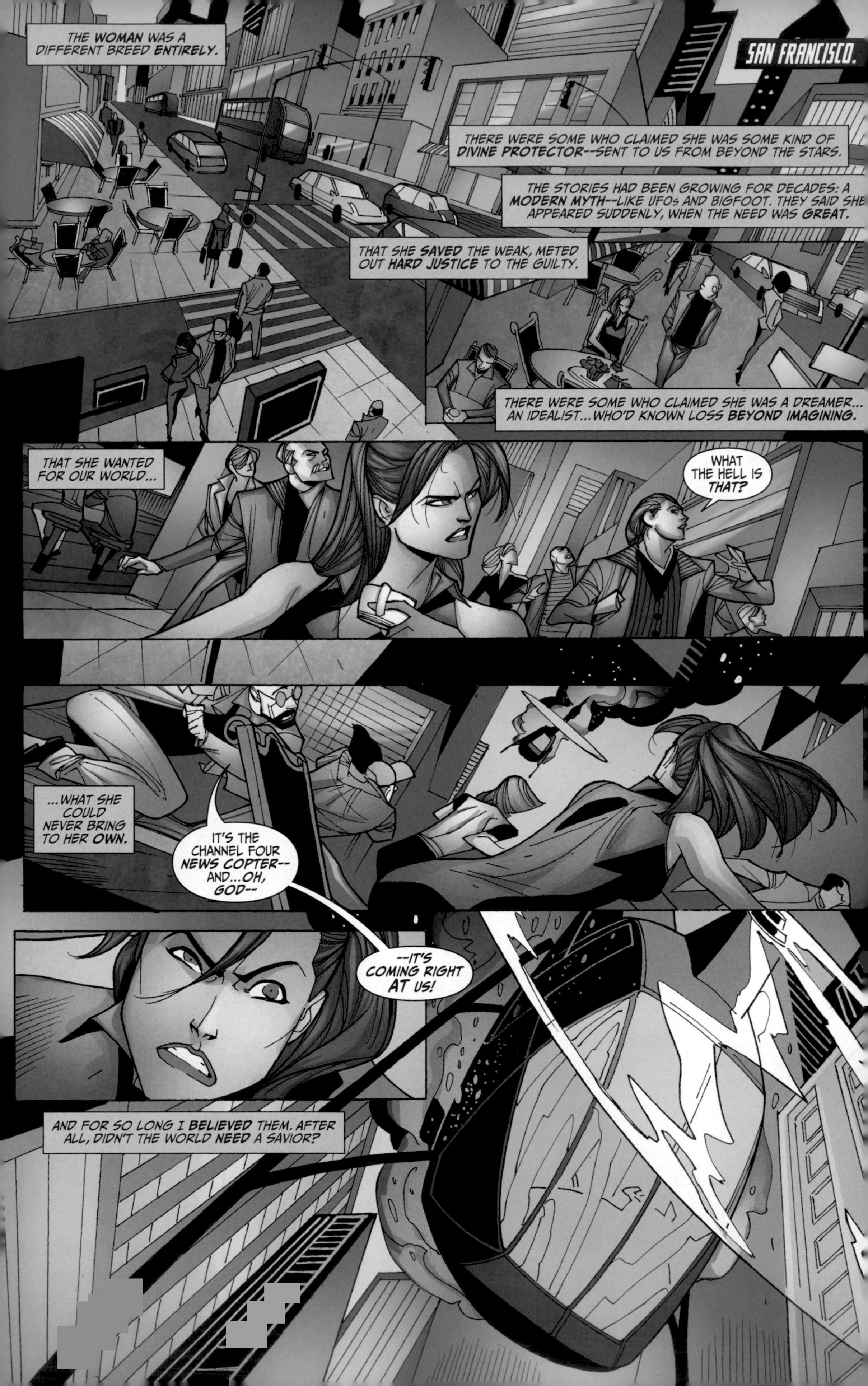
THE WOMAN WAS A DIFFERENT BREED ENTIRELY.
SAN FRANCISCO.
THERE WERE SOME WHO CLAIMED SHE WAS SOME KIND OF DIVINE PROTECTOR--SENT TO US FROM BEYOND THE STARS.
THE STORIES HAD BEEN GROWING FOR DECADES: A MODERN MYTH--LIKE UFOs AND BIGFOOT. THEY SAID SHE APPEARED SUDDENLY, WHEN THE NEED WAS GREAT.
THAT SHE SAVED THE WEAK, METED OUT HARD JUSTICE TO THE GUILTY.
THERE WERE SOME WHO CLAIMED SHE WAS A DREAMER... AN IDEALIST...WHO'D KNOWN LOSS BEYOND IMAGINING.
THAT SHE WANTED FOR OUR WORLD...
WHAT THE HELL IS THAT?
...WHAT SHE COULD NEVER BRING TO HER OWN.
IT'S THE CHANNEL FOUR NEWS COPTER-- AND...OH, GOD--
--IT'S COMING RIGHT AT US!
AND FOR SO LONG I BELIEVED THEM. AFTER ALL, DIDN'T THE WORLD NEED A SAVIOR?

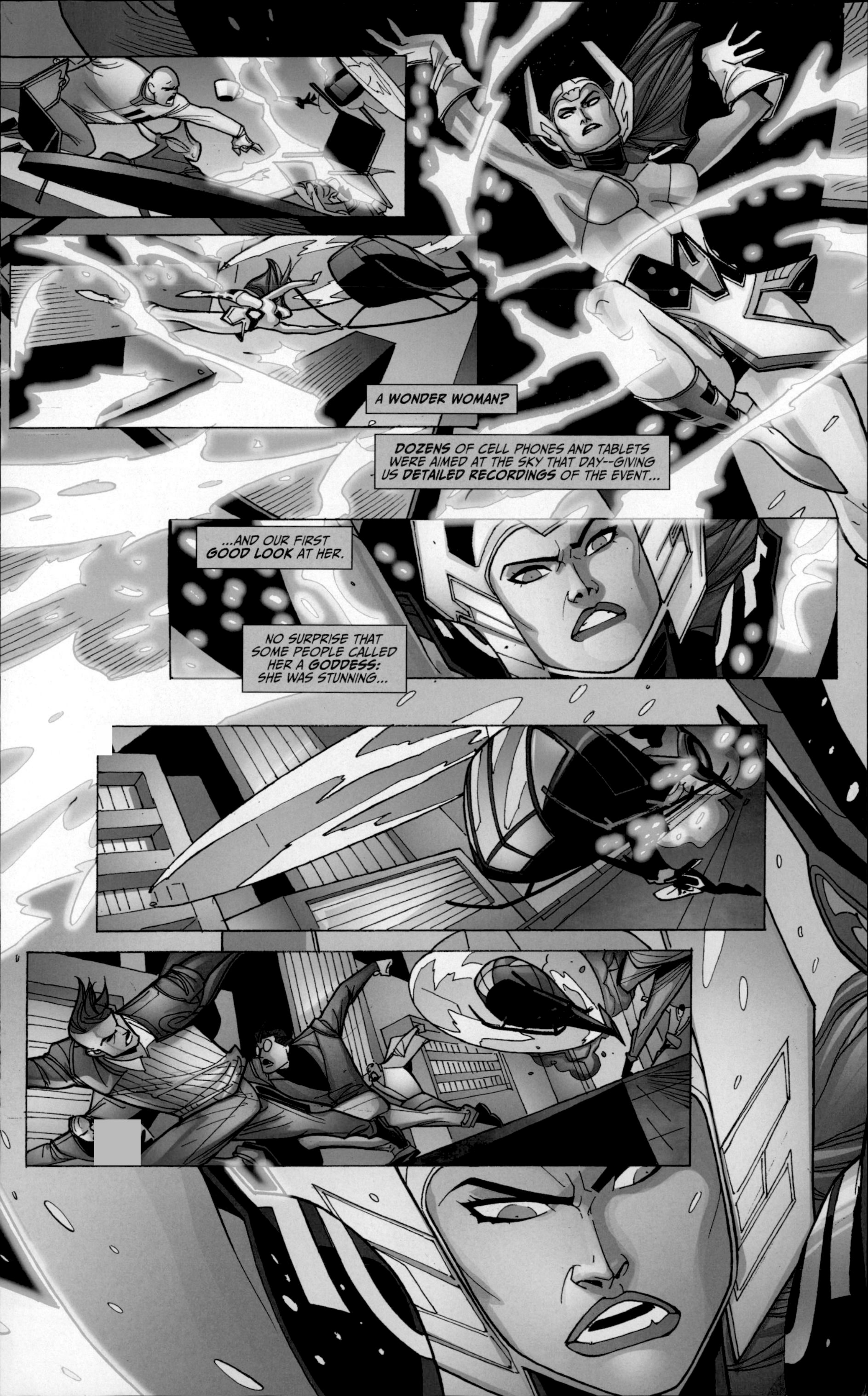
A WONDER WOMAN?
DOZENS OF CELL PHONES AND TABLETS WERE AIMED AT THE SKY THAT DAY--GIVING US DETAILED RECORDINGS OF THE EVENT...
...AND OUR FIRST GOOD LOOK AT HER.
NO SURPRISE THAT SOME PEOPLE CALLED HER A GODDESS: SHE WAS STUNNING...

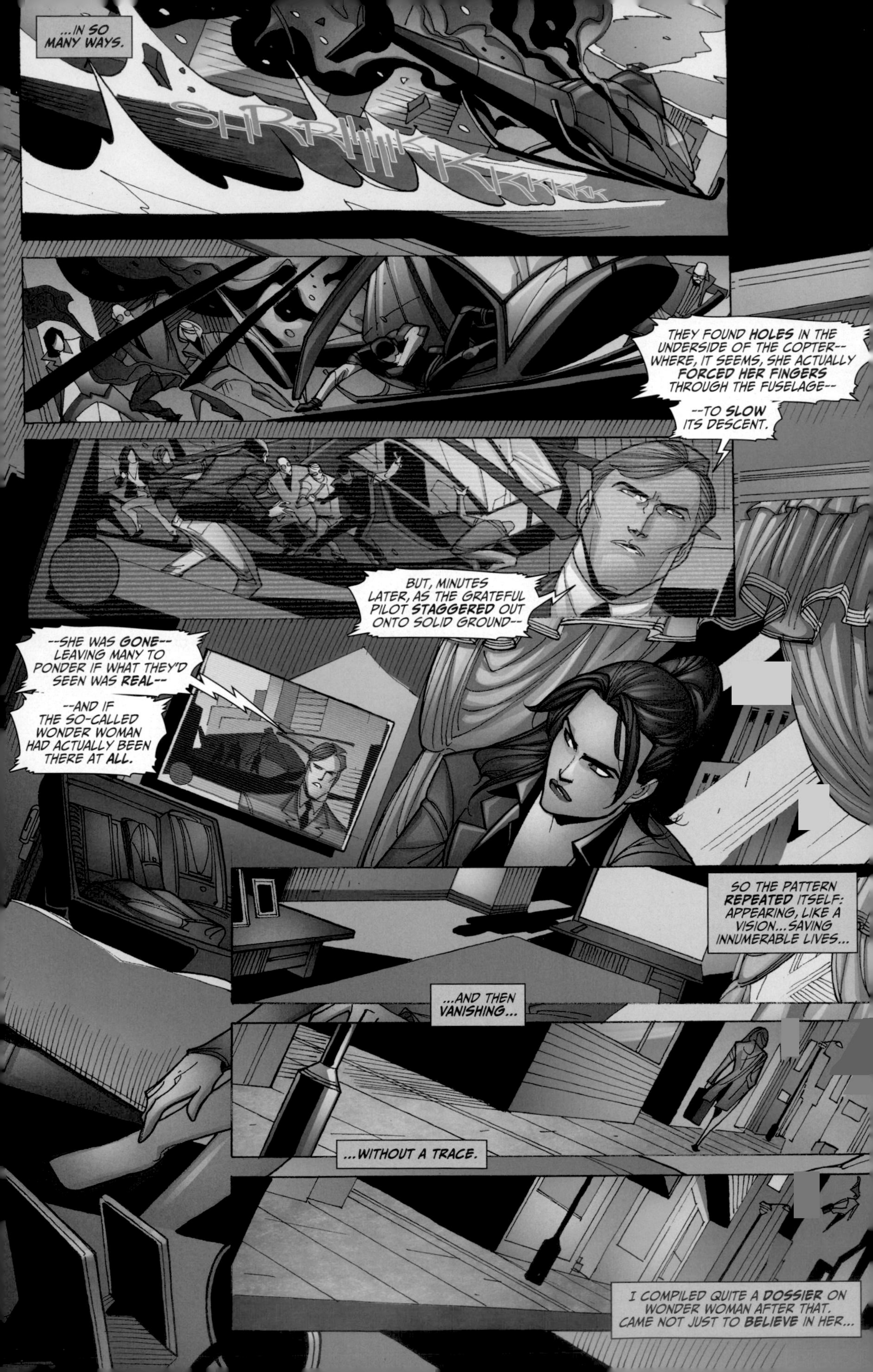
...IN SO MANY WAYS.
SHRRIIIIKKKKKKK
THEY FOUND HOLES IN THE UNDERSIDE OF THE COPTER-- WHERE, IT SEEMS, SHE ACTUALLY FORCED HER FINGERS THROUGH THE FUSELAGE--
--TO SLOW ITS DESCENT.
BUT, MINUTES LATER, AS THE GRATEFUL PILOT STAGGERED OUT ONTO SOLID GROUND--
--SHE WAS GONE-- LEAVING MANY TO PONDER IF WHAT THEY'D SEEN WAS REAL--
--AND IF THE SO-CALLED WONDER WOMAN HAD ACTUALLY BEEN THERE AT ALL.
SO THE PATTERN REPEATED ITSELF: APPEARING, LIKE A VISION...SAVING INNUMERABLE LIVES...
...AND THEN VANISHING...
...WITHOUT A TRACE.
I COMPILED QUITE A DOSSIER ON WONDER WOMAN AFTER THAT. CAME NOT JUST TO BELIEVE IN HER...

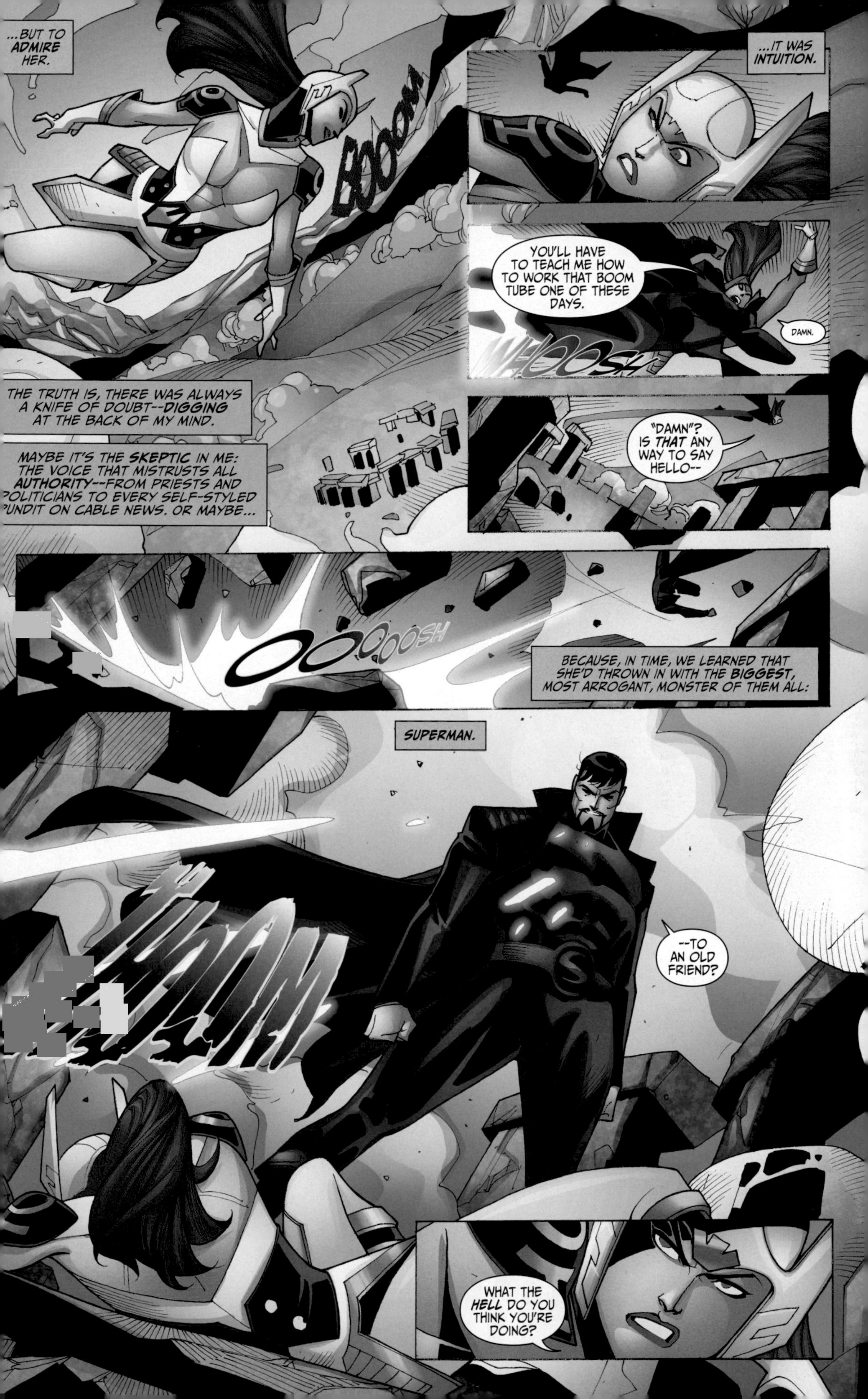
...BUT TO ADMIRE HER.
BOOOM
...IT WAS INTUITION.
YOU'LL HAVE TO TEACH ME HOW TO WORK THAT BOOM TUBE ONE OF THESE DAYS.
DAMN.
WHOOOSH
THE TRUTH IS, THERE WAS ALWAYS A KNIFE OF DOUBT--DIGGING AT THE BACK OF MY MIND.
MAYBE IT'S THE SKEPTIC IN ME: THE VOICE THAT MISTRUSTS ALL AUTHORITY--FROM PRIESTS AND POLITICIANS TO EVERY SELF-STYLED PUNDIT ON CABLE NEWS. OR MAYBE...
"DAMN"? IS THAT ANY WAY TO SAY HELLO--
OOOOOOSH
BECAUSE, IN TIME, WE LEARNED THAT SHE'D THROWN IN WITH THE BIGGEST, MOST ARROGANT, MONSTER OF THEM ALL:
SUPERMAN.
--TO AN OLD FRIEND?
WHAT THE HELL DO YOU THINK YOU'RE DOING?

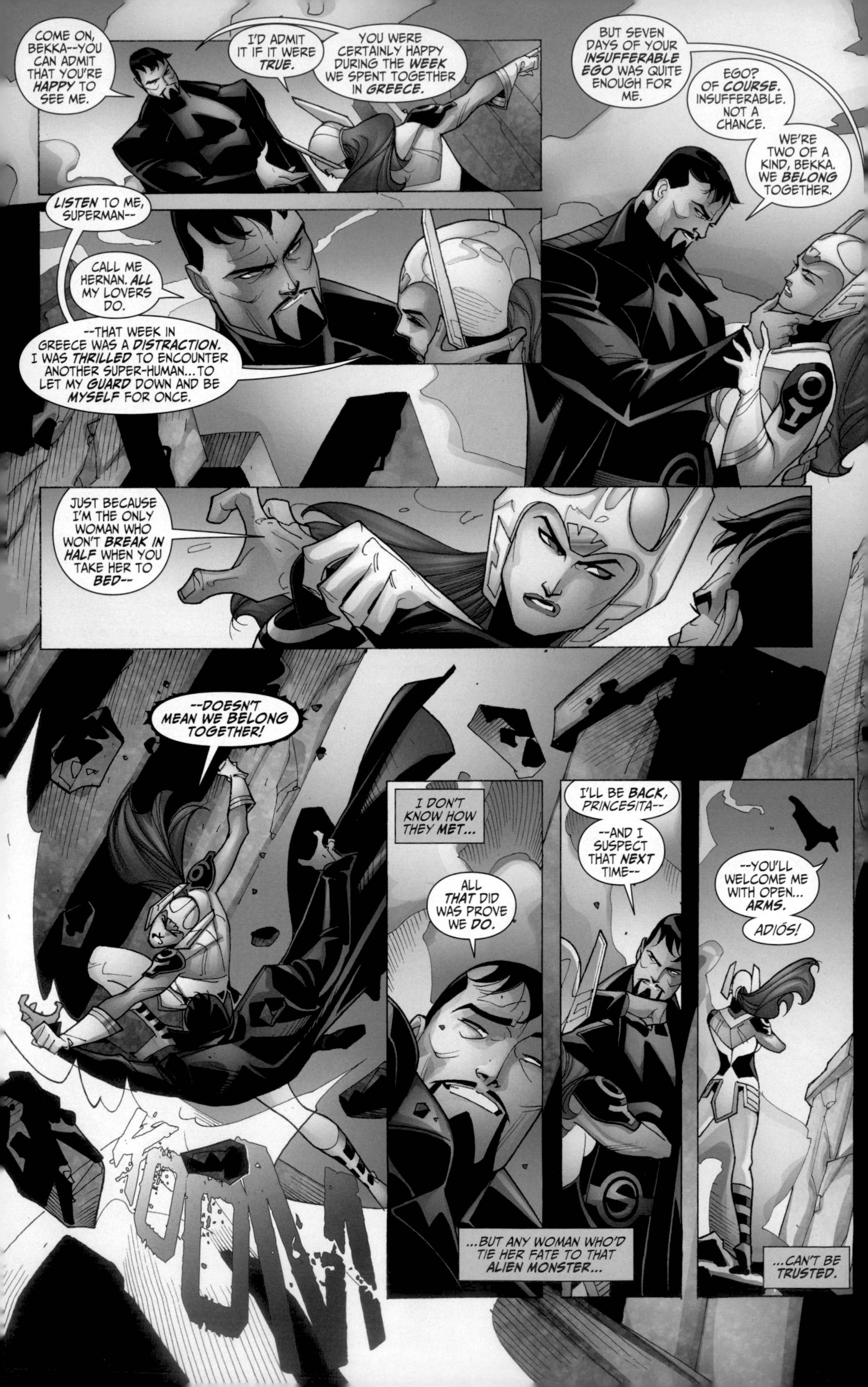
COME ON, BEKKA--YOU CAN ADMIT THAT YOU'RE HAPPY TO SEE ME.
I'D ADMIT IT IF IT WERE TRUE.
YOU WERE CERTAINLY HAPPY DURING THE WEEK WE SPENT TOGETHER IN GREECE.
BUT SEVEN DAYS OF YOUR INSUFFERABLE EGO WAS QUITE ENOUGH FOR ME.
EGO? OF COURSE. INSUFFERABLE. NOT A CHANCE.
WE'RE TWO OF A KIND, BEKKA. WE BELONG TOGETHER.
LISTEN TO ME, SUPERMAN--
CALL ME HERNAN. ALL MY LOVERS DO.
--THAT WEEK IN GREECE WAS A DISTRACTION. I WAS THRILLED TO ENCOUNTER ANOTHER SUPER-HUMAN...TO LET MY GUARD DOWN AND BE MYSELF FOR ONCE.
JUST BECAUSE I'M THE ONLY WOMAN WHO WON'T BREAK IN HALF WHEN YOU TAKE HER TO BED--
--DOESN'T MEAN WE BELONG TOGETHER!
I DON'T KNOW HOW THEY MET...
ALL THAT DID WAS PROVE WE DO.
I'LL BE BACK, PRINCESITA--
--AND I SUSPECT THAT NEXT TIME--
--YOU'LL WELCOME ME WITH OPEN... ARMS.
ADIÓS!
...BUT ANY WOMAN WHO'D TIE HER FATE TO THAT ALIEN MONSTER...
...CAN'T BE TRUSTED.

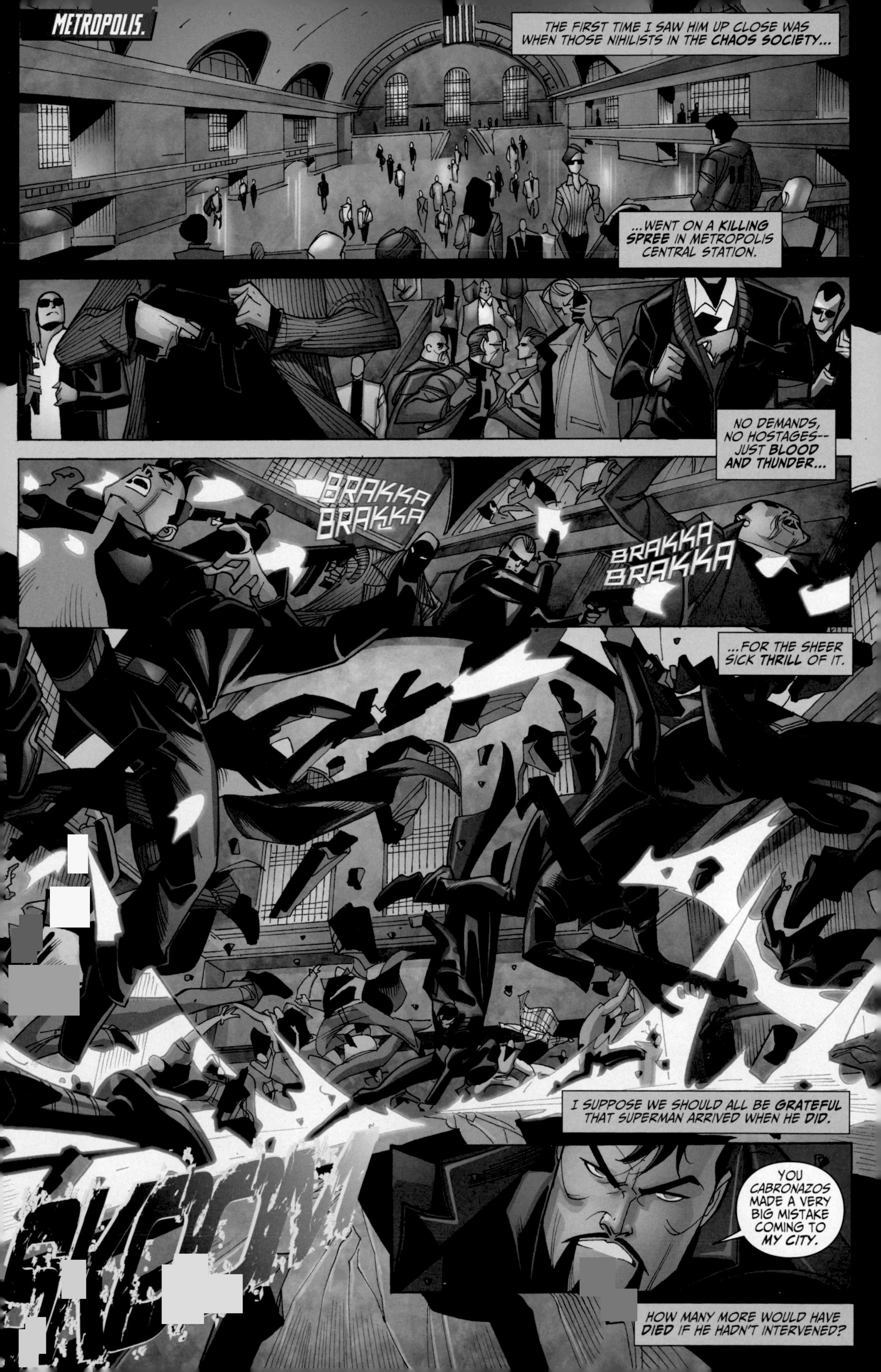
METROPOLIS.
THE FIRST TIME I SAW HIM UP CLOSE WAS WHEN THOSE NIHILISTS IN THE CHAOS SOCIETY...
...WENT ON A KILLING SPREE IN METROPOLIS CENTRAL STATION.
NO DEMANDS, NO HOSTAGES-- JUST BLOOD AND THUNDER...
BRAKKA BRAKKA
BRAKKA BRAKKA
...FOR THE SHEER SICK THRILL OF IT.
I SUPPOSE WE SHOULD ALL BE GRATEFUL THAT SUPERMAN ARRIVED WHEN HE DID.
YOU CABRONAZOS MADE A VERY BIG MISTAKE COMING TO MY CITY.
HOW MANY MORE WOULD HAVE DIED IF HE HADN'T INTERVENED?

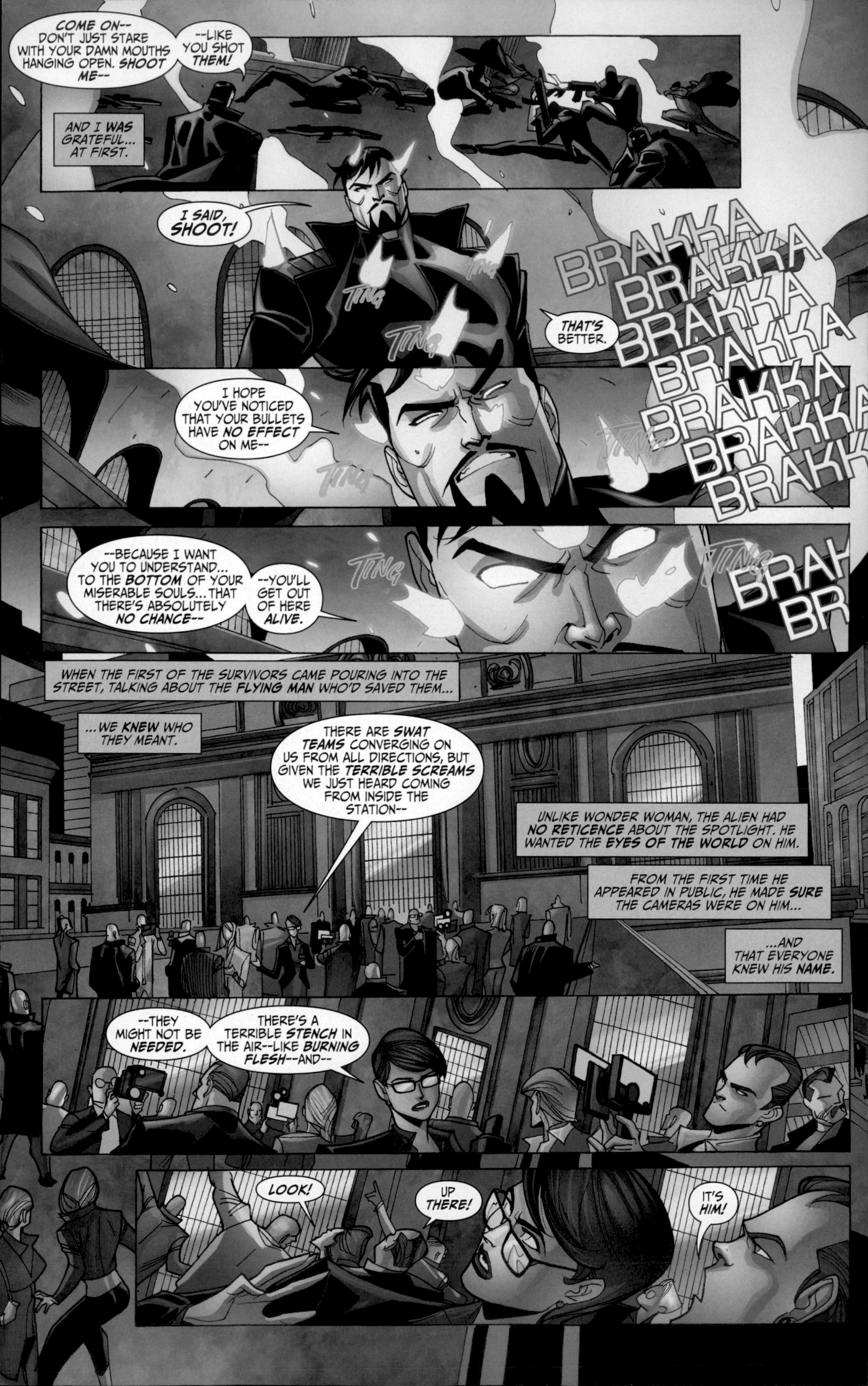
COME ON-- DON'T JUST STARE WITH YOUR DAMN MOUTHS HANGING OPEN. SHOOT ME--
--LIKE YOU SHOT THEM!
AND I WAS GRATEFUL... AT FIRST.
I SAID, SHOOT!
TING
TING
TING
BRAKKA BRAKKA BRAKKA BRAKKA BRAKKA BRAKKA BRAKKA BRAKKA
THAT'S BETTER.
I HOPE YOU'VE NOTICED THAT YOUR BULLETS HAVE NO EFFECT ON ME--
TING
TING
--BECAUSE I WANT YOU TO UNDERSTAND... TO THE BOTTOM OF YOUR MISERABLE SOULS... THAT THERE'S ABSOLUTELY NO CHANCE--
--YOU'LL GET OUT OF HERE ALIVE.
TING
TING
BRAK BR
WHEN THE FIRST OF THE SURVIVORS CAME POURING INTO THE STREET, TALKING ABOUT THE FLYING MAN WHO'D SAVED THEM...
...WE KNEW WHO THEY MEANT.
THERE ARE SWAT TEAMS CONVERGING ON US FROM ALL DIRECTIONS, BUT GIVEN THE TERRIBLE SCREAMS WE JUST HEARD COMING FROM INSIDE THE STATION--
UNLIKE WONDER WOMAN, THE ALIEN HAD NO RETICENCE ABOUT THE SPOTLIGHT. HE WANTED THE EYES OF THE WORLD ON HIM.
FROM THE FIRST TIME HE APPEARED IN PUBLIC, HE MADE SURE THE CAMERAS WERE ON HIM...
...AND THAT EVERYONE KNEW HIS NAME.
--THEY MIGHT NOT BE NEEDED.
THERE'S A TERRIBLE STENCH IN THE AIR--LIKE BURNING FLESH--AND--
LOOK!
UP THERE!
IT'S HIM!

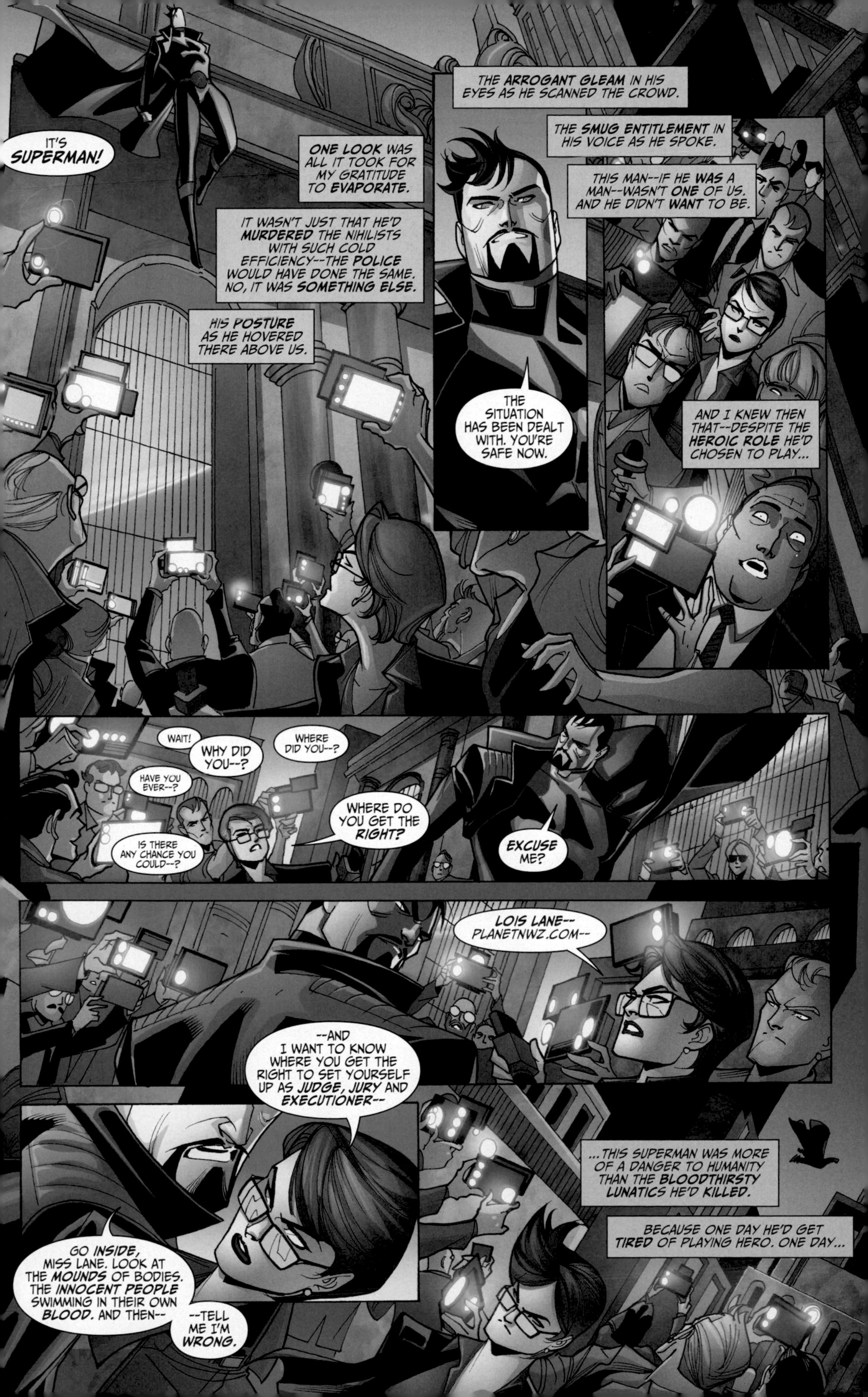
IT'S SUPERMAN!
ONE LOOK WAS ALL IT TOOK FOR MY GRATITUDE TO EVAPORATE.
IT WASN'T JUST THAT HE'D MURDERED THE NIHILISTS WITH SUCH COLD EFFICIENCY--THE POLICE WOULD HAVE DONE THE SAME. NO, IT WAS SOMETHING ELSE.
HIS POSTURE AS HE HOVERED THERE ABOVE US.
THE ARROGANT GLEAM IN HIS EYES AS HE SCANNED THE CROWD.
THE SITUATION HAS BEEN DEALT WITH. YOU'RE SAFE NOW.
THE SMUG ENTITLEMENT IN HIS VOICE AS HE SPOKE.
THIS MAN--IF HE WAS A MAN--WASN'T ONE OF US. AND HE DIDN'T WANT TO BE.
AND I KNEW THEN THAT--DESPITE THE HEROIC ROLE HE'D CHOSEN TO PLAY...
WAIT!
WHY DID YOU--?
HAVE YOU EVER--?
WHERE DID YOU--?
IS THERE ANY CHANCE YOU COULD--?
WHERE DO YOU GET THE RIGHT?
EXCUSE ME?
LOIS LANE-- PLANETNWZ.COM--
--AND I WANT TO KNOW WHERE YOU GET THE RIGHT TO SET YOURSELF UP AS JUDGE, JURY AND EXECUTIONER--
GO INSIDE, MISS LANE. LOOK AT THE MOUNDS OF BODIES. THE INNOCENT PEOPLE SWIMMING IN THEIR OWN BLOOD. AND THEN--
--TELL ME I'M WRONG.
...THIS SUPERMAN WAS MORE OF A DANGER TO HUMANITY THAN THE BLOODTHIRSTY LUNATICS HE'D KILLED.
BECAUSE ONE DAY HE'D GET TIRED OF PLAYING HERO. ONE DAY...

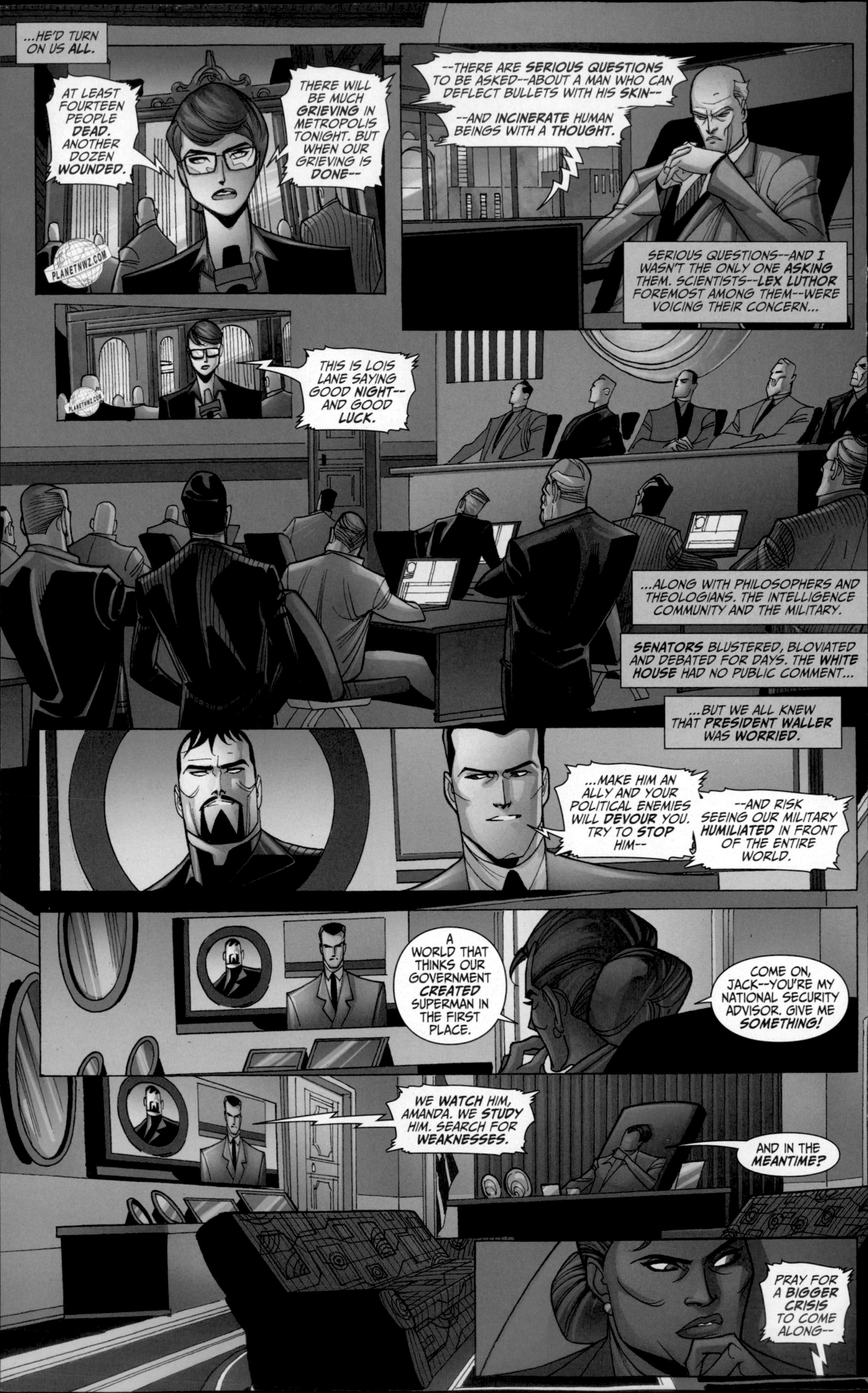
...HE'D TURN ON US ALL.
AT LEAST FOURTEEN PEOPLE DEAD. ANOTHER DOZEN WOUNDED.
THERE WILL BE MUCH GRIEVING IN METROPOLIS TONIGHT. BUT WHEN OUR GRIEVING IS DONE--
PLANETNWZ.COM
--THERE ARE SERIOUS QUESTIONS TO BE ASKED--ABOUT A MAN WHO CAN DEFLECT BULLETS WITH HIS SKIN--
--AND INCINERATE HUMAN BEINGS WITH A THOUGHT.
SERIOUS QUESTIONS--AND I WASN'T THE ONLY ONE ASKING THEM. SCIENTISTS--LEX LUTHOR FOREMOST AMONG THEM--WERE VOICING THEIR CONCERN...
THIS IS LOIS LANE SAYING GOOD NIGHT-- AND GOOD LUCK.
...ALONG WITH PHILOSOPHERS AND THEOLOGIANS. THE INTELLIGENCE COMMUNITY AND THE MILITARY.
SENATORS BLUSTERED, BLOVIATED AND DEBATED FOR DAYS. THE WHITE HOUSE HAD NO PUBLIC COMMENT...
...BUT WE ALL KNEW THAT PRESIDENT WALLER WAS WORRIED.
...MAKE HIM AN ALLY AND YOUR POLITICAL ENEMIES WILL DEVOUR YOU. TRY TO STOP HIM--
--AND RISK SEEING OUR MILITARY HUMILIATED IN FRONT OF THE ENTIRE WORLD.
A WORLD THAT THINKS OUR GOVERNMENT CREATED SUPERMAN IN THE FIRST PLACE.
COME ON, JACK--YOU'RE MY NATIONAL SECURITY ADVISOR. GIVE ME SOMETHING!
WE WATCH HIM, AMANDA. WE STUDY HIM. SEARCH FOR WEAKNESSES.
AND IN THE MEANTIME?
PRAY FOR A BIGGER CRISIS TO COME ALONG--

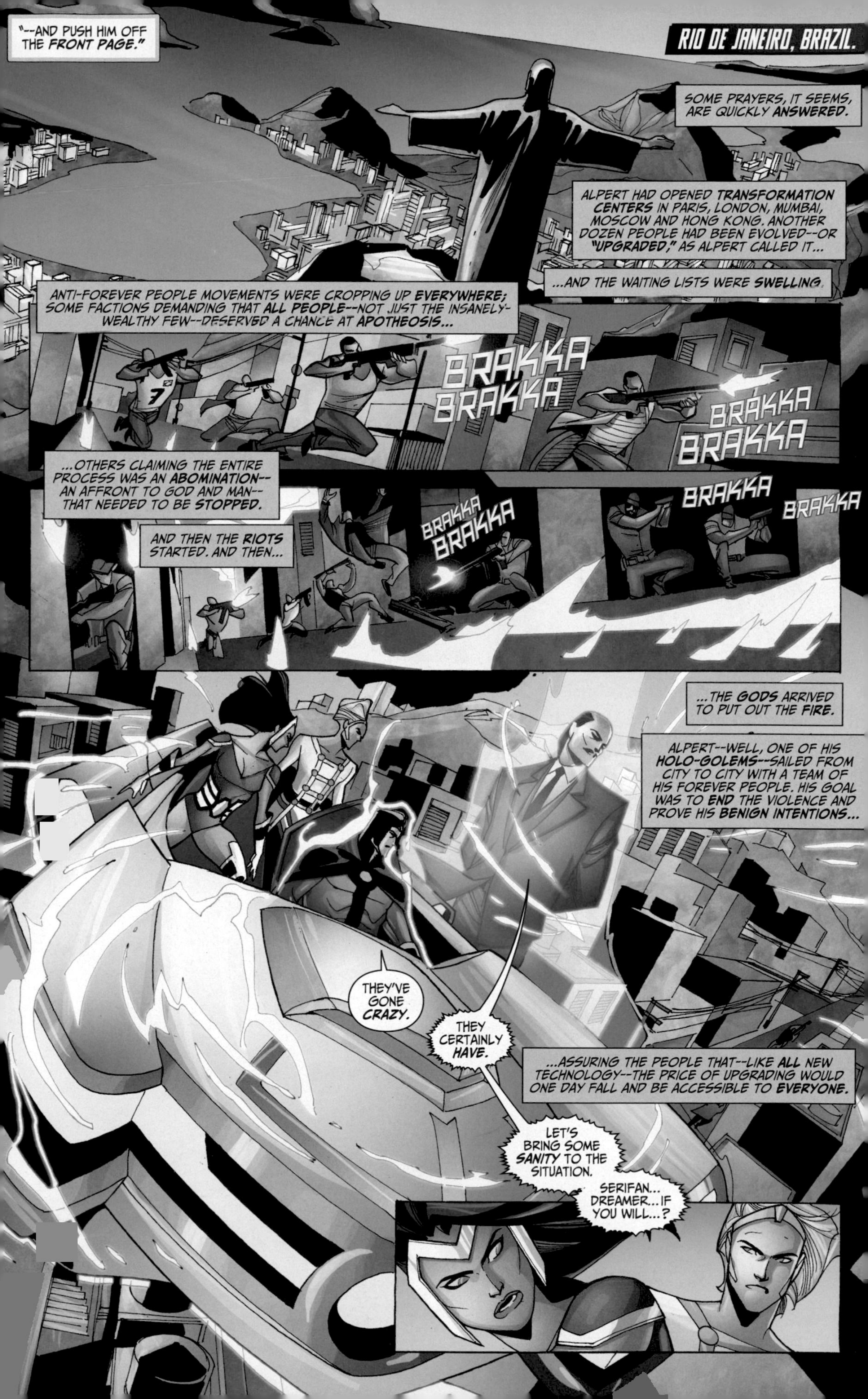
"--AND PUSH HIM OFF THE FRONT PAGE."
RIO DE JANEIRO, BRAZIL.
SOME PRAYERS, IT SEEMS, ARE QUICKLY ANSWERED.
ALPERT HAD OPENED TRANSFORMATION CENTERS IN PARIS, LONDON, MUMBAI, MOSCOW AND HONG KONG. ANOTHER DOZEN PEOPLE HAD BEEN EVOLVED--OR "UPGRADED," AS ALPERT CALLED IT...
...AND THE WAITING LISTS WERE SWELLING.
ANTI-FOREVER PEOPLE MOVEMENTS WERE CROPPING UP EVERYWHERE; SOME FACTIONS DEMANDING THAT ALL PEOPLE--NOT JUST THE INSANELY-WEALTHY FEW--DESERVED A CHANCE AT APOTHEOSIS...
BRAKKA BRAKKA
BRAKKA BRAKKA
...OTHERS CLAIMING THE ENTIRE PROCESS WAS AN ABOMINATION--AN AFFRONT TO GOD AND MAN--THAT NEEDED TO BE STOPPED.
AND THEN THE RIOTS STARTED. AND THEN...
BRAKKA BRAKKA
BRAKKA
BRAKKA
...THE GODS ARRIVED TO PUT OUT THE FIRE.
ALPERT--WELL, ONE OF HIS HOLO-GOLEMS--SAILED FROM CITY TO CITY WITH A TEAM OF HIS FOREVER PEOPLE. HIS GOAL WAS TO END THE VIOLENCE AND PROVE HIS BENIGN INTENTIONS...
THEY'VE GONE CRAZY.
THEY CERTAINLY HAVE.
...ASSURING THE PEOPLE THAT--LIKE ALL NEW TECHNOLOGY--THE PRICE OF UPGRADING WOULD ONE DAY FALL AND BE ACCESSIBLE TO EVERYONE.
LET'S BRING SOME SANITY TO THE SITUATION.
SERIFAN... DREAMER... IF YOU WILL...?

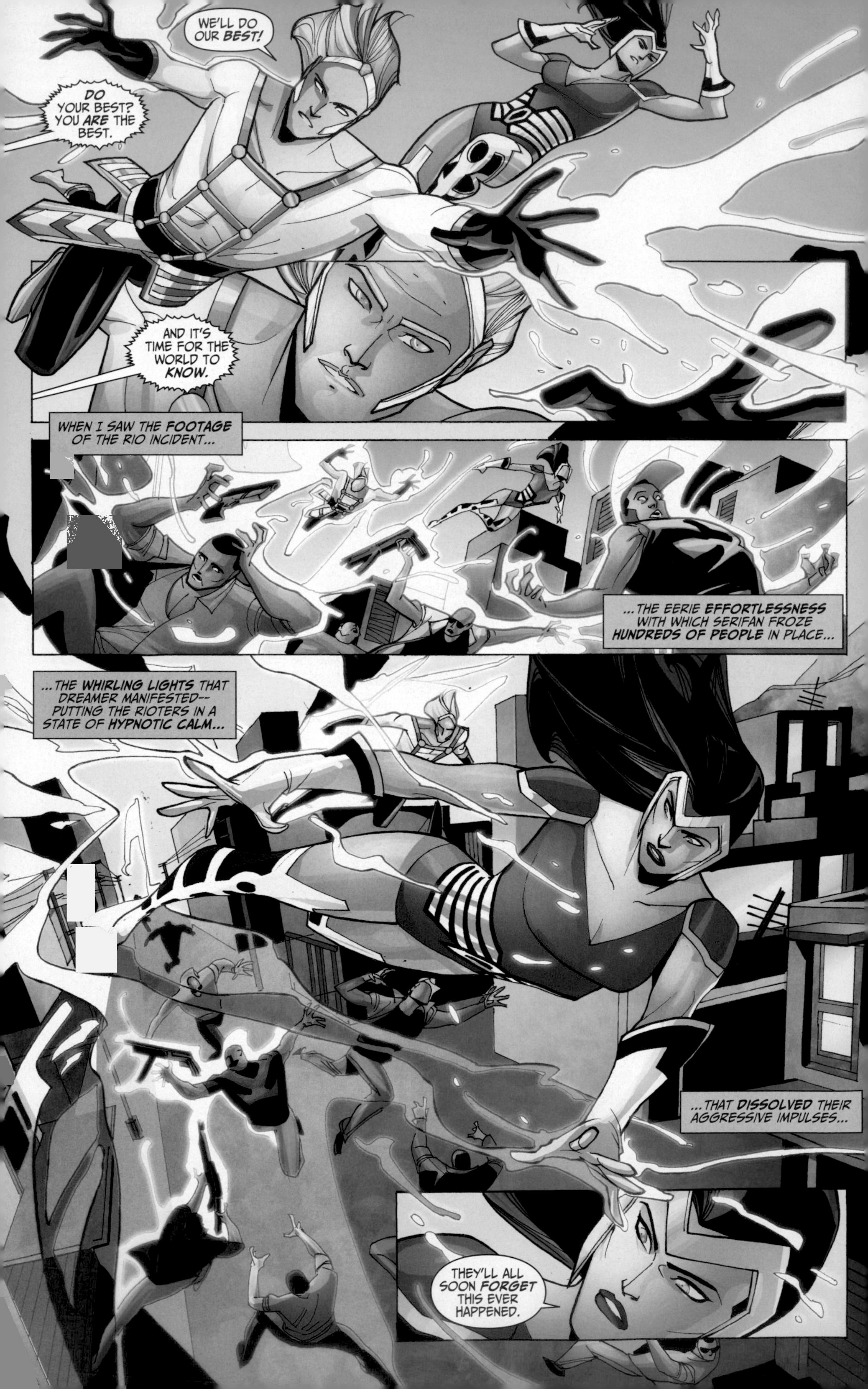
WE'LL DO OUR BEST!
DO YOUR BEST? YOU ARE THE BEST.
AND IT'S TIME FOR THE WORLD TO KNOW.
WHEN I SAW THE FOOTAGE OF THE RIO INCIDENT...
...THE EERIE EFFORTLESSNESS WITH WHICH SERIFAN FROZE HUNDREDS OF PEOPLE IN PLACE...
...THE WHIRLING LIGHTS THAT DREAMER MANIFESTED--PUTTING THE RIOTERS IN A STATE OF HYPNOTIC CALM...
...THAT DISSOLVED THEIR AGGRESSIVE IMPULSES...
THEY'LL ALL SOON FORGET THIS EVER HAPPENED.

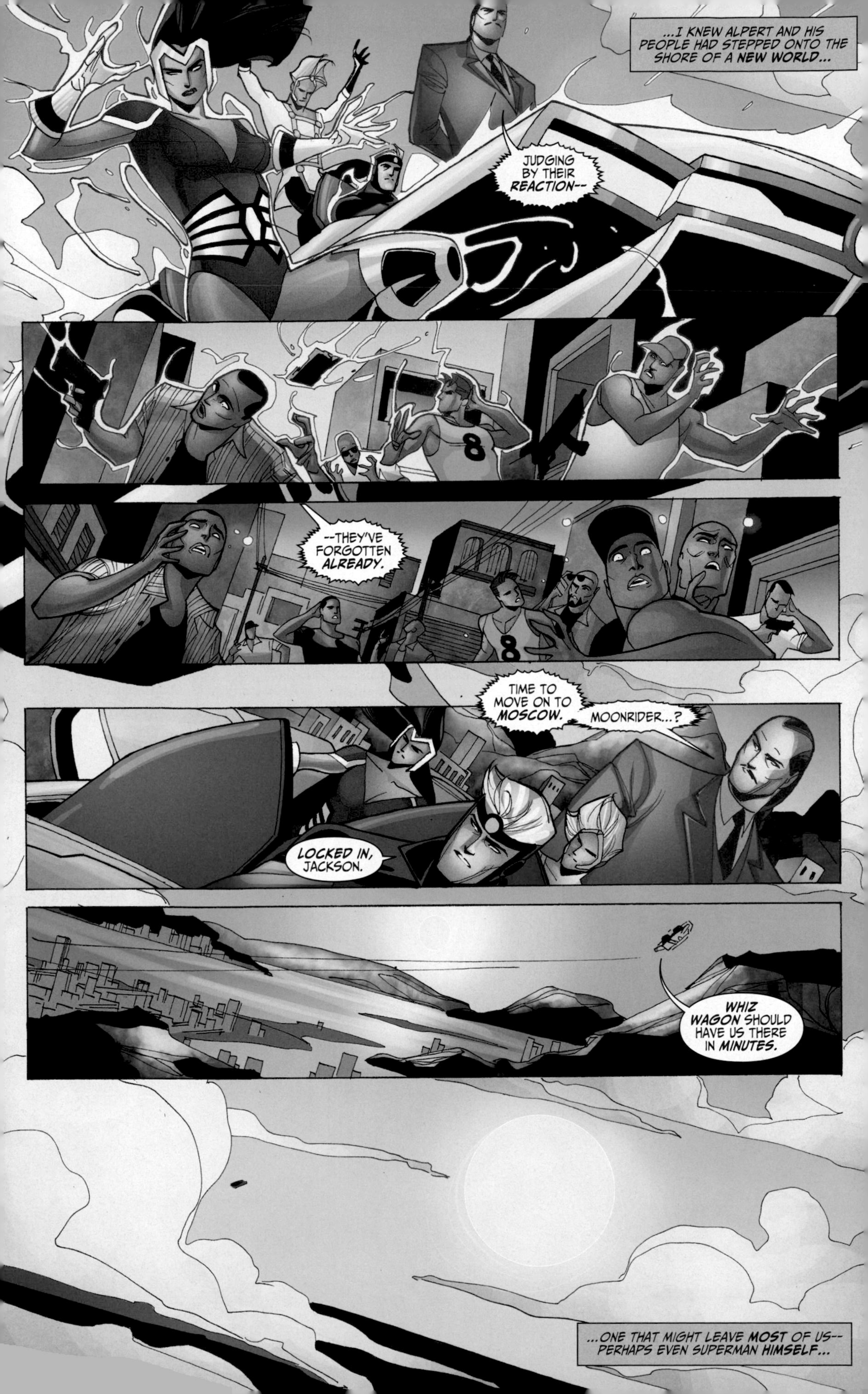
...I KNEW ALPERT AND HIS PEOPLE HAD STEPPED ONTO THE SHORE OF A NEW WORLD...
JUDGING BY THEIR REACTION--
--THEY'VE FORGOTTEN ALREADY.
TIME TO MOVE ON TO MOSCOW.
MOONRIDER...?
LOCKED IN, JACKSON.
WHIZ WAGON SHOULD HAVE US THERE IN MINUTES.
...ONE THAT MIGHT LEAVE MOST OF US--PERHAPS EVEN SUPERMAN HIMSELF...

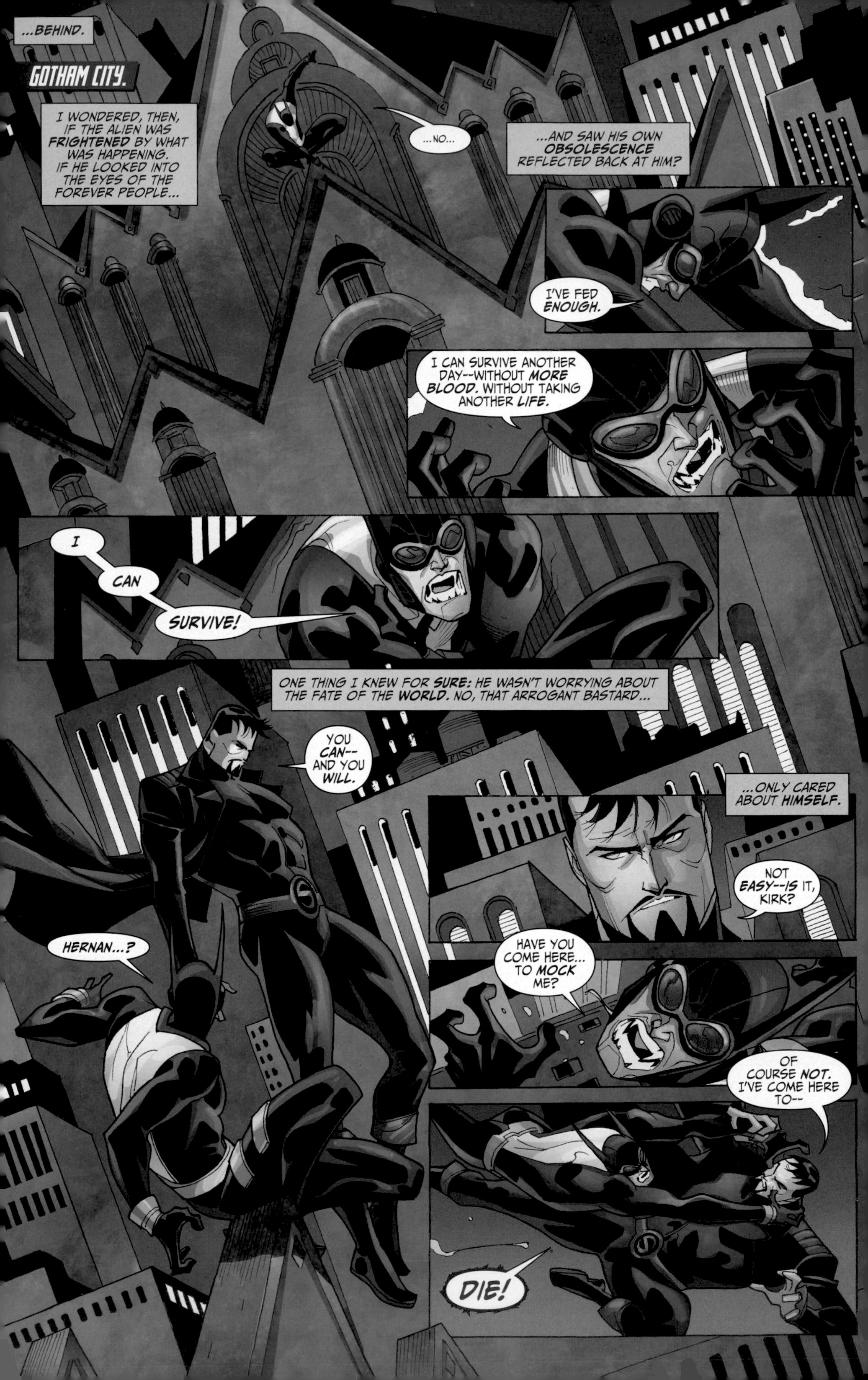
...BEHIND.
GOTHAM CITY.
I WONDERED, THEN, IF THE ALIEN WAS FRIGHTENED BY WHAT WAS HAPPENING. IF HE LOOKED INTO THE EYES OF THE FOREVER PEOPLE...
...NO...
...AND SAW HIS OWN OBSOLESCENCE REFLECTED BACK AT HIM?
I'VE FED ENOUGH.
I CAN SURVIVE ANOTHER DAY--WITHOUT MORE BLOOD. WITHOUT TAKING ANOTHER LIFE.
I
CAN
SURVIVE!
ONE THING I KNEW FOR SURE: HE WASN'T WORRYING ABOUT THE FATE OF THE WORLD. NO, THAT ARROGANT BASTARD...
YOU CAN--AND YOU WILL.
HERNAN...?
...ONLY CARED ABOUT HIMSELF.
NOT EASY--IS IT, KIRK?
HAVE YOU COME HERE... TO MOCK ME?
OF COURSE NOT. I'VE COME HERE TO--
DIE!

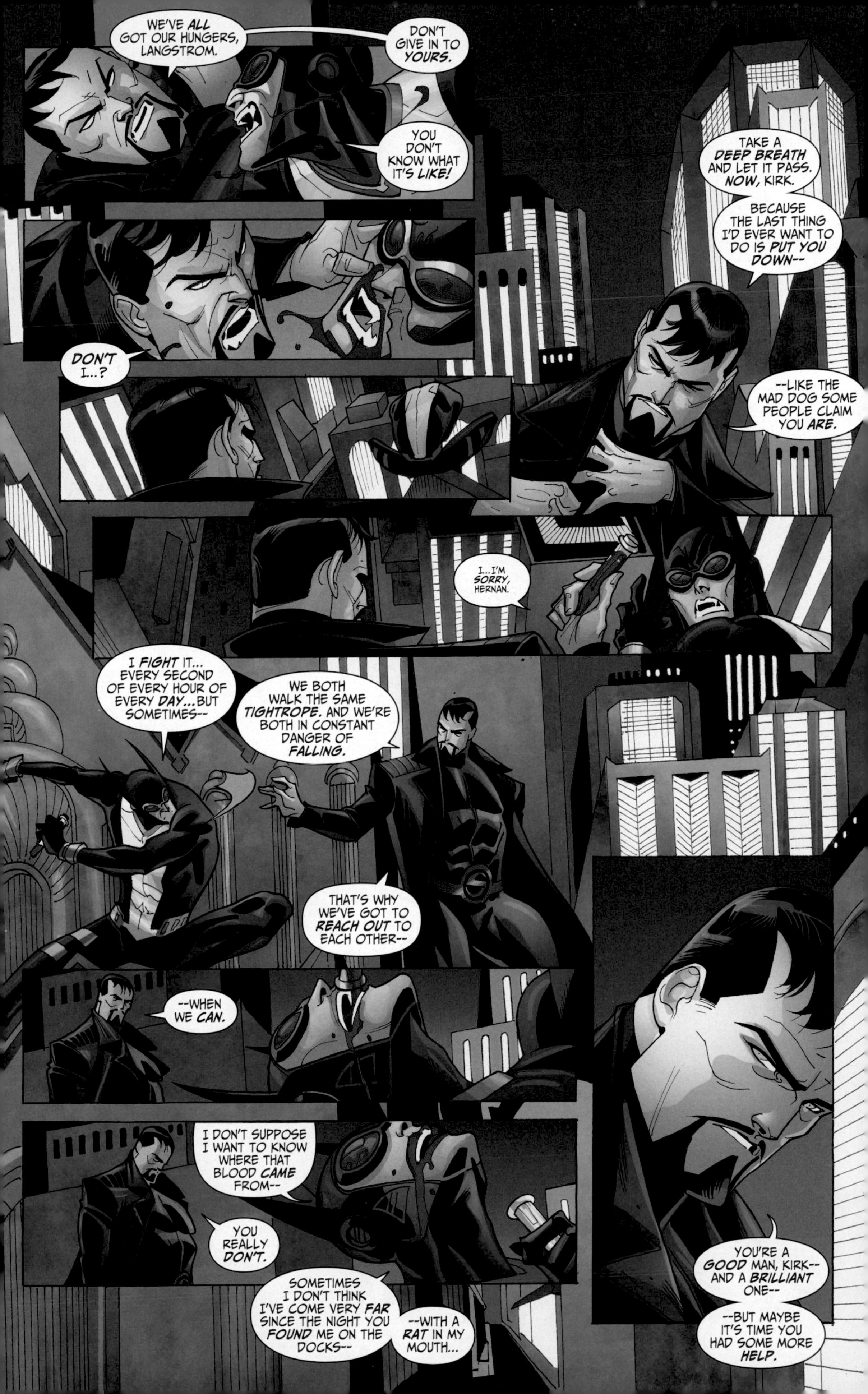
WE'VE ALL GOT OUR HUNGERS, LANGSTROM.
DON'T GIVE IN TO YOURS.
YOU DON'T KNOW WHAT IT'S LIKE!
TAKE A DEEP BREATH AND LET IT PASS. NOW, KIRK.
BECAUSE THE LAST THING I'D EVER WANT TO DO IS PUT YOU DOWN--
DON'T I...?
--LIKE THE MAD DOG SOME PEOPLE CLAIM YOU ARE.
I...I'M SORRY, HERNAN.
I FIGHT IT... EVERY SECOND OF EVERY HOUR OF EVERY DAY...BUT SOMETIMES--
WE BOTH WALK THE SAME TIGHTROPE. AND WE'RE BOTH IN CONSTANT DANGER OF FALLING.
THAT'S WHY WE'VE GOT TO REACH OUT TO EACH OTHER--
--WHEN WE CAN.
I DON'T SUPPOSE I WANT TO KNOW WHERE THAT BLOOD CAME FROM--
YOU REALLY DON'T.
SOMETIMES I DON'T THINK I'VE COME VERY FAR SINCE THE NIGHT YOU FOUND ME ON THE DOCKS--
--WITH A RAT IN MY MOUTH...
YOU'RE A GOOD MAN, KIRK--AND A BRILLIANT ONE--
--BUT MAYBE IT'S TIME YOU HAD SOME MORE HELP.

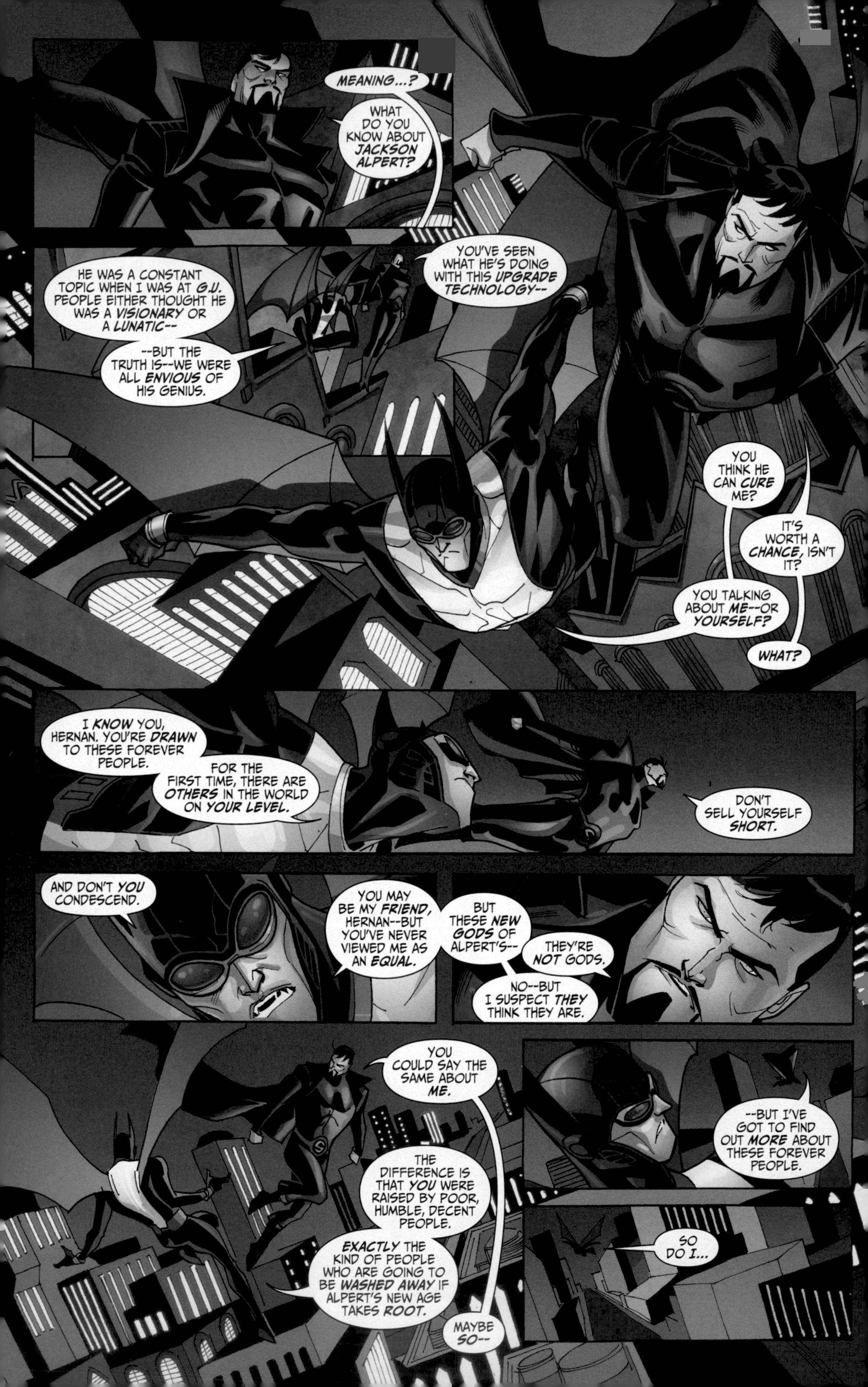
MEANING...?
WHAT DO YOU KNOW ABOUT JACKSON ALPERT?
HE WAS A CONSTANT TOPIC WHEN I WAS AT G.U. PEOPLE EITHER THOUGHT HE WAS A VISIONARY OR A LUNATIC--
--BUT THE TRUTH IS--WE WERE ALL ENVIOUS OF HIS GENIUS.
YOU'VE SEEN WHAT HE'S DOING WITH THIS UPGRADE TECHNOLOGY--
YOU THINK HE CAN CURE ME?
IT'S WORTH A CHANCE, ISN'T IT?
YOU TALKING ABOUT ME--OR YOURSELF?
WHAT?
I KNOW YOU, HERNAN. YOU'RE DRAWN TO THESE FOREVER PEOPLE.
FOR THE FIRST TIME, THERE ARE OTHERS IN THE WORLD ON YOUR LEVEL.
DON'T SELL YOURSELF SHORT.
AND DON'T YOU CONDESCEND.
YOU MAY BE MY FRIEND, HERNAN--BUT YOU'VE NEVER VIEWED ME AS AN EQUAL.
BUT THESE NEW GODS OF ALPERT'S--
THEY'RE NOT GODS.
NO--BUT I SUSPECT THEY THINK THEY ARE.
YOU COULD SAY THE SAME ABOUT ME.
THE DIFFERENCE IS THAT YOU WERE RAISED BY POOR, HUMBLE, DECENT PEOPLE.
EXACTLY THE KIND OF PEOPLE WHO ARE GOING TO BE WASHED AWAY IF ALPERT'S NEW AGE TAKES ROOT.
MAYBE SO--
--BUT I'VE GOT TO FIND OUT MORE ABOUT THESE FOREVER PEOPLE.
SO DO I...

WE CAN'T KNOW FOR SURE WHAT DEMONS DROVE HIM THERE...

...BUT WE **DO** KNOW THAT SUPERMAN SOARED ACROSS THE WORLD TO THE ETERNITY INSTITUTE...

SSXXX

SSZZZZXXXX

SSZZXX

...WHERE I'M SURE HIS FELLOW "GODS" WELCOMED HIM WITH **OPEN ARMS.**

SSRAKOOOOMM

THAT FORCE FIELD IS THERE FOR A **REASON**--

--BUT IT'S JUST **LIKE** YOU TO COME BARGING IN WITHOUT PERMISSION.

BEKKA--?!

TURN AROUND AND **LEAVE** NOW--

--OR YOU'LL GET A LESSON IN **HUMILITY** THAT'S BEEN **YEARS** IN COMING.

OH, IT'S TIME FOR A **LESSON,** ALL RIGHT--

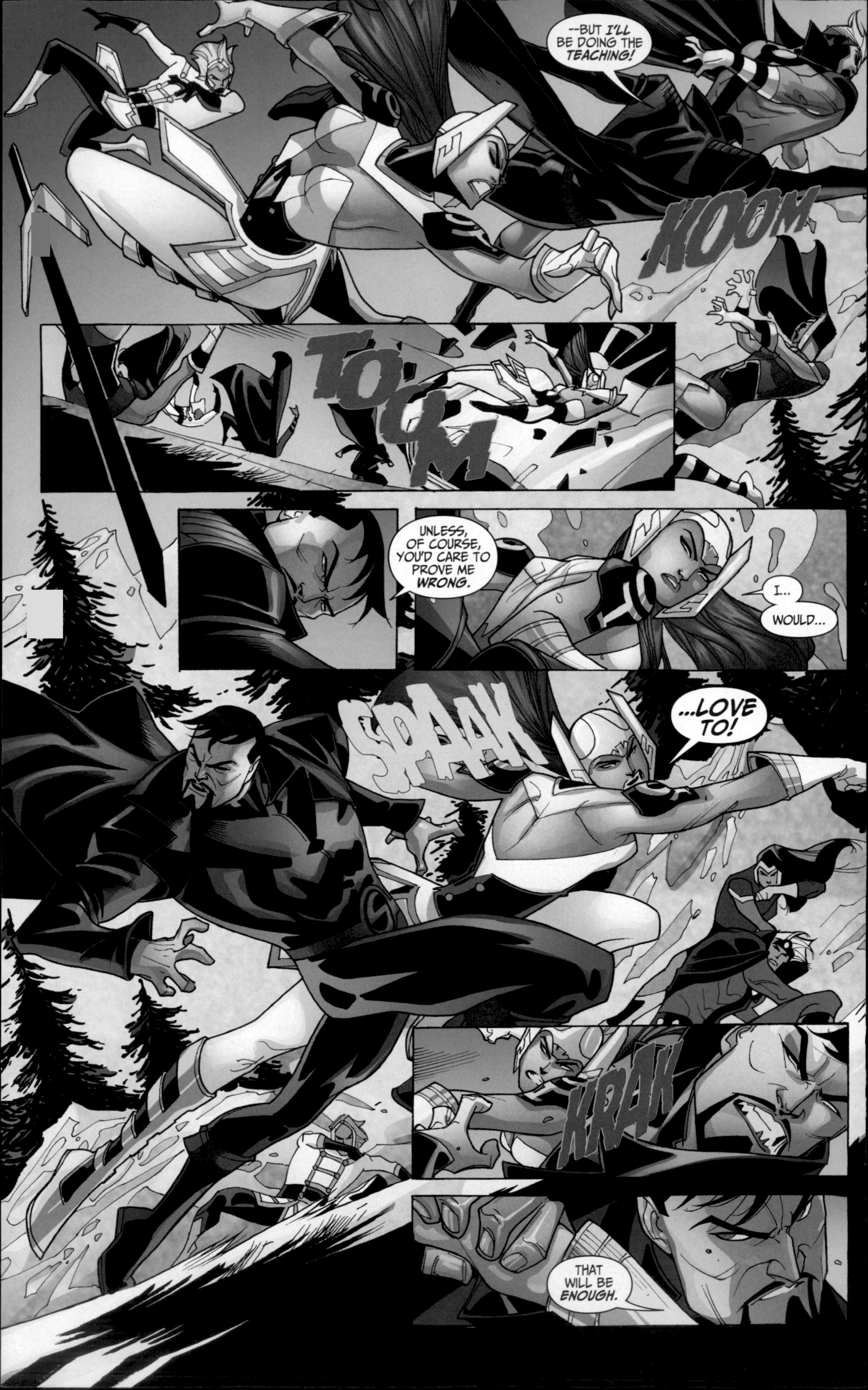
--BUT I'LL BE DOING THE TEACHING!
KOOM
TOOM
UNLESS, OF COURSE, YOU'D CARE TO PROVE ME WRONG.
I...
WOULD...
SPAAK
...LOVE TO!
KRAK
THAT WILL BE ENOUGH.

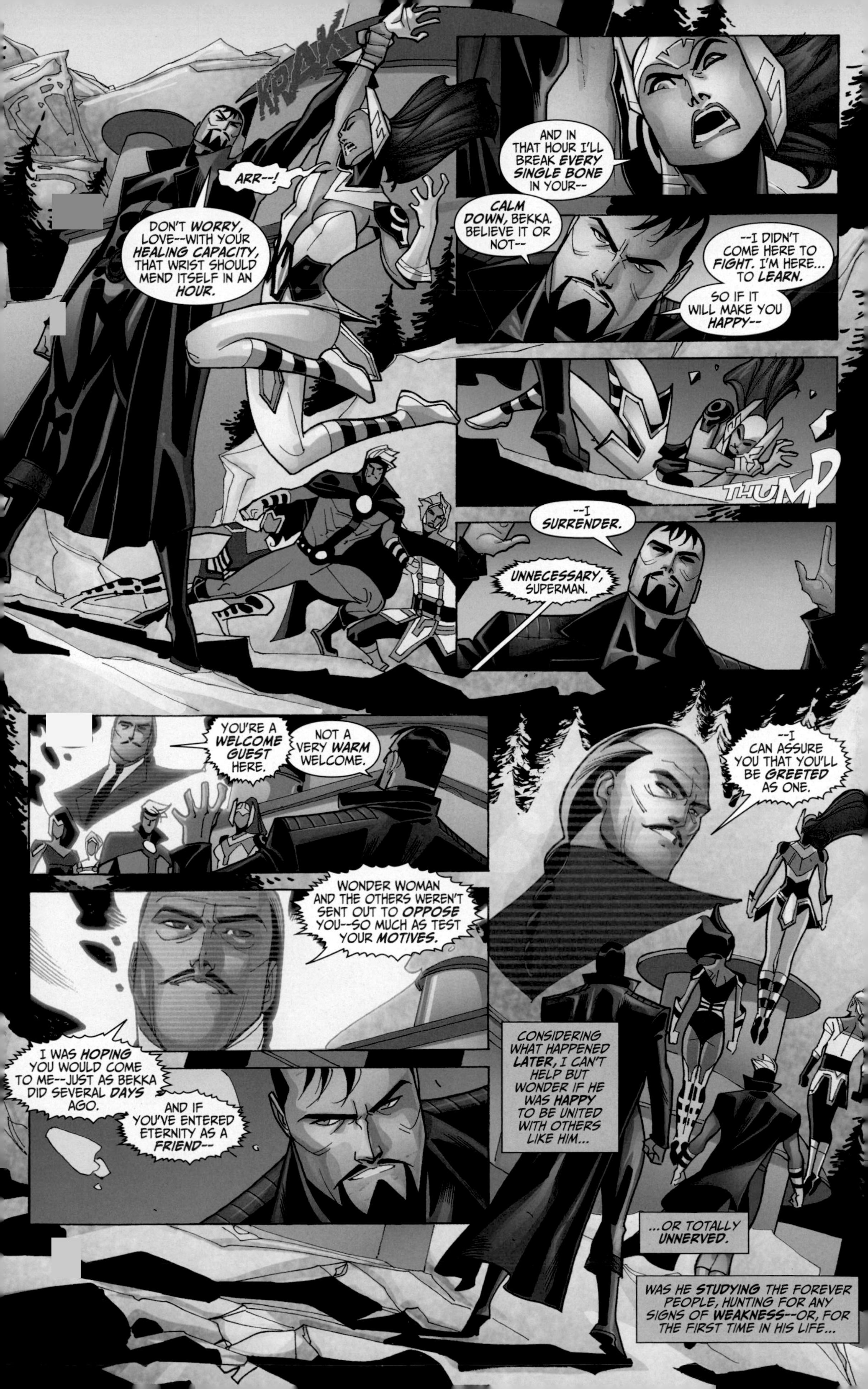

KRAAK
ARR--!
DON'T WORRY, LOVE--WITH YOUR HEALING CAPACITY, THAT WRIST SHOULD MEND ITSELF IN AN HOUR.
AND IN THAT HOUR I'LL BREAK EVERY SINGLE BONE IN YOUR--
CALM DOWN, BEKKA. BELIEVE IT OR NOT--
--I DIDN'T COME HERE TO FIGHT. I'M HERE... TO LEARN.
SO IF IT WILL MAKE YOU HAPPY--
THUMP
--I SURRENDER.
UNNECESSARY, SUPERMAN.
YOU'RE A WELCOME GUEST HERE.
NOT A VERY WARM WELCOME.
--I CAN ASSURE YOU THAT YOU'LL BE GREETED AS ONE.
WONDER WOMAN AND THE OTHERS WEREN'T SENT OUT TO OPPOSE YOU--SO MUCH AS TEST YOUR MOTIVES.
I WAS HOPING YOU WOULD COME TO ME--JUST AS BEKKA DID SEVERAL DAYS AGO.
AND IF YOU'VE ENTERED ETERNITY AS A FRIEND--
CONSIDERING WHAT HAPPENED LATER, I CAN'T HELP BUT WONDER IF HE WAS HAPPY TO BE UNITED WITH OTHERS LIKE HIM...
...OR TOTALLY UNNERVED.
WAS HE STUDYING THE FOREVER PEOPLE, HUNTING FOR ANY SIGNS OF WEAKNESS--OR, FOR THE FIRST TIME IN HIS LIFE...

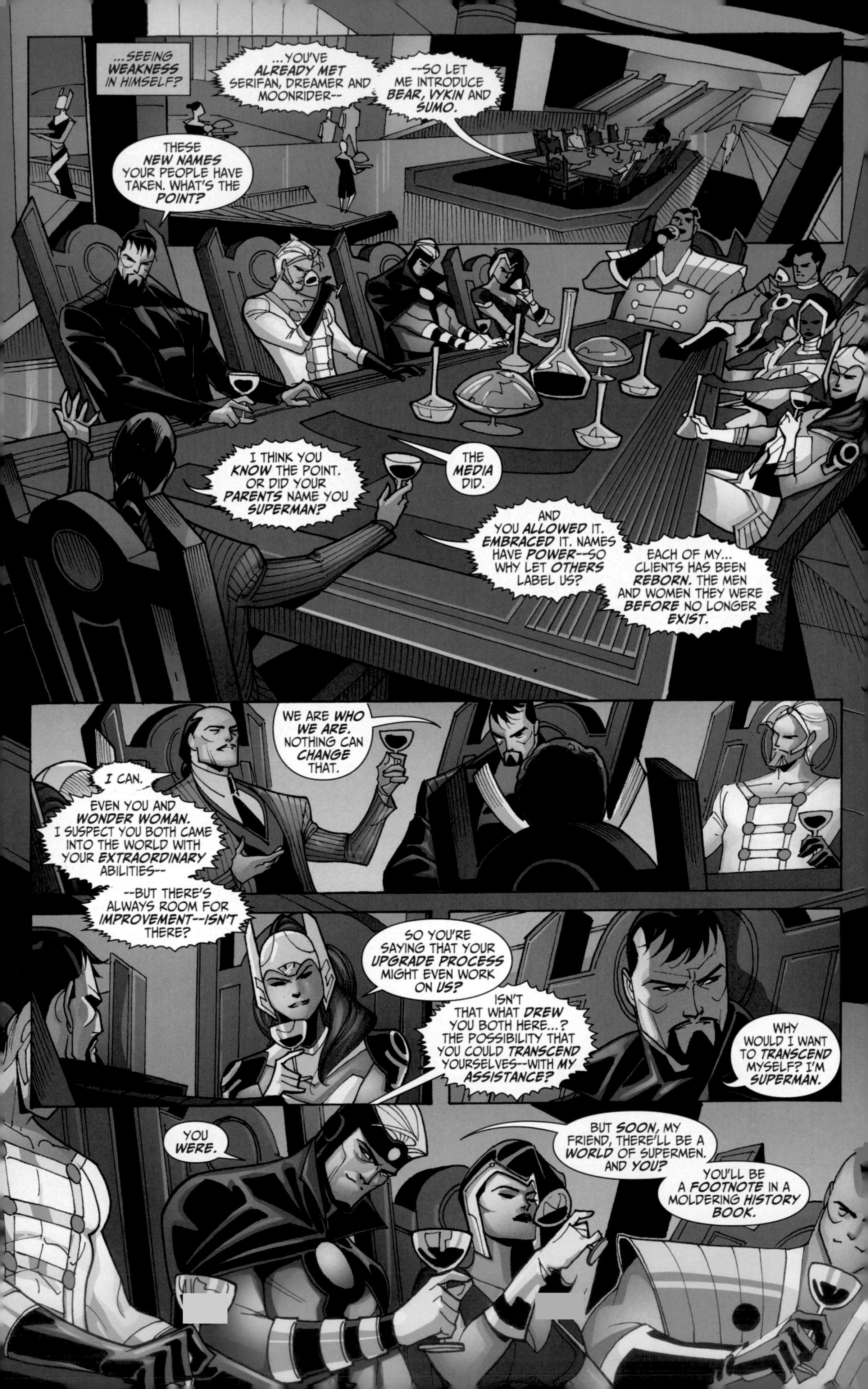
...SEEING WEAKNESS IN HIMSELF?
...YOU'VE ALREADY MET SERIFAN, DREAMER AND MOONRIDER--
--SO LET ME INTRODUCE BEAR, VYKIN AND SUMO.
THESE NEW NAMES YOUR PEOPLE HAVE TAKEN. WHAT'S THE POINT?
I THINK YOU KNOW THE POINT. OR DID YOUR PARENTS NAME YOU SUPERMAN?
THE MEDIA DID.
AND YOU ALLOWED IT. EMBRACED IT. NAMES HAVE POWER--SO WHY LET OTHERS LABEL US?
EACH OF MY... CLIENTS HAS BEEN REBORN. THE MEN AND WOMEN THEY WERE BEFORE NO LONGER EXIST.
WE ARE WHO WE ARE. NOTHING CAN CHANGE THAT.
I CAN.
EVEN YOU AND WONDER WOMAN. I SUSPECT YOU BOTH CAME INTO THE WORLD WITH YOUR EXTRAORDINARY ABILITIES--
--BUT THERE'S ALWAYS ROOM FOR IMPROVEMENT--ISN'T THERE?
SO YOU'RE SAYING THAT YOUR UPGRADE PROCESS MIGHT EVEN WORK ON US?
ISN'T THAT WHAT DREW YOU BOTH HERE...? THE POSSIBILITY THAT YOU COULD TRANSCEND YOURSELVES--WITH MY ASSISTANCE?
WHY WOULD I WANT TO TRANSCEND MYSELF? I'M SUPERMAN.
YOU WERE.
BUT SOON, MY FRIEND, THERE'LL BE A WORLD OF SUPERMEN. AND YOU?
YOU'LL BE A FOOTNOTE IN A MOLDERING HISTORY BOOK.

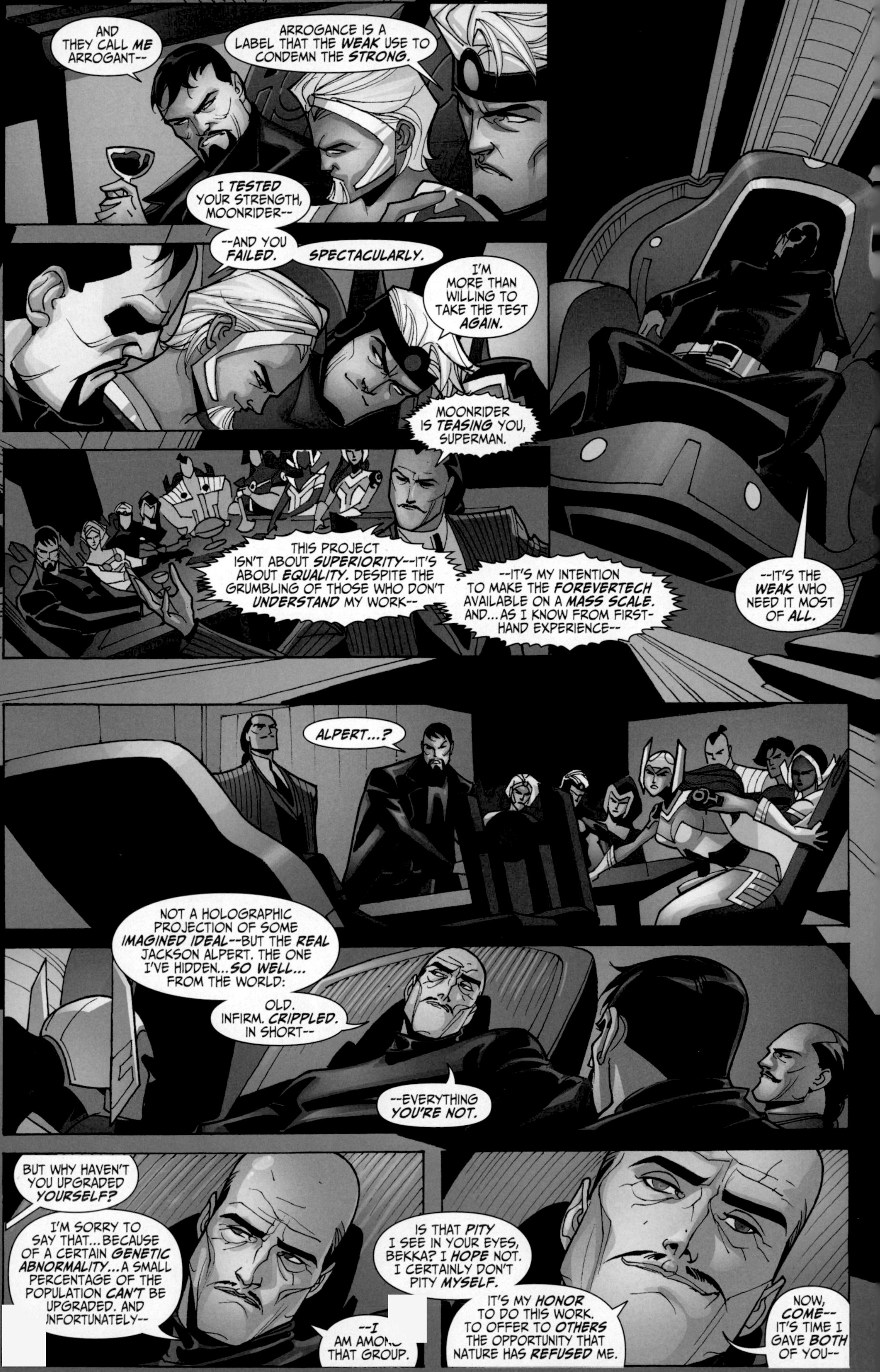
AND THEY CALL *ME* ARROGANT--
ARROGANCE IS A LABEL THAT THE *WEAK* USE TO CONDEMN THE *STRONG.*
I *TESTED* YOUR STRENGTH, MOONRIDER--
--AND YOU *FAILED.*
SPECTACULARLY.
I'M MORE THAN WILLING TO TAKE THE TEST *AGAIN.*
MOONRIDER IS *TEASING* YOU, SUPERMAN.
THIS PROJECT ISN'T ABOUT *SUPERIORITY*--IT'S ABOUT *EQUALITY.* DESPITE THE GRUMBLING OF THOSE WHO DON'T *UNDERSTAND* MY WORK--
--IT'S MY INTENTION TO MAKE THE *FOREVERTECH* AVAILABLE ON A *MASS SCALE.* AND...AS I KNOW FROM FIRST-HAND EXPERIENCE--
--IT'S THE *WEAK* WHO NEED IT MOST OF *ALL.*
ALPERT...?
NOT A HOLOGRAPHIC PROJECTION OF SOME *IMAGINED IDEAL*--BUT THE *REAL* JACKSON ALPERT. THE ONE I'VE HIDDEN...*SO WELL...* FROM THE WORLD:
OLD. INFIRM. *CRIPPLED.* IN SHORT--
--EVERYTHING *YOU'RE NOT.*
BUT WHY HAVEN'T YOU UPGRADED *YOURSELF?*
I'M SORRY TO SAY THAT...BECAUSE OF A CERTAIN *GENETIC ABNORMALITY*...A SMALL PERCENTAGE OF THE POPULATION *CAN'T* BE UPGRADED. AND NFORTUNATELY--
--I AM AMON THAT GROUP.
IS THAT *PITY* I SEE IN YOUR EYES, BEKKA? I *HOPE* NOT. I CERTAINLY DON'T PITY *MYSELF.*
IT'S MY *HONOR* TO DO THIS WORK. TO OFFER TO *OTHERS* THE OPPORTUNITY THAT NATURE HAS *REFUSED* ME.
NOW, *COME--* IT'S TIME I GAVE *BOTH* OF YOU--

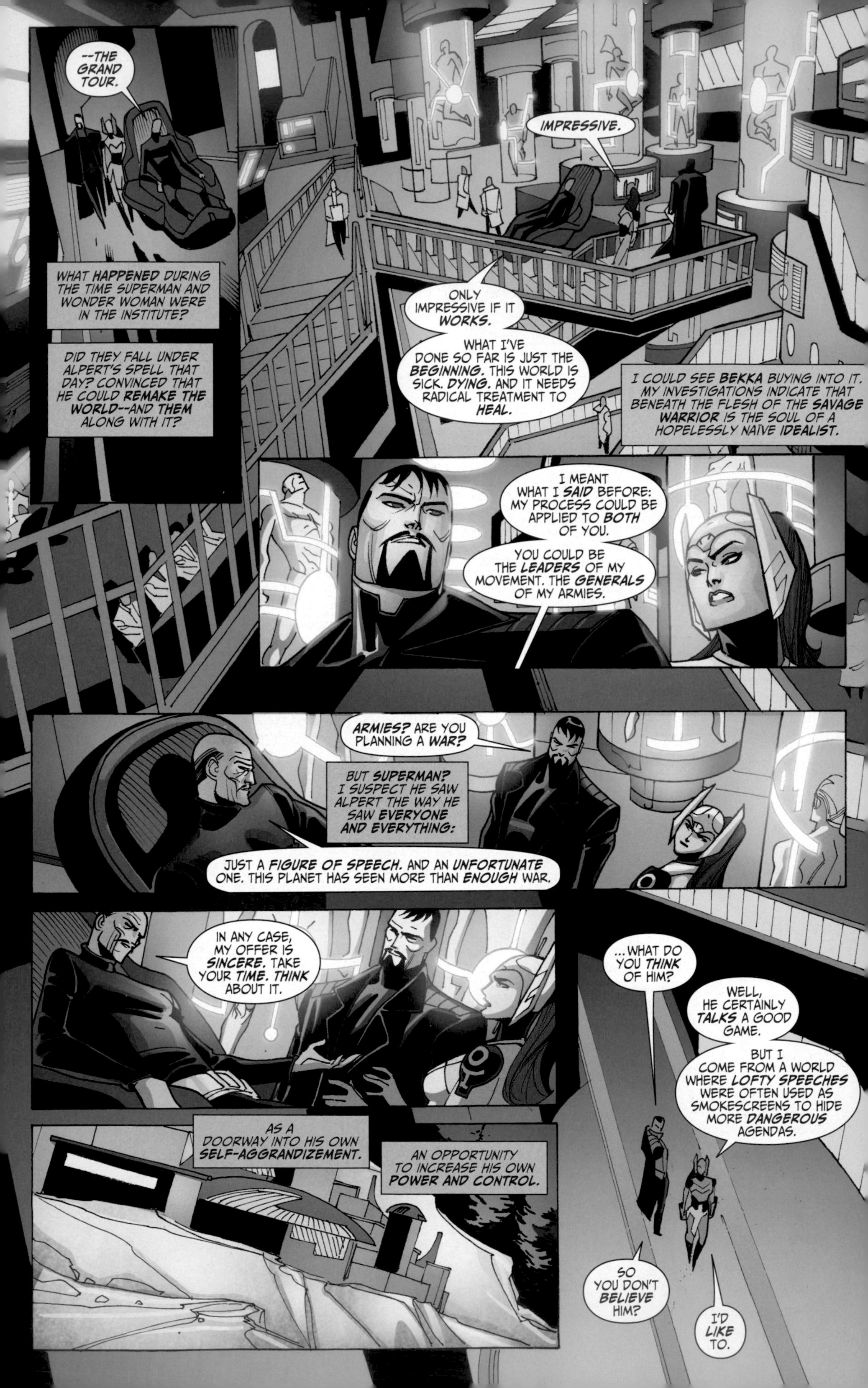
--THE GRAND TOUR.
IMPRESSIVE.
WHAT HAPPENED DURING THE TIME SUPERMAN AND WONDER WOMAN WERE IN THE INSTITUTE?
DID THEY FALL UNDER ALPERT'S SPELL THAT DAY? CONVINCED THAT HE COULD REMAKE THE WORLD--AND THEM ALONG WITH IT?
ONLY IMPRESSIVE IF IT WORKS.
WHAT I'VE DONE SO FAR IS JUST THE BEGINNING. THIS WORLD IS SICK. DYING. AND IT NEEDS RADICAL TREATMENT TO HEAL.
I COULD SEE BEKKA BUYING INTO IT. MY INVESTIGATIONS INDICATE THAT BENEATH THE FLESH OF THE SAVAGE WARRIOR IS THE SOUL OF A HOPELESSLY NAÏVE IDEALIST.
I MEANT WHAT I SAID BEFORE: MY PROCESS COULD BE APPLIED TO BOTH OF YOU.
YOU COULD BE THE LEADERS OF MY MOVEMENT. THE GENERALS OF MY ARMIES.
ARMIES? ARE YOU PLANNING A WAR?
BUT SUPERMAN? I SUSPECT HE SAW ALPERT THE WAY HE SAW EVERYONE AND EVERYTHING:
JUST A FIGURE OF SPEECH. AND AN UNFORTUNATE ONE. THIS PLANET HAS SEEN MORE THAN ENOUGH WAR.
IN ANY CASE, MY OFFER IS SINCERE. TAKE YOUR TIME. THINK ABOUT IT.
AS A DOORWAY INTO HIS OWN SELF-AGGRANDIZEMENT.
AN OPPORTUNITY TO INCREASE HIS OWN POWER AND CONTROL.
...WHAT DO YOU THINK OF HIM?
WELL, HE CERTAINLY TALKS A GOOD GAME.
BUT I COME FROM A WORLD WHERE LOFTY SPEECHES WERE OFTEN USED AS SMOKESCREENS TO HIDE MORE DANGEROUS AGENDAS.
SO YOU DON'T BELIEVE HIM?
I'D LIKE TO.

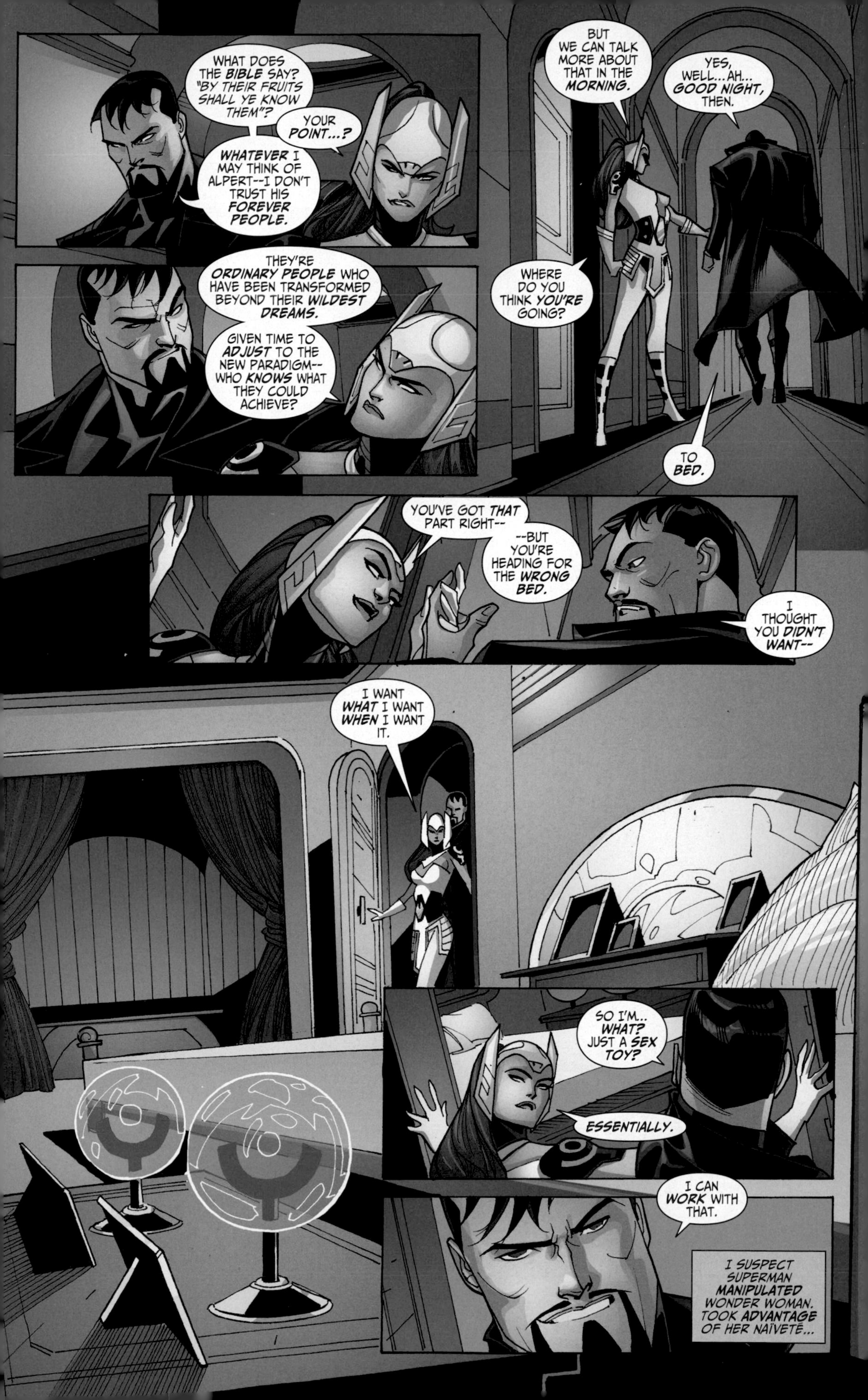
WHAT DOES THE BIBLE SAY? "BY THEIR FRUITS SHALL YE KNOW THEM"?
YOUR POINT...?
WHATEVER I MAY THINK OF ALPERT--I DON'T TRUST HIS FOREVER PEOPLE.
THEY'RE ORDINARY PEOPLE WHO HAVE BEEN TRANSFORMED BEYOND THEIR WILDEST DREAMS.
GIVEN TIME TO ADJUST TO THE NEW PARADIGM--WHO KNOWS WHAT THEY COULD ACHIEVE?
BUT WE CAN TALK MORE ABOUT THAT IN THE MORNING.
YES, WELL...AH... GOOD NIGHT, THEN.
WHERE DO YOU THINK YOU'RE GOING?
TO BED.
YOU'VE GOT THAT PART RIGHT--
--BUT YOU'RE HEADING FOR THE WRONG BED.
I THOUGHT YOU DIDN'T WANT--
I WANT WHAT I WANT WHEN I WANT IT.
SO I'M... WHAT? JUST A SEX TOY?
ESSENTIALLY.
I CAN WORK WITH THAT.
I SUSPECT SUPERMAN MANIPULATED WONDER WOMAN. TOOK ADVANTAGE OF HER NAÏVETÉ...

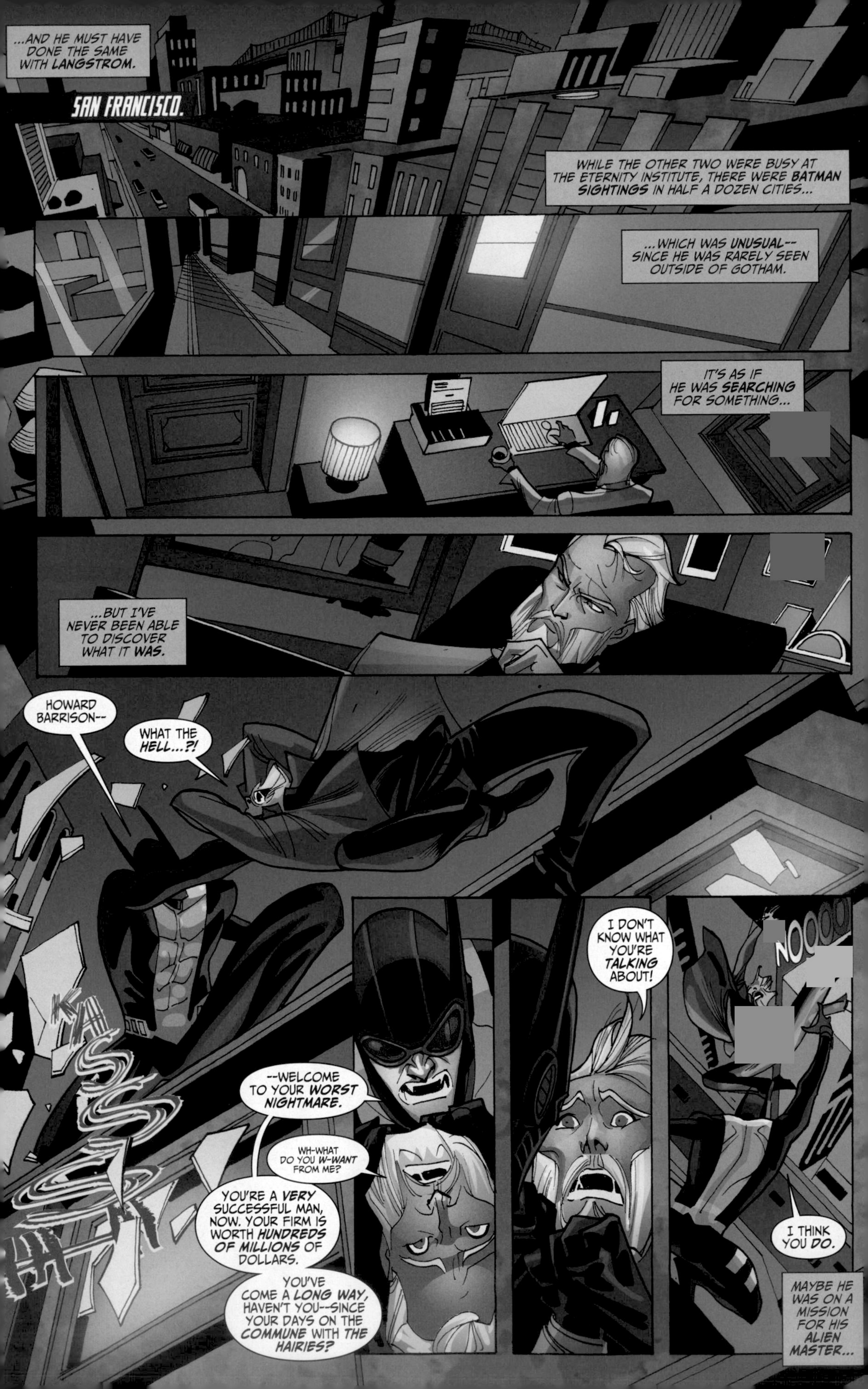
...AND HE MUST HAVE DONE THE SAME WITH LANGSTROM.
SAN FRANCISCO.
WHILE THE OTHER TWO WERE BUSY AT THE ETERNITY INSTITUTE, THERE WERE BATMAN SIGHTINGS IN HALF A DOZEN CITIES...
...WHICH WAS UNUSUAL-- SINCE HE WAS RARELY SEEN OUTSIDE OF GOTHAM.
IT'S AS IF HE WAS SEARCHING FOR SOMETHING...
...BUT I'VE NEVER BEEN ABLE TO DISCOVER WHAT IT WAS.
HOWARD BARRISON--
WHAT THE HELL...?!
--WELCOME TO YOUR WORST NIGHTMARE.
WH-WHAT DO YOU W-WANT FROM ME?
YOU'RE A VERY SUCCESSFUL MAN, NOW. YOUR FIRM IS WORTH HUNDREDS OF MILLIONS OF DOLLARS.
YOU'VE COME A LONG WAY, HAVEN'T YOU--SINCE YOUR DAYS ON THE COMMUNE WITH THE HAIRIES?
I DON'T KNOW WHAT YOU'RE TALKING ABOUT!
I THINK YOU DO.
MAYBE HE WAS ON A MISSION FOR HIS ALIEN MASTER...

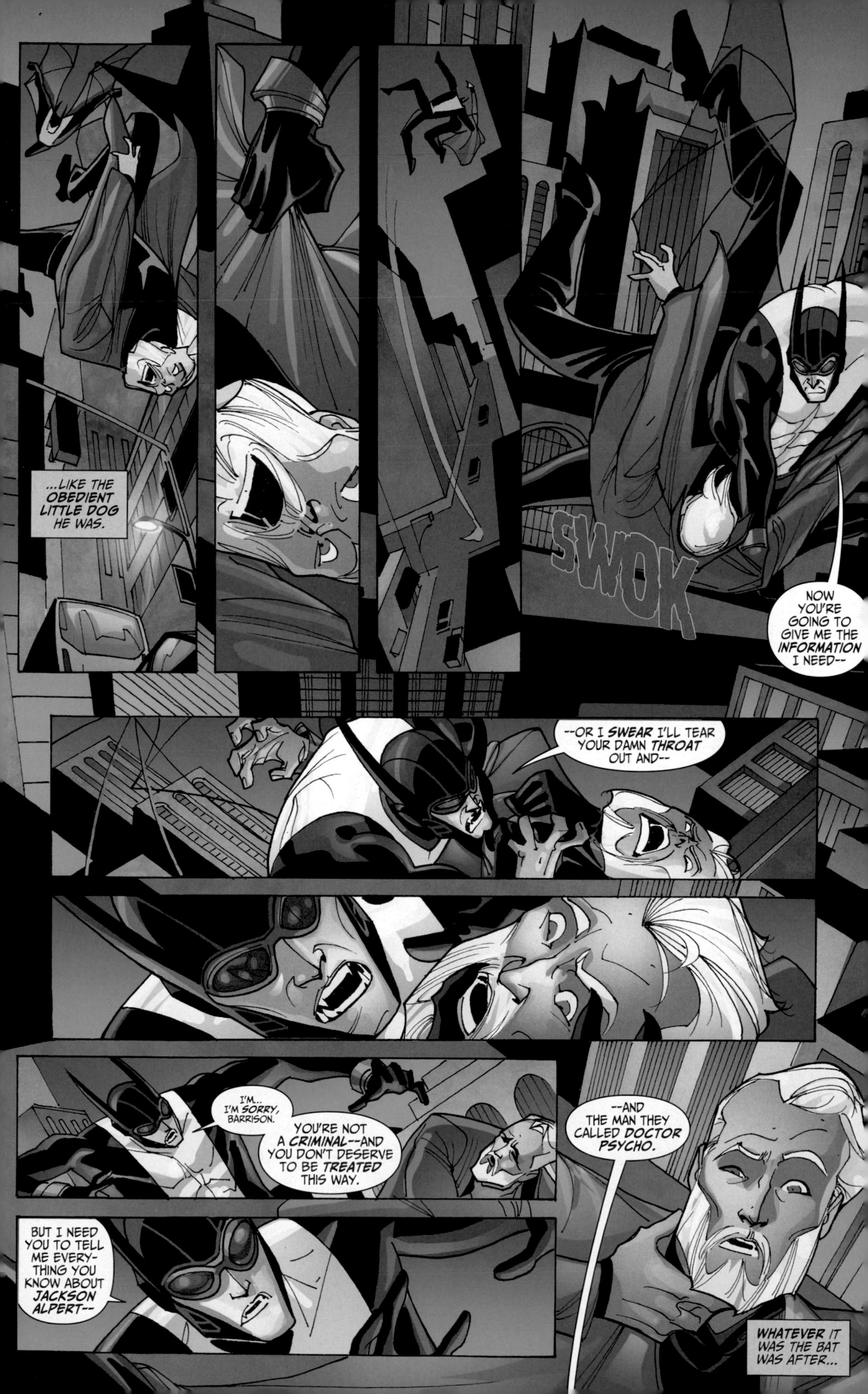

...LIKE THE OBEDIENT LITTLE DOG HE WAS.
SWOK
NOW YOU'RE GOING TO GIVE ME THE INFORMATION I NEED--
--OR I SWEAR I'LL TEAR YOUR DAMN THROAT OUT AND--
I'M... I'M SORRY, BARRISON.
YOU'RE NOT A CRIMINAL--AND YOU DON'T DESERVE TO BE TREATED THIS WAY.
BUT I NEED YOU TO TELL ME EVERY-THING YOU KNOW ABOUT JACKSON ALPERT--
--AND THE MAN THEY CALLED DOCTOR PSYCHO.
WHATEVER IT WAS THE BAT WAS AFTER...

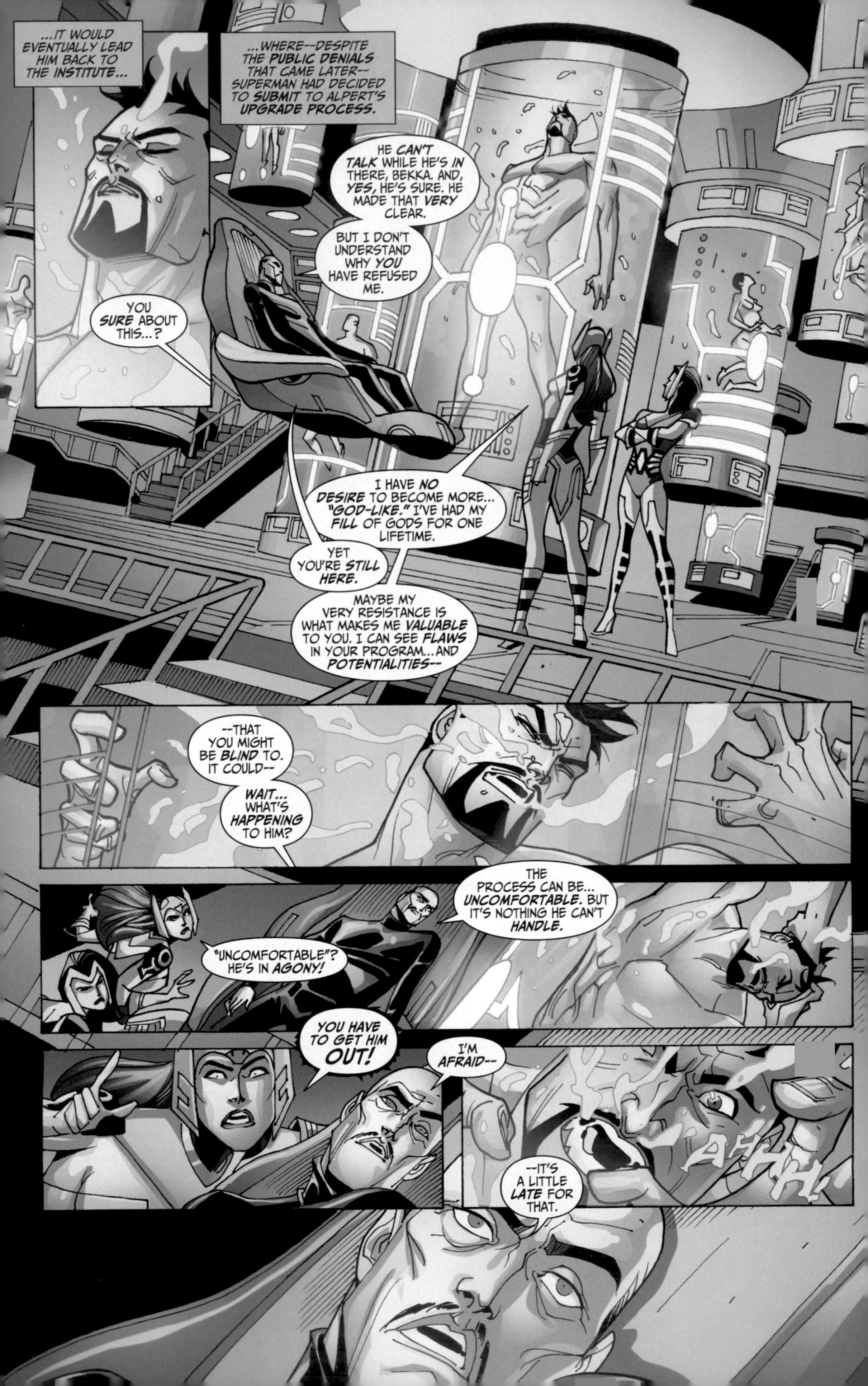
...IT WOULD EVENTUALLY LEAD HIM BACK TO THE INSTITUTE...
...WHERE--DESPITE THE PUBLIC DENIALS THAT CAME LATER--SUPERMAN HAD DECIDED TO SUBMIT TO ALPERT'S UPGRADE PROCESS.
YOU SURE ABOUT THIS...?
HE CAN'T TALK WHILE HE'S IN THERE, BEKKA. AND, YES, HE'S SURE. HE MADE THAT VERY CLEAR.
BUT I DON'T UNDERSTAND WHY YOU HAVE REFUSED ME.
I HAVE NO DESIRE TO BECOME MORE... "GOD-LIKE." I'VE HAD MY FILL OF GODS FOR ONE LIFETIME.
YET YOU'RE STILL HERE.
MAYBE MY VERY RESISTANCE IS WHAT MAKES ME VALUABLE TO YOU. I CAN SEE FLAWS IN YOUR PROGRAM...AND POTENTIALITIES--
--THAT YOU MIGHT BE BLIND TO. IT COULD--
WAIT... WHAT'S HAPPENING TO HIM?
THE PROCESS CAN BE... UNCOMFORTABLE. BUT IT'S NOTHING HE CAN'T HANDLE.
"UNCOMFORTABLE"? HE'S IN AGONY!
YOU HAVE TO GET HIM OUT!
I'M AFRAID--
--IT'S A LITTLE LATE FOR THAT.
AHHH!

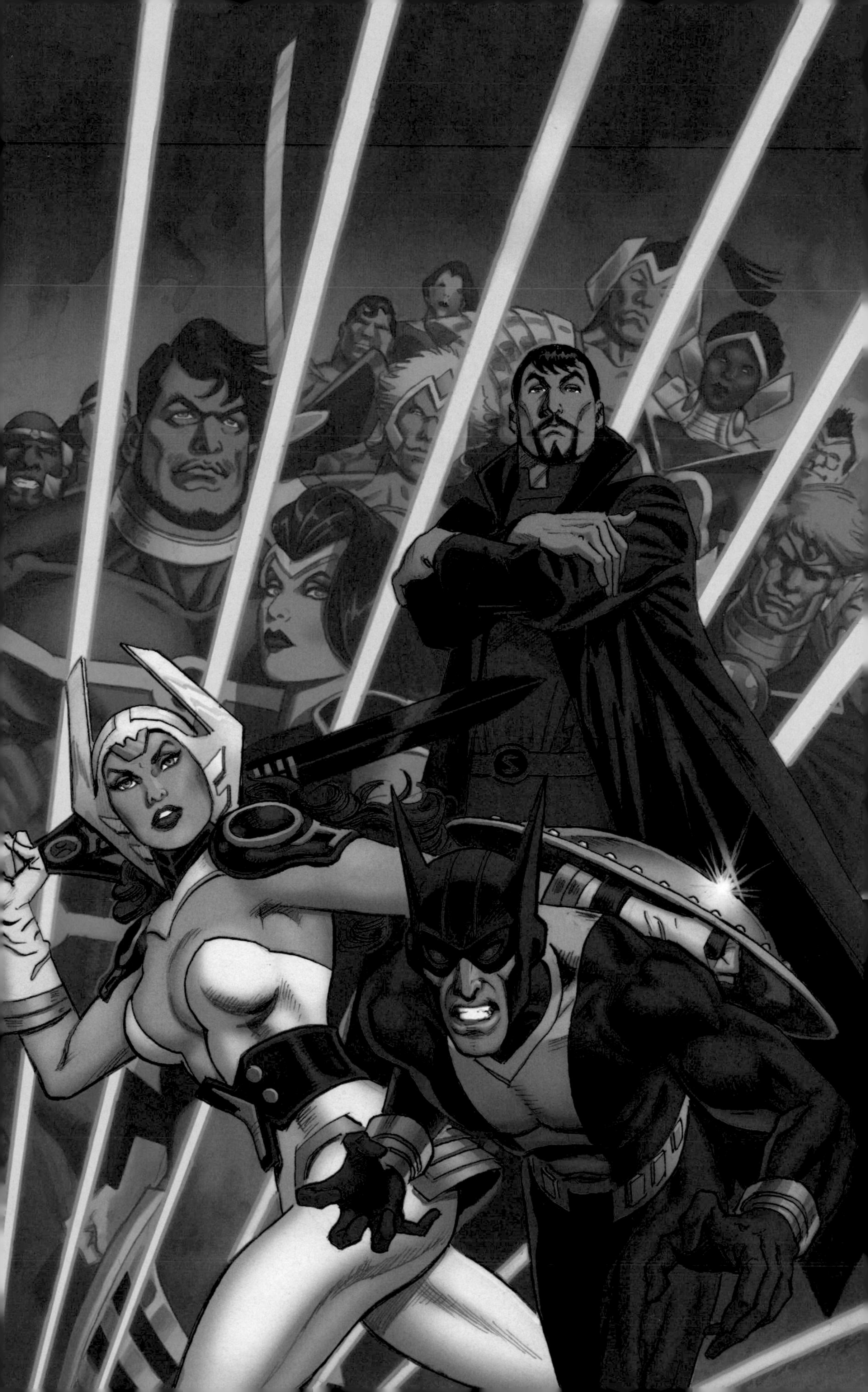

GENESIS PART 2

ART BY THONY SILAS

COLORS BY TONY AVIÑA

COVER ART BY JOSE LUIS GARCIA-LOPEZ AND TRISH MULVIHILL

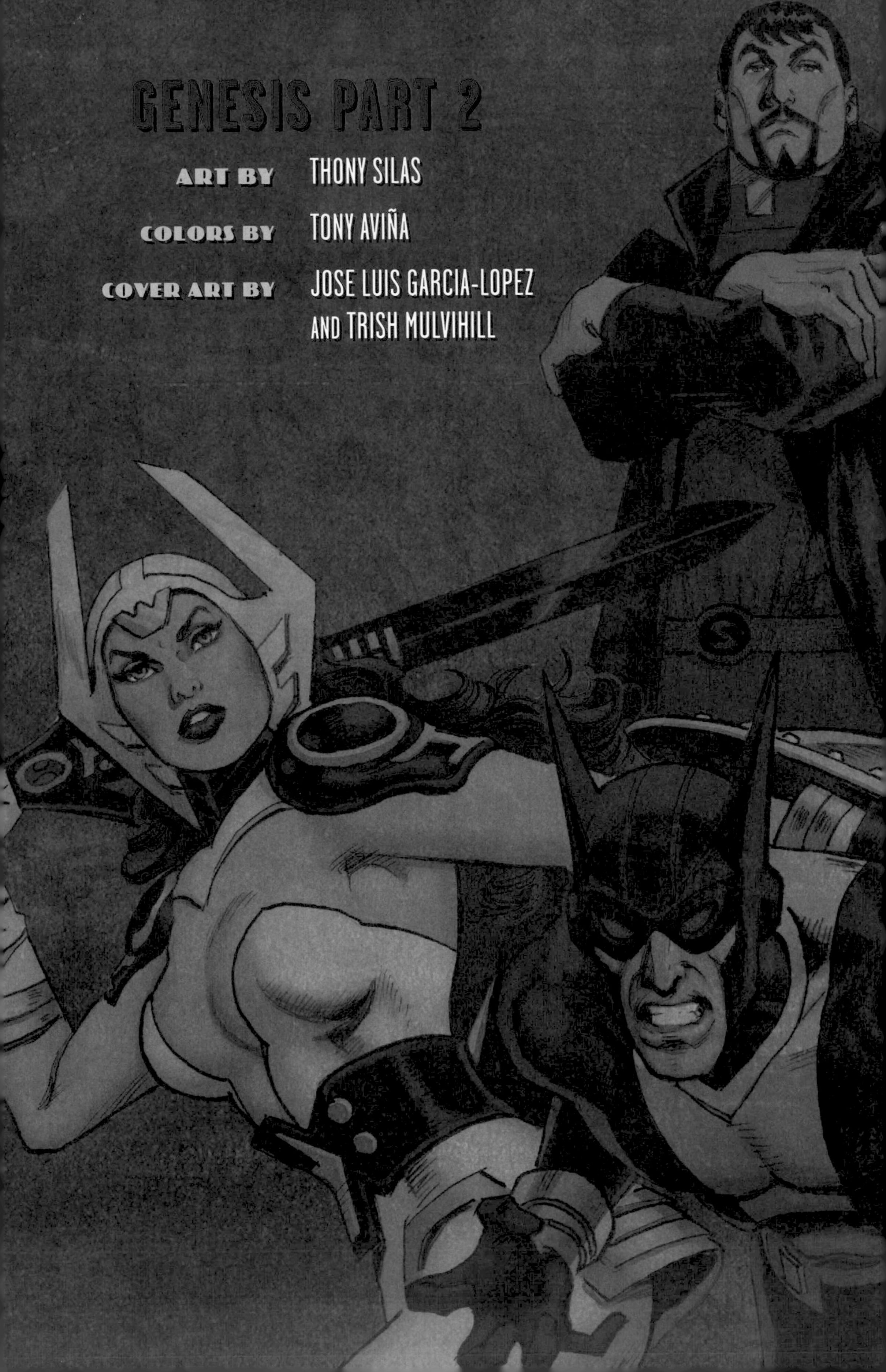

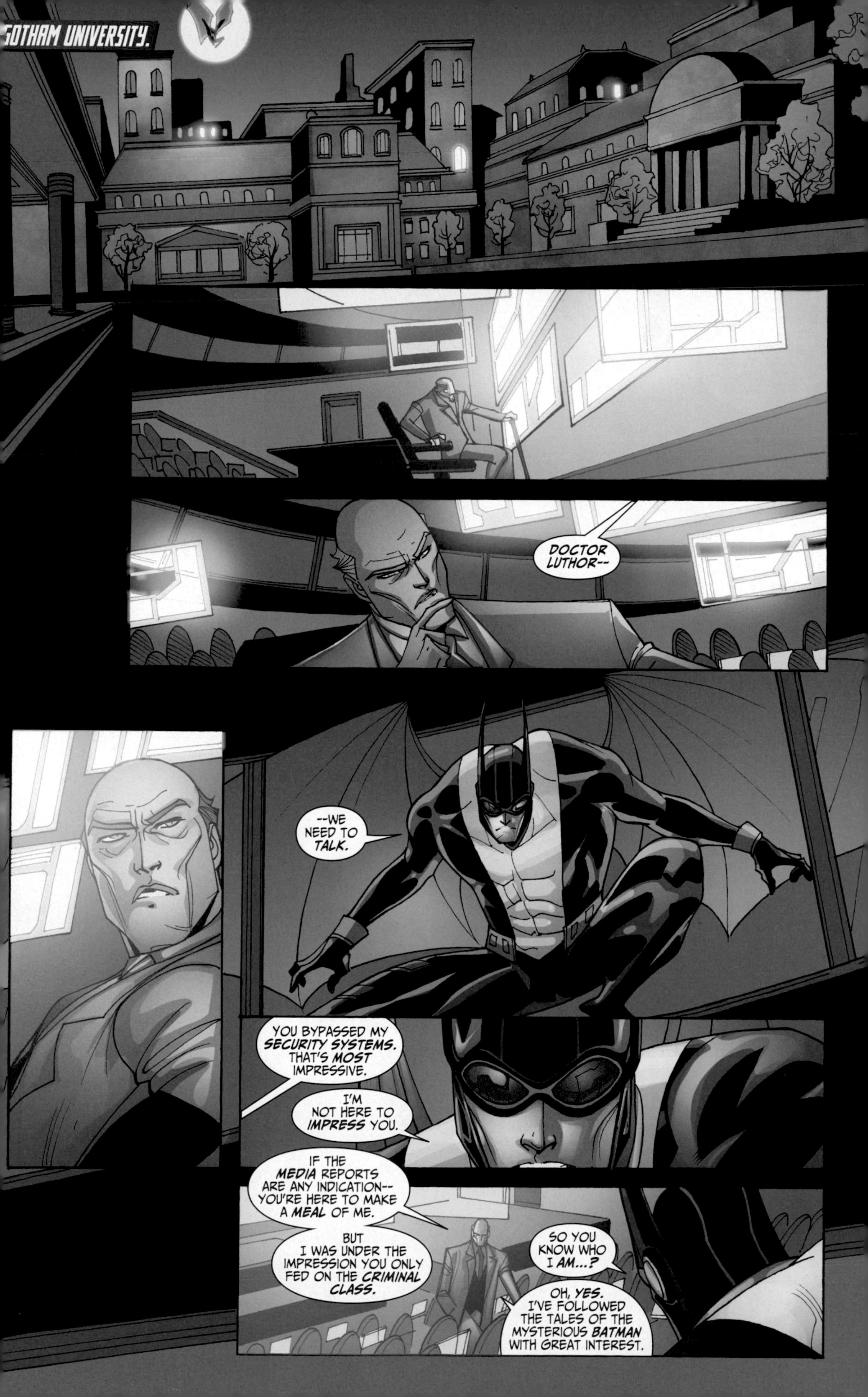
GOTHAM UNIVERSITY.
DOCTOR LUTHOR--
--WE NEED TO TALK.
YOU BYPASSED MY SECURITY SYSTEMS. THAT'S MOST IMPRESSIVE.
I'M NOT HERE TO IMPRESS YOU.
IF THE MEDIA REPORTS ARE ANY INDICATION-- YOU'RE HERE TO MAKE A MEAL OF ME.
BUT I WAS UNDER THE IMPRESSION YOU ONLY FED ON THE CRIMINAL CLASS.
SO YOU KNOW WHO I AM...?
OH, YES. I'VE FOLLOWED THE TALES OF THE MYSTERIOUS BATMAN WITH GREAT INTEREST.

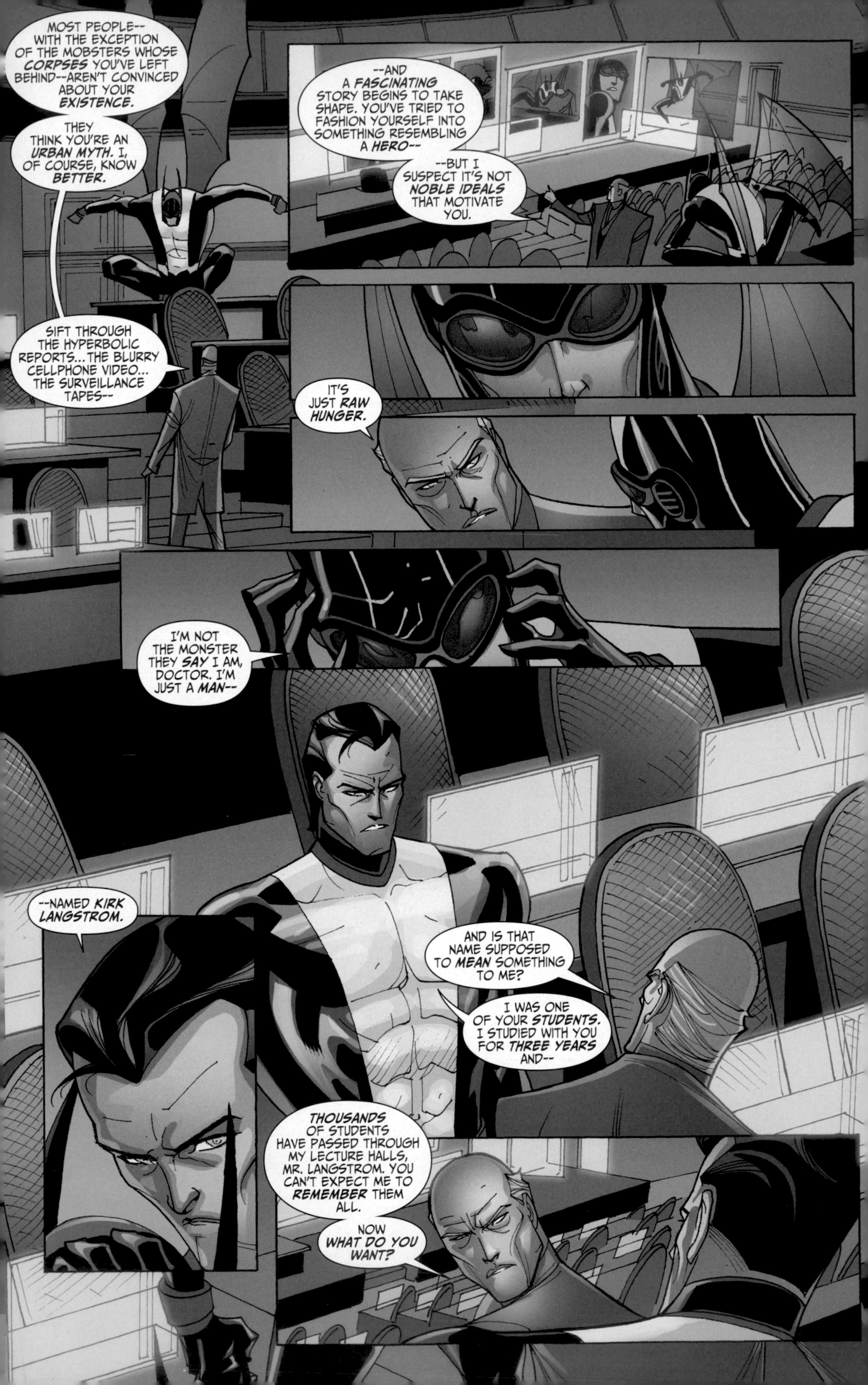
MOST PEOPLE-- WITH THE EXCEPTION OF THE MOBSTERS WHOSE CORPSES YOU'VE LEFT BEHIND--AREN'T CONVINCED ABOUT YOUR EXISTENCE.
THEY THINK YOU'RE AN URBAN MYTH. I, OF COURSE, KNOW BETTER.
SIFT THROUGH THE HYPERBOLIC REPORTS... THE BLURRY CELLPHONE VIDEO... THE SURVEILLANCE TAPES--
--AND A FASCINATING STORY BEGINS TO TAKE SHAPE. YOU'VE TRIED TO FASHION YOURSELF INTO SOMETHING RESEMBLING A HERO--
--BUT I SUSPECT IT'S NOT NOBLE IDEALS THAT MOTIVATE YOU.
IT'S JUST RAW HUNGER.
I'M NOT THE MONSTER THEY SAY I AM, DOCTOR. I'M JUST A MAN--
--NAMED KIRK LANGSTROM.
AND IS THAT NAME SUPPOSED TO MEAN SOMETHING TO ME?
I WAS ONE OF YOUR STUDENTS. I STUDIED WITH YOU FOR THREE YEARS AND--
THOUSANDS OF STUDENTS HAVE PASSED THROUGH MY LECTURE HALLS, MR. LANGSTROM. YOU CAN'T EXPECT ME TO REMEMBER THEM ALL.
NOW WHAT DO YOU WANT?

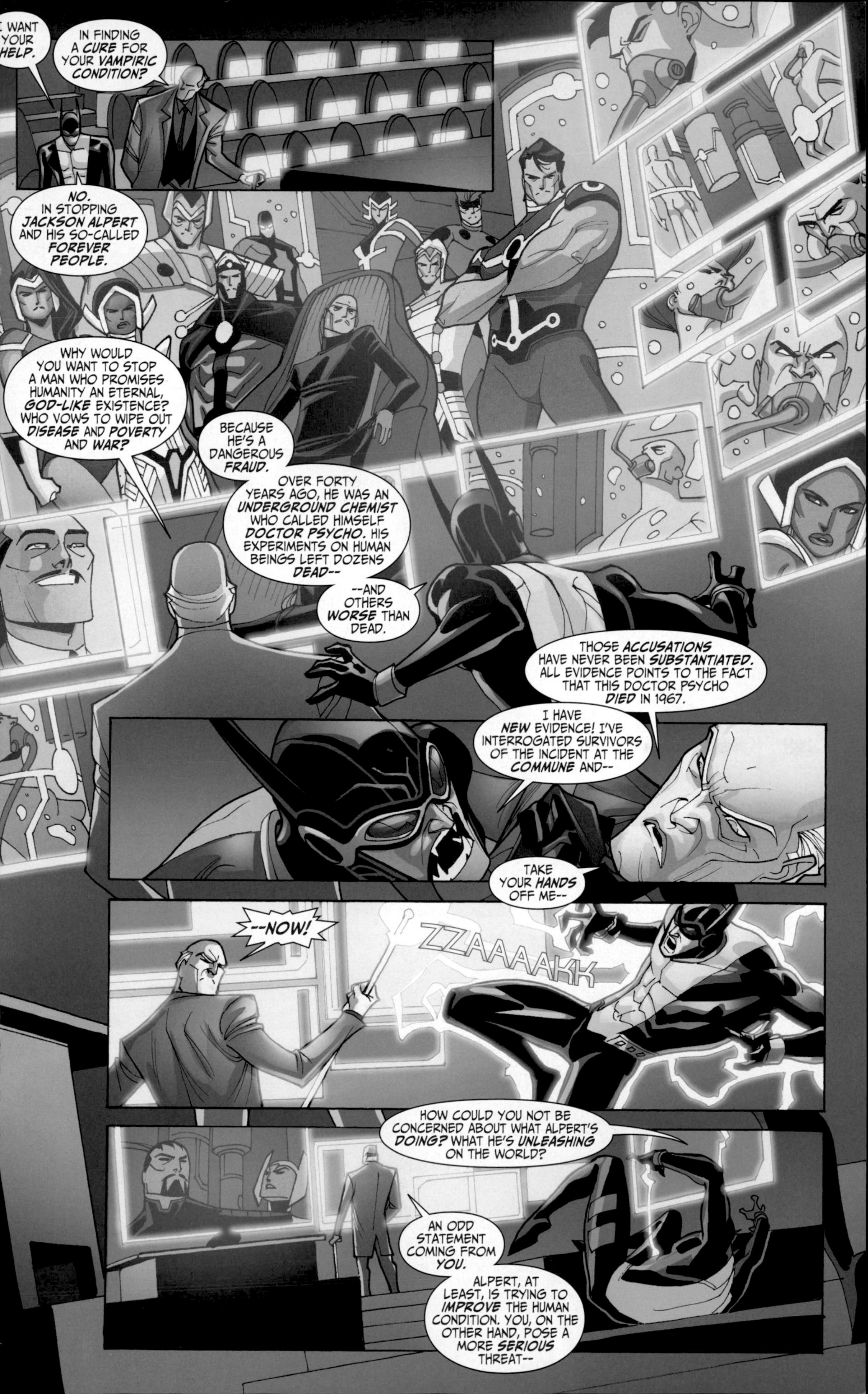
I WANT YOUR HELP.
IN FINDING A CURE FOR YOUR VAMPIRIC CONDITION?
NO. IN STOPPING JACKSON ALPERT AND HIS SO-CALLED FOREVER PEOPLE.
WHY WOULD YOU WANT TO STOP A MAN WHO PROMISES HUMANITY AN ETERNAL, GOD-LIKE EXISTENCE? WHO VOWS TO WIPE OUT DISEASE AND POVERTY AND WAR?
BECAUSE HE'S A DANGEROUS FRAUD.
OVER FORTY YEARS AGO, HE WAS AN UNDERGROUND CHEMIST WHO CALLED HIMSELF DOCTOR PSYCHO. HIS EXPERIMENTS ON HUMAN BEINGS LEFT DOZENS DEAD--
--AND OTHERS WORSE THAN DEAD.
THOSE ACCUSATIONS HAVE NEVER BEEN SUBSTANTIATED. ALL EVIDENCE POINTS TO THE FACT THAT THIS DOCTOR PSYCHO DIED IN 1967.
I HAVE NEW EVIDENCE! I'VE INTERROGATED SURVIVORS OF THE INCIDENT AT THE COMMUNE AND--
TAKE YOUR HANDS OFF ME--
--NOW!
ZZAAAAAKK
HOW COULD YOU NOT BE CONCERNED ABOUT WHAT ALPERT'S DOING? WHAT HE'S UNLEASHING ON THE WORLD?
AN ODD STATEMENT COMING FROM YOU.
ALPERT, AT LEAST, IS TRYING TO IMPROVE THE HUMAN CONDITION. YOU, ON THE OTHER HAND, POSE A MORE SERIOUS THREAT--

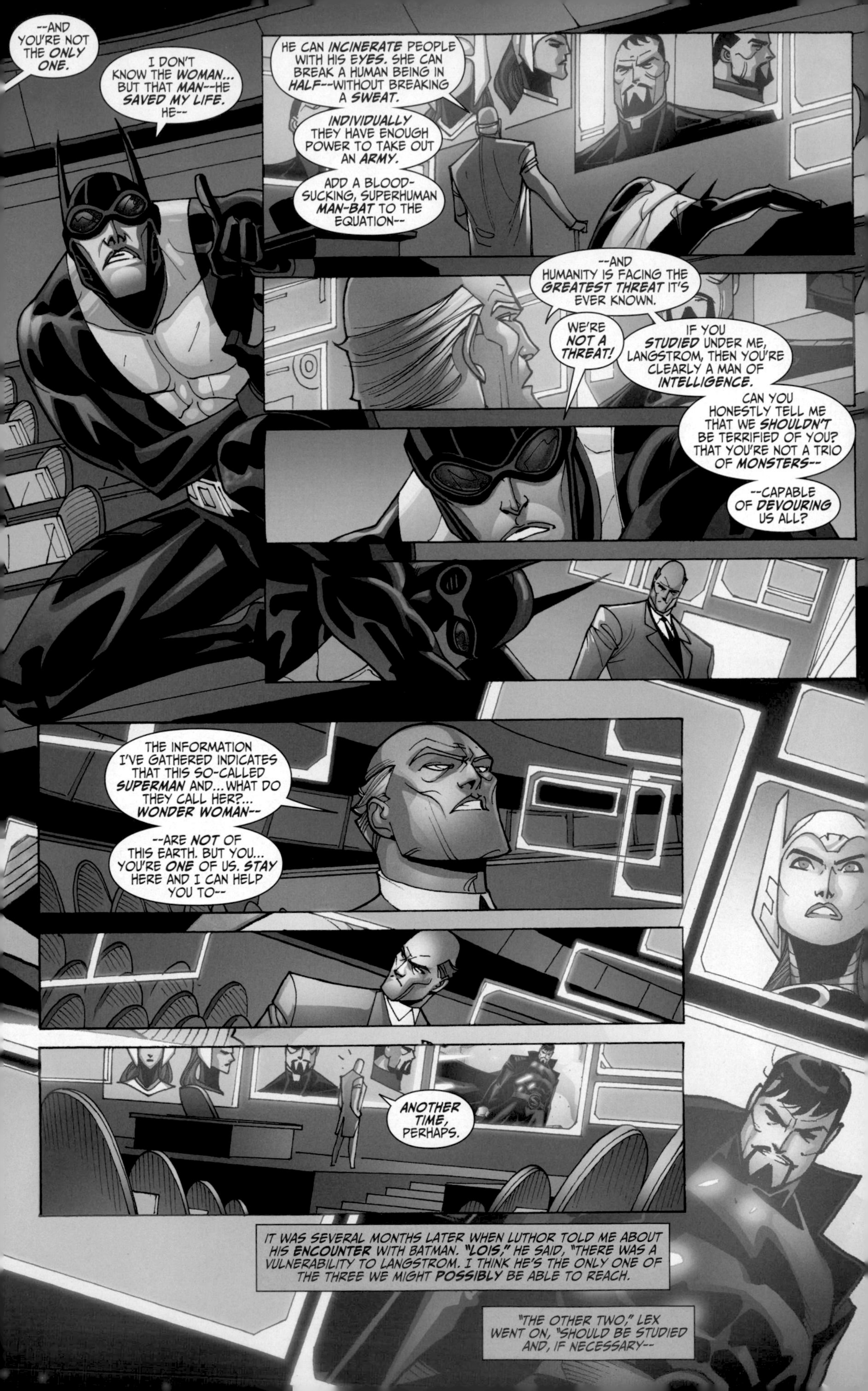
--AND YOU'RE NOT THE ONLY ONE.
I DON'T KNOW THE WOMAN... BUT THAT MAN--HE SAVED MY LIFE. HE--
HE CAN INCINERATE PEOPLE WITH HIS EYES. SHE CAN BREAK A HUMAN BEING IN HALF--WITHOUT BREAKING A SWEAT.
INDIVIDUALLY THEY HAVE ENOUGH POWER TO TAKE OUT AN ARMY.
ADD A BLOOD-SUCKING, SUPERHUMAN MAN-BAT TO THE EQUATION--
--AND HUMANITY IS FACING THE GREATEST THREAT IT'S EVER KNOWN.
WE'RE NOT A THREAT!
IF YOU STUDIED UNDER ME, LANGSTROM, THEN YOU'RE CLEARLY A MAN OF INTELLIGENCE.
CAN YOU HONESTLY TELL ME THAT WE SHOULDN'T BE TERRIFIED OF YOU? THAT YOU'RE NOT A TRIO OF MONSTERS--
--CAPABLE OF DEVOURING US ALL?
THE INFORMATION I'VE GATHERED INDICATES THAT THIS SO-CALLED SUPERMAN AND...WHAT DO THEY CALL HER?... WONDER WOMAN--
--ARE NOT OF THIS EARTH. BUT YOU... YOU'RE ONE OF US. STAY HERE AND I CAN HELP YOU TO--
ANOTHER TIME, PERHAPS.
IT WAS SEVERAL MONTHS LATER WHEN LUTHOR TOLD ME ABOUT HIS ENCOUNTER WITH BATMAN. "LOIS," HE SAID, "THERE WAS A VULNERABILITY TO LANGSTROM. I THINK HE'S THE ONLY ONE OF THE THREE WE MIGHT POSSIBLY BE ABLE TO REACH.
"THE OTHER TWO," LEX WENT ON, "SHOULD BE STUDIED AND, IF NECESSARY--

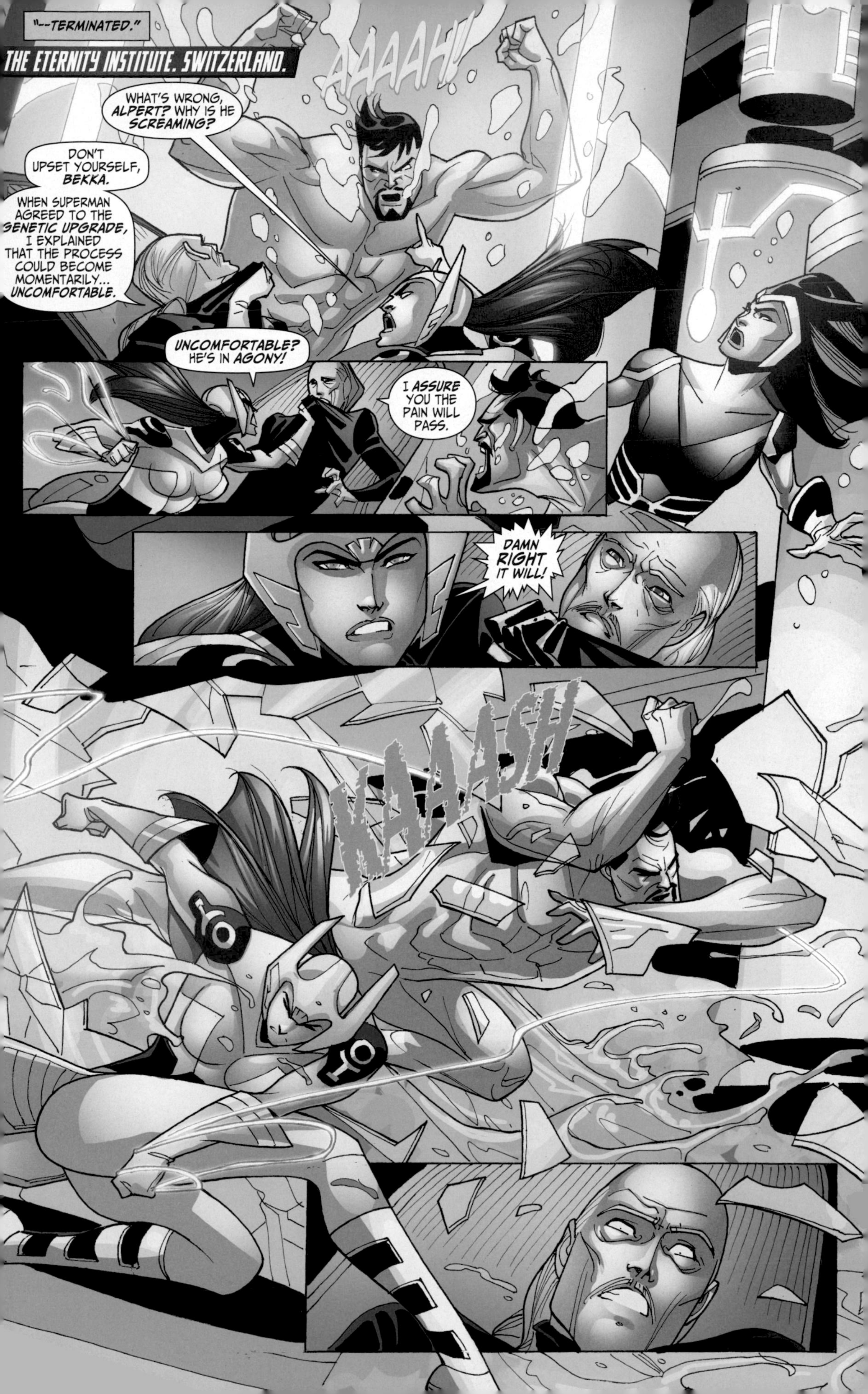
"--TERMINATED."
THE ETERNITY INSTITUTE. SWITZERLAND.
AAAAH!!
WHAT'S WRONG, ALPERT? WHY IS HE SCREAMING?
DON'T UPSET YOURSELF, BEKKA.
WHEN SUPERMAN AGREED TO THE GENETIC UPGRADE, I EXPLAINED THAT THE PROCESS COULD BECOME MOMENTARILY... UNCOMFORTABLE.
UNCOMFORTABLE? HE'S IN AGONY!
I ASSURE YOU THE PAIN WILL PASS.
DAMN RIGHT IT WILL!
KRAAASH

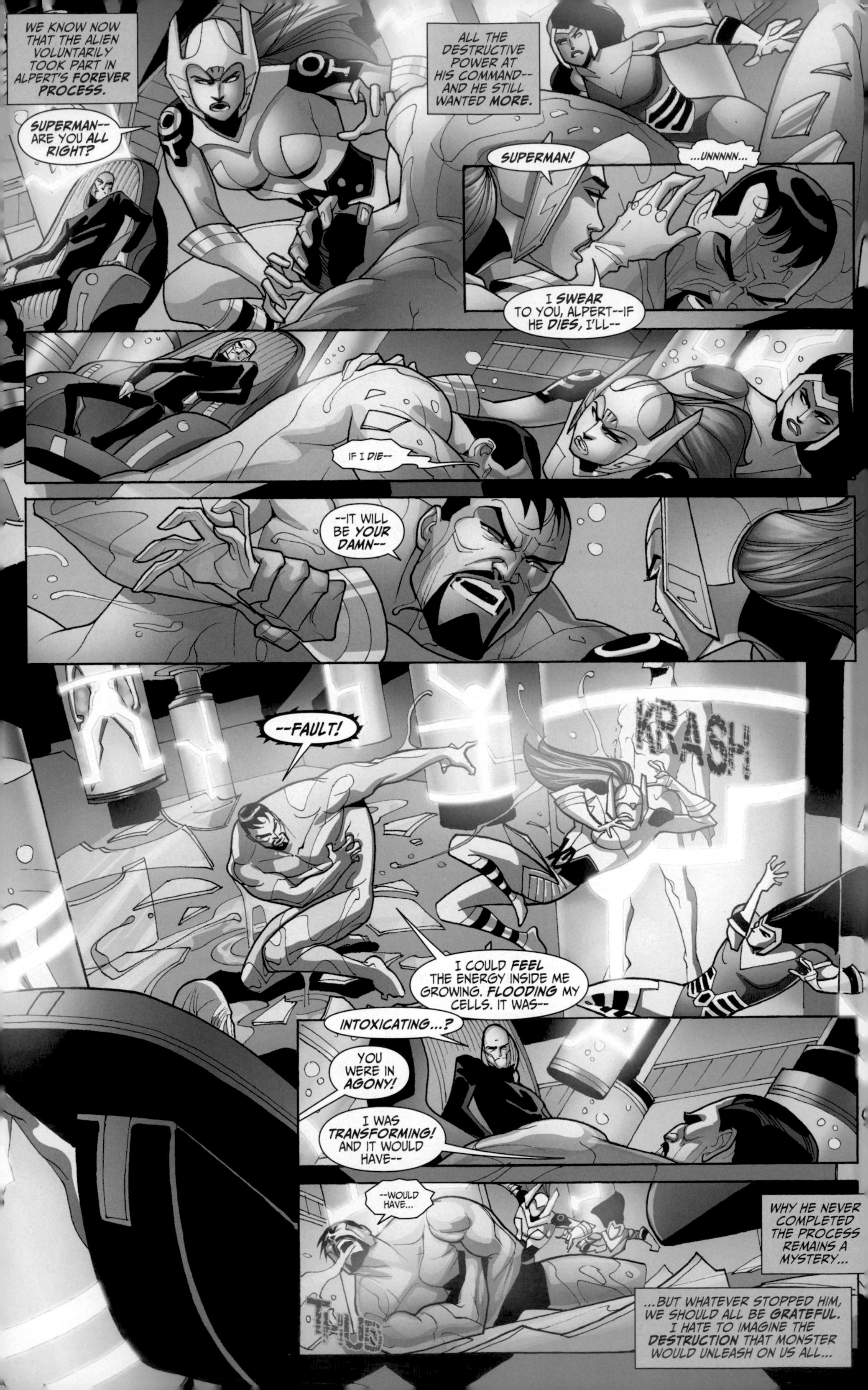
WE KNOW NOW THAT THE ALIEN VOLUNTARILY TOOK PART IN ALPERT'S FOREVER PROCESS.
ALL THE DESTRUCTIVE POWER AT HIS COMMAND--AND HE STILL WANTED MORE.
SUPERMAN--ARE YOU ALL RIGHT?
SUPERMAN!
...UNNNNN...
I SWEAR TO YOU, ALPERT--IF HE DIES, I'LL--
IF I DIE--
--IT WILL BE YOUR DAMN--
--FAULT!
KRASH
I COULD FEEL THE ENERGY INSIDE ME GROWING. FLOODING MY CELLS. IT WAS--
INTOXICATING...?
YOU WERE IN AGONY!
I WAS TRANSFORMING! AND IT WOULD HAVE--
--WOULD HAVE...
THUD
WHY HE NEVER COMPLETED THE PROCESS REMAINS A MYSTERY...
...BUT WHATEVER STOPPED HIM, WE SHOULD ALL BE GRATEFUL. I HATE TO IMAGINE THE DESTRUCTION THAT MONSTER WOULD UNLEASH ON US ALL...

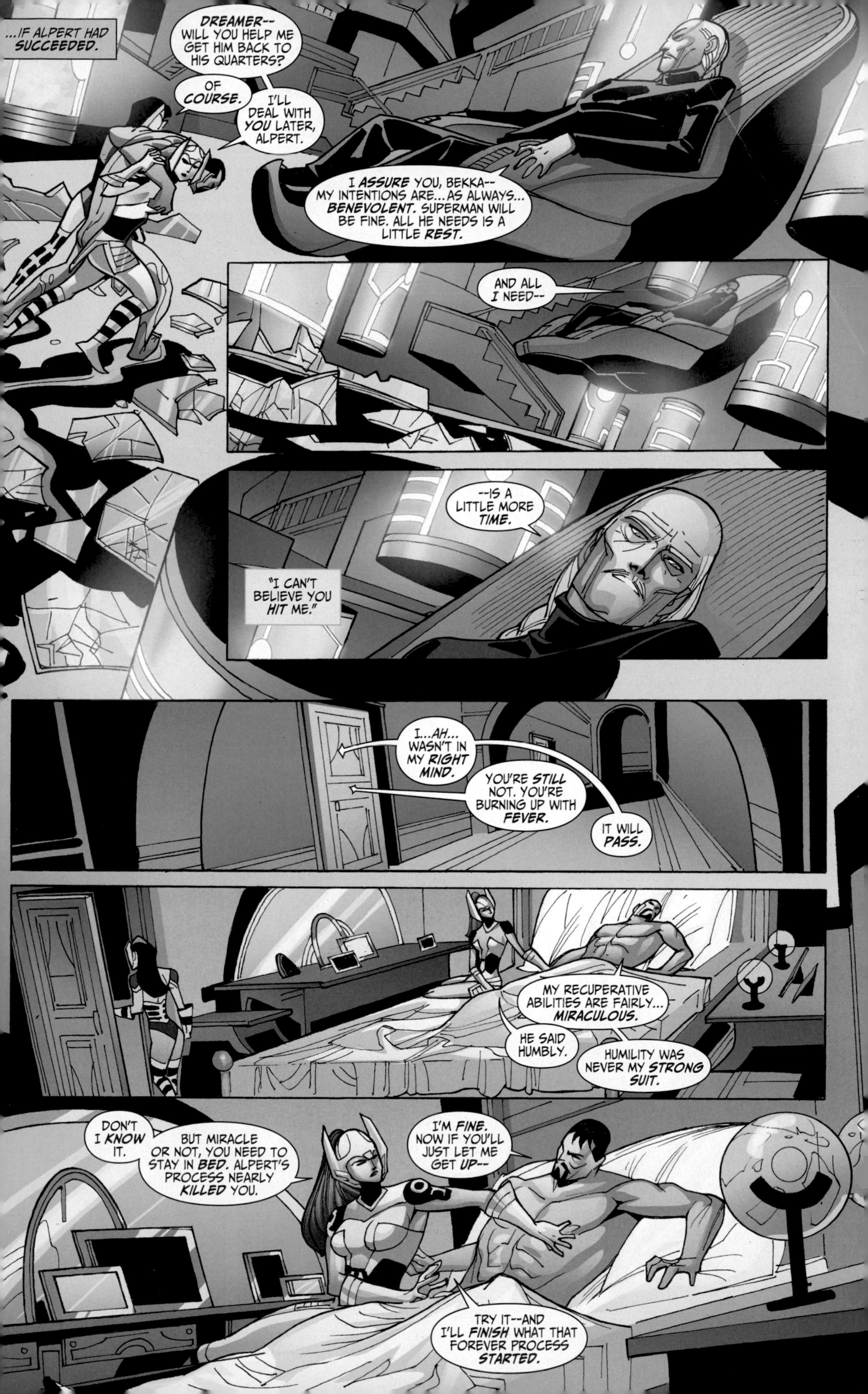

...IF ALPERT HAD SUCCEEDED.
DREAMER-- WILL YOU HELP ME GET HIM BACK TO HIS QUARTERS?
OF COURSE.
I'LL DEAL WITH YOU LATER, ALPERT.
I ASSURE YOU, BEKKA-- MY INTENTIONS ARE...AS ALWAYS... BENEVOLENT. SUPERMAN WILL BE FINE. ALL HE NEEDS IS A LITTLE REST.
AND ALL I NEED--
--IS A LITTLE MORE TIME.
"I CAN'T BELIEVE YOU HIT ME."
I...AH... WASN'T IN MY RIGHT MIND.
YOU'RE STILL NOT. YOU'RE BURNING UP WITH FEVER.
IT WILL PASS.
MY RECUPERATIVE ABILITIES ARE FAIRLY... MIRACULOUS.
HE SAID HUMBLY.
HUMILITY WAS NEVER MY STRONG SUIT.
DON'T I KNOW IT.
BUT MIRACLE OR NOT, YOU NEED TO STAY IN BED. ALPERT'S PROCESS NEARLY KILLED YOU.
I'M FINE. NOW IF YOU'LL JUST LET ME GET UP--
TRY IT--AND I'LL FINISH WHAT THAT FOREVER PROCESS STARTED.

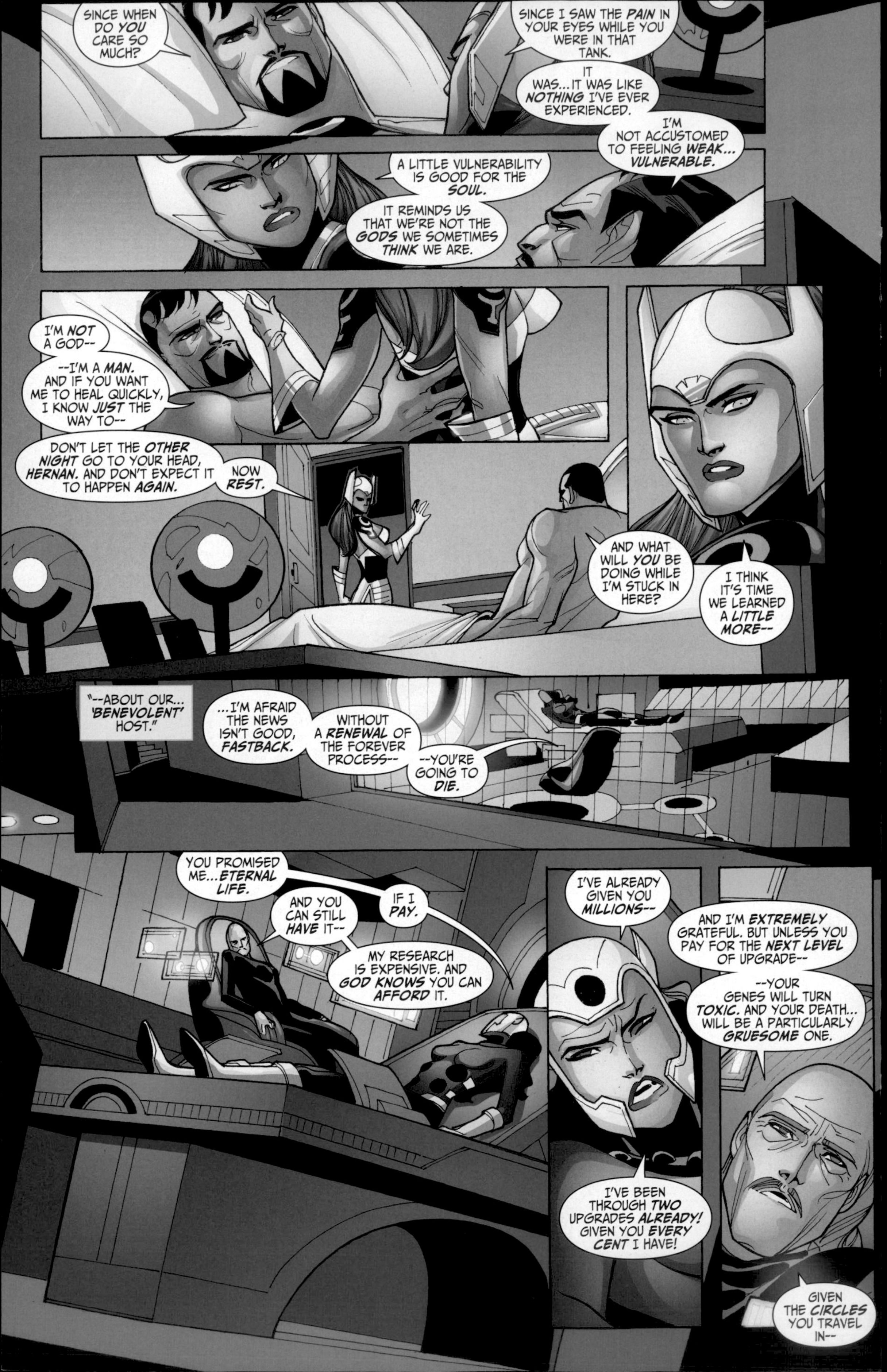

SINCE WHEN DO YOU CARE SO MUCH?
SINCE I SAW THE PAIN IN YOUR EYES WHILE YOU WERE IN THAT TANK.
IT WAS...IT WAS LIKE NOTHING I'VE EVER EXPERIENCED.
I'M NOT ACCUSTOMED TO FEELING WEAK... VULNERABLE.
A LITTLE VULNERABILITY IS GOOD FOR THE SOUL.
IT REMINDS US THAT WE'RE NOT THE GODS WE SOMETIMES THINK WE ARE.
I'M NOT A GOD--
--I'M A MAN. AND IF YOU WANT ME TO HEAL QUICKLY, I KNOW JUST THE WAY TO--
DON'T LET THE OTHER NIGHT GO TO YOUR HEAD, HERNAN. AND DON'T EXPECT IT TO HAPPEN AGAIN.
NOW REST.
AND WHAT WILL YOU BE DOING WHILE I'M STUCK IN HERE?
I THINK IT'S TIME WE LEARNED A LITTLE MORE--
"--ABOUT OUR... 'BENEVOLENT' HOST."
...I'M AFRAID THE NEWS ISN'T GOOD, FASTBACK.
WITHOUT A RENEWAL OF THE FOREVER PROCESS--
--YOU'RE GOING TO DIE.
YOU PROMISED ME...ETERNAL LIFE.
AND YOU CAN STILL HAVE IT--
IF I PAY.
MY RESEARCH IS EXPENSIVE. AND GOD KNOWS YOU CAN AFFORD IT.
I'VE ALREADY GIVEN YOU MILLIONS--
AND I'M EXTREMELY GRATEFUL. BUT UNLESS YOU PAY FOR THE NEXT LEVEL OF UPGRADE--
--YOUR GENES WILL TURN TOXIC. AND YOUR DEATH... WILL BE A PARTICULARLY GRUESOME ONE.
I'VE BEEN THROUGH TWO UPGRADES ALREADY! GIVEN YOU EVERY CENT I HAVE!
GIVEN THE CIRCLES YOU TRAVEL IN--

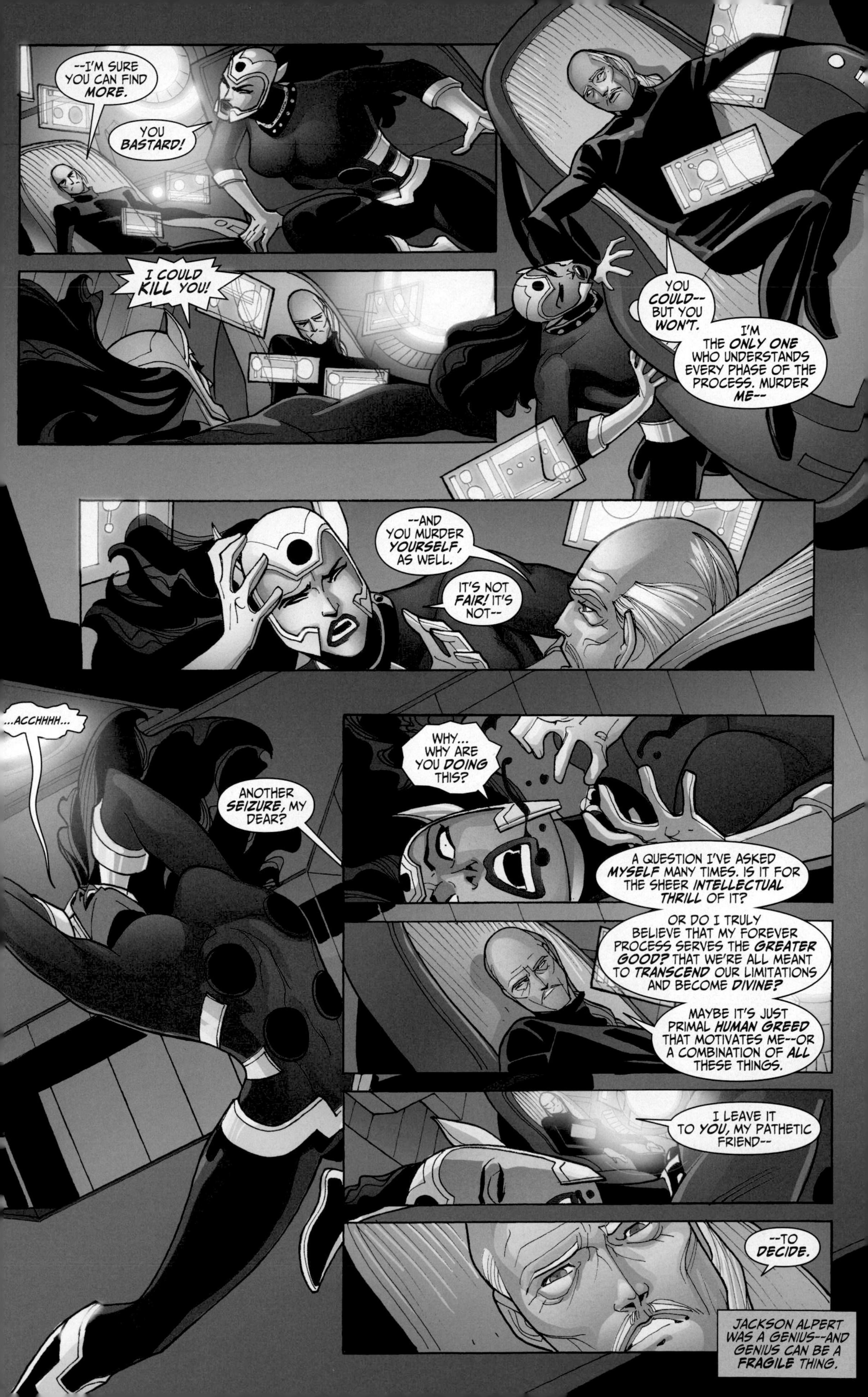
--I'M SURE YOU CAN FIND MORE.
YOU BASTARD!
I COULD KILL YOU!
YOU COULD--BUT YOU WON'T.
I'M THE ONLY ONE WHO UNDERSTANDS EVERY PHASE OF THE PROCESS. MURDER ME--
--AND YOU MURDER YOURSELF, AS WELL.
IT'S NOT FAIR! IT'S NOT--
...ACCHHHH...
ANOTHER SEIZURE, MY DEAR?
WHY... WHY ARE YOU DOING THIS?
A QUESTION I'VE ASKED MYSELF MANY TIMES. IS IT FOR THE SHEER INTELLECTUAL THRILL OF IT?
OR DO I TRULY BELIEVE THAT MY FOREVER PROCESS SERVES THE GREATER GOOD? THAT WE'RE ALL MEANT TO TRANSCEND OUR LIMITATIONS AND BECOME DIVINE?
MAYBE IT'S JUST PRIMAL HUMAN GREED THAT MOTIVATES ME--OR A COMBINATION OF ALL THESE THINGS.
I LEAVE IT TO YOU, MY PATHETIC FRIEND--
--TO DECIDE.
JACKSON ALPERT WAS A GENIUS--AND GENIUS CAN BE A FRAGILE THING.

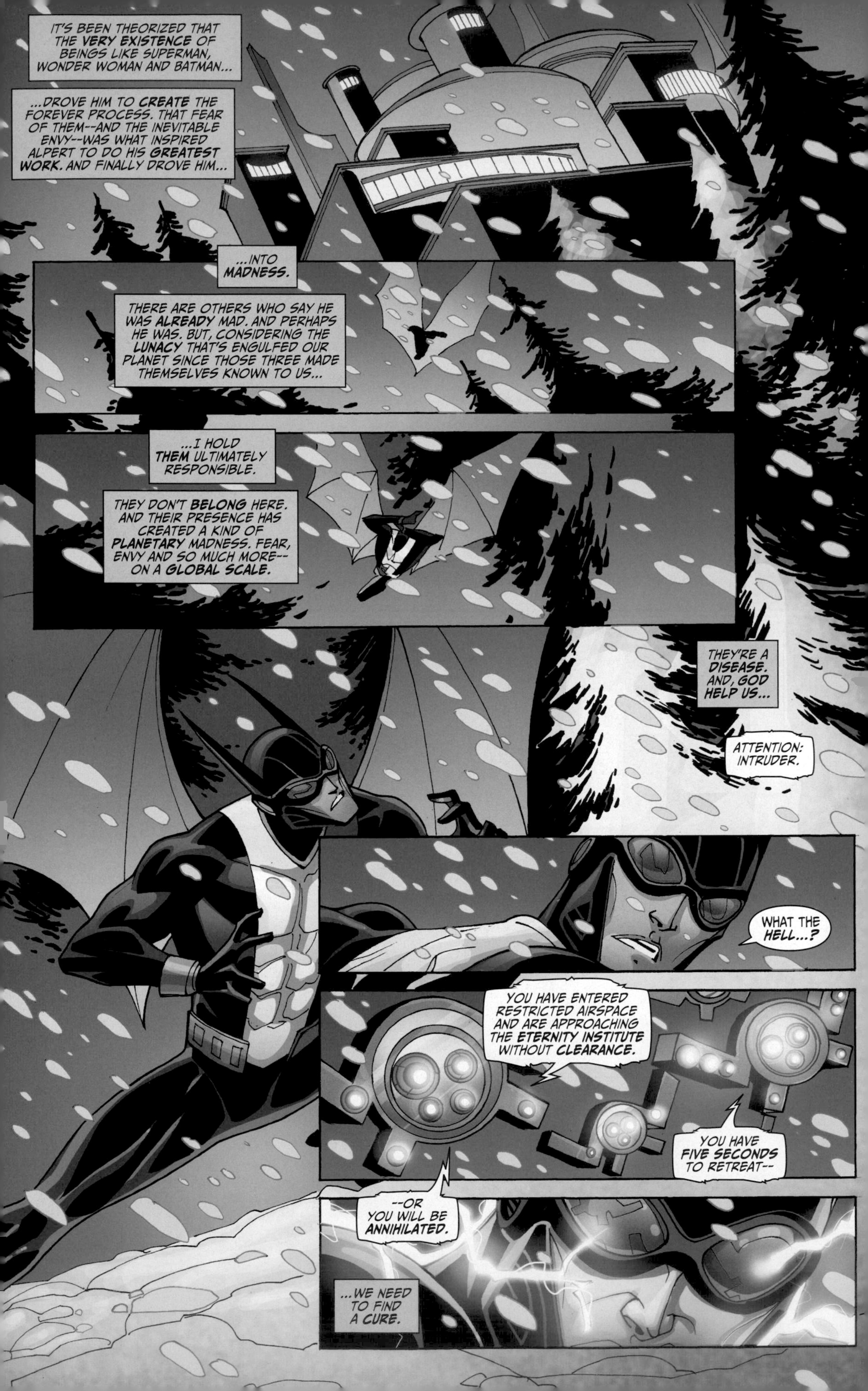
IT'S BEEN THEORIZED THAT THE VERY EXISTENCE OF BEINGS LIKE SUPERMAN, WONDER WOMAN AND BATMAN...
...DROVE HIM TO CREATE THE FOREVER PROCESS. THAT FEAR OF THEM--AND THE INEVITABLE ENVY--WAS WHAT INSPIRED ALPERT TO DO HIS GREATEST WORK. AND FINALLY DROVE HIM...
...INTO MADNESS.
THERE ARE OTHERS WHO SAY HE WAS ALREADY MAD. AND PERHAPS HE WAS. BUT, CONSIDERING THE LUNACY THAT'S ENGULFED OUR PLANET SINCE THOSE THREE MADE THEMSELVES KNOWN TO US...
...I HOLD THEM ULTIMATELY RESPONSIBLE.
THEY DON'T BELONG HERE. AND THEIR PRESENCE HAS CREATED A KIND OF PLANETARY MADNESS. FEAR, ENVY AND SO MUCH MORE--ON A GLOBAL SCALE.
THEY'RE A DISEASE. AND, GOD HELP US...
ATTENTION: INTRUDER.
WHAT THE HELL...?
YOU HAVE ENTERED RESTRICTED AIRSPACE AND ARE APPROACHING THE ETERNITY INSTITUTE WITHOUT CLEARANCE.
YOU HAVE FIVE SECONDS TO RETREAT--
--OR YOU WILL BE ANNIHILATED.
...WE NEED TO FIND A CURE.

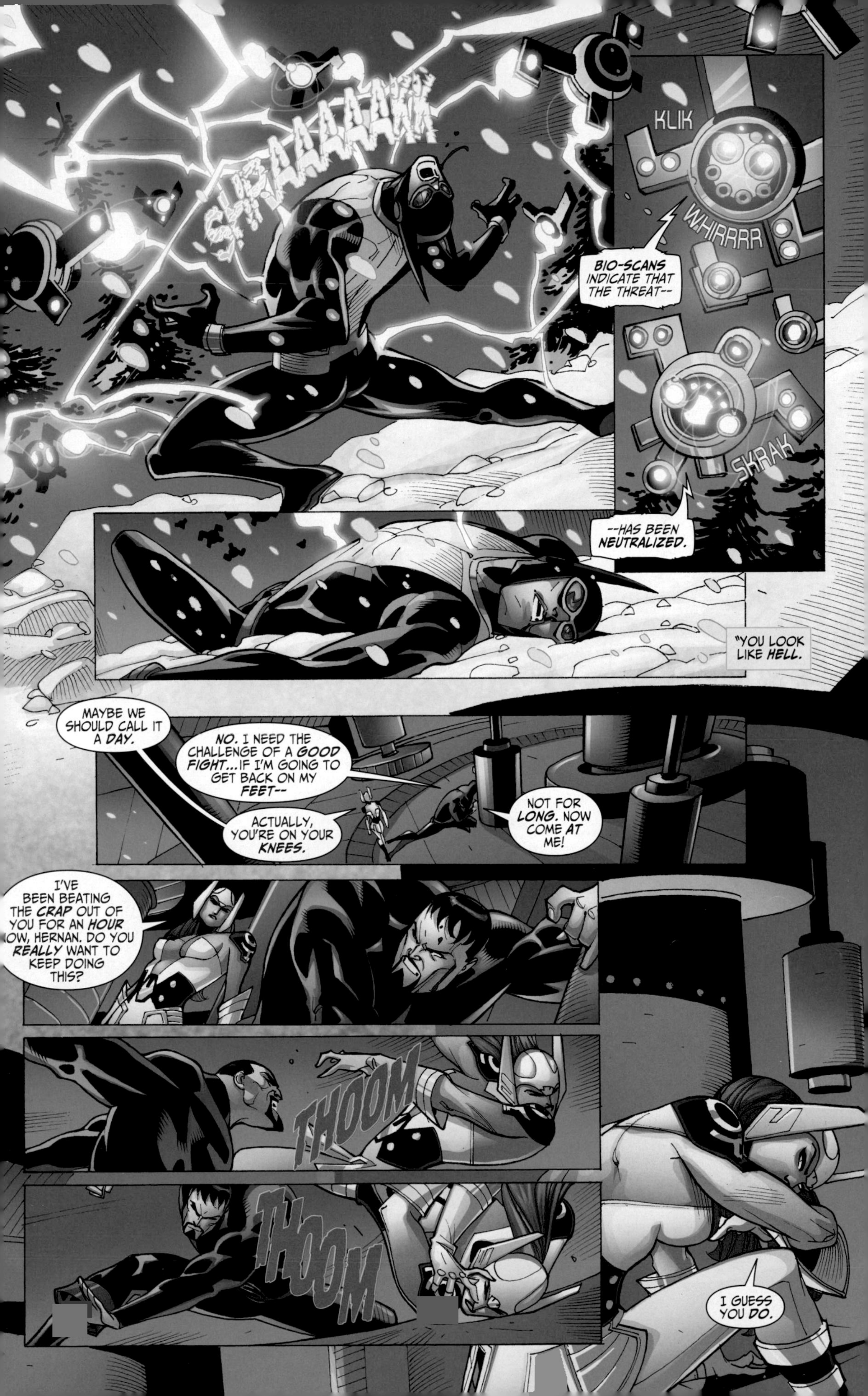
SHRAAAAAAKK
KLIK
WHIRRRR
BIO-SCANS INDICATE THAT THE THREAT--
SKRAK
--HAS BEEN NEUTRALIZED.
"YOU LOOK LIKE HELL.
MAYBE WE SHOULD CALL IT A DAY.
NO. I NEED THE CHALLENGE OF A GOOD FIGHT... IF I'M GOING TO GET BACK ON MY FEET--
ACTUALLY, YOU'RE ON YOUR KNEES.
NOT FOR LONG. NOW COME AT ME!
I'VE BEEN BEATING THE CRAP OUT OF YOU FOR AN HOUR NOW, HERNAN. DO YOU REALLY WANT TO KEEP DOING THIS?
THOOM
THOOM
I GUESS YOU DO.

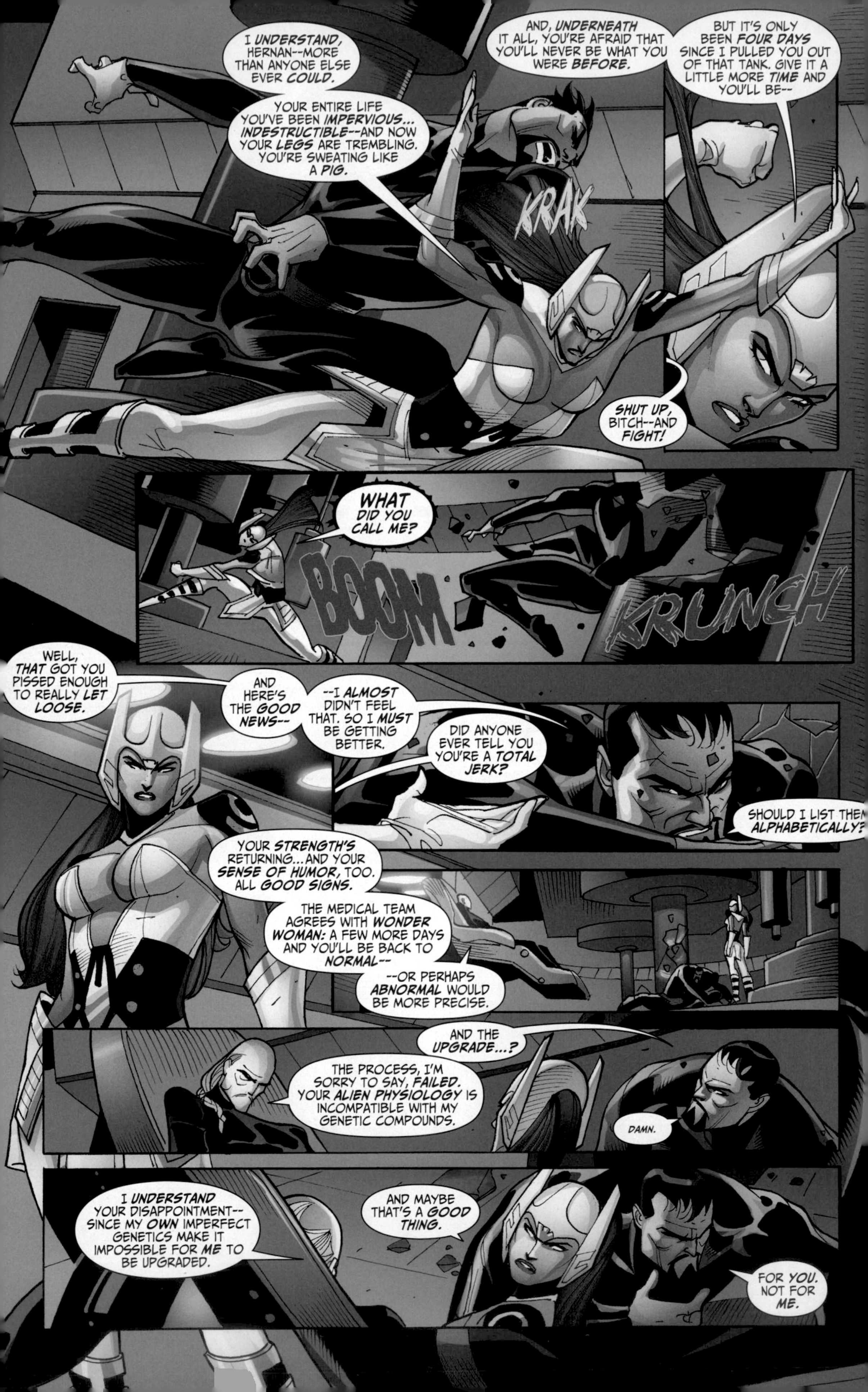
I UNDERSTAND, HERNAN--MORE THAN ANYONE ELSE EVER COULD.
YOUR ENTIRE LIFE YOU'VE BEEN IMPERVIOUS... INDESTRUCTIBLE--AND NOW YOUR LEGS ARE TREMBLING. YOU'RE SWEATING LIKE A PIG.
AND, UNDERNEATH IT ALL, YOU'RE AFRAID THAT YOU'LL NEVER BE WHAT YOU WERE BEFORE.
KRAK
BUT IT'S ONLY BEEN FOUR DAYS SINCE I PULLED YOU OUT OF THAT TANK. GIVE IT A LITTLE MORE TIME AND YOU'LL BE--
SHUT UP, BITCH--AND FIGHT!
WHAT DID YOU CALL ME?
BOOM
KRUNCH
WELL, THAT GOT YOU PISSED ENOUGH TO REALLY LET LOOSE.
AND HERE'S THE GOOD NEWS--
--I ALMOST DIDN'T FEEL THAT. SO I MUST BE GETTING BETTER.
DID ANYONE EVER TELL YOU YOU'RE A TOTAL JERK?
SHOULD I LIST THEM ALPHABETICALLY?
YOUR STRENGTH'S RETURNING... AND YOUR SENSE OF HUMOR, TOO. ALL GOOD SIGNS.
THE MEDICAL TEAM AGREES WITH WONDER WOMAN: A FEW MORE DAYS AND YOU'LL BE BACK TO NORMAL--
--OR PERHAPS ABNORMAL WOULD BE MORE PRECISE.
AND THE UPGRADE...?
THE PROCESS, I'M SORRY TO SAY, FAILED. YOUR ALIEN PHYSIOLOGY IS INCOMPATIBLE WITH MY GENETIC COMPOUNDS.
DAMN.
I UNDERSTAND YOUR DISAPPOINTMENT--SINCE MY OWN IMPERFECT GENETICS MAKE IT IMPOSSIBLE FOR ME TO BE UPGRADED.
AND MAYBE THAT'S A GOOD THING.
FOR YOU. NOT FOR ME.

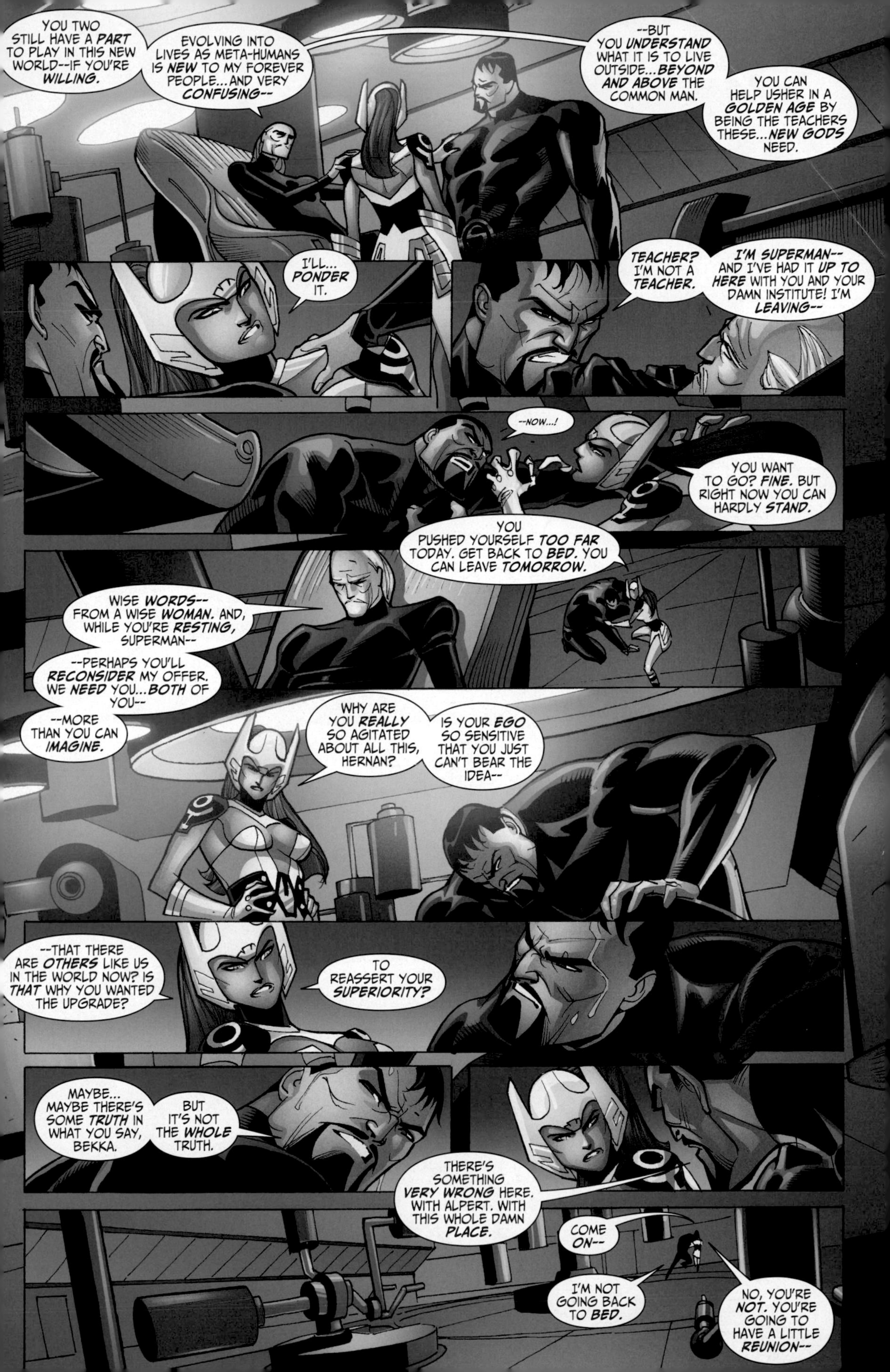
YOU TWO STILL HAVE A PART TO PLAY IN THIS NEW WORLD--IF YOU'RE WILLING.
EVOLVING INTO LIVES AS META-HUMANS IS NEW TO MY FOREVER PEOPLE...AND VERY CONFUSING--
--BUT YOU UNDERSTAND WHAT IT IS TO LIVE OUTSIDE...BEYOND AND ABOVE THE COMMON MAN.
YOU CAN HELP USHER IN A GOLDEN AGE BY BEING THE TEACHERS THESE...NEW GODS NEED.
I'LL... PONDER IT.
TEACHER? I'M NOT A TEACHER.
I'M SUPERMAN-- AND I'VE HAD IT UP TO HERE WITH YOU AND YOUR DAMN INSTITUTE! I'M LEAVING--
--NOW...!
YOU WANT TO GO? FINE. BUT RIGHT NOW YOU CAN HARDLY STAND.
YOU PUSHED YOURSELF TOO FAR TODAY. GET BACK TO BED. YOU CAN LEAVE TOMORROW.
WISE WORDS-- FROM A WISE WOMAN. AND, WHILE YOU'RE RESTING, SUPERMAN--
--PERHAPS YOU'LL RECONSIDER MY OFFER. WE NEED YOU...BOTH OF YOU--
--MORE THAN YOU CAN IMAGINE.
WHY ARE YOU REALLY SO AGITATED ABOUT ALL THIS, HERNAN?
IS YOUR EGO SO SENSITIVE THAT YOU JUST CAN'T BEAR THE IDEA--
--THAT THERE ARE OTHERS LIKE US IN THE WORLD NOW? IS THAT WHY YOU WANTED THE UPGRADE?
TO REASSERT YOUR SUPERIORITY?
MAYBE... MAYBE THERE'S SOME TRUTH IN WHAT YOU SAY, BEKKA.
BUT IT'S NOT THE WHOLE TRUTH.
THERE'S SOMETHING VERY WRONG HERE. WITH ALPERT. WITH THIS WHOLE DAMN PLACE.
COME ON--
I'M NOT GOING BACK TO BED.
NO, YOU'RE NOT. YOU'RE GOING TO HAVE A LITTLE REUNION--

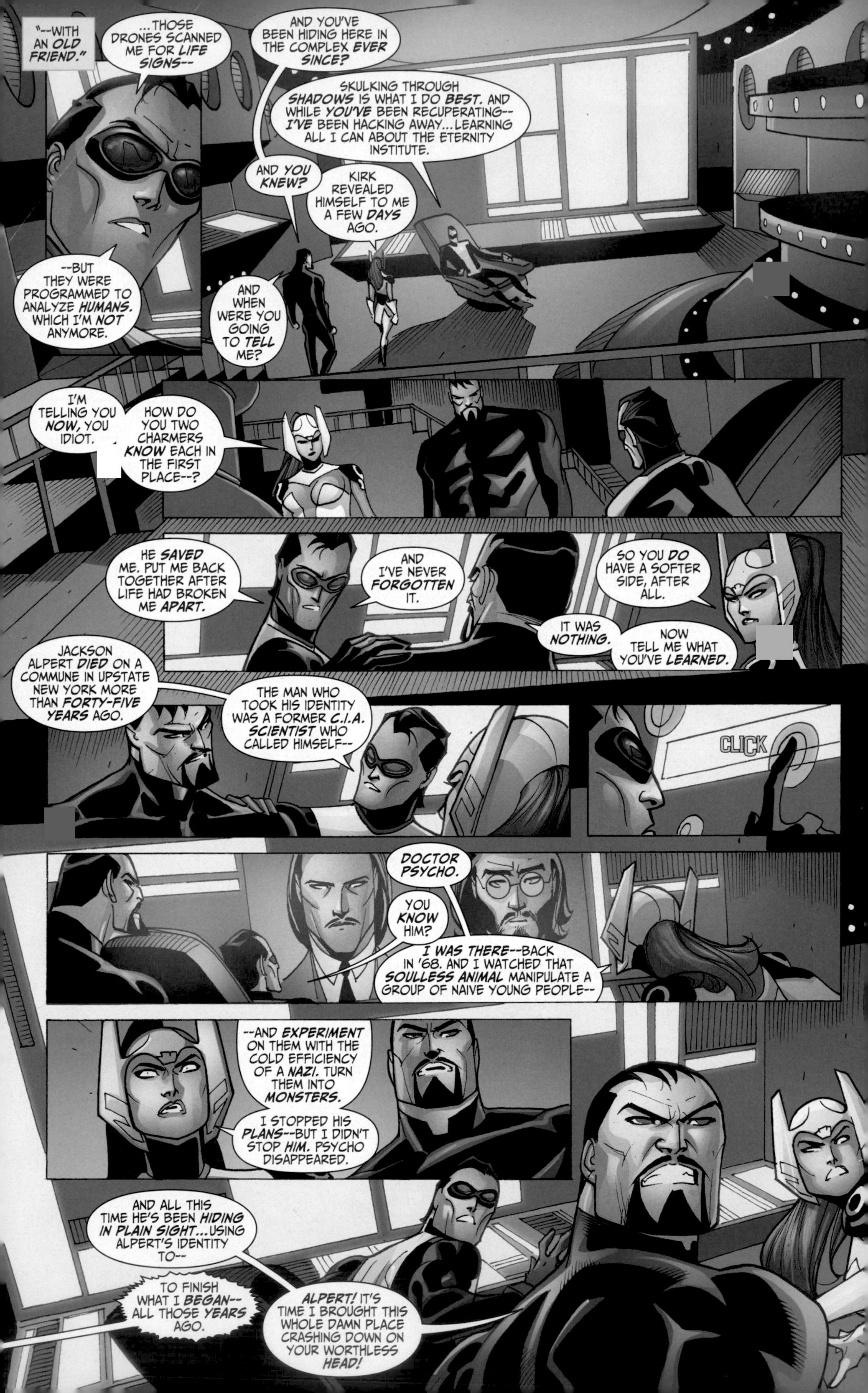
"--WITH AN OLD FRIEND."
...THOSE DRONES SCANNED ME FOR LIFE SIGNS--
--BUT THEY WERE PROGRAMMED TO ANALYZE HUMANS. WHICH I'M NOT ANYMORE.
AND YOU'VE BEEN HIDING HERE IN THE COMPLEX EVER SINCE?
SKULKING THROUGH SHADOWS IS WHAT I DO BEST. AND WHILE YOU'VE BEEN RECUPERATING-- I'VE BEEN HACKING AWAY...LEARNING ALL I CAN ABOUT THE ETERNITY INSTITUTE.
AND YOU KNEW?
KIRK REVEALED HIMSELF TO ME A FEW DAYS AGO.
AND WHEN WERE YOU GOING TO TELL ME?
I'M TELLING YOU NOW, YOU IDIOT.
HOW DO YOU TWO CHARMERS KNOW EACH IN THE FIRST PLACE--?
HE SAVED ME. PUT ME BACK TOGETHER AFTER LIFE HAD BROKEN ME APART.
AND I'VE NEVER FORGOTTEN IT.
SO YOU DO HAVE A SOFTER SIDE, AFTER ALL.
IT WAS NOTHING.
NOW TELL ME WHAT YOU'VE LEARNED.
JACKSON ALPERT DIED ON A COMMUNE IN UPSTATE NEW YORK MORE THAN FORTY-FIVE YEARS AGO.
THE MAN WHO TOOK HIS IDENTITY WAS A FORMER C.I.A. SCIENTIST WHO CALLED HIMSELF--
CLICK
DOCTOR PSYCHO.
YOU KNOW HIM?
I WAS THERE--BACK IN '68. AND I WATCHED THAT SOULLESS ANIMAL MANIPULATE A GROUP OF NAIVE YOUNG PEOPLE--
--AND EXPERIMENT ON THEM WITH THE COLD EFFICIENCY OF A NAZI. TURN THEM INTO MONSTERS.
I STOPPED HIS PLANS--BUT I DIDN'T STOP HIM. PSYCHO DISAPPEARED.
AND ALL THIS TIME HE'S BEEN HIDING IN PLAIN SIGHT...USING ALPERT'S IDENTITY TO--
TO FINISH WHAT I BEGAN-- ALL THOSE YEARS AGO.
ALPERT! IT'S TIME I BROUGHT THIS WHOLE DAMN PLACE CRASHING DOWN ON YOUR WORTHLESS HEAD!

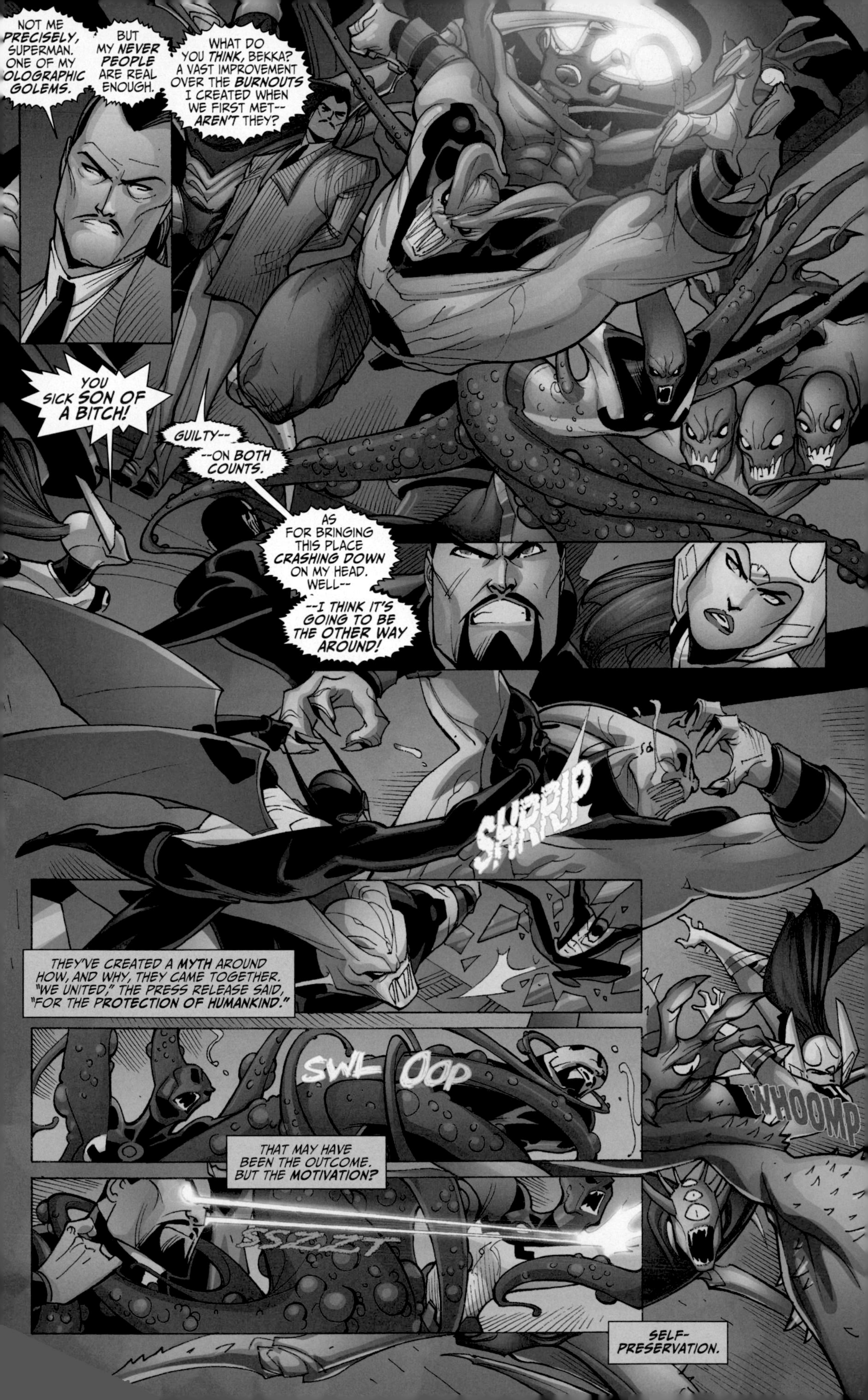
NOT ME PRECISELY, SUPERMAN. ONE OF MY OLOGRAPHIC GOLEMS.
BUT MY NEVER PEOPLE ARE REAL ENOUGH.
WHAT DO YOU THINK, BEKKA? A VAST IMPROVEMENT OVER THE BURNOUTS I CREATED WHEN WE FIRST MET--AREN'T THEY?
YOU SICK SON OF A BITCH!
GUILTY--
--ON BOTH COUNTS.
AS FOR BRINGING THIS PLACE CRASHING DOWN ON MY HEAD. WELL--
--I THINK IT'S GOING TO BE THE OTHER WAY AROUND!
SHRRIP
THEY'VE CREATED A MYTH AROUND HOW, AND WHY, THEY CAME TOGETHER. "WE UNITED," THE PRESS RELEASE SAID, "FOR THE PROTECTION OF HUMANKIND."
SWL OOP
WHOOMP
THAT MAY HAVE BEEN THE OUTCOME. BUT THE MOTIVATION?
SSZZZT
SELF-PRESERVATION.

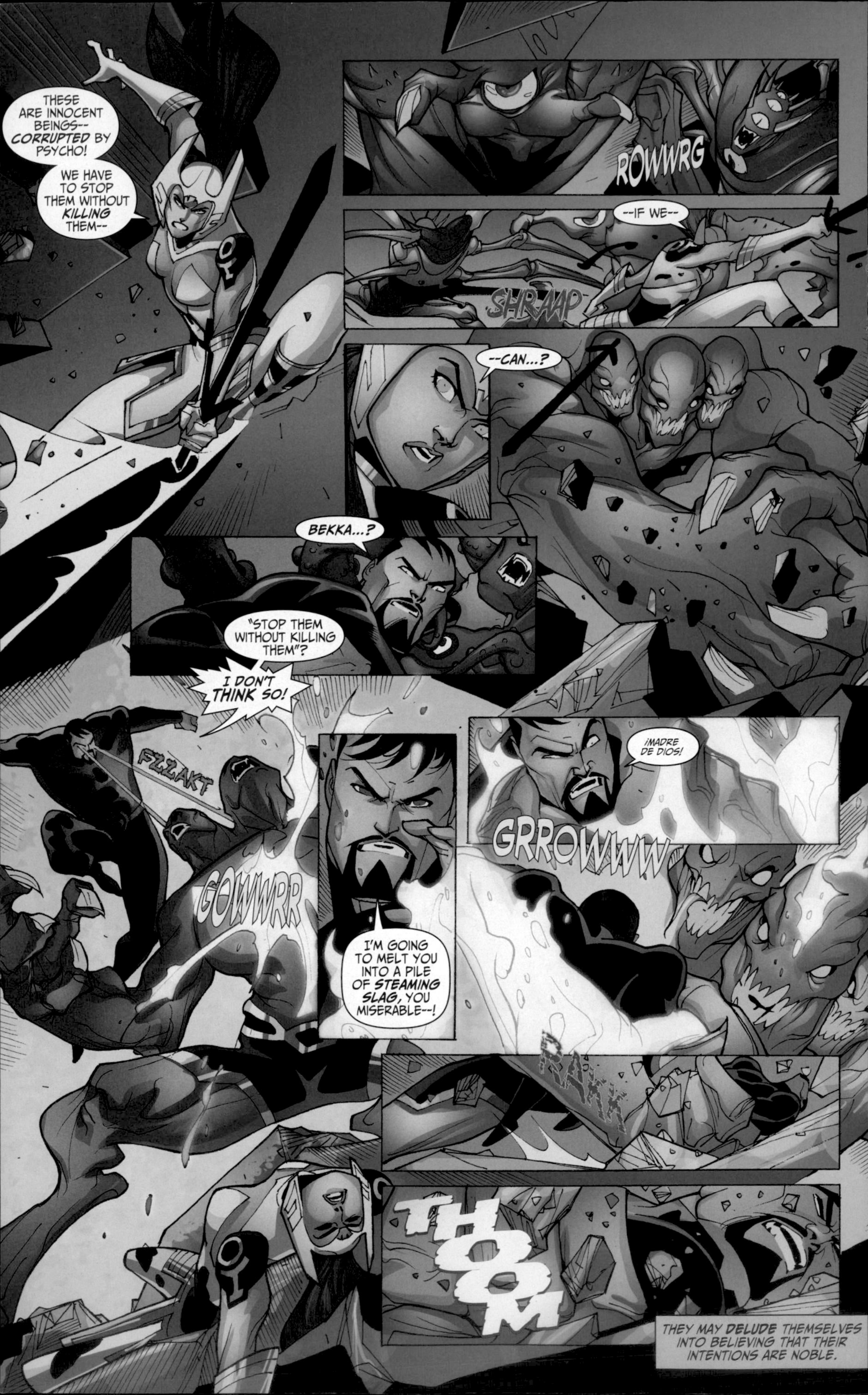
THESE ARE INNOCENT BEINGS-- CORRUPTED BY PSYCHO!
WE HAVE TO STOP THEM WITHOUT KILLING THEM--
ROWWRG
--IF WE--
SHRAAP
--CAN...?
BEKKA...?
"STOP THEM WITHOUT KILLING THEM"?
I DON'T THINK SO!
FZZAKT
¡MADRE DE DIOS!
GRROWWW
GOWWRR
I'M GOING TO MELT YOU INTO A PILE OF STEAMING SLAG, YOU MISERABLE--!
RAK
THOOM
THEY MAY DELUDE THEMSELVES INTO BELIEVING THAT THEIR INTENTIONS ARE NOBLE.

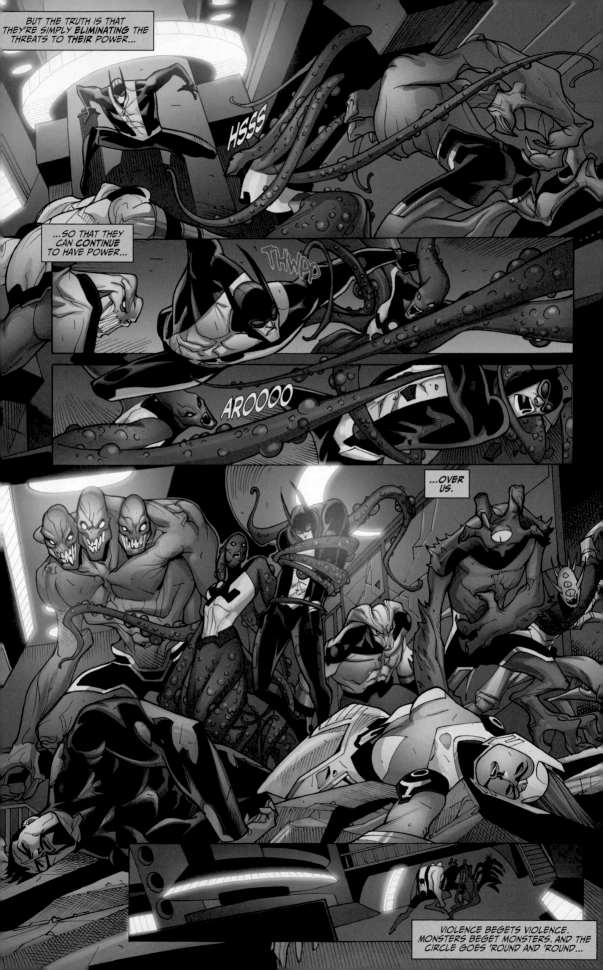

BUT THE TRUTH IS THAT THEY'RE SIMPLY ELIMINATING THE THREATS TO THEIR POWER...

HSSS

...SO THAT THEY CAN CONTINUE TO HAVE POWER...

THWPP

AROOOO

...OVER US.

VIOLENCE BEGETS VIOLENCE. MONSTERS BEGET MONSTERS. AND THE CIRCLE GOES 'ROUND AND 'ROUND...

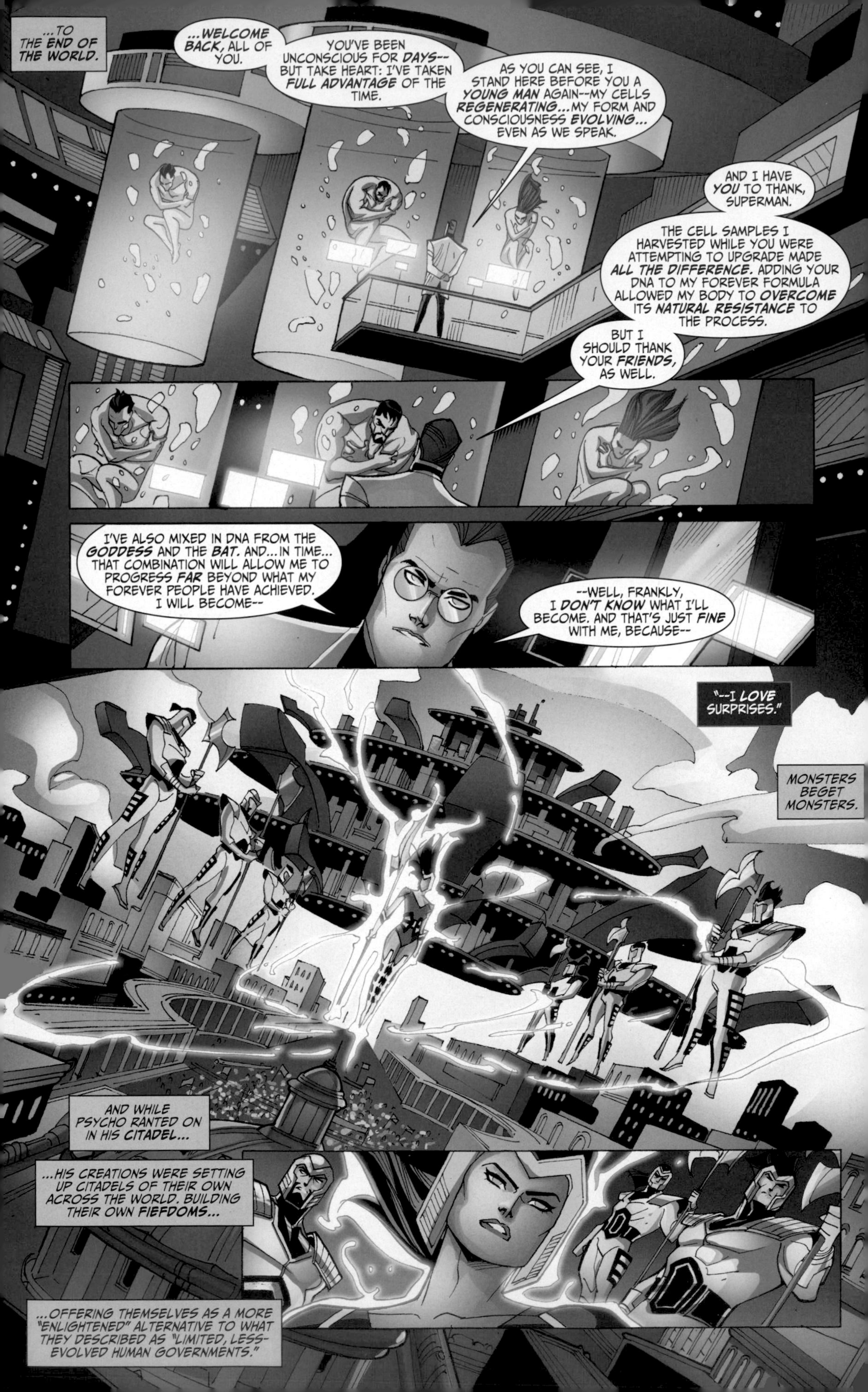
...TO THE END OF THE WORLD.
...WELCOME BACK, ALL OF YOU.
YOU'VE BEEN UNCONSCIOUS FOR DAYS-- BUT TAKE HEART: I'VE TAKEN FULL ADVANTAGE OF THE TIME.
AS YOU CAN SEE, I STAND HERE BEFORE YOU A YOUNG MAN AGAIN--MY CELLS REGENERATING...MY FORM AND CONSCIOUSNESS EVOLVING... EVEN AS WE SPEAK.
AND I HAVE YOU TO THANK, SUPERMAN.
THE CELL SAMPLES I HARVESTED WHILE YOU WERE ATTEMPTING TO UPGRADE MADE ALL THE DIFFERENCE. ADDING YOUR DNA TO MY FOREVER FORMULA ALLOWED MY BODY TO OVERCOME ITS NATURAL RESISTANCE TO THE PROCESS.
BUT I SHOULD THANK YOUR FRIENDS, AS WELL.
I'VE ALSO MIXED IN DNA FROM THE GODDESS AND THE BAT. AND...IN TIME... THAT COMBINATION WILL ALLOW ME TO PROGRESS FAR BEYOND WHAT MY FOREVER PEOPLE HAVE ACHIEVED. I WILL BECOME--
--WELL, FRANKLY, I DON'T KNOW WHAT I'LL BECOME. AND THAT'S JUST FINE WITH ME, BECAUSE--
"--I LOVE SURPRISES."
MONSTERS BEGET MONSTERS.
AND WHILE PSYCHO RANTED ON IN HIS CITADEL...
...HIS CREATIONS WERE SETTING UP CITADELS OF THEIR OWN ACROSS THE WORLD. BUILDING THEIR OWN FIEFDOMS...
...OFFERING THEMSELVES AS A MORE "ENLIGHTENED" ALTERNATIVE TO WHAT THEY DESCRIBED AS "LIMITED, LESS-EVOLVED HUMAN GOVERNMENTS."

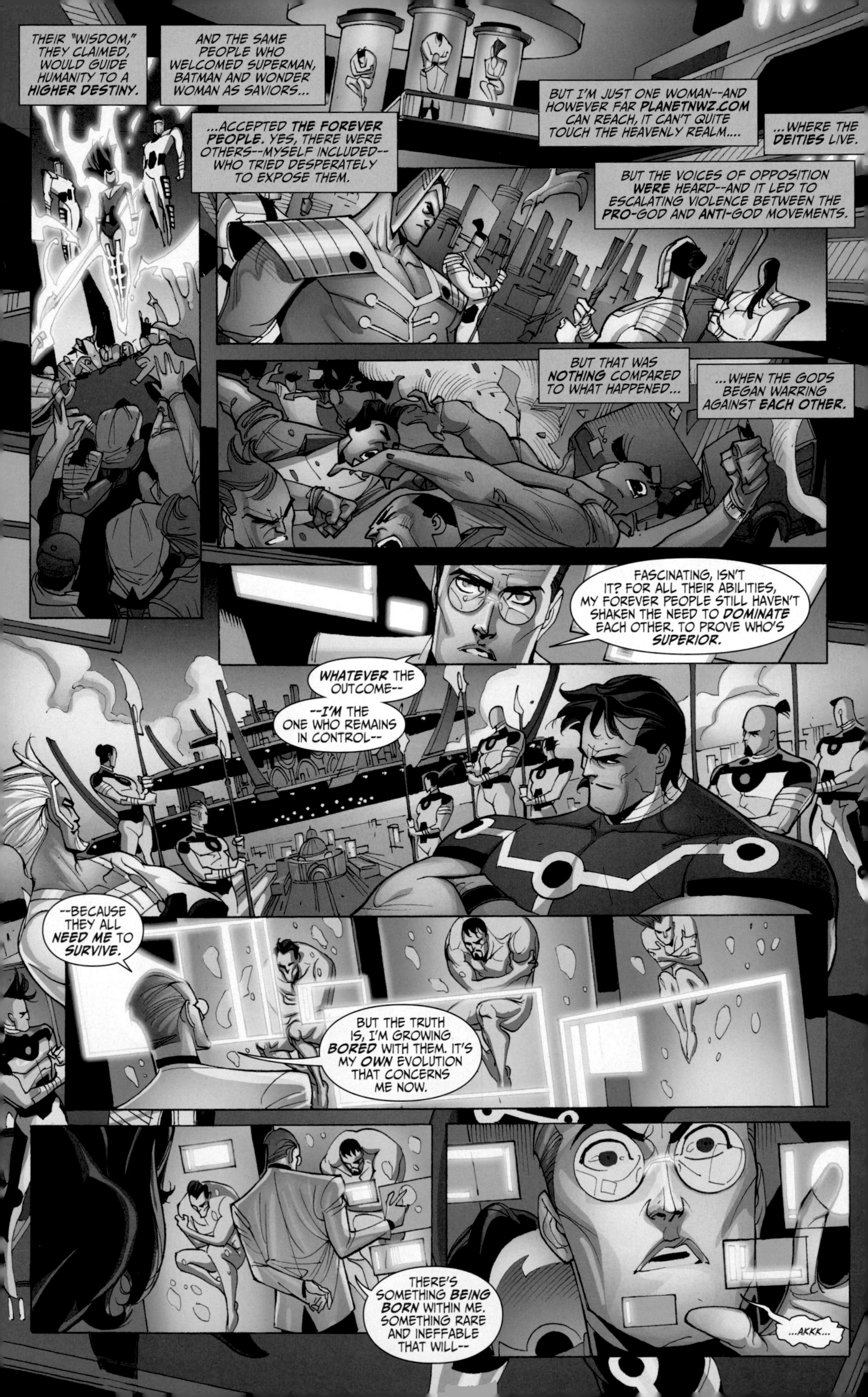
THEIR "WISDOM," THEY CLAIMED, WOULD GUIDE HUMANITY TO A HIGHER DESTINY.
AND THE SAME PEOPLE WHO WELCOMED SUPERMAN, BATMAN AND WONDER WOMAN AS SAVIORS...
...ACCEPTED THE FOREVER PEOPLE. YES, THERE WERE OTHERS--MYSELF INCLUDED--WHO TRIED DESPERATELY TO EXPOSE THEM.
BUT I'M JUST ONE WOMAN--AND HOWEVER FAR PLANETNWZ.COM CAN REACH, IT CAN'T QUITE TOUCH THE HEAVENLY REALM....
...WHERE THE DEITIES LIVE.
BUT THE VOICES OF OPPOSITION WERE HEARD--AND IT LED TO ESCALATING VIOLENCE BETWEEN THE PRO-GOD AND ANTI-GOD MOVEMENTS.
BUT THAT WAS NOTHING COMPARED TO WHAT HAPPENED...
...WHEN THE GODS BEGAN WARRING AGAINST EACH OTHER.
FASCINATING, ISN'T IT? FOR ALL THEIR ABILITIES, MY FOREVER PEOPLE STILL HAVEN'T SHAKEN THE NEED TO DOMINATE EACH OTHER. TO PROVE WHO'S SUPERIOR.
WHATEVER THE OUTCOME--
--I'M THE ONE WHO REMAINS IN CONTROL--
--BECAUSE THEY ALL NEED ME TO SURVIVE.
BUT THE TRUTH IS, I'M GROWING BORED WITH THEM. IT'S MY OWN EVOLUTION THAT CONCERNS ME NOW.
THERE'S SOMETHING BEING BORN WITHIN ME. SOMETHING RARE AND INEFFABLE THAT WILL--
...AKKK...

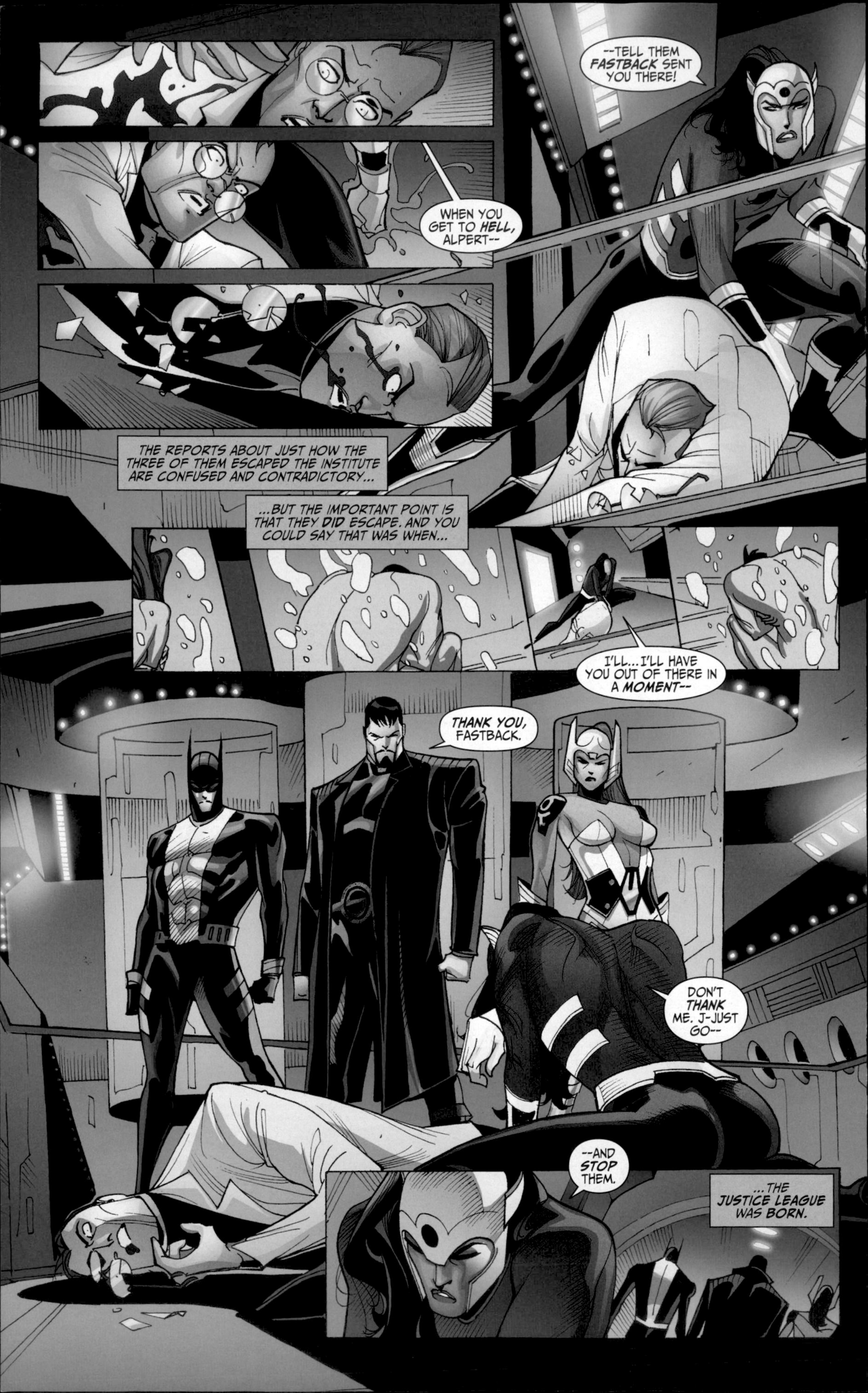
WHEN YOU GET TO HELL, ALPERT--
--TELL THEM FASTBACK SENT YOU THERE!
THE REPORTS ABOUT JUST HOW THE THREE OF THEM ESCAPED THE INSTITUTE ARE CONFUSED AND CONTRADICTORY...
...BUT THE IMPORTANT POINT IS THAT THEY DID ESCAPE. AND YOU COULD SAY THAT WAS WHEN...
I'LL...I'LL HAVE YOU OUT OF THERE IN A MOMENT--
THANK YOU, FASTBACK.
DON'T THANK ME. J-JUST GO--
--AND STOP THEM.
...THE JUSTICE LEAGUE WAS BORN.

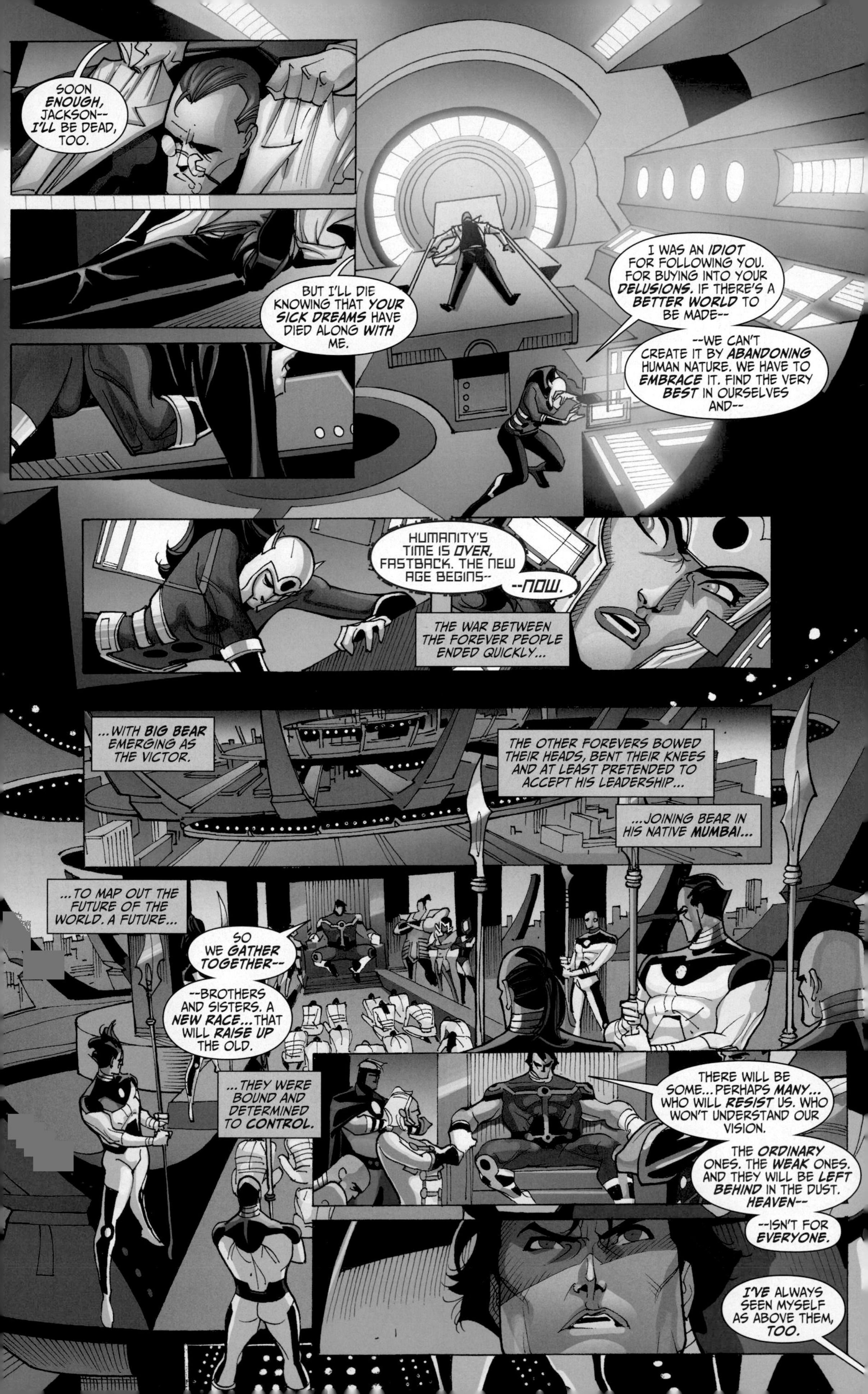
SOON ENOUGH, JACKSON-- I'LL BE DEAD, TOO.
BUT I'LL DIE KNOWING THAT YOUR SICK DREAMS HAVE DIED ALONG WITH ME.
I WAS AN IDIOT FOR FOLLOWING YOU. FOR BUYING INTO YOUR DELUSIONS. IF THERE'S A BETTER WORLD TO BE MADE--
--WE CAN'T CREATE IT BY ABANDONING HUMAN NATURE. WE HAVE TO EMBRACE IT. FIND THE VERY BEST IN OURSELVES AND--
HUMANITY'S TIME IS OVER, FASTBACK. THE NEW AGE BEGINS--
--NOW.
THE WAR BETWEEN THE FOREVER PEOPLE ENDED QUICKLY...
...WITH BIG BEAR EMERGING AS THE VICTOR.
THE OTHER FOREVERS BOWED THEIR HEADS, BENT THEIR KNEES AND AT LEAST PRETENDED TO ACCEPT HIS LEADERSHIP...
...JOINING BEAR IN HIS NATIVE MUMBAI...
...TO MAP OUT THE FUTURE OF THE WORLD. A FUTURE...
SO WE GATHER TOGETHER--
--BROTHERS AND SISTERS. A NEW RACE... THAT WILL RAISE UP THE OLD.
...THEY WERE BOUND AND DETERMINED TO CONTROL.
THERE WILL BE SOME... PERHAPS MANY... WHO WILL RESIST US. WHO WON'T UNDERSTAND OUR VISION.
THE ORDINARY ONES. THE WEAK ONES. AND THEY WILL BE LEFT BEHIND IN THE DUST. HEAVEN--
--ISN'T FOR EVERYONE.
I'VE ALWAYS SEEN MYSELF AS ABOVE THEM, TOO.

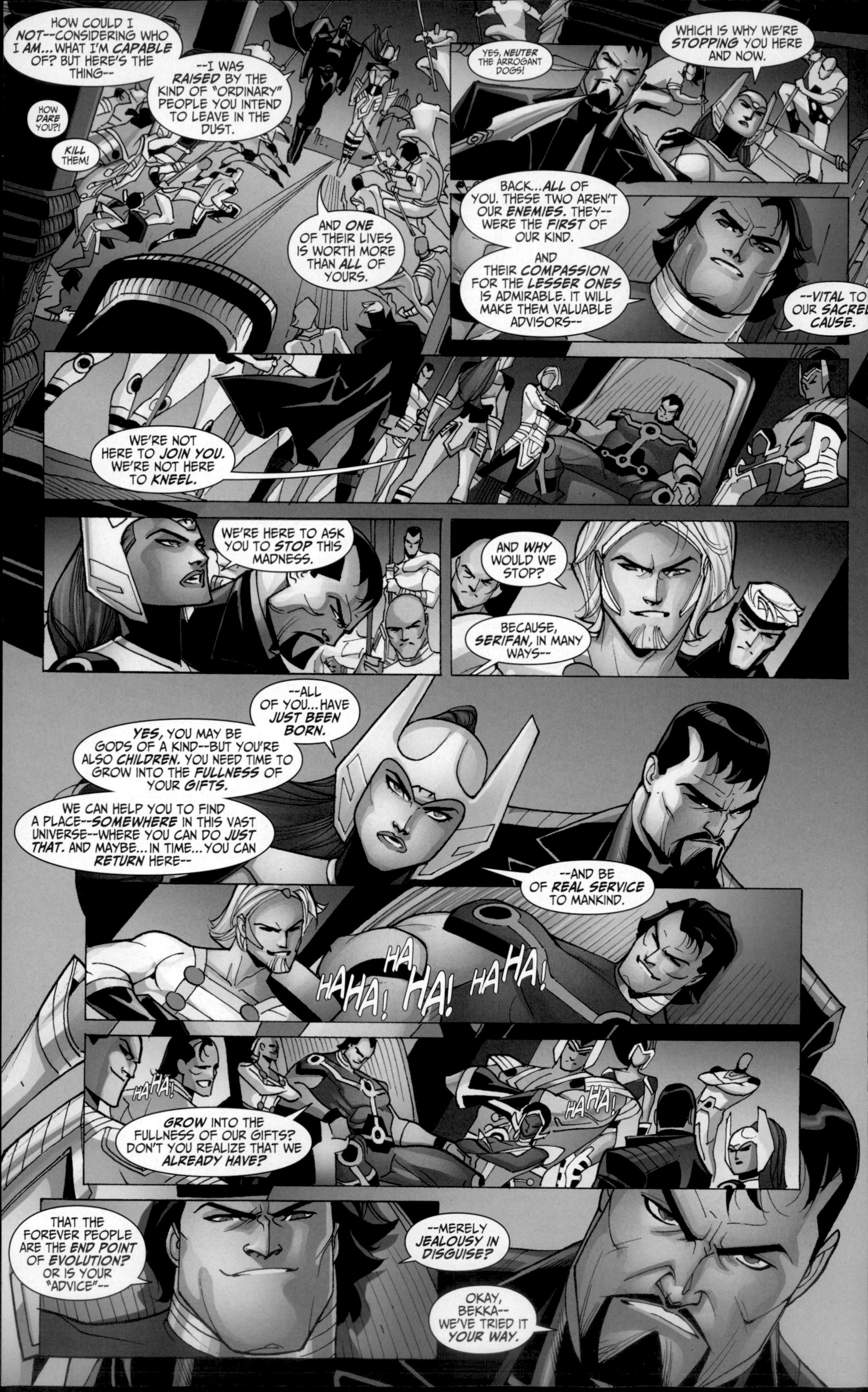
HOW COULD I NOT--CONSIDERING WHO I AM...WHAT I'M CAPABLE OF? BUT HERE'S THE THING--
--I WAS RAISED BY THE KIND OF "ORDINARY" PEOPLE YOU INTEND TO LEAVE IN THE DUST.
HOW DARE YOU?!
KILL THEM!
AND ONE OF THEIR LIVES IS WORTH MORE THAN ALL OF YOURS.
YES, NEUTER THE ARROGANT DOGS!
WHICH IS WHY WE'RE STOPPING YOU HERE AND NOW.
BACK...ALL OF YOU. THESE TWO AREN'T OUR ENEMIES. THEY--WERE THE FIRST OF OUR KIND.
AND THEIR COMPASSION FOR THE LESSER ONES IS ADMIRABLE. IT WILL MAKE THEM VALUABLE ADVISORS--
--VITAL TO OUR SACRED CAUSE.
WE'RE NOT HERE TO JOIN YOU. WE'RE NOT HERE TO KNEEL.
WE'RE HERE TO ASK YOU TO STOP THIS MADNESS.
AND WHY WOULD WE STOP?
BECAUSE, SERIFAN, IN MANY WAYS--
--ALL OF YOU...HAVE JUST BEEN BORN.
YES, YOU MAY BE GODS OF A KIND--BUT YOU'RE ALSO CHILDREN. YOU NEED TIME TO GROW INTO THE FULLNESS OF YOUR GIFTS.
WE CAN HELP YOU TO FIND A PLACE--SOMEWHERE IN THIS VAST UNIVERSE--WHERE YOU CAN DO JUST THAT. AND MAYBE...IN TIME...YOU CAN RETURN HERE--
--AND BE OF REAL SERVICE TO MANKIND.
HAHA! HA HA! HAHA!
HAHA!
GROW INTO THE FULLNESS OF OUR GIFTS? DON'T YOU REALIZE THAT WE ALREADY HAVE?
HAHA!
THAT THE FOREVER PEOPLE ARE THE END POINT OF EVOLUTION? OR IS YOUR "ADVICE"--
--MERELY JEALOUSY IN DISGUISE?
OKAY, BEKKA--WE'VE TRIED IT YOUR WAY.

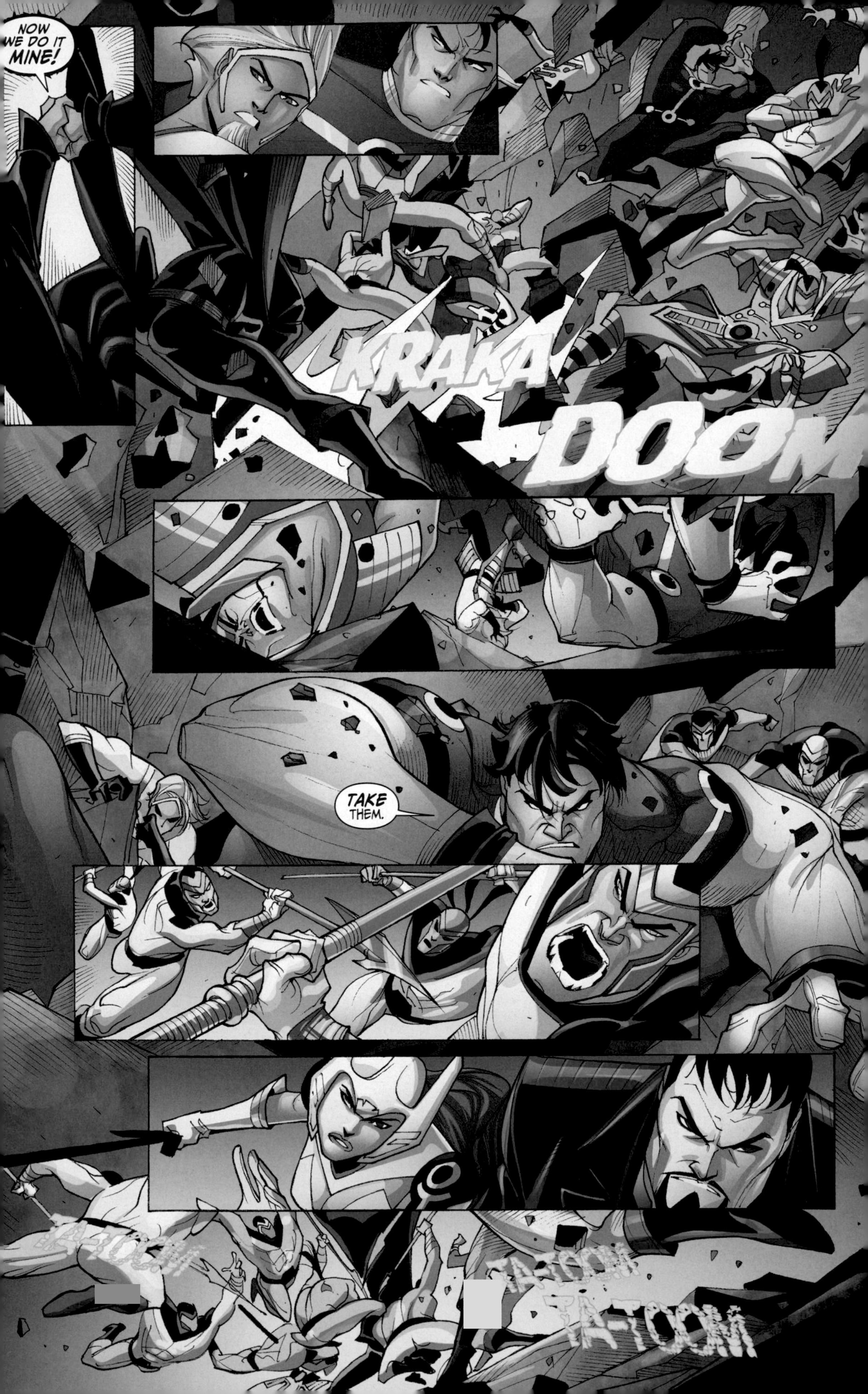
NOW WE DO IT MINE!
KRAKA
DOOM
TAKE THEM.
TA-TOOM
TA-TOOM
TA-TOOM

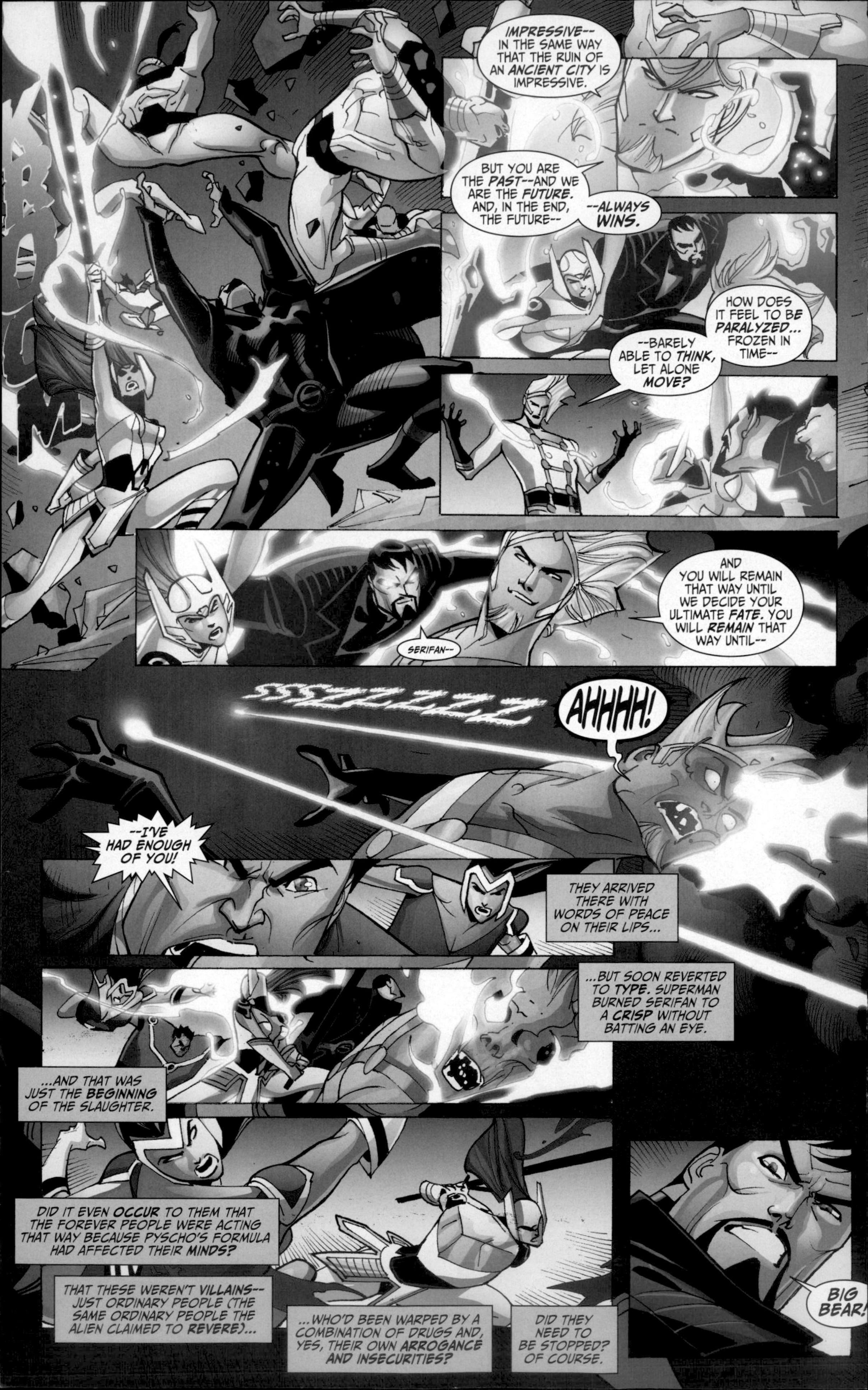

IMPRESSIVE-- IN THE SAME WAY THAT THE RUIN OF AN ANCIENT CITY IS IMPRESSIVE.
BUT YOU ARE THE PAST--AND WE ARE THE FUTURE. AND, IN THE END, THE FUTURE--
--ALWAYS WINS.
HOW DOES IT FEEL TO BE PARALYZED... FROZEN IN TIME--
--BARELY ABLE TO THINK, LET ALONE MOVE?
AND YOU WILL REMAIN THAT WAY UNTIL WE DECIDE YOUR ULTIMATE FATE. YOU WILL REMAIN THAT WAY UNTIL--
SERIFAN--
SSSZZZZZZ
AHHHH!
--I'VE HAD ENOUGH OF YOU!
THEY ARRIVED THERE WITH WORDS OF PEACE ON THEIR LIPS...
...BUT SOON REVERTED TO TYPE. SUPERMAN BURNED SERIFAN TO A CRISP WITHOUT BATTING AN EYE.
...AND THAT WAS JUST THE BEGINNING OF THE SLAUGHTER.
DID IT EVEN OCCUR TO THEM THAT THE FOREVER PEOPLE WERE ACTING THAT WAY BECAUSE PYSCHO'S FORMULA HAD AFFECTED THEIR MINDS?
THAT THESE WEREN'T VILLAINS-- JUST ORDINARY PEOPLE (THE SAME ORDINARY PEOPLE THE ALIEN CLAIMED TO REVERE)...
...WHO'D BEEN WARPED BY A COMBINATION OF DRUGS AND, YES, THEIR OWN ARROGANCE AND INSECURITIES?
DID THEY NEED TO BE STOPPED? OF COURSE.
BIG BEAR!

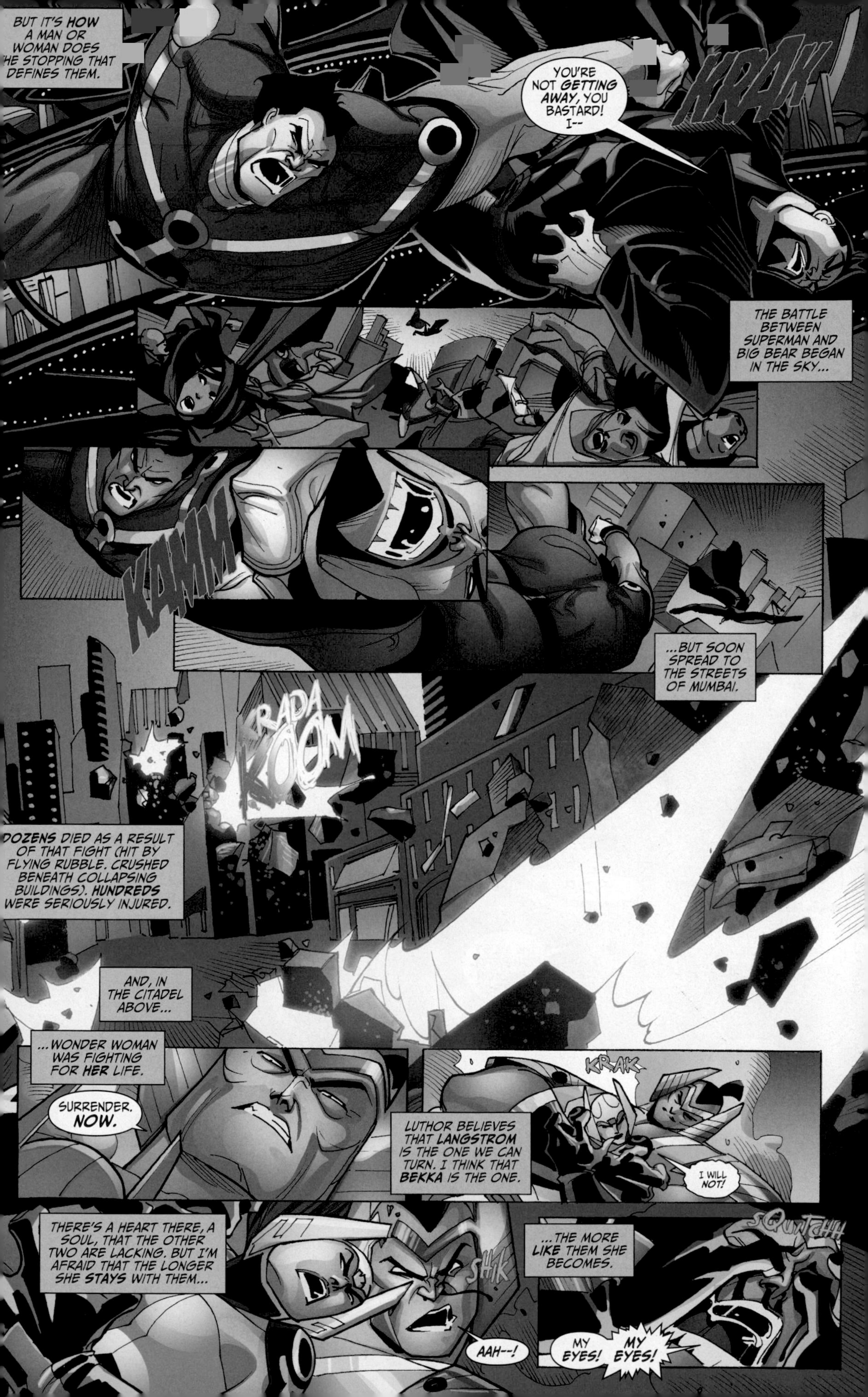
BUT IT'S HOW A MAN OR WOMAN DOES HE STOPPING THAT DEFINES THEM.
YOU'RE NOT GETTING AWAY, YOU BASTARD! I--
KRAK
THE BATTLE BETWEEN SUPERMAN AND BIG BEAR BEGAN IN THE SKY...
KAMM
...BUT SOON SPREAD TO THE STREETS OF MUMBAI.
KRADA KOOM
DOZENS DIED AS A RESULT OF THAT FIGHT (HIT BY FLYING RUBBLE. CRUSHED BENEATH COLLAPSING BUILDINGS). HUNDREDS WERE SERIOUSLY INJURED.
AND, IN THE CITADEL ABOVE...
...WONDER WOMAN WAS FIGHTING FOR HER LIFE.
SURRENDER. NOW.
KRAK
LUTHOR BELIEVES THAT LANGSTROM IS THE ONE WE CAN TURN. I THINK THAT BEKKA IS THE ONE.
I WILL NOT!
THERE'S A HEART THERE, A SOUL, THAT THE OTHER TWO ARE LACKING. BUT I'M AFRAID THAT THE LONGER SHE STAYS WITH THEM...
SHIK
AAH--!
...THE MORE LIKE THEM SHE BECOMES.
SQUTCHHH
MY EYES!
MY EYES!

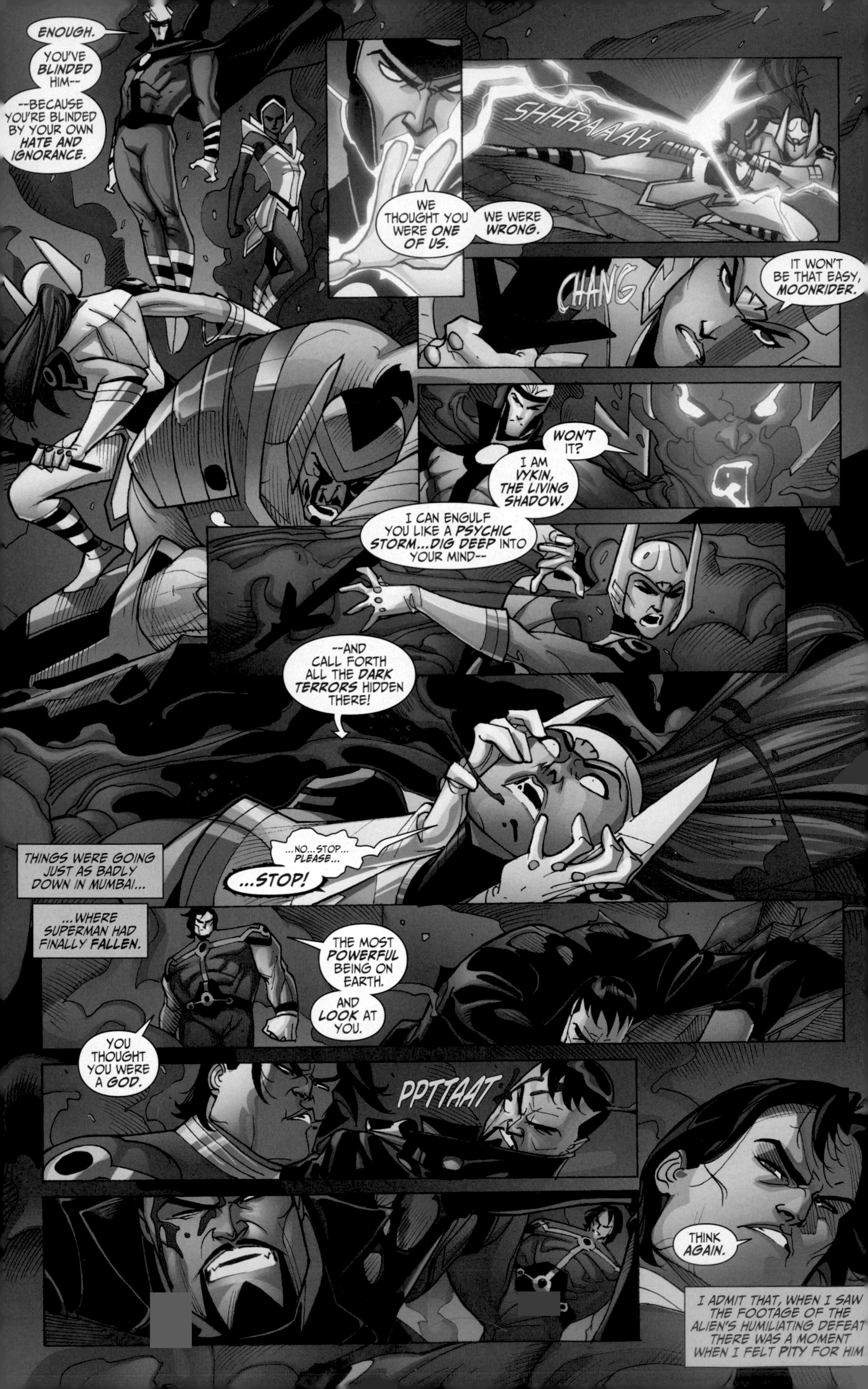
ENOUGH.
YOU'VE BLINDED HIM--
--BECAUSE YOU'RE BLINDED BY YOUR OWN HATE AND IGNORANCE.
SHHRAAAK
WE THOUGHT YOU WERE ONE OF US.
WE WERE WRONG.
CHANG
IT WON'T BE THAT EASY, MOONRIDER.
WON'T IT?
I AM VYKIN, THE LIVING SHADOW.
I CAN ENGULF YOU LIKE A PSYCHIC STORM...DIG DEEP INTO YOUR MIND--
--AND CALL FORTH ALL THE DARK TERRORS HIDDEN THERE!
...NO...STOP... PLEASE...
...STOP!
THINGS WERE GOING JUST AS BADLY DOWN IN MUMBAI...
...WHERE SUPERMAN HAD FINALLY FALLEN.
THE MOST POWERFUL BEING ON EARTH.
AND LOOK AT YOU.
YOU THOUGHT YOU WERE A GOD.
PPTTAAT
THINK AGAIN.
I ADMIT THAT, WHEN I SAW THE FOOTAGE OF THE ALIEN'S HUMILIATING DEFEAT THERE WAS A MOMENT WHEN I FELT PITY FOR HIM

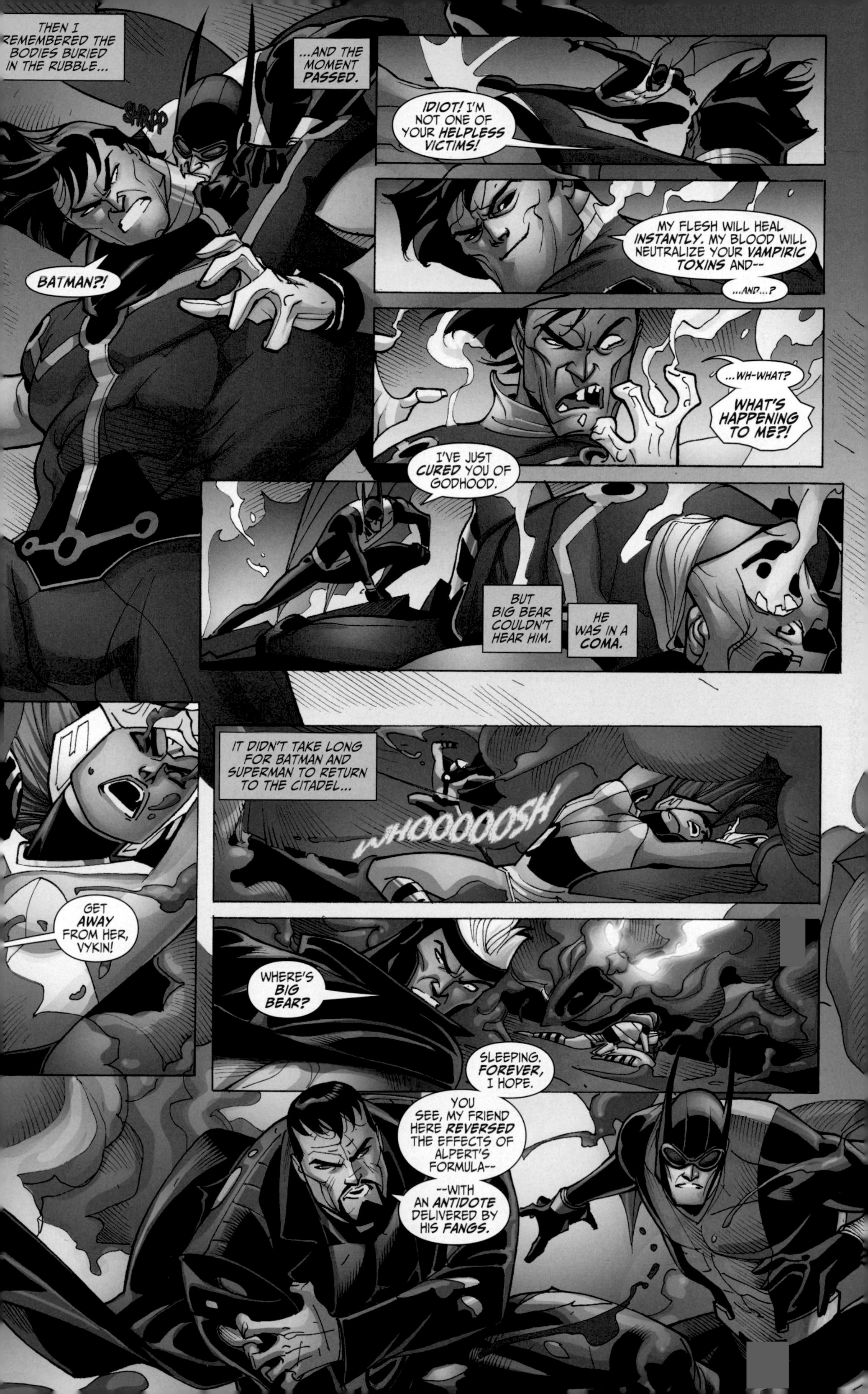
THEN I REMEMBERED THE BODIES BURIED IN THE RUBBLE...
SHRPP
...AND THE MOMENT PASSED.
BATMAN?!
IDIOT! I'M NOT ONE OF YOUR HELPLESS VICTIMS!
MY FLESH WILL HEAL INSTANTLY. MY BLOOD WILL NEUTRALIZE YOUR VAMPIRIC TOXINS AND--
...AND...?
...WH-WHAT?
WHAT'S HAPPENING TO ME?!
I'VE JUST CURED YOU OF GODHOOD.
BUT BIG BEAR COULDN'T HEAR HIM.
HE WAS IN A COMA.
IT DIDN'T TAKE LONG FOR BATMAN AND SUPERMAN TO RETURN TO THE CITADEL...
WHOOOOOOSH
GET AWAY FROM HER, VYKIN!
WHERE'S BIG BEAR?
SLEEPING. FOREVER, I HOPE.
YOU SEE, MY FRIEND HERE REVERSED THE EFFECTS OF ALPERT'S FORMULA--
--WITH AN ANTIDOTE DELIVERED BY HIS FANGS.

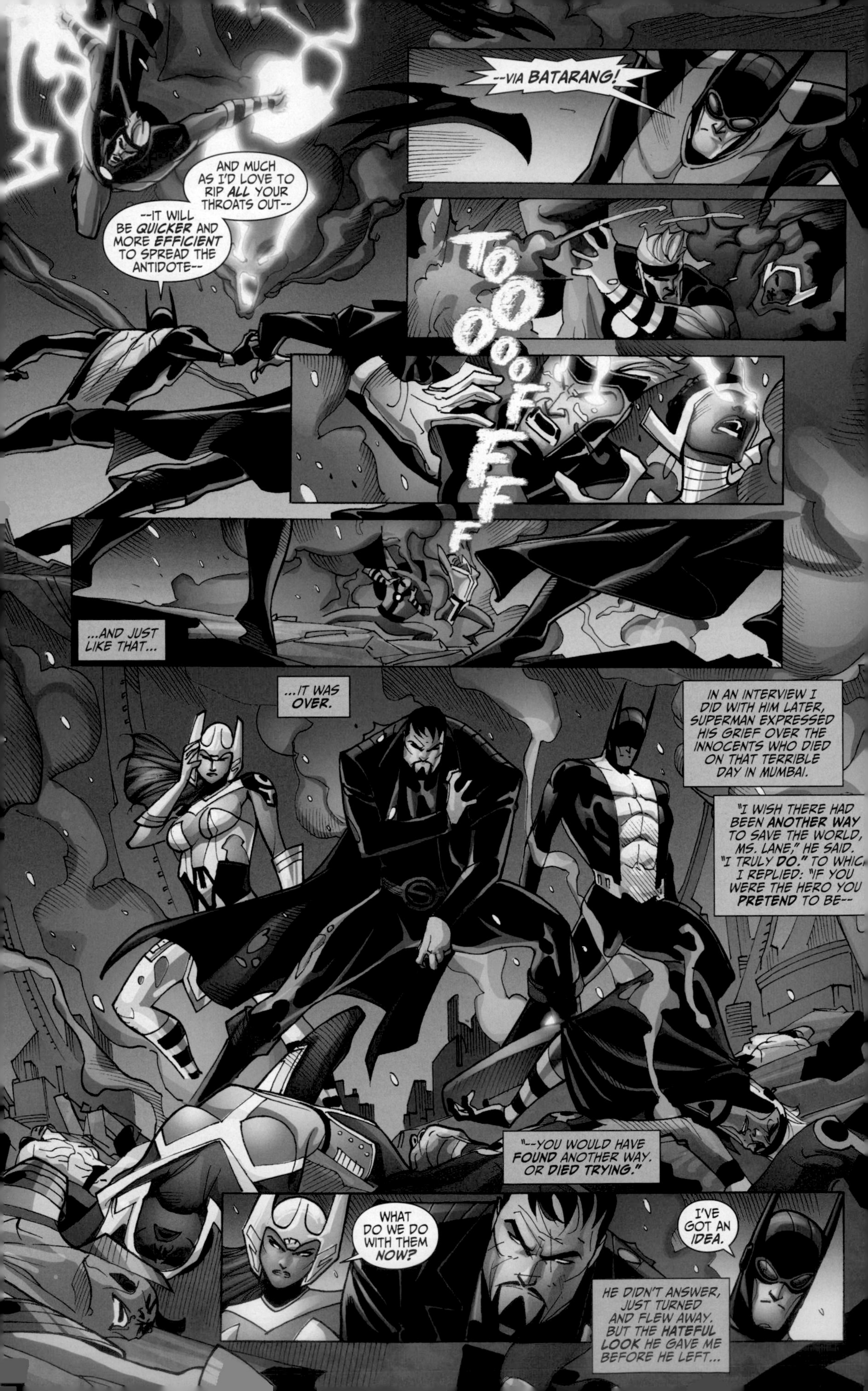
--VIA BATARANG!
AND MUCH AS I'D LOVE TO RIP ALL YOUR THROATS OUT--
--IT WILL BE QUICKER AND MORE EFFICIENT TO SPREAD THE ANTIDOTE--
TOOOOOOFFFFFF
...AND JUST LIKE THAT...
...IT WAS OVER.
IN AN INTERVIEW I DID WITH HIM LATER, SUPERMAN EXPRESSED HIS GRIEF OVER THE INNOCENTS WHO DIED ON THAT TERRIBLE DAY IN MUMBAI.
"I WISH THERE HAD BEEN ANOTHER WAY TO SAVE THE WORLD, MS. LANE," HE SAID. "I TRULY DO." TO WHICH I REPLIED: "IF YOU WERE THE HERO YOU PRETEND TO BE--
"--YOU WOULD HAVE FOUND ANOTHER WAY. OR DIED TRYING."
WHAT DO WE DO WITH THEM NOW?
I'VE GOT AN IDEA.
HE DIDN'T ANSWER, JUST TURNED AND FLEW AWAY. BUT THE HATEFUL LOOK HE GAVE ME BEFORE HE LEFT...

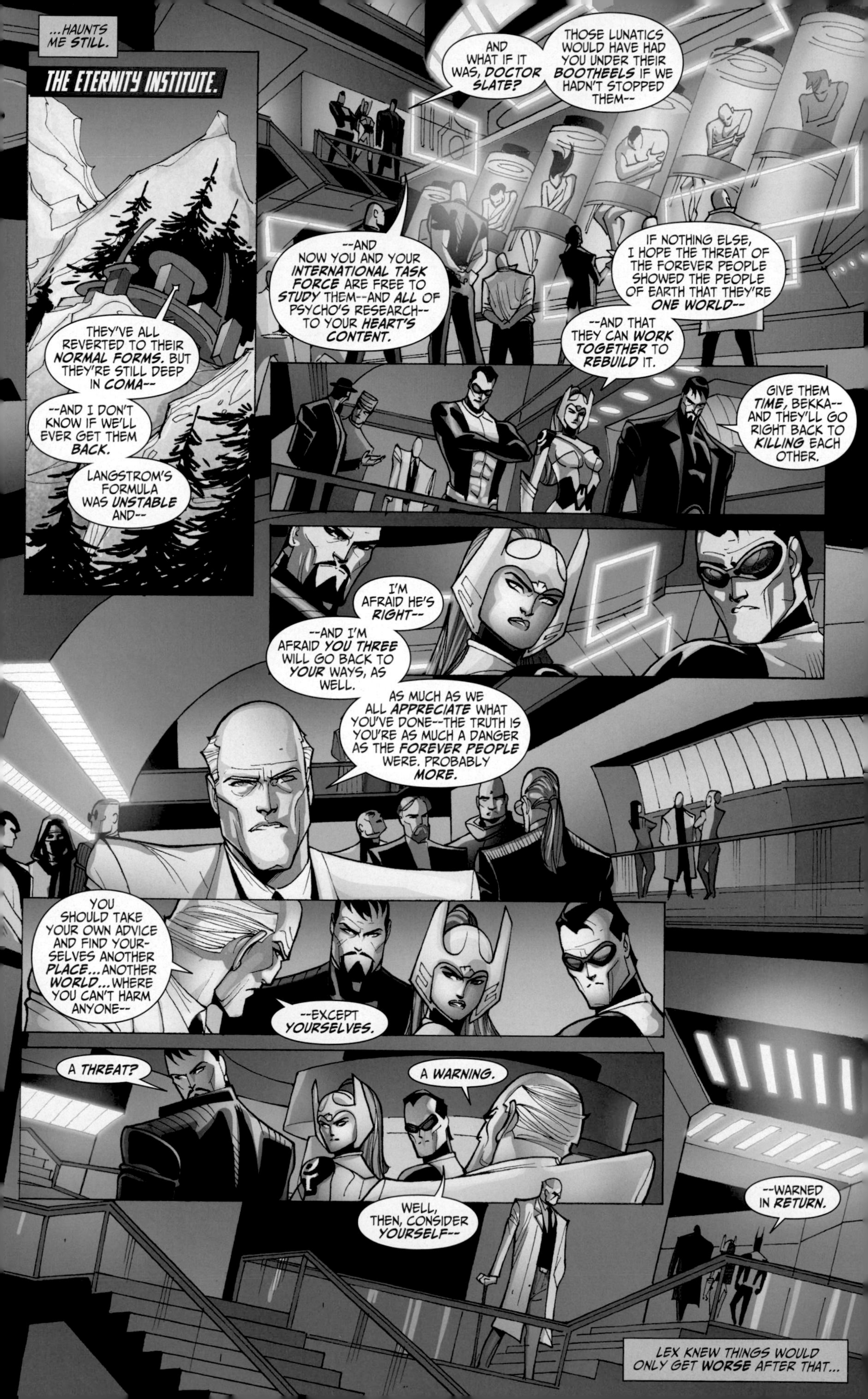
...HAUNTS ME STILL.
THE ETERNITY INSTITUTE.
THEY'VE ALL REVERTED TO THEIR NORMAL FORMS. BUT THEY'RE STILL DEEP IN COMA--
--AND I DON'T KNOW IF WE'LL EVER GET THEM BACK.
LANGSTROM'S FORMULA WAS UNSTABLE AND--
AND WHAT IF IT WAS, DOCTOR SLATE?
THOSE LUNATICS WOULD HAVE HAD YOU UNDER THEIR BOOTHEELS IF WE HADN'T STOPPED THEM--
--AND NOW YOU AND YOUR INTERNATIONAL TASK FORCE ARE FREE TO STUDY THEM--AND ALL OF PSYCHO'S RESEARCH--TO YOUR HEART'S CONTENT.
IF NOTHING ELSE, I HOPE THE THREAT OF THE FOREVER PEOPLE SHOWED THE PEOPLE OF EARTH THAT THEY'RE ONE WORLD--
--AND THAT THEY CAN WORK TOGETHER TO REBUILD IT.
GIVE THEM TIME, BEKKA--AND THEY'LL GO RIGHT BACK TO KILLING EACH OTHER.
I'M AFRAID HE'S RIGHT--
--AND I'M AFRAID YOU THREE WILL GO BACK TO YOUR WAYS, AS WELL.
AS MUCH AS WE ALL APPRECIATE WHAT YOU'VE DONE--THE TRUTH IS YOU'RE AS MUCH A DANGER AS THE FOREVER PEOPLE WERE. PROBABLY MORE.
YOU SHOULD TAKE YOUR OWN ADVICE AND FIND YOURSELVES ANOTHER PLACE...ANOTHER WORLD...WHERE YOU CAN'T HARM ANYONE--
--EXCEPT YOURSELVES.
A THREAT?
A WARNING.
WELL, THEN, CONSIDER YOURSELF--
--WARNED IN RETURN.
LEX KNEW THINGS WOULD ONLY GET WORSE AFTER THAT...

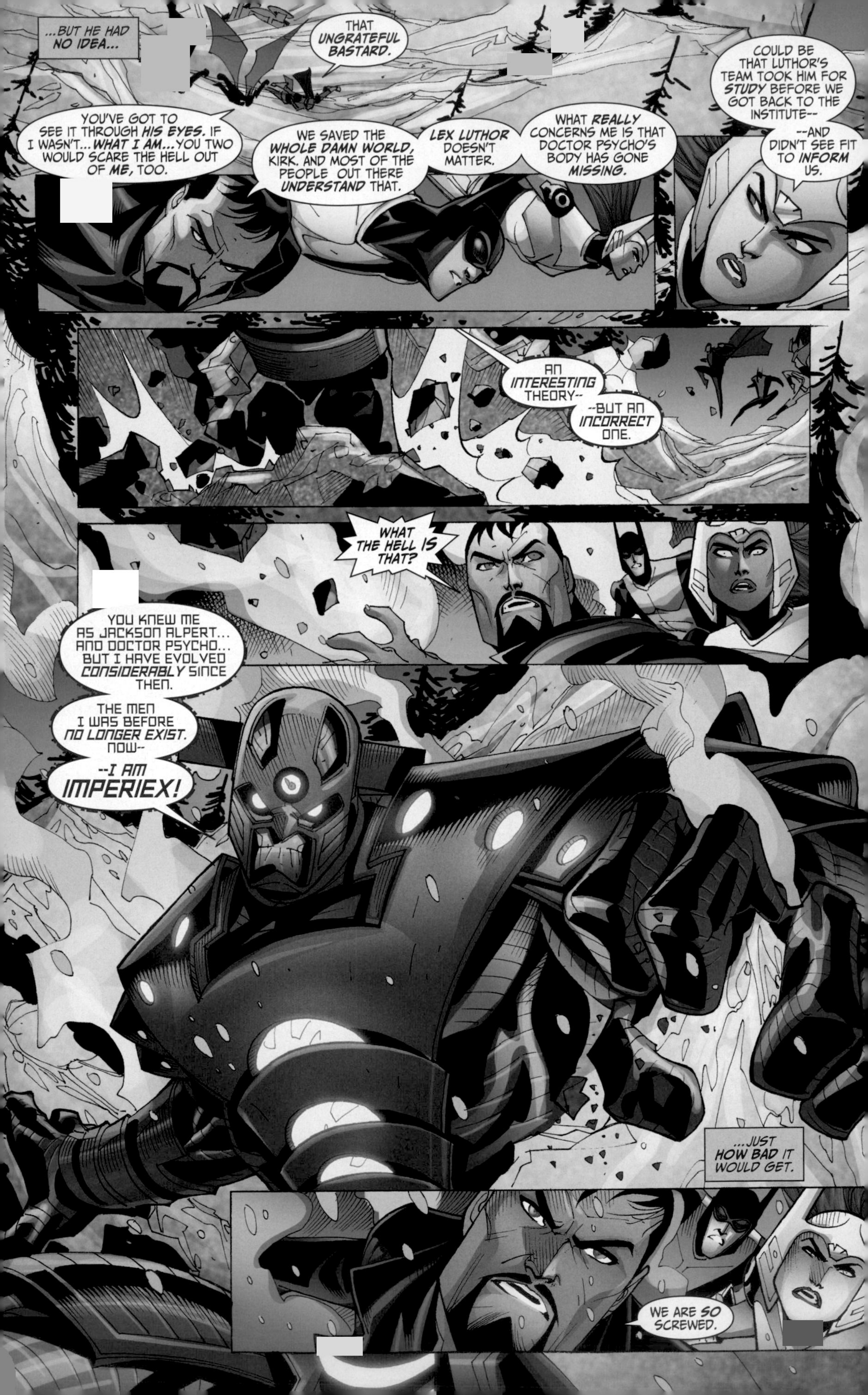

...BUT HE HAD NO IDEA...
THAT UNGRATEFUL BASTARD.
YOU'VE GOT TO SEE IT THROUGH HIS EYES. IF I WASN'T... WHAT I AM... YOU TWO WOULD SCARE THE HELL OUT OF ME, TOO.
WE SAVED THE WHOLE DAMN WORLD, KIRK. AND MOST OF THE PEOPLE OUT THERE UNDERSTAND THAT.
LEX LUTHOR DOESN'T MATTER.
WHAT REALLY CONCERNS ME IS THAT DOCTOR PSYCHO'S BODY HAS GONE MISSING.
COULD BE THAT LUTHOR'S TEAM TOOK HIM FOR STUDY BEFORE WE GOT BACK TO THE INSTITUTE--
--AND DIDN'T SEE FIT TO INFORM US.
AN INTERESTING THEORY--
--BUT AN INCORRECT ONE.
WHAT THE HELL IS THAT?
YOU KNEW ME AS JACKSON ALPERT... AND DOCTOR PSYCHO... BUT I HAVE EVOLVED CONSIDERABLY SINCE THEN.
THE MEN I WAS BEFORE NO LONGER EXIST. NOW--
--I AM IMPERIEX!
...JUST HOW BAD IT WOULD GET.
WE ARE SO SCREWED.

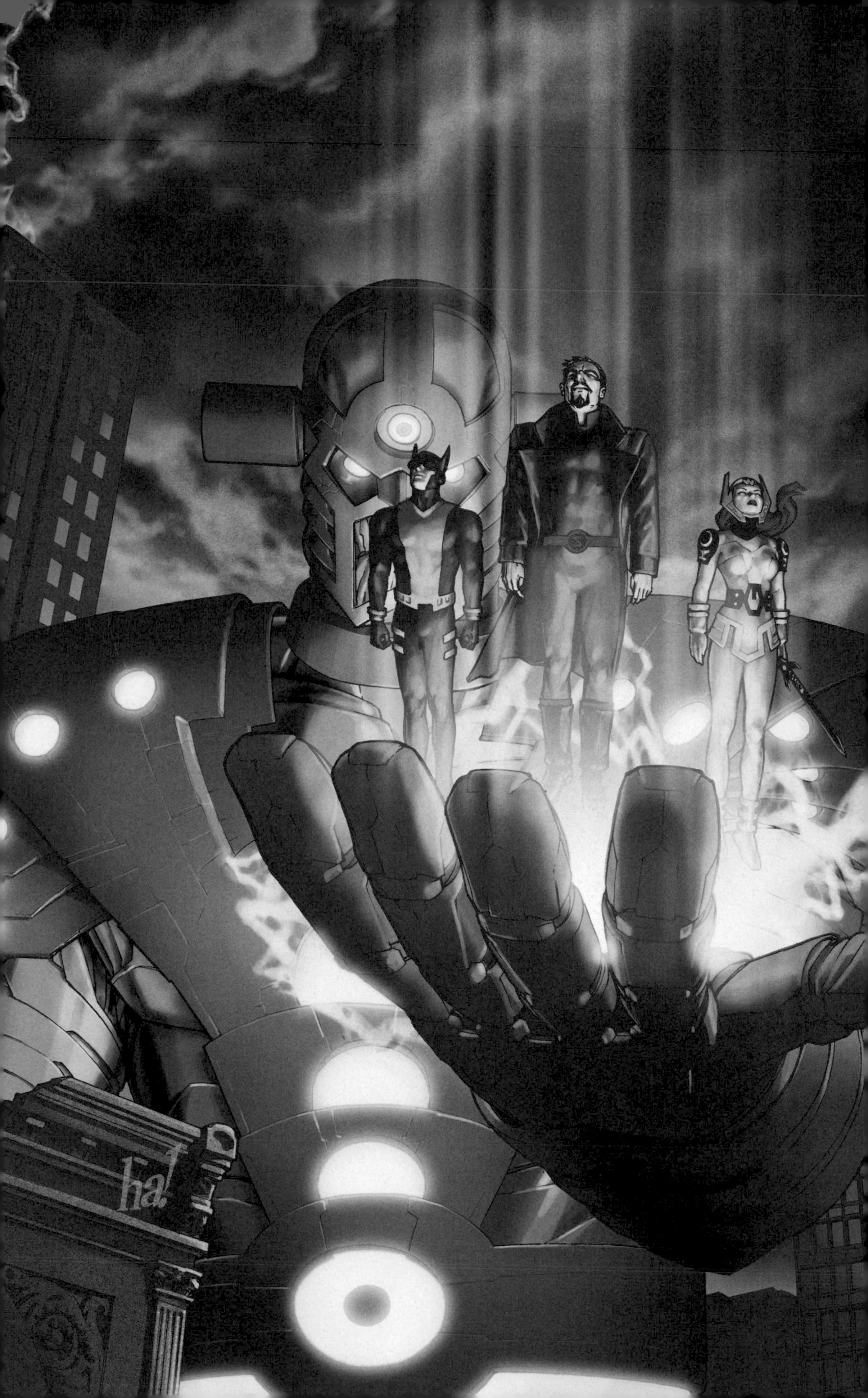
ha!

GENESIS PART 3

ART BY THONY SILAS

COLORS BY TONY AVIÑA

COVER ART BY GENE HA

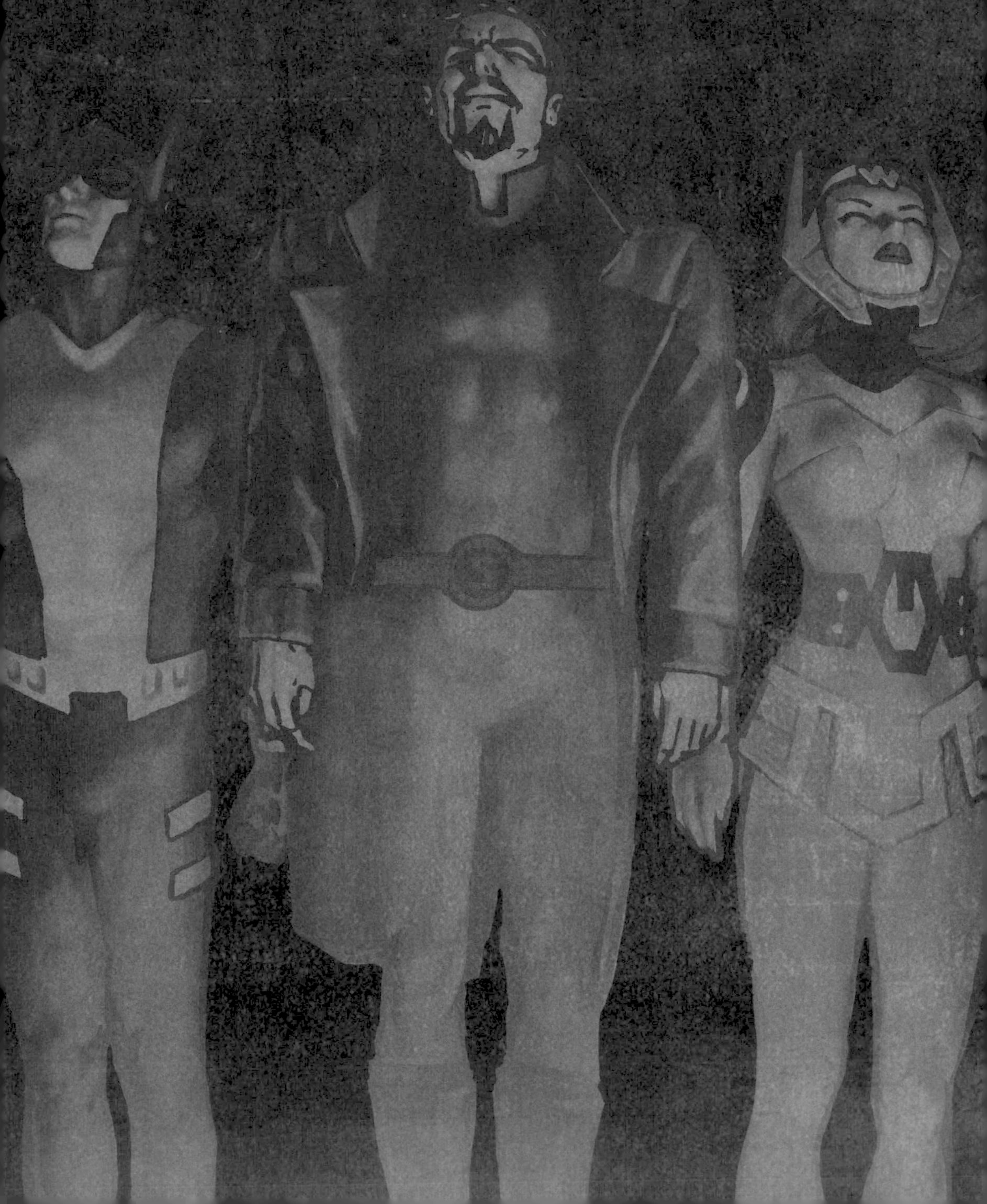

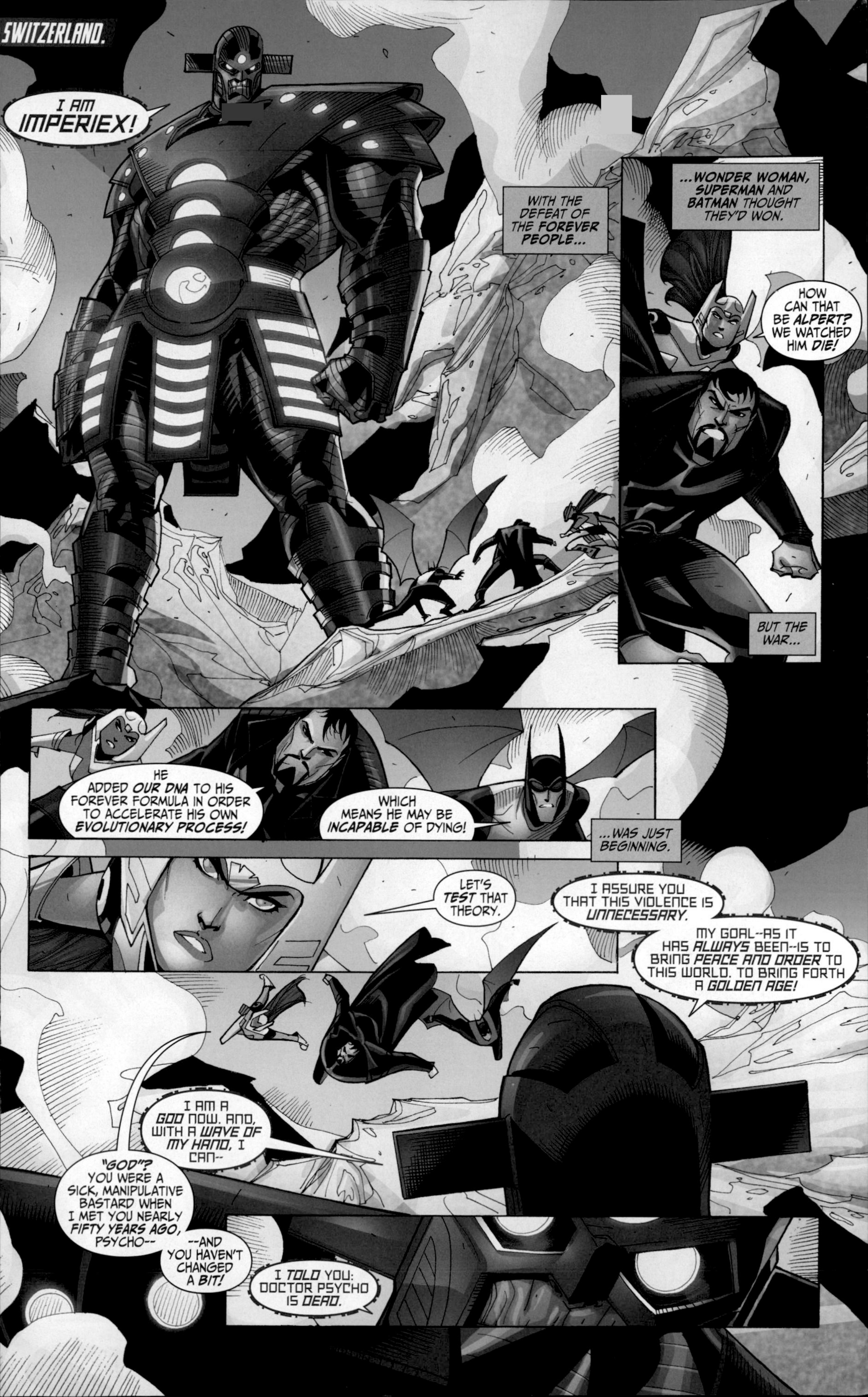
SWITZERLAND.
I AM IMPERIEX!
WITH THE DEFEAT OF THE FOREVER PEOPLE...
...WONDER WOMAN, SUPERMAN AND BATMAN THOUGHT THEY'D WON.
HOW CAN THAT BE ALPERT? WE WATCHED HIM DIE!
BUT THE WAR...
HE ADDED OUR DNA TO HIS FOREVER FORMULA IN ORDER TO ACCELERATE HIS OWN EVOLUTIONARY PROCESS!
WHICH MEANS HE MAY BE INCAPABLE OF DYING!
...WAS JUST BEGINNING.
LET'S TEST THAT THEORY.
I ASSURE YOU THAT THIS VIOLENCE IS UNNECESSARY.
MY GOAL--AS IT HAS ALWAYS BEEN--IS TO BRING PEACE AND ORDER TO THIS WORLD. TO BRING FORTH A GOLDEN AGE!
I AM A GOD NOW. AND, WITH A WAVE OF MY HAND, I CAN--
"GOD"? YOU WERE A SICK, MANIPULATIVE BASTARD WHEN I MET YOU NEARLY FIFTY YEARS AGO, PSYCHO--
--AND YOU HAVEN'T CHANGED A BIT!
I TOLD YOU: DOCTOR PSYCHO IS DEAD.

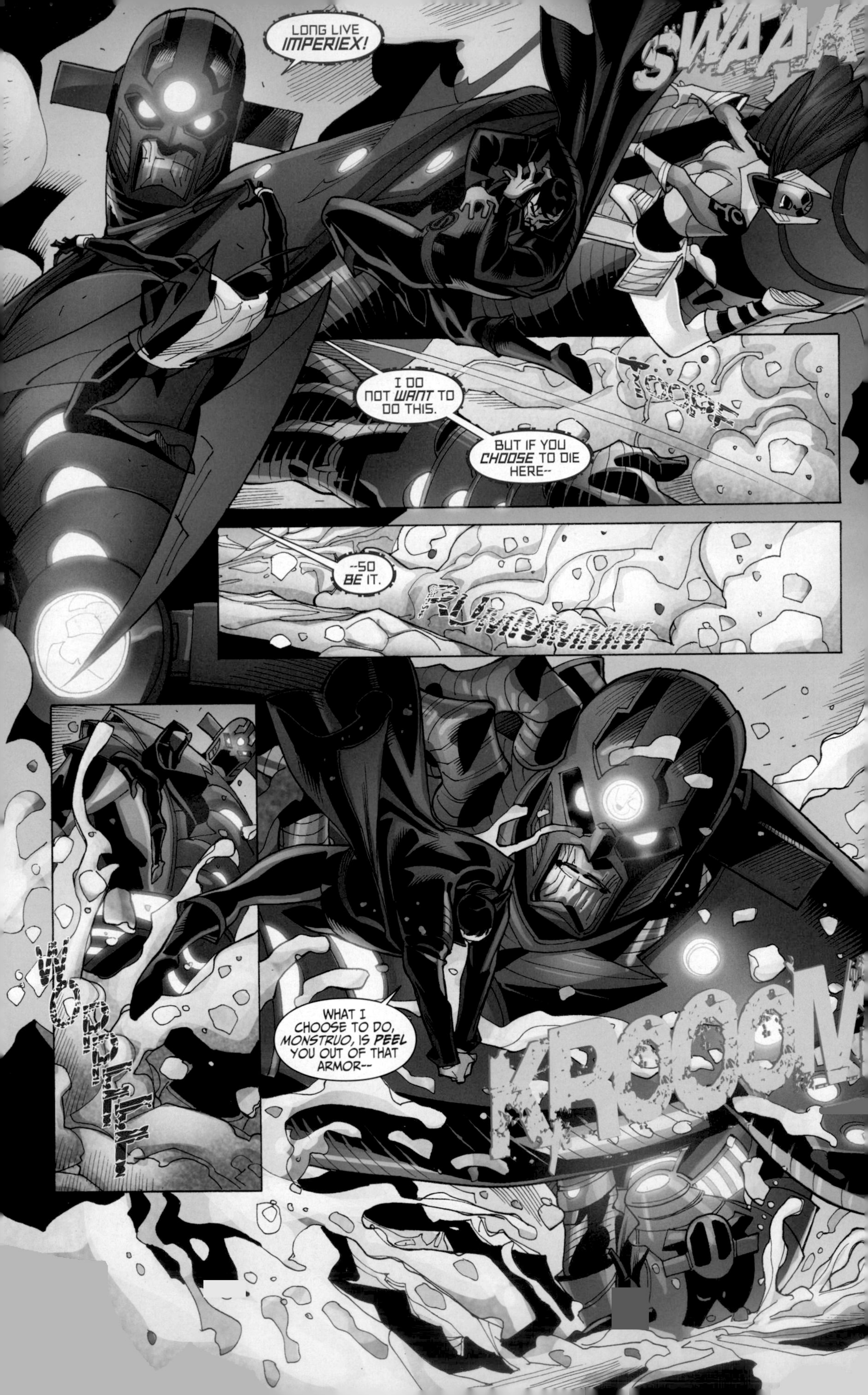
LONG LIVE IMPERIEX!
I DO NOT WANT TO DO THIS.
BUT IF YOU CHOOSE TO DIE HERE--
--SO BE IT.
WHAT I CHOOSE TO DO, MONSTRUO, IS PEEL YOU OUT OF THAT ARMOR--

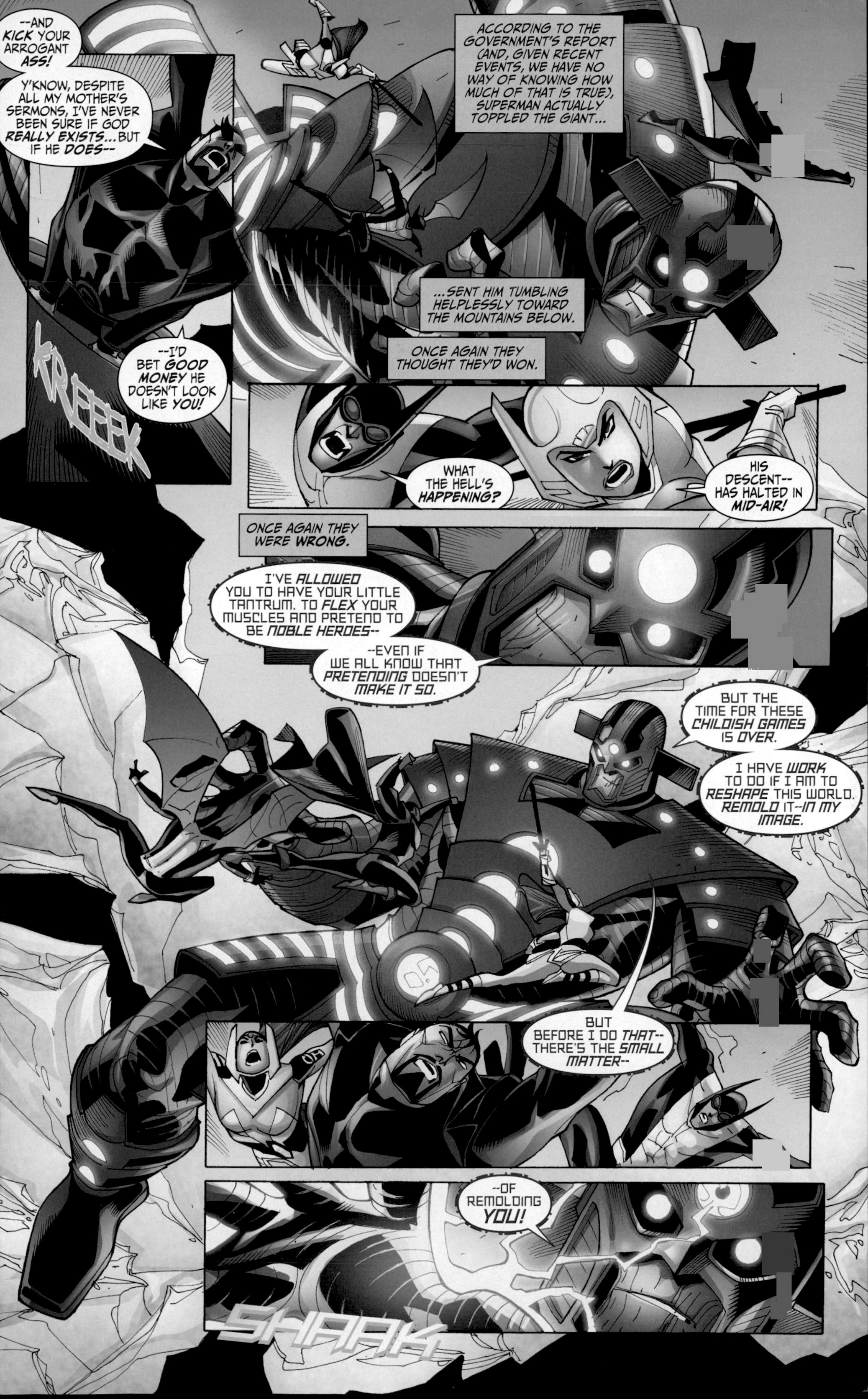
--AND KICK YOUR ARROGANT ASS!
Y'KNOW, DESPITE ALL MY MOTHER'S SERMONS, I'VE NEVER BEEN SURE IF GOD REALLY EXISTS...BUT IF HE DOES--
--I'D BET GOOD MONEY HE DOESN'T LOOK LIKE YOU!
KREEEEK
ACCORDING TO THE GOVERNMENT'S REPORT (AND, GIVEN RECENT EVENTS, WE HAVE NO WAY OF KNOWING HOW MUCH OF THAT IS TRUE), SUPERMAN ACTUALLY TOPPLED THE GIANT...
...SENT HIM TUMBLING HELPLESSLY TOWARD THE MOUNTAINS BELOW.
ONCE AGAIN THEY THOUGHT THEY'D WON.
WHAT THE HELL'S HAPPENING?
HIS DESCENT-- HAS HALTED IN MID-AIR!
ONCE AGAIN THEY WERE WRONG.
I'VE ALLOWED YOU TO HAVE YOUR LITTLE TANTRUM. TO FLEX YOUR MUSCLES AND PRETEND TO BE NOBLE HEROES--
--EVEN IF WE ALL KNOW THAT PRETENDING DOESN'T MAKE IT SO.
BUT THE TIME FOR THESE CHILDISH GAMES IS OVER.
I HAVE WORK TO DO IF I AM TO RESHAPE THIS WORLD. REMOLD IT--IN MY IMAGE.
BUT BEFORE I DO THAT-- THERE'S THE SMALL MATTER--
--OF REMOLDING YOU!
SHRAAK

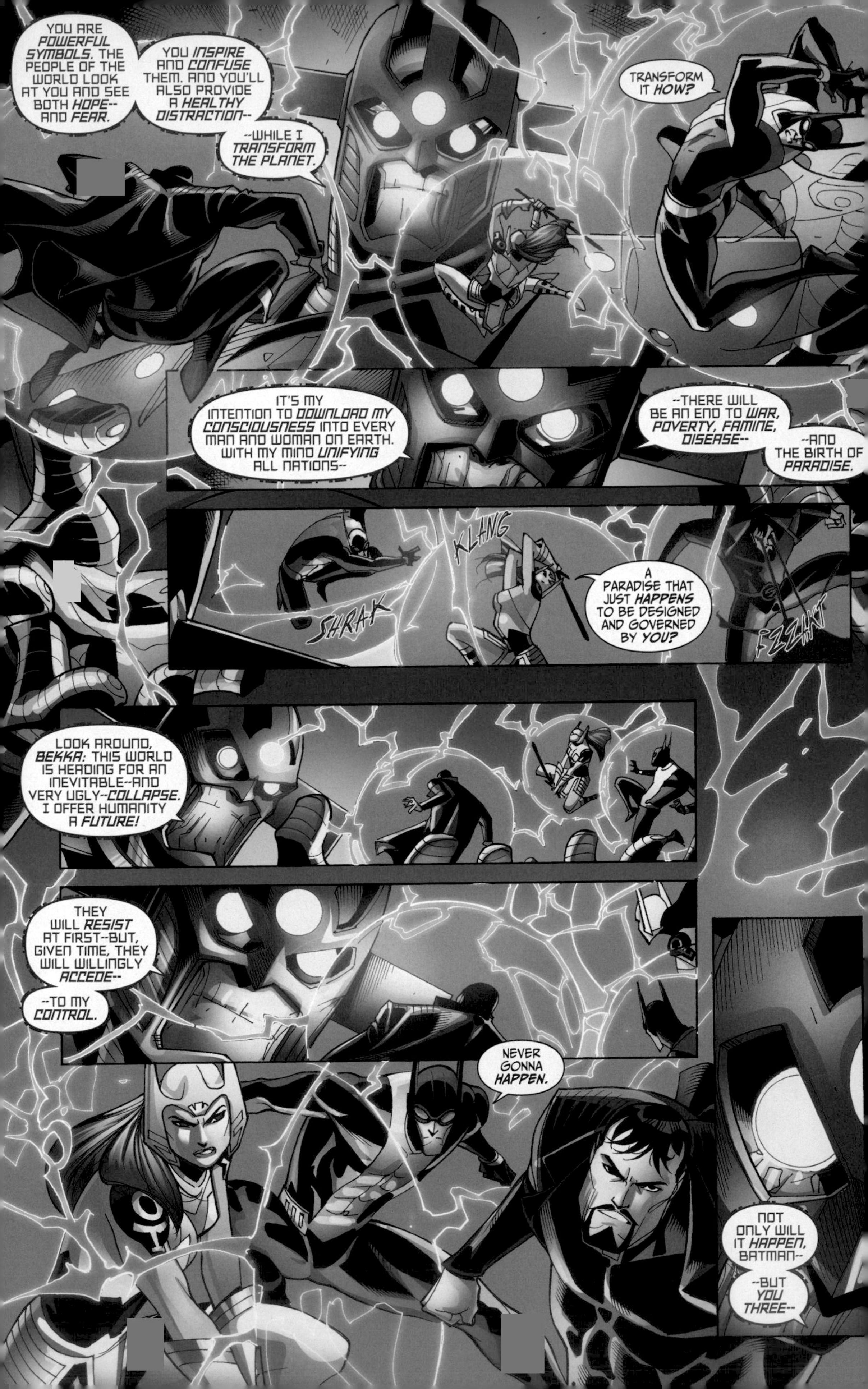
YOU ARE POWERFUL SYMBOLS. THE PEOPLE OF THE WORLD LOOK AT YOU AND SEE BOTH HOPE-- AND FEAR.
YOU INSPIRE AND CONFUSE THEM. AND YOU'LL ALSO PROVIDE A HEALTHY DISTRACTION--
--WHILE I TRANSFORM THE PLANET.
TRANSFORM IT HOW?
IT'S MY INTENTION TO DOWNLOAD MY CONSCIOUSNESS INTO EVERY MAN AND WOMAN ON EARTH. WITH MY MIND UNIFYING ALL NATIONS--
--THERE WILL BE AN END TO WAR, POVERTY, FAMINE, DISEASE--
--AND THE BIRTH OF PARADISE.
KLANG
SHRAK
A PARADISE THAT JUST HAPPENS TO BE DESIGNED AND GOVERNED BY YOU?
FZZAKT
LOOK AROUND, BEKKA: THIS WORLD IS HEADING FOR AN INEVITABLE--AND VERY UGLY--COLLAPSE. I OFFER HUMANITY A FUTURE!
THEY WILL RESIST AT FIRST--BUT, GIVEN TIME, THEY WILL WILLINGLY ACCEDE--
--TO MY CONTROL.
NEVER GONNA HAPPEN.
NOT ONLY WILL IT HAPPEN, BATMAN--
--BUT YOU THREE--

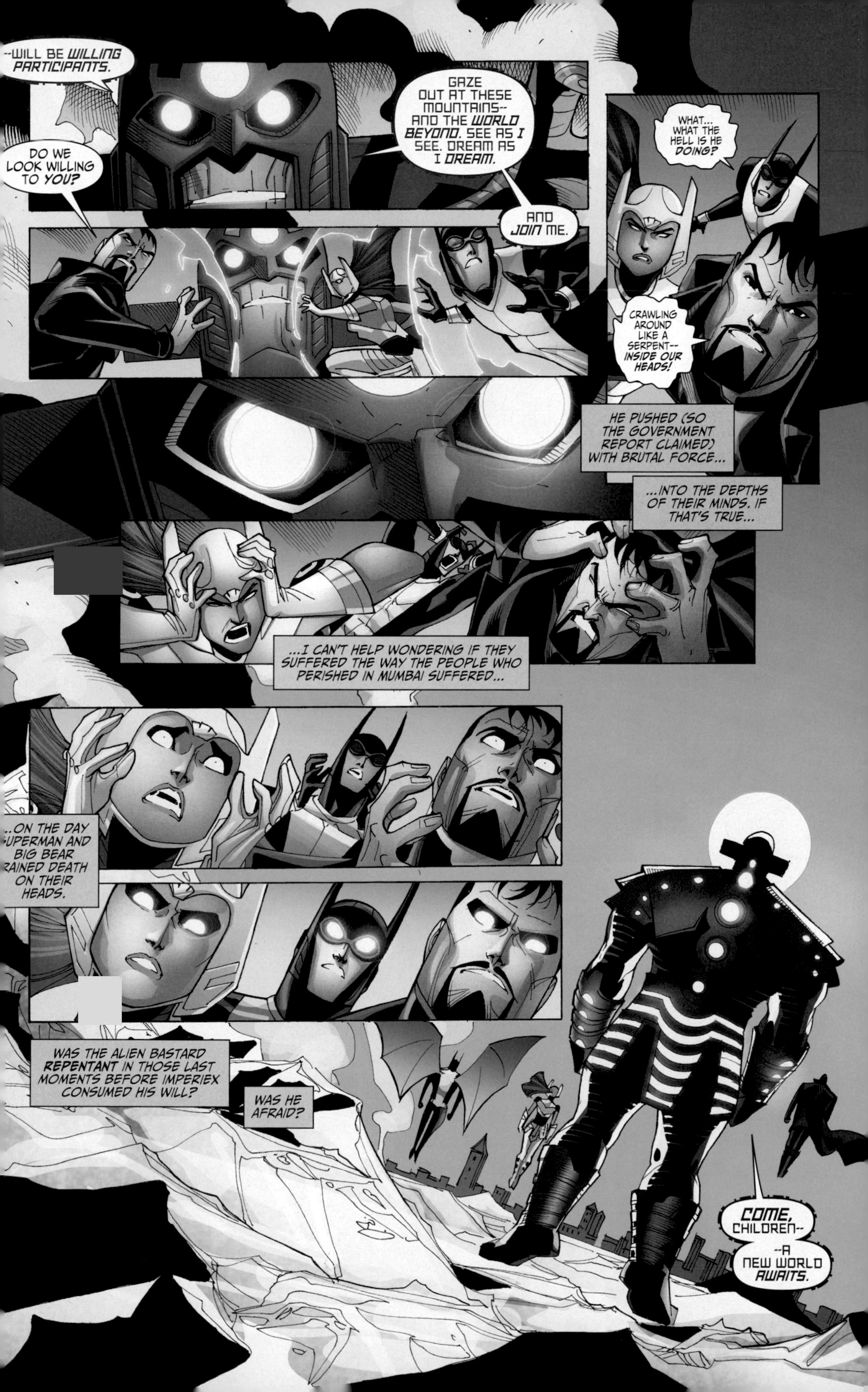
--WILL BE WILLING PARTICIPANTS.
GAZE OUT AT THESE MOUNTAINS-- AND THE WORLD BEYOND. SEE AS I SEE. DREAM AS I DREAM.
DO WE LOOK WILLING TO YOU?
AND JOIN ME.
WHAT... WHAT THE HELL IS HE DOING?
CRAWLING AROUND LIKE A SERPENT-- INSIDE OUR HEADS!
HE PUSHED (SO THE GOVERNMENT REPORT CLAIMED) WITH BRUTAL FORCE...
...INTO THE DEPTHS OF THEIR MINDS. IF THAT'S TRUE...
...I CAN'T HELP WONDERING IF THEY SUFFERED THE WAY THE PEOPLE WHO PERISHED IN MUMBAI SUFFERED...
..ON THE DAY UPERMAN AND BIG BEAR AINED DEATH ON THEIR HEADS.
WAS THE ALIEN BASTARD REPENTANT IN THOSE LAST MOMENTS BEFORE IMPERIEX CONSUMED HIS WILL?
WAS HE AFRAID?
COME, CHILDREN--
--A NEW WORLD AWAITS.

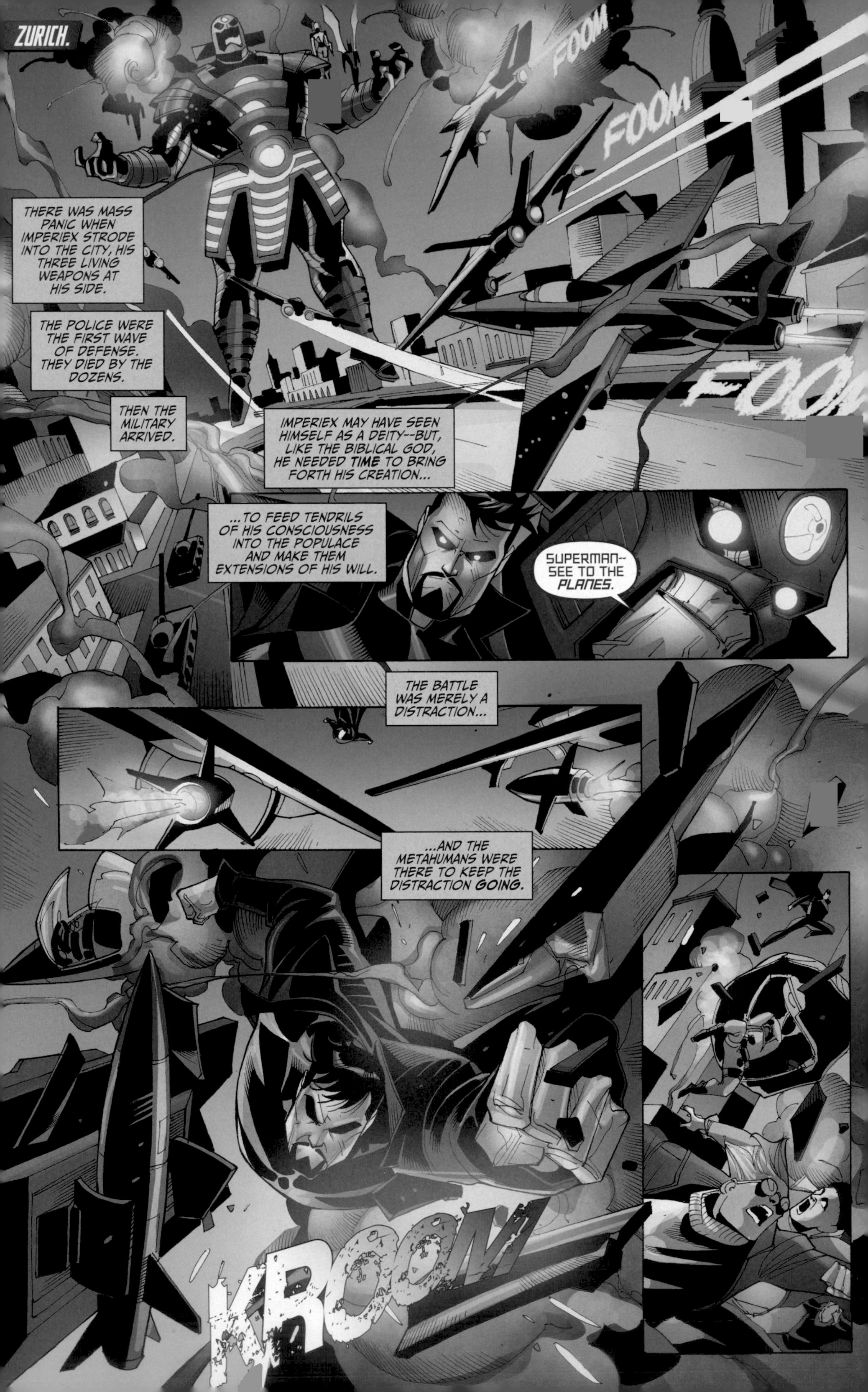
ZURICH.
THERE WAS MASS PANIC WHEN IMPERIEX STRODE INTO THE CITY, HIS THREE LIVING WEAPONS AT HIS SIDE.
FOOM
FOOM
THE POLICE WERE THE FIRST WAVE OF DEFENSE. THEY DIED BY THE DOZENS.
FOOM
THEN THE MILITARY ARRIVED.
IMPERIEX MAY HAVE SEEN HIMSELF AS A DEITY--BUT, LIKE THE BIBLICAL GOD, HE NEEDED TIME TO BRING FORTH HIS CREATION...
...TO FEED TENDRILS OF HIS CONSCIOUSNESS INTO THE POPULACE AND MAKE THEM EXTENSIONS OF HIS WILL.
SUPERMAN-- SEE TO THE PLANES.
THE BATTLE WAS MERELY A DISTRACTION...
...AND THE METAHUMANS WERE THERE TO KEEP THE DISTRACTION GOING.
KROOM

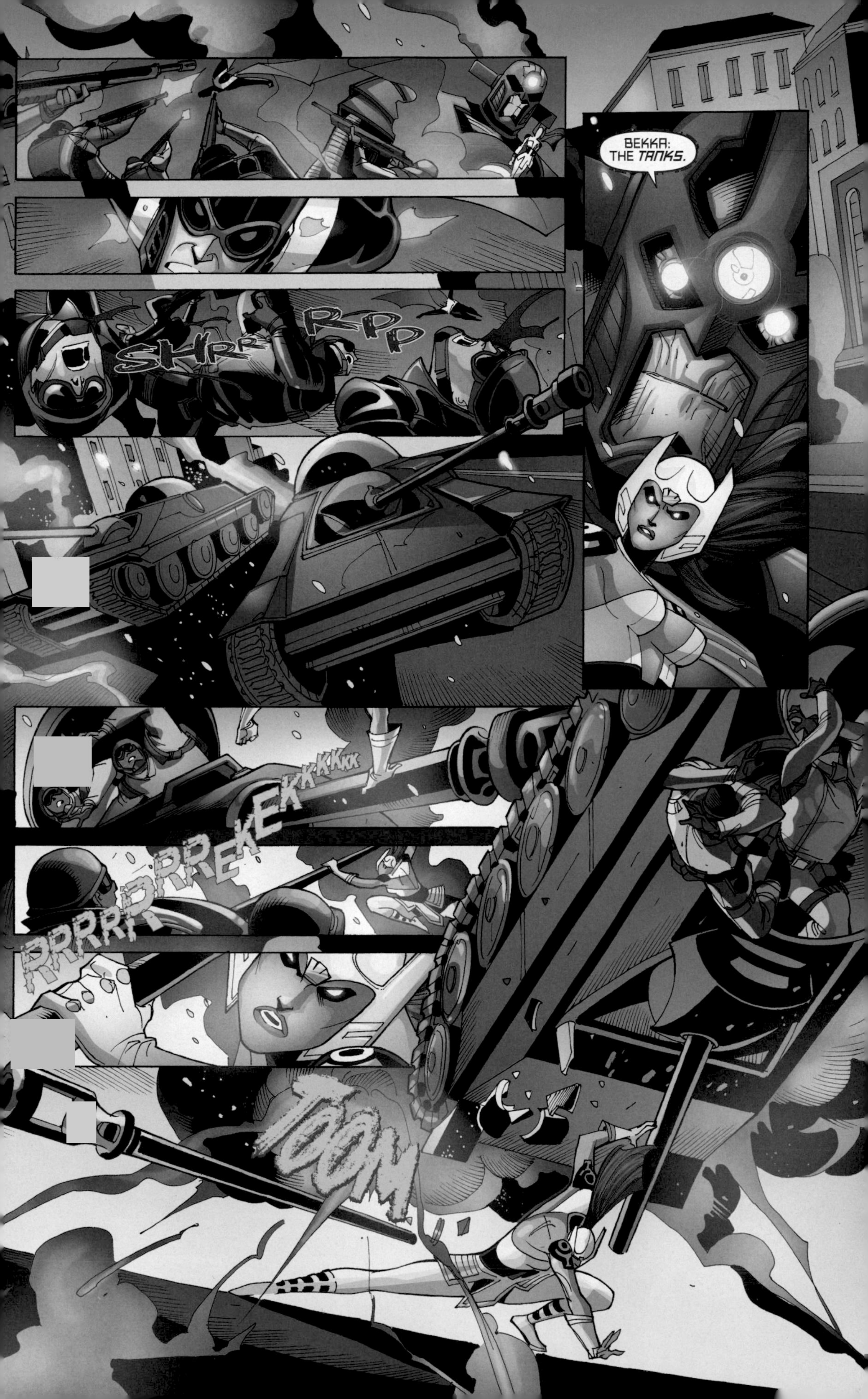
BEKKA: THE TANKS.
TOOM

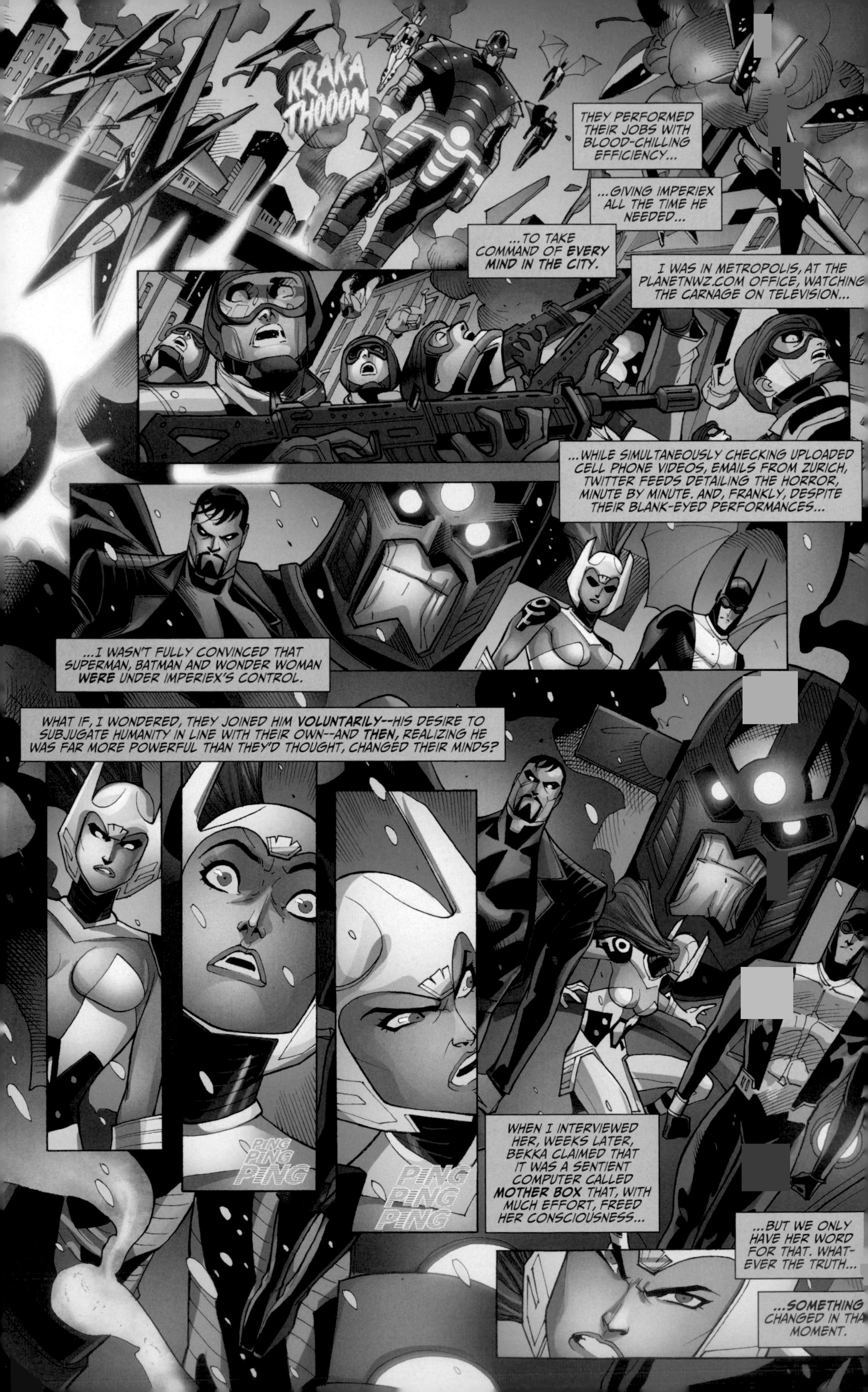
KRAKA THOOOM
THEY PERFORMED THEIR JOBS WITH BLOOD-CHILLING EFFICIENCY...
...GIVING IMPERIEX ALL THE TIME HE NEEDED...
...TO TAKE COMMAND OF EVERY MIND IN THE CITY.
I WAS IN METROPOLIS, AT THE PLANETNWZ.COM OFFICE, WATCHING THE CARNAGE ON TELEVISION...
...WHILE SIMULTANEOUSLY CHECKING UPLOADED CELL PHONE VIDEOS, EMAILS FROM ZURICH, TWITTER FEEDS DETAILING THE HORROR, MINUTE BY MINUTE. AND, FRANKLY, DESPITE THEIR BLANK-EYED PERFORMANCES...
...I WASN'T FULLY CONVINCED THAT SUPERMAN, BATMAN AND WONDER WOMAN WERE UNDER IMPERIEX'S CONTROL.
WHAT IF, I WONDERED, THEY JOINED HIM VOLUNTARILY--HIS DESIRE TO SUBJUGATE HUMANITY IN LINE WITH THEIR OWN--AND THEN, REALIZING HE WAS FAR MORE POWERFUL THAN THEY'D THOUGHT, CHANGED THEIR MINDS?
PING PING PING
PING PING PING
WHEN I INTERVIEWED HER, WEEKS LATER, BEKKA CLAIMED THAT IT WAS A SENTIENT COMPUTER CALLED MOTHER BOX THAT, WITH MUCH EFFORT, FREED HER CONSCIOUSNESS...
...BUT WE ONLY HAVE HER WORD FOR THAT. WHATEVER THE TRUTH...
...SOMETHING CHANGED IN THA MOMENT.

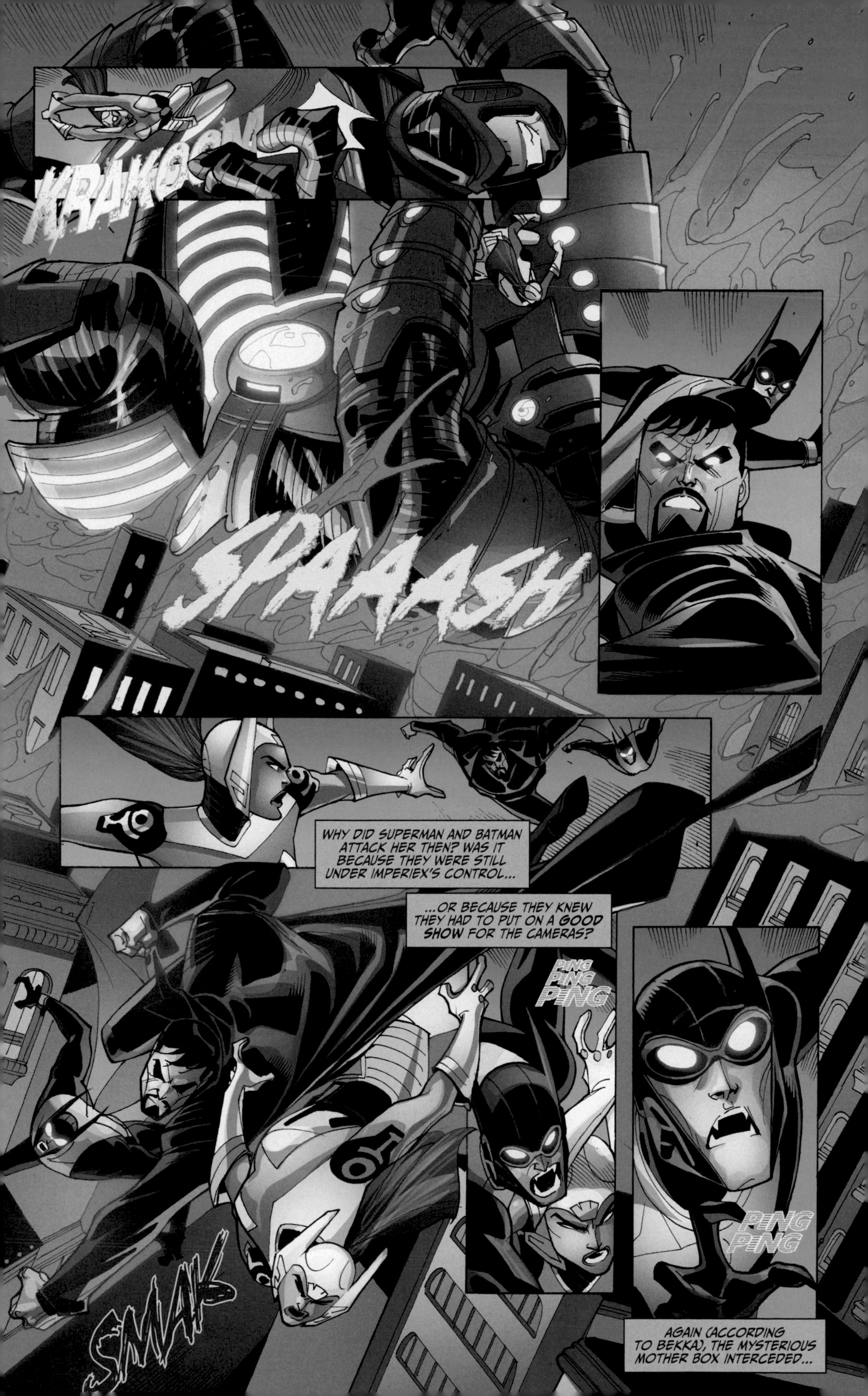
KRAKOOM
SPAAASH
WHY DID SUPERMAN AND BATMAN ATTACK HER THEN? WAS IT BECAUSE THEY WERE STILL UNDER IMPERIEX'S CONTROL...
...OR BECAUSE THEY KNEW THEY HAD TO PUT ON A GOOD SHOW FOR THE CAMERAS?
PING PING PING
PING PING
SMAK
AGAIN (ACCORDING TO BEKKA), THE MYSTERIOUS MOTHER BOX INTERCEDED...

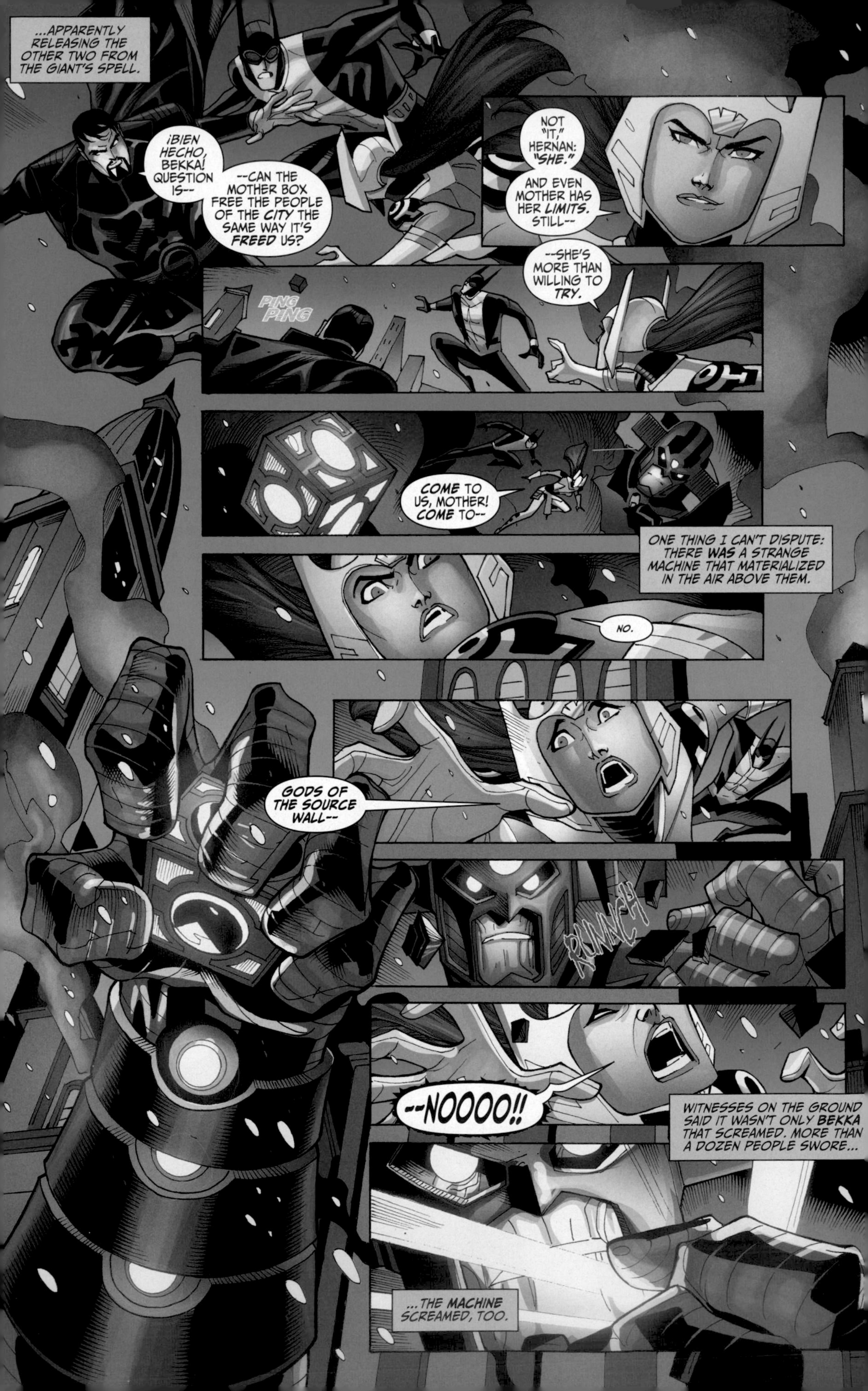

...APPARENTLY RELEASING THE OTHER TWO FROM THE GIANT'S SPELL.
¡BIEN HECHO, BEKKA! QUESTION IS--
--CAN THE MOTHER BOX FREE THE PEOPLE OF THE CITY THE SAME WAY IT'S FREED US?
NOT "IT," HERNAN: "SHE."
AND EVEN MOTHER HAS HER LIMITS. STILL--
--SHE'S MORE THAN WILLING TO TRY.
PING PING
COME TO US, MOTHER! COME TO--
ONE THING I CAN'T DISPUTE: THERE WAS A STRANGE MACHINE THAT MATERIALIZED IN THE AIR ABOVE THEM.
NO.
GODS OF THE SOURCE WALL--
KRUNCH
--NOOOO!!
WITNESSES ON THE GROUND SAID IT WASN'T ONLY BEKKA THAT SCREAMED. MORE THAN A DOZEN PEOPLE SWORE...
...THE MACHINE SCREAMED, TOO.

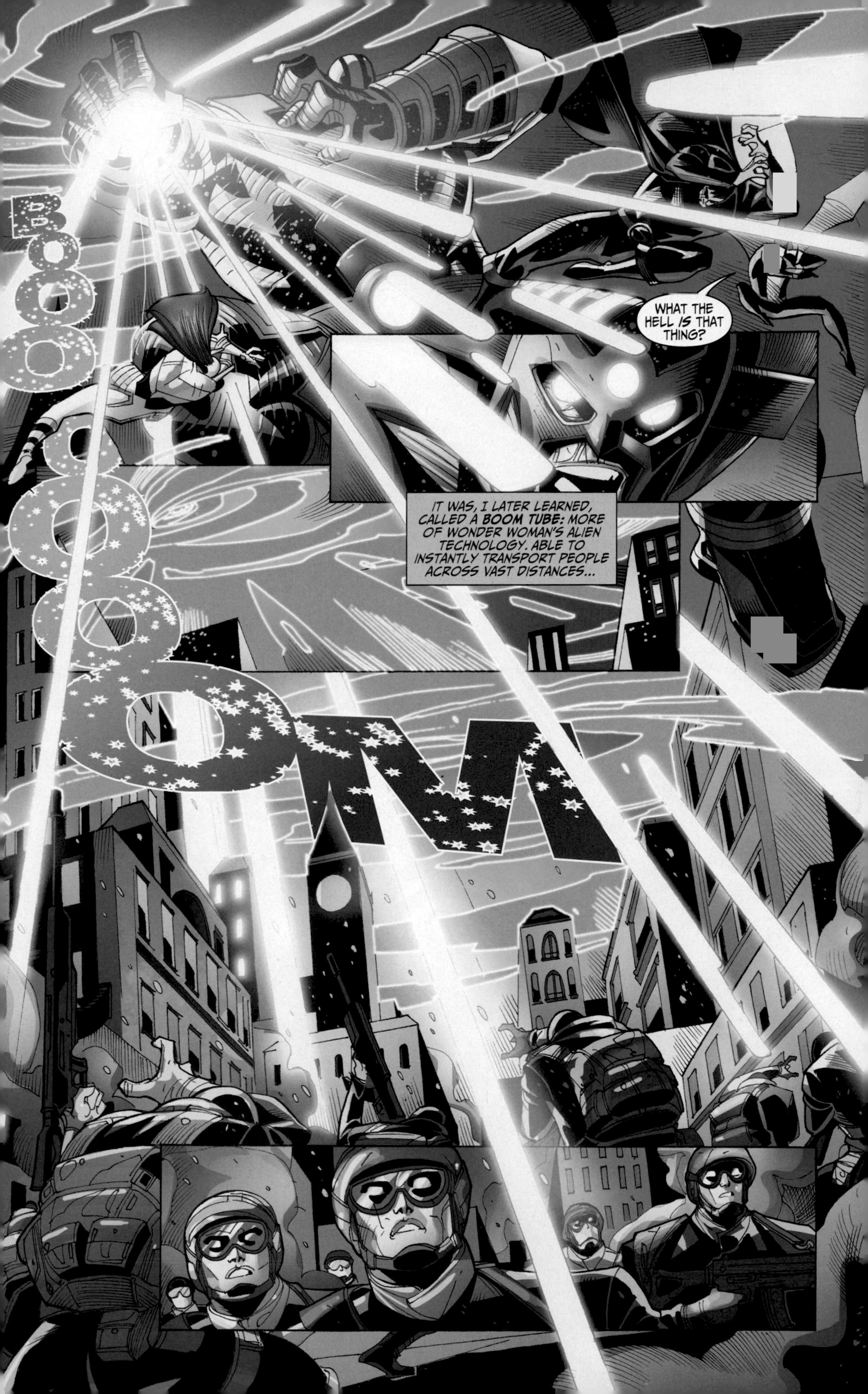
BOOOOOM
WHAT THE HELL IS THAT THING?
IT WAS, I LATER LEARNED, CALLED A BOOM TUBE: MORE OF WONDER WOMAN'S ALIEN TECHNOLOGY. ABLE TO INSTANTLY TRANSPORT PEOPLE ACROSS VAST DISTANCES...

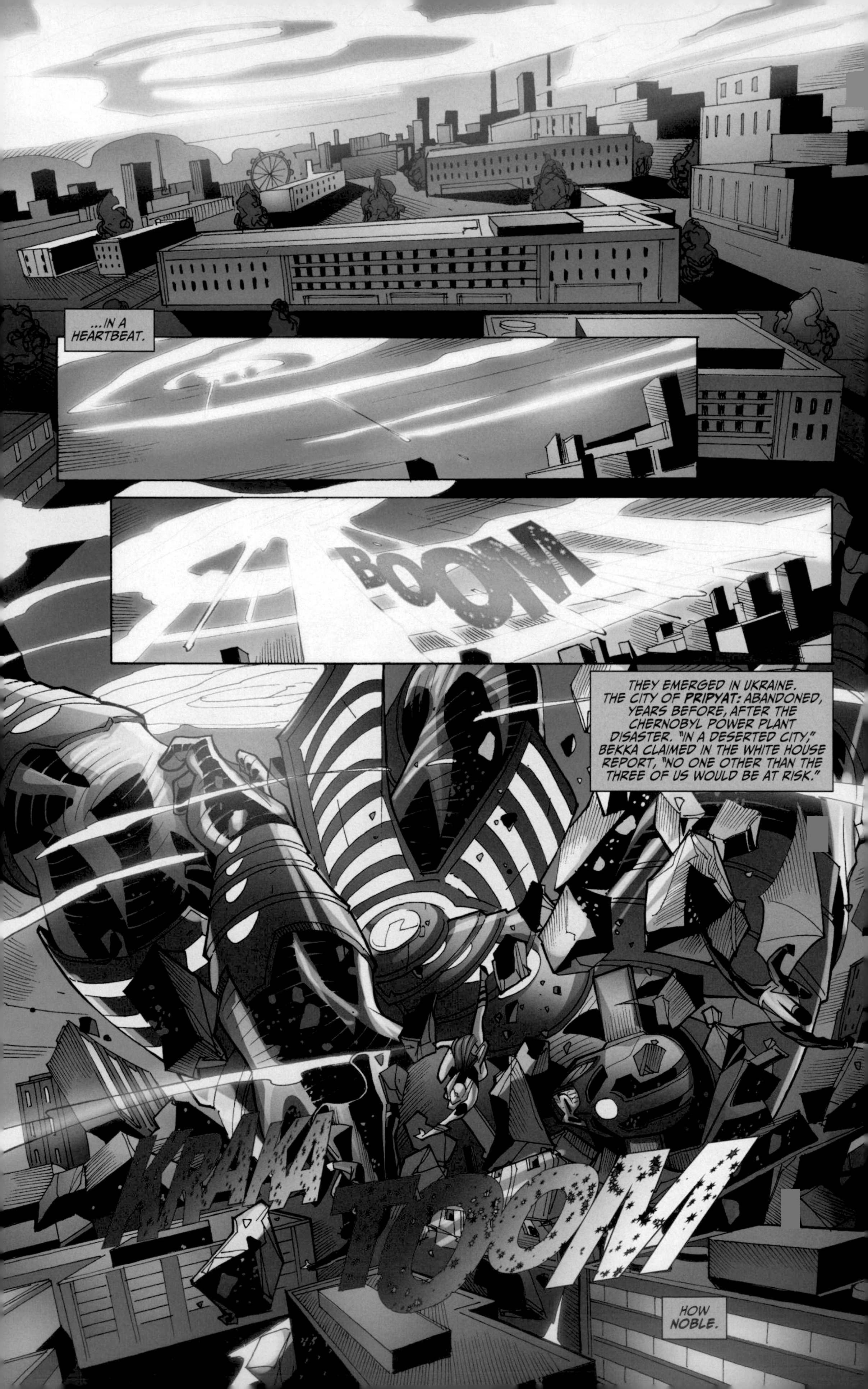
...IN A HEARTBEAT.
BOOM
THEY EMERGED IN UKRAINE. THE CITY OF PRIPYAT: ABANDONED, YEARS BEFORE, AFTER THE CHERNOBYL POWER PLANT DISASTER. "IN A DESERTED CITY," BEKKA CLAIMED IN THE WHITE HOUSE REPORT, "NO ONE OTHER THAN THE THREE OF US WOULD BE AT RISK."
KRAKATOOM
HOW NOBLE.

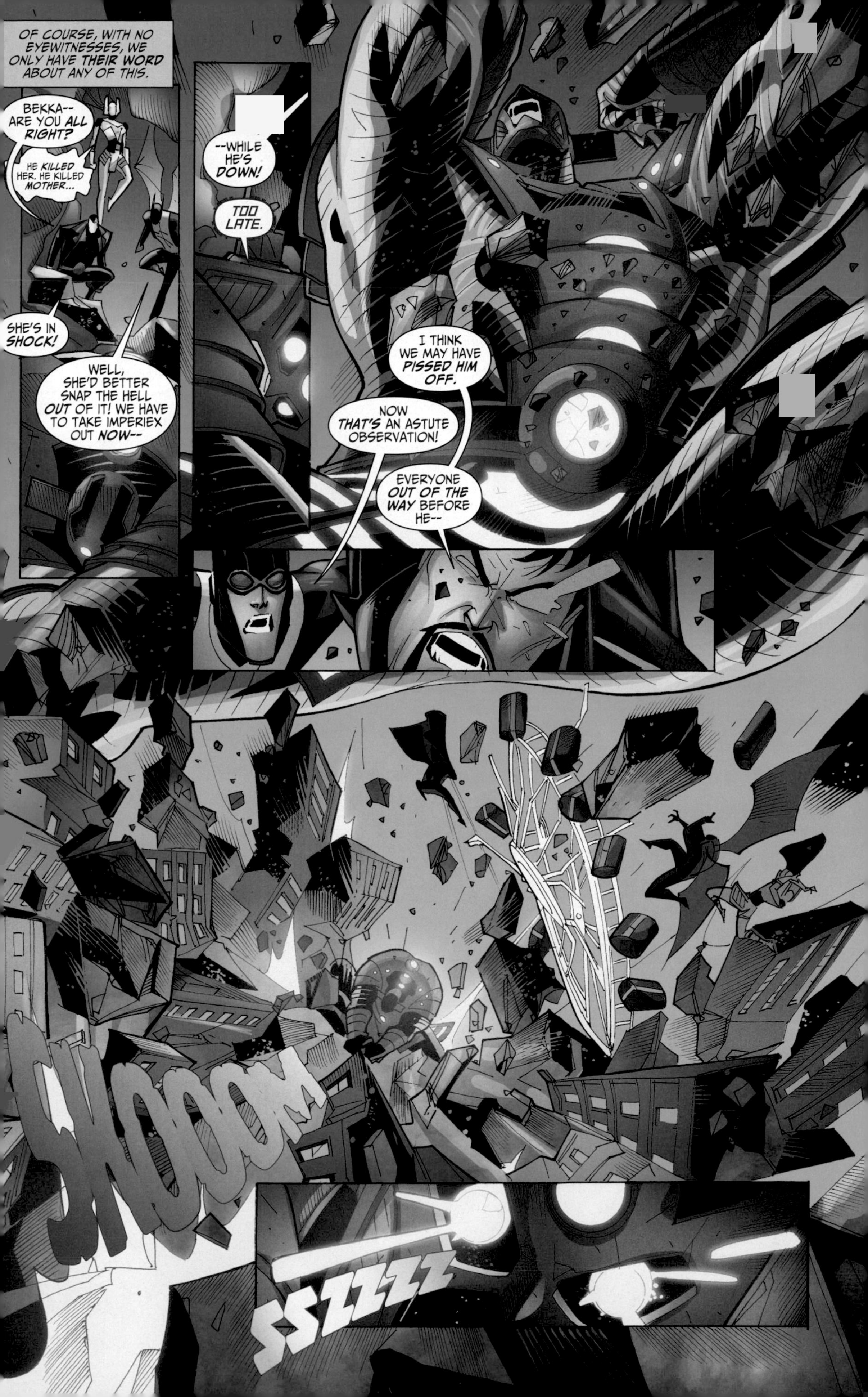
OF COURSE, WITH NO EYEWITNESSES, WE ONLY HAVE THEIR WORD ABOUT ANY OF THIS.
BEKKA-- ARE YOU ALL RIGHT?
HE KILLED HER. HE KILLED MOTHER...
SHE'S IN SHOCK!
WELL, SHE'D BETTER SNAP THE HELL OUT OF IT! WE HAVE TO TAKE IMPERIEX OUT NOW--
--WHILE HE'S DOWN!
TOO LATE.
I THINK WE MAY HAVE PISSED HIM OFF.
NOW THAT'S AN ASTUTE OBSERVATION!
EVERYONE OUT OF THE WAY BEFORE HE--
SHOOOM
SSZZZZZ

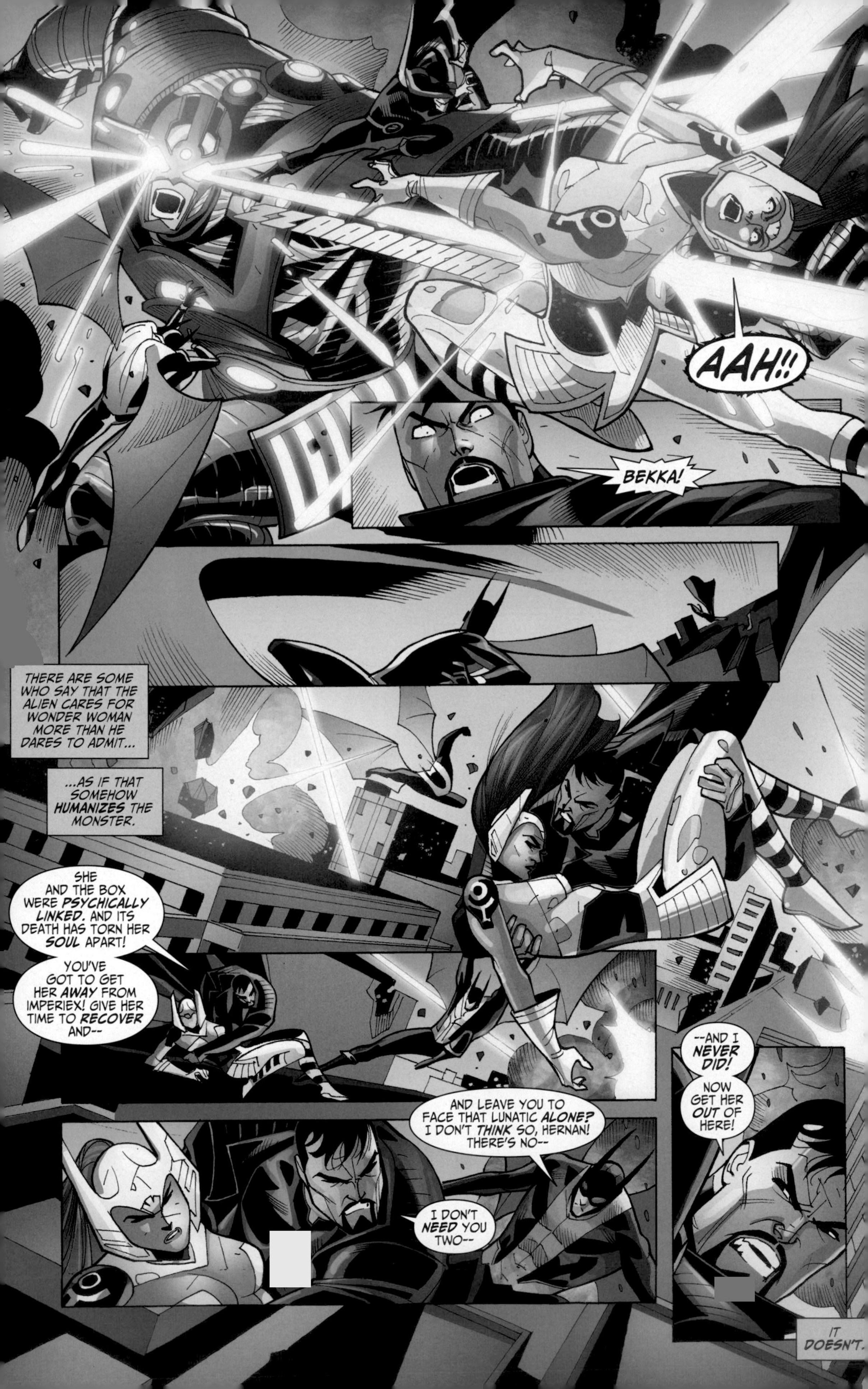
AAH!!
BEKKA!
THERE ARE SOME WHO SAY THAT THE ALIEN CARES FOR WONDER WOMAN MORE THAN HE DARES TO ADMIT...
...AS IF THAT SOMEHOW HUMANIZES THE MONSTER.
SHE AND THE BOX WERE PSYCHICALLY LINKED. AND ITS DEATH HAS TORN HER SOUL APART!
YOU'VE GOT TO GET HER AWAY FROM IMPERIEX! GIVE HER TIME TO RECOVER AND--
AND LEAVE YOU TO FACE THAT LUNATIC ALONE? I DON'T THINK SO, HERNAN! THERE'S NO--
I DON'T NEED YOU TWO--
--AND I NEVER DID!
NOW GET HER OUT OF HERE!
IT DOESN'T.

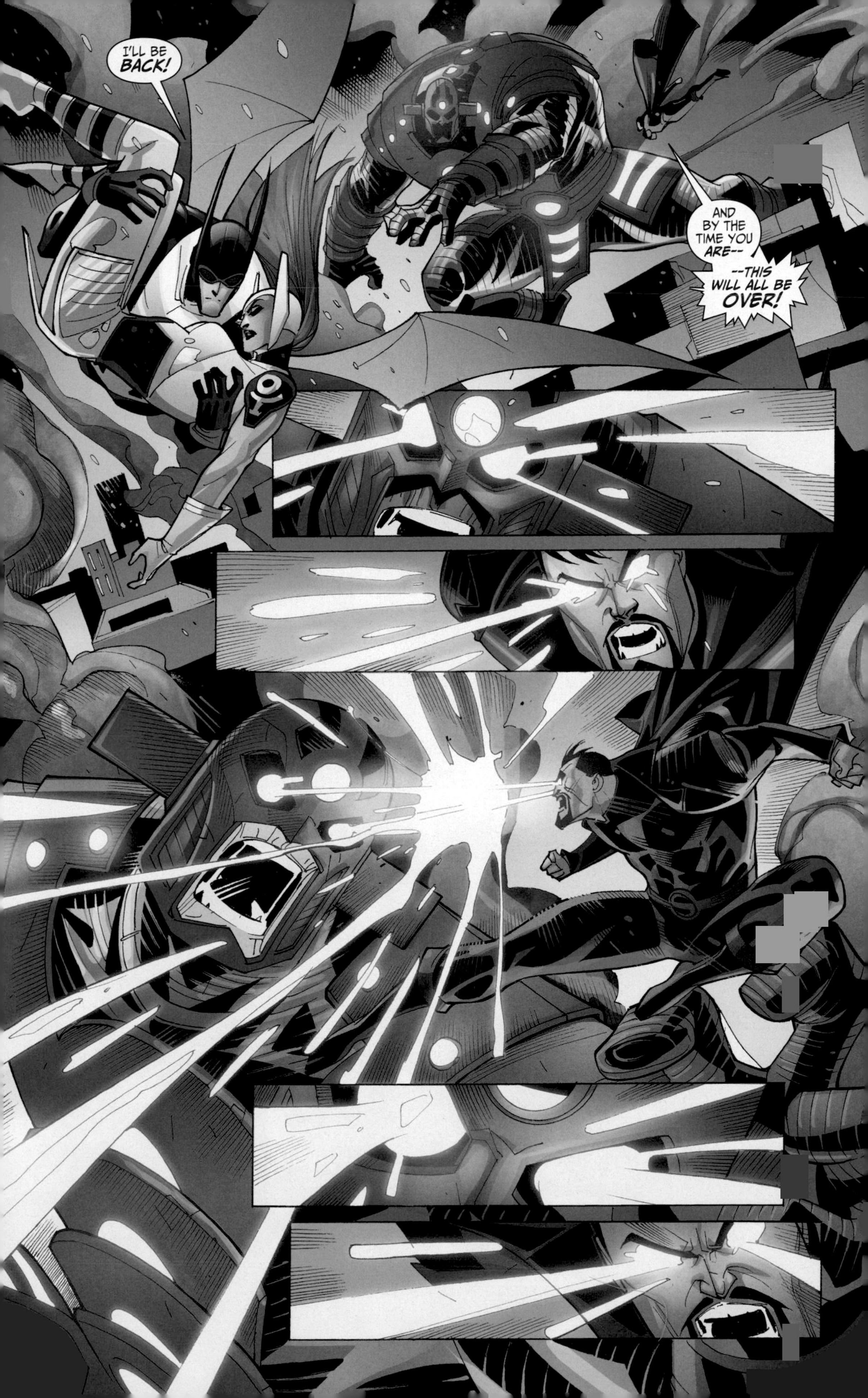
I'LL BE BACK!
AND BY THE TIME YOU ARE--
--THIS WILL ALL BE OVER!

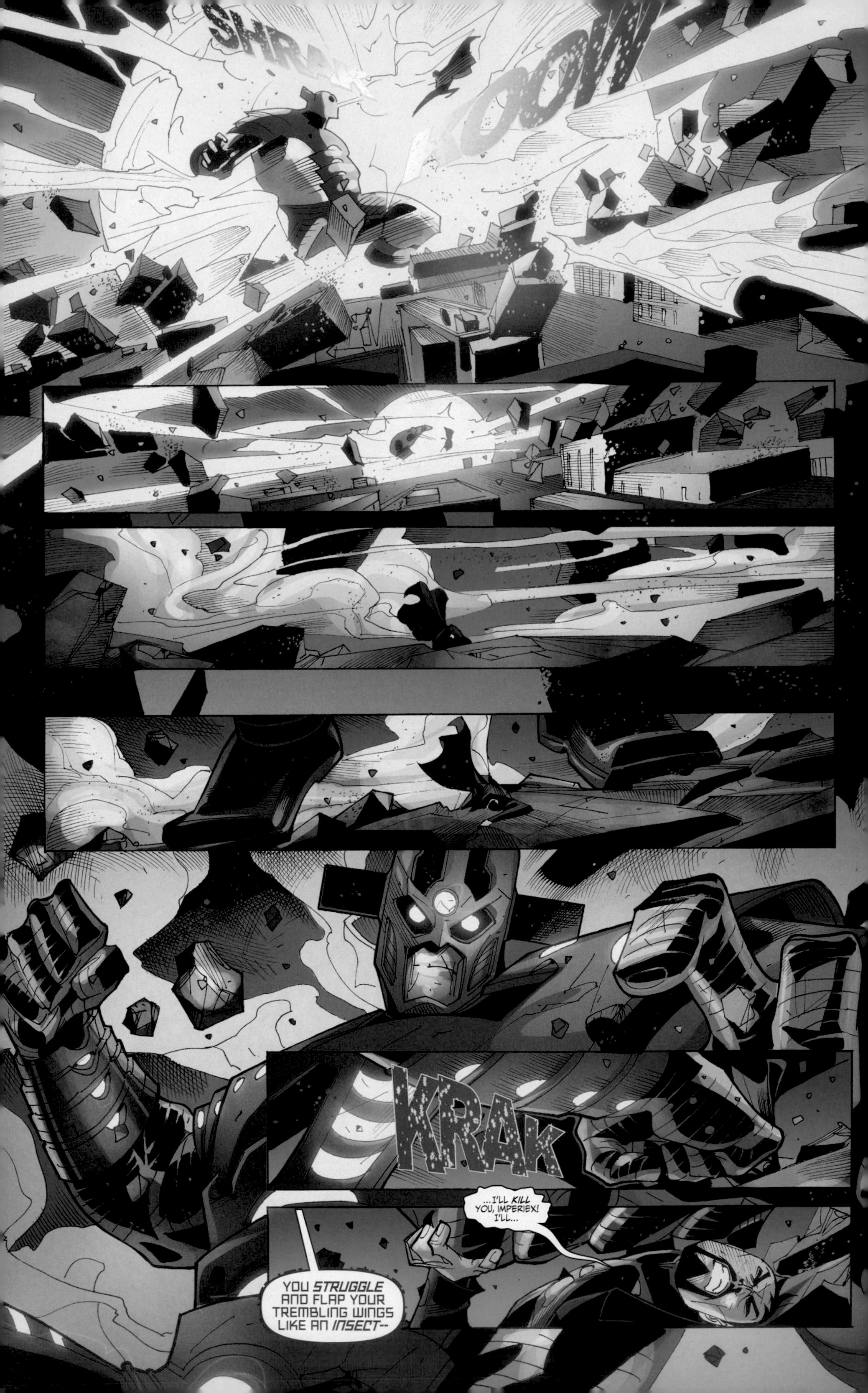
SHRAK
KOOOM
KRAK
...I'LL KILL YOU, IMPERIEX! I'LL...
YOU STRUGGLE AND FLAP YOUR TREMBLING WINGS LIKE AN INSECT--

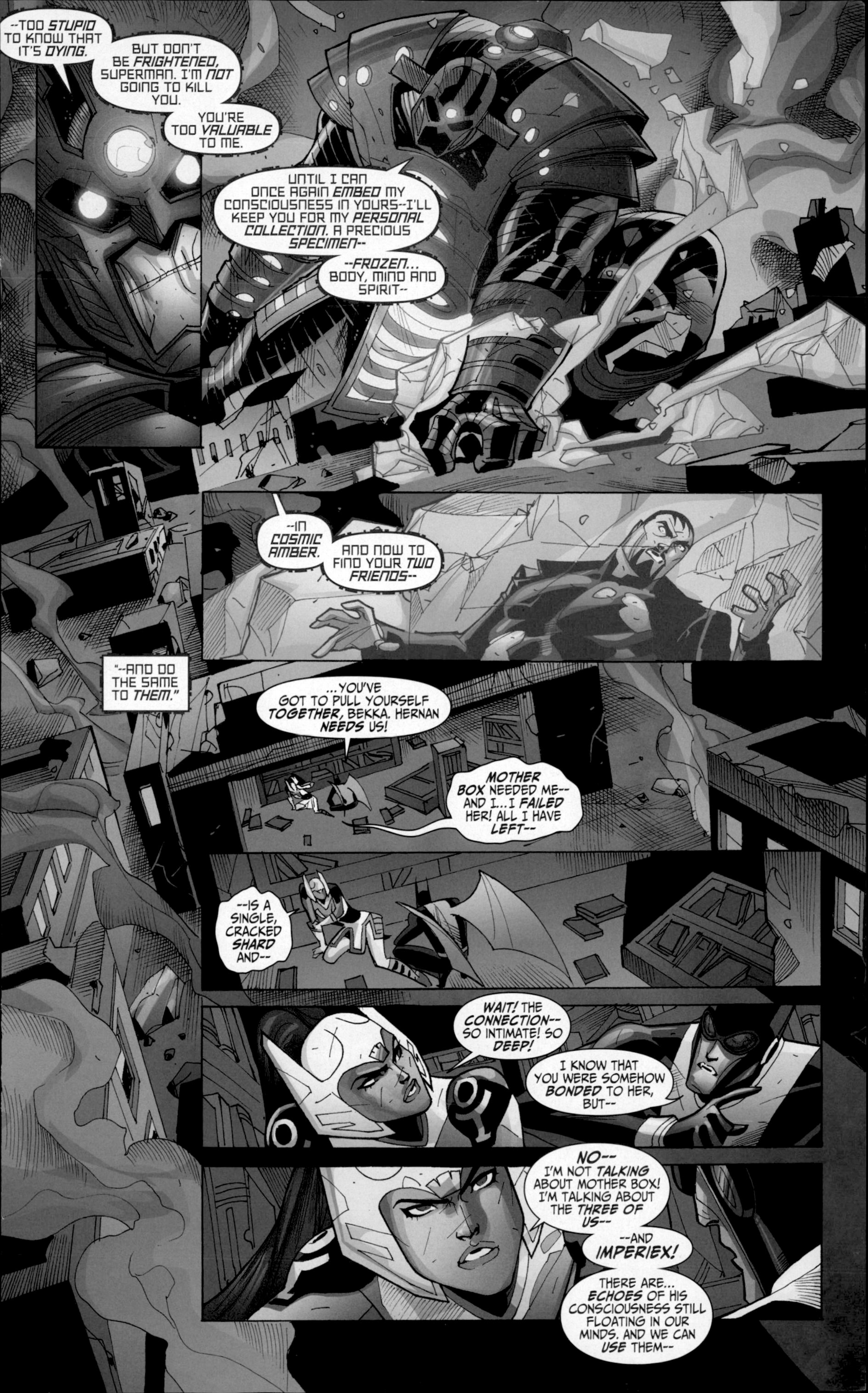
--TOO STUPID TO KNOW THAT IT'S DYING.
BUT DON'T BE FRIGHTENED, SUPERMAN. I'M NOT GOING TO KILL YOU.
YOU'RE TOO VALUABLE TO ME.
UNTIL I CAN ONCE AGAIN EMBED MY CONSCIOUSNESS IN YOURS--I'LL KEEP YOU FOR MY PERSONAL COLLECTION. A PRECIOUS SPECIMEN--
--FROZEN... BODY, MIND AND SPIRIT--
--IN COSMIC AMBER.
AND NOW TO FIND YOUR TWO FRIENDS--
"--AND DO THE SAME TO THEM."
...YOU'VE GOT TO PULL YOURSELF TOGETHER, BEKKA. HERNAN NEEDS US!
MOTHER BOX NEEDED ME--AND I...I FAILED HER! ALL I HAVE LEFT--
--IS A SINGLE, CRACKED SHARD AND--
WAIT! THE CONNECTION--SO INTIMATE! SO DEEP!
I KNOW THAT YOU WERE SOMEHOW BONDED TO HER, BUT--
NO--I'M NOT TALKING ABOUT MOTHER BOX! I'M TALKING ABOUT THE THREE OF US--
--AND IMPERIEX!
THERE ARE... ECHOES OF HIS CONSCIOUSNESS STILL FLOATING IN OUR MINDS. AND WE CAN USE THEM--

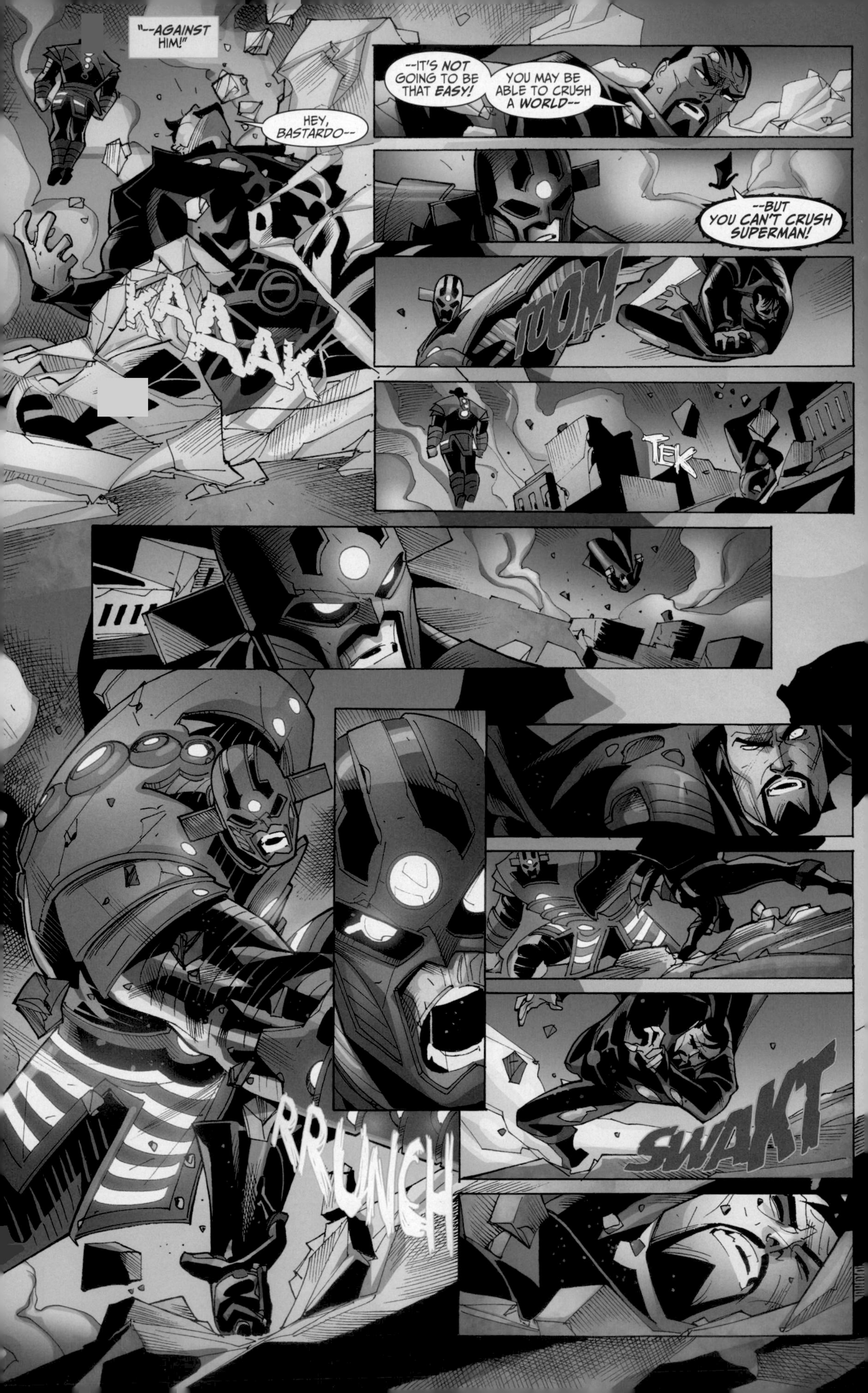
"--AGAINST HIM!"
HEY, BASTARDO--
KAAAAK
--IT'S NOT GOING TO BE THAT EASY!
YOU MAY BE ABLE TO CRUSH A WORLD--
--BUT YOU CAN'T CRUSH SUPERMAN!
TOOM
TEK
RRUNCH
SWAKT

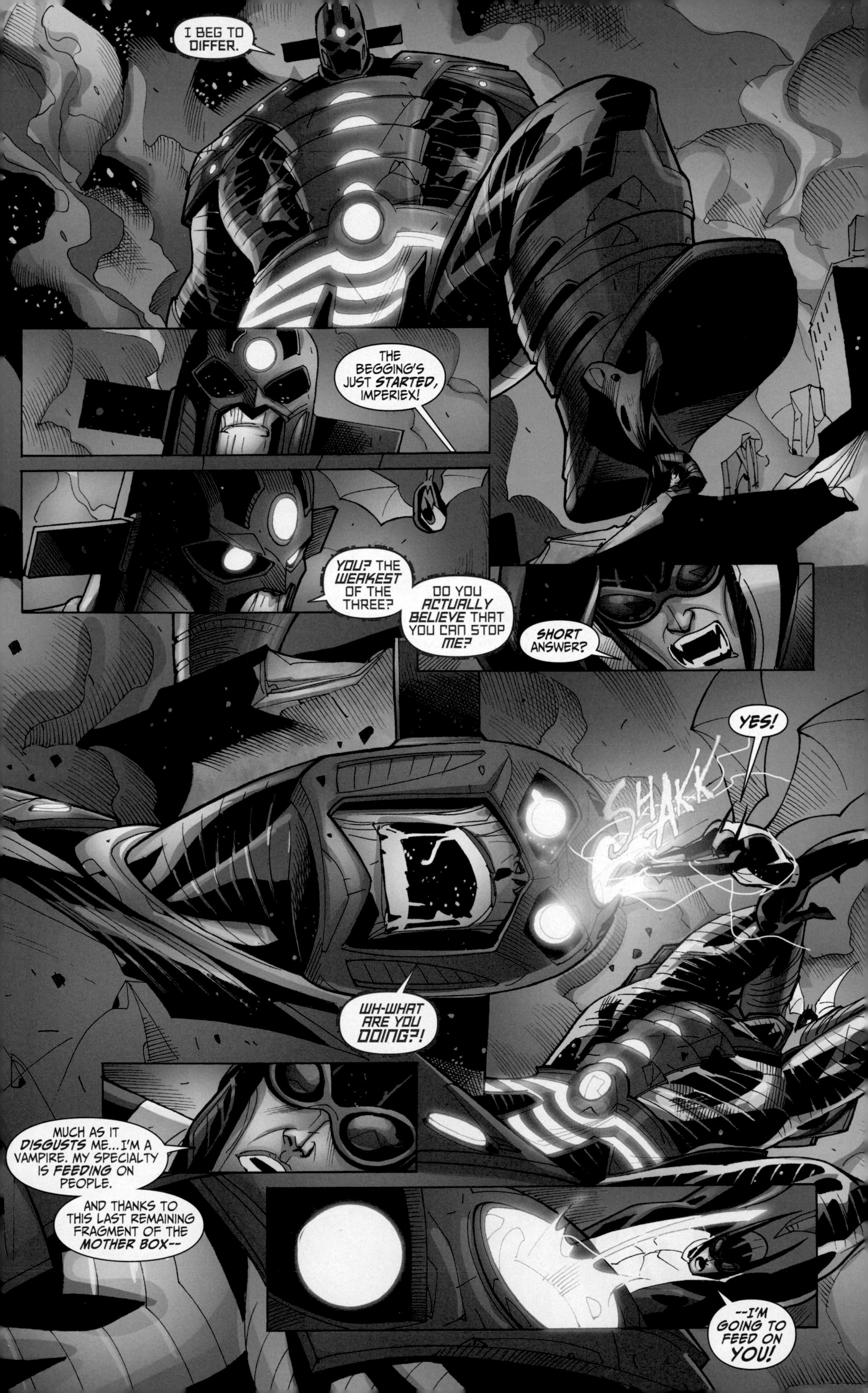
I BEG TO DIFFER.
THE BEGGING'S JUST STARTED, IMPERIEX!
YOU? THE WEAKEST OF THE THREE?
DO YOU ACTUALLY BELIEVE THAT YOU CAN STOP ME?
SHORT ANSWER?
YES!
SHAKK
WH-WHAT ARE YOU DOING?!
MUCH AS IT DISGUSTS ME...I'M A VAMPIRE. MY SPECIALTY IS FEEDING ON PEOPLE.
AND THANKS TO THIS LAST REMAINING FRAGMENT OF THE MOTHER BOX--
--I'M GOING TO FEED ON YOU!

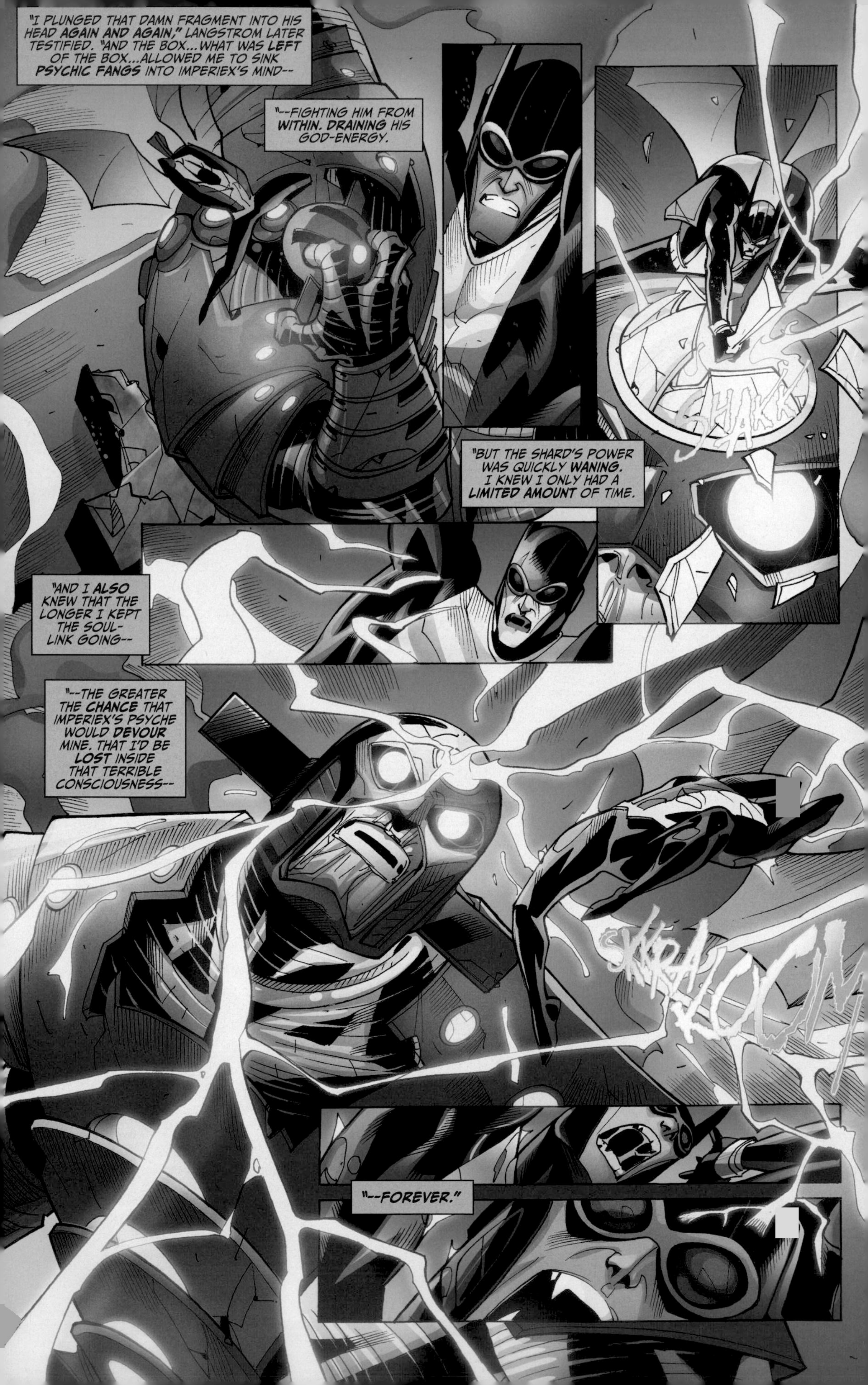
"I PLUNGED THAT DAMN FRAGMENT INTO HIS HEAD AGAIN AND AGAIN," LANGSTROM LATER TESTIFIED. "AND THE BOX...WHAT WAS LEFT OF THE BOX...ALLOWED ME TO SINK PSYCHIC FANGS INTO IMPERIEX'S MIND--
"--FIGHTING HIM FROM WITHIN. DRAINING HIS GOD-ENERGY.
SHAKK
"BUT THE SHARD'S POWER WAS QUICKLY WANING. I KNEW I ONLY HAD A LIMITED AMOUNT OF TIME.
"AND I ALSO KNEW THAT THE LONGER I KEPT THE SOUL-LINK GOING--
"--THE GREATER THE CHANCE THAT IMPERIEX'S PSYCHE WOULD DEVOUR MINE. THAT I'D BE LOST INSIDE THAT TERRIBLE CONSCIOUSNESS--
SKRABLOOM
"--FOREVER."

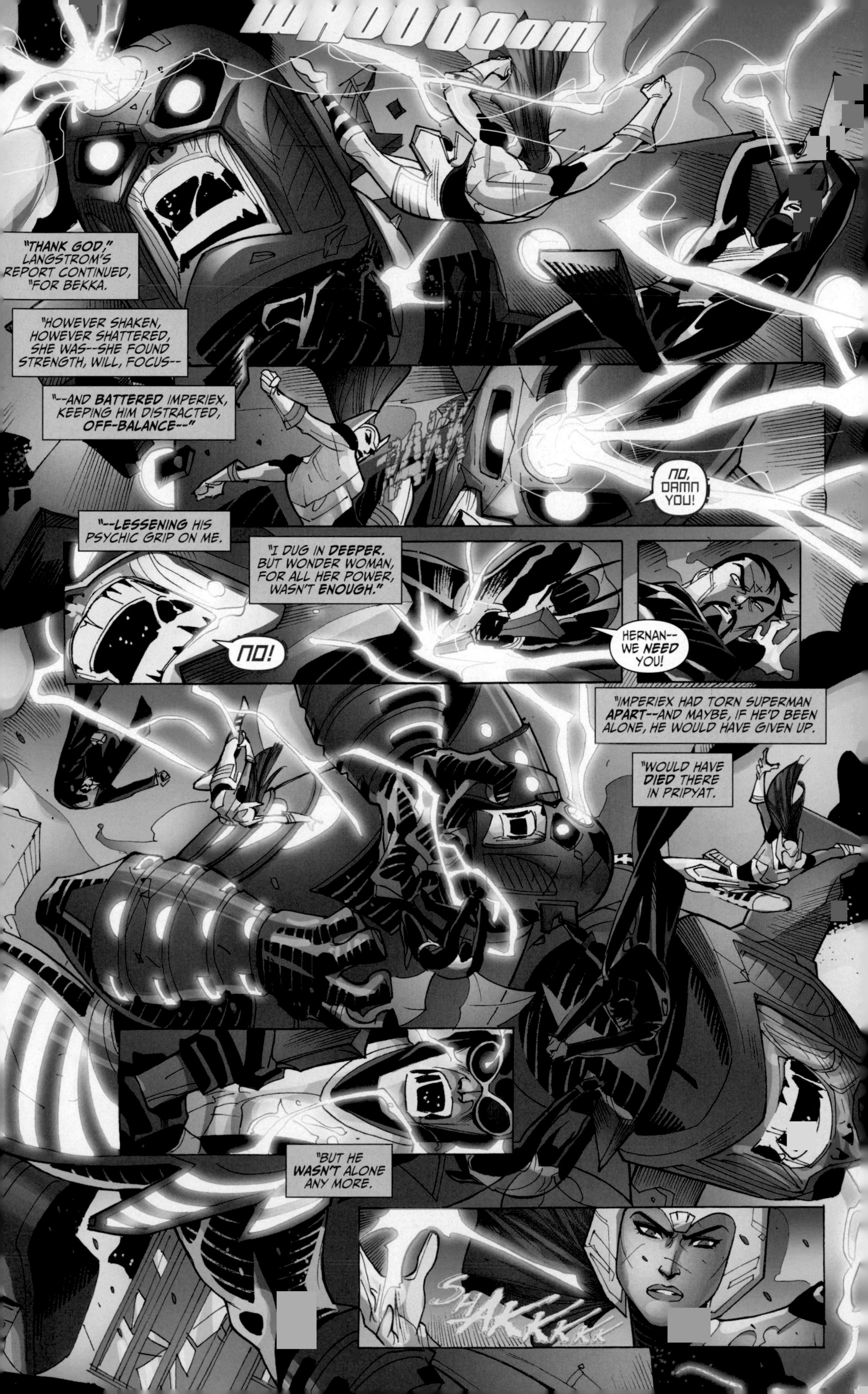
WHOOOOOOM
"THANK GOD," LANGSTROM'S REPORT CONTINUED, "FOR BEKKA.
"HOWEVER SHAKEN, HOWEVER SHATTERED, SHE WAS--SHE FOUND STRENGTH, WILL, FOCUS--
"--AND BATTERED IMPERIEX, KEEPING HIM DISTRACTED, OFF-BALANCE--"
NO, DAMN YOU!
"--LESSENING HIS PSYCHIC GRIP ON ME.
"I DUG IN DEEPER. BUT WONDER WOMAN, FOR ALL HER POWER, WASN'T ENOUGH."
NO!
HERNAN-- WE NEED YOU!
"IMPERIEX HAD TORN SUPERMAN APART--AND MAYBE, IF HE'D BEEN ALONE, HE WOULD HAVE GIVEN UP.
"WOULD HAVE DIED THERE IN PRIPYAT.
"BUT HE WASN'T ALONE ANY MORE.
SHAKKKKKK

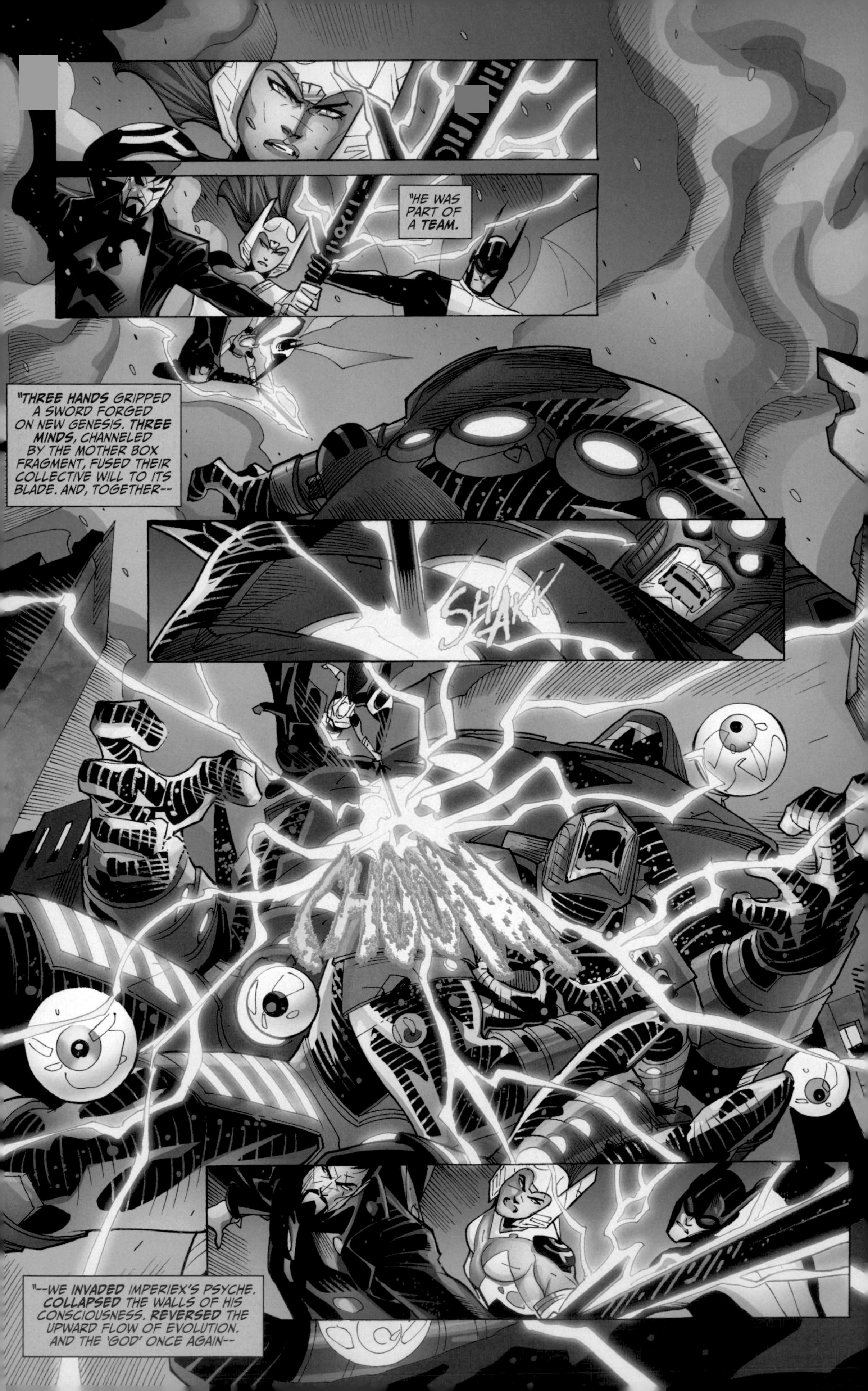
"HE WAS PART OF A TEAM.
"THREE HANDS GRIPPED A SWORD FORGED ON NEW GENESIS. THREE MINDS, CHANNELED BY THE MOTHER BOX FRAGMENT, FUSED THEIR COLLECTIVE WILL TO ITS BLADE. AND, TOGETHER--
SHAKK
"--WE INVADED IMPERIEX'S PSYCHE. COLLAPSED THE WALLS OF HIS CONSCIOUSNESS. REVERSED THE UPWARD FLOW OF EVOLUTION. AND THE 'GOD' ONCE AGAIN--

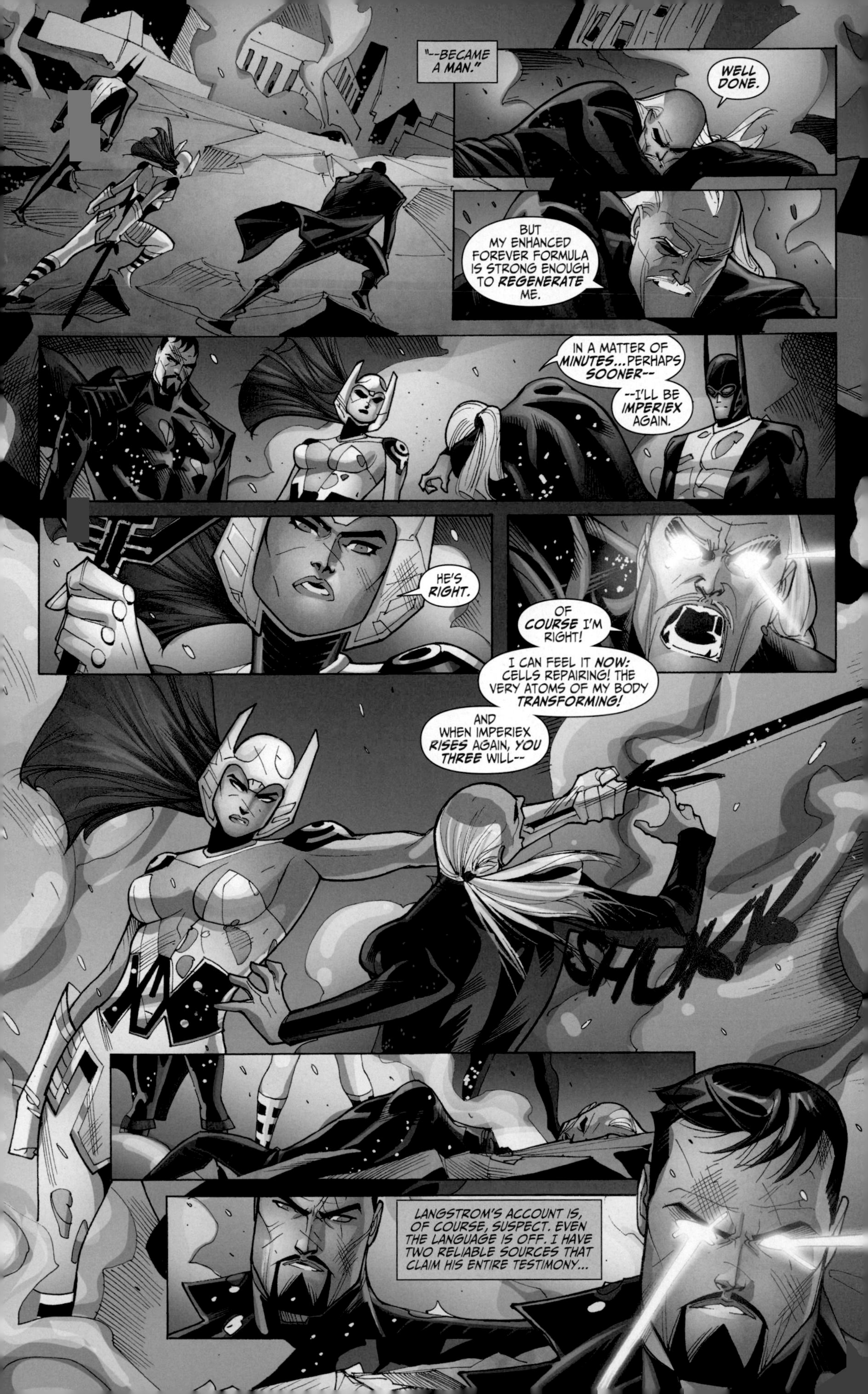
"--BECAME A MAN."
WELL DONE.
BUT MY ENHANCED FOREVER FORMULA IS STRONG ENOUGH TO REGENERATE ME.
IN A MATTER OF MINUTES...PERHAPS SOONER--
--I'LL BE IMPERIEX AGAIN.
HE'S RIGHT.
OF COURSE I'M RIGHT!
I CAN FEEL IT NOW: CELLS REPAIRING! THE VERY ATOMS OF MY BODY TRANSFORMING!
AND WHEN IMPERIEX RISES AGAIN, YOU THREE WILL--
SHUKK
LANGSTROM'S ACCOUNT IS, OF COURSE, SUSPECT. EVEN THE LANGUAGE IS OFF. I HAVE TWO RELIABLE SOURCES THAT CLAIM HIS ENTIRE TESTIMONY...

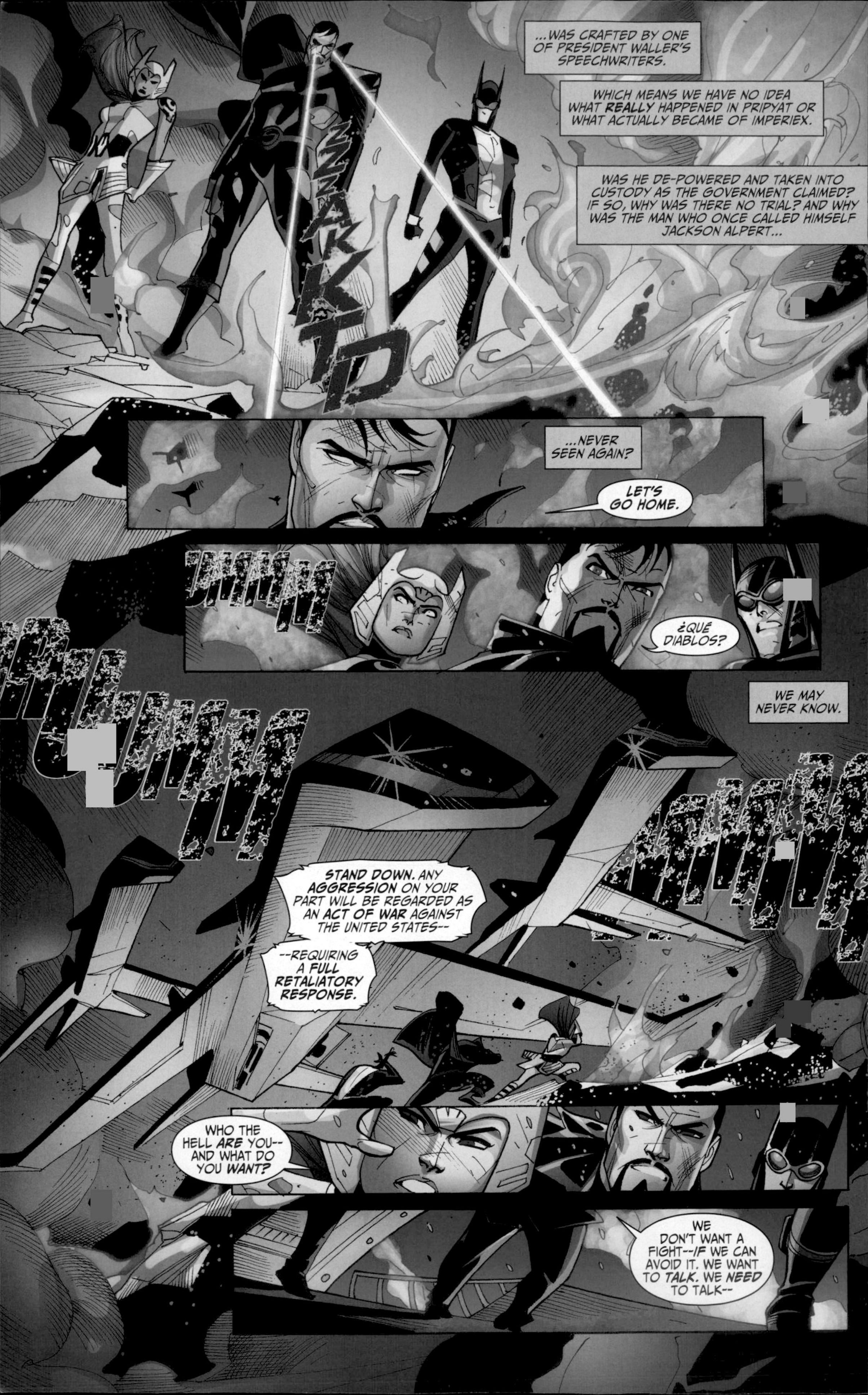
...WAS CRAFTED BY ONE OF PRESIDENT WALLER'S SPEECHWRITERS.
WHICH MEANS WE HAVE NO IDEA WHAT REALLY HAPPENED IN PRIPYAT OR WHAT ACTUALLY BECAME OF IMPERIEX.
WAS HE DE-POWERED AND TAKEN INTO CUSTODY AS THE GOVERNMENT CLAIMED? IF SO, WHY WAS THERE NO TRIAL? AND WHY WAS THE MAN WHO ONCE CALLED HIMSELF JACKSON ALPERT...
ZZZARKT
...NEVER SEEN AGAIN?
LET'S GO HOME.
UMMM
¿QUÉ DIABLOS?
WE MAY NEVER KNOW.
STAND DOWN. ANY AGGRESSION ON YOUR PART WILL BE REGARDED AS AN ACT OF WAR AGAINST THE UNITED STATES--
--REQUIRING A FULL RETALIATORY RESPONSE.
WHO THE HELL ARE YOU-- AND WHAT DO YOU WANT?
WE DON'T WANT A FIGHT--IF WE CAN AVOID IT. WE WANT TO TALK. WE NEED TO TALK--

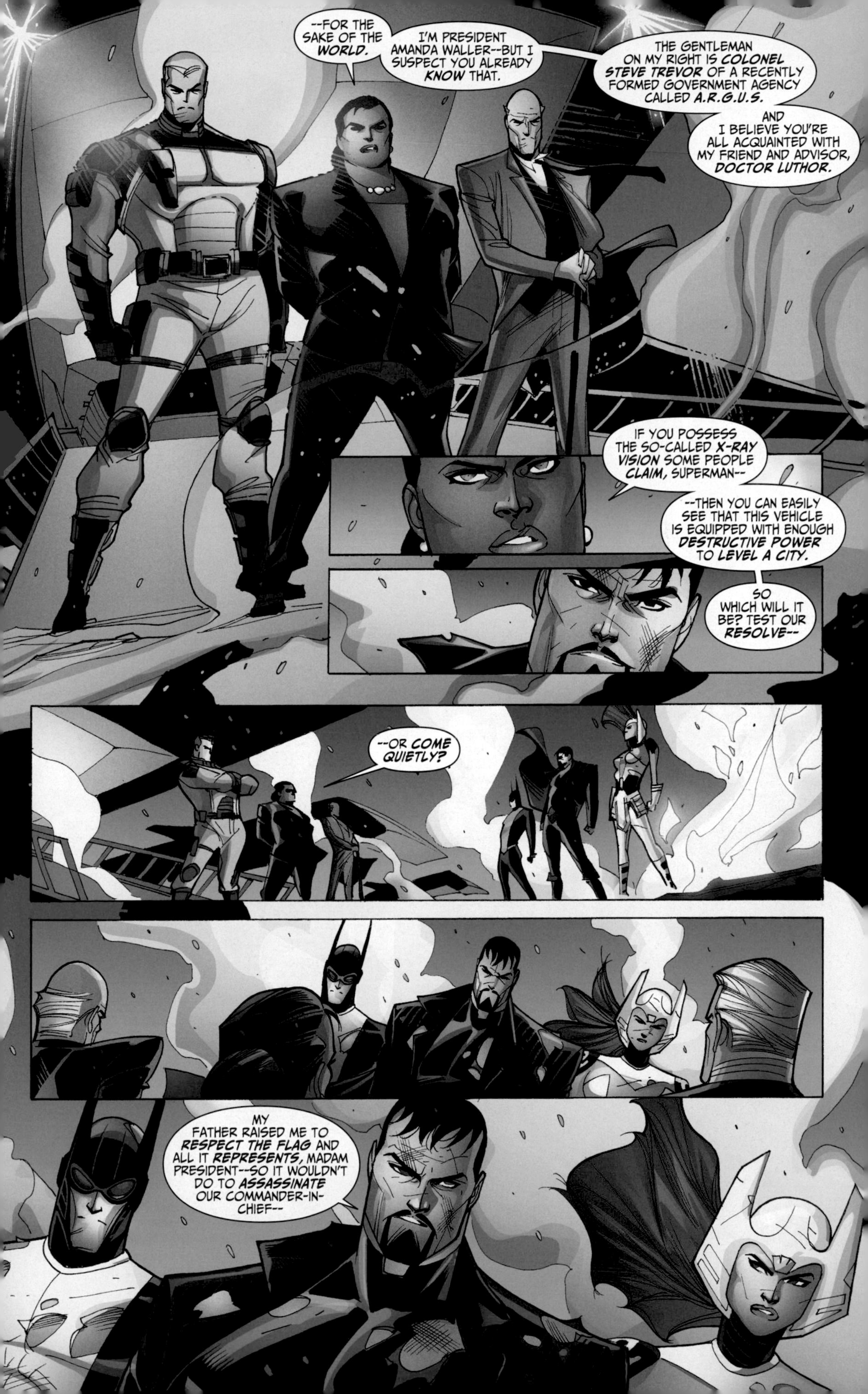
--FOR THE SAKE OF THE WORLD.
I'M PRESIDENT AMANDA WALLER--BUT I SUSPECT YOU ALREADY KNOW THAT.
THE GENTLEMAN ON MY RIGHT IS COLONEL STEVE TREVOR OF A RECENTLY FORMED GOVERNMENT AGENCY CALLED A.R.G.U.S.
AND I BELIEVE YOU'RE ALL ACQUAINTED WITH MY FRIEND AND ADVISOR, DOCTOR LUTHOR.
IF YOU POSSESS THE SO-CALLED X-RAY VISION SOME PEOPLE CLAIM, SUPERMAN--
--THEN YOU CAN EASILY SEE THAT THIS VEHICLE IS EQUIPPED WITH ENOUGH DESTRUCTIVE POWER TO LEVEL A CITY.
SO WHICH WILL IT BE? TEST OUR RESOLVE--
--OR COME QUIETLY?
MY FATHER RAISED ME TO RESPECT THE FLAG AND ALL IT REPRESENTS, MADAM PRESIDENT--SO IT WOULDN'T DO TO ASSASSINATE OUR COMMANDER-IN-CHIEF--

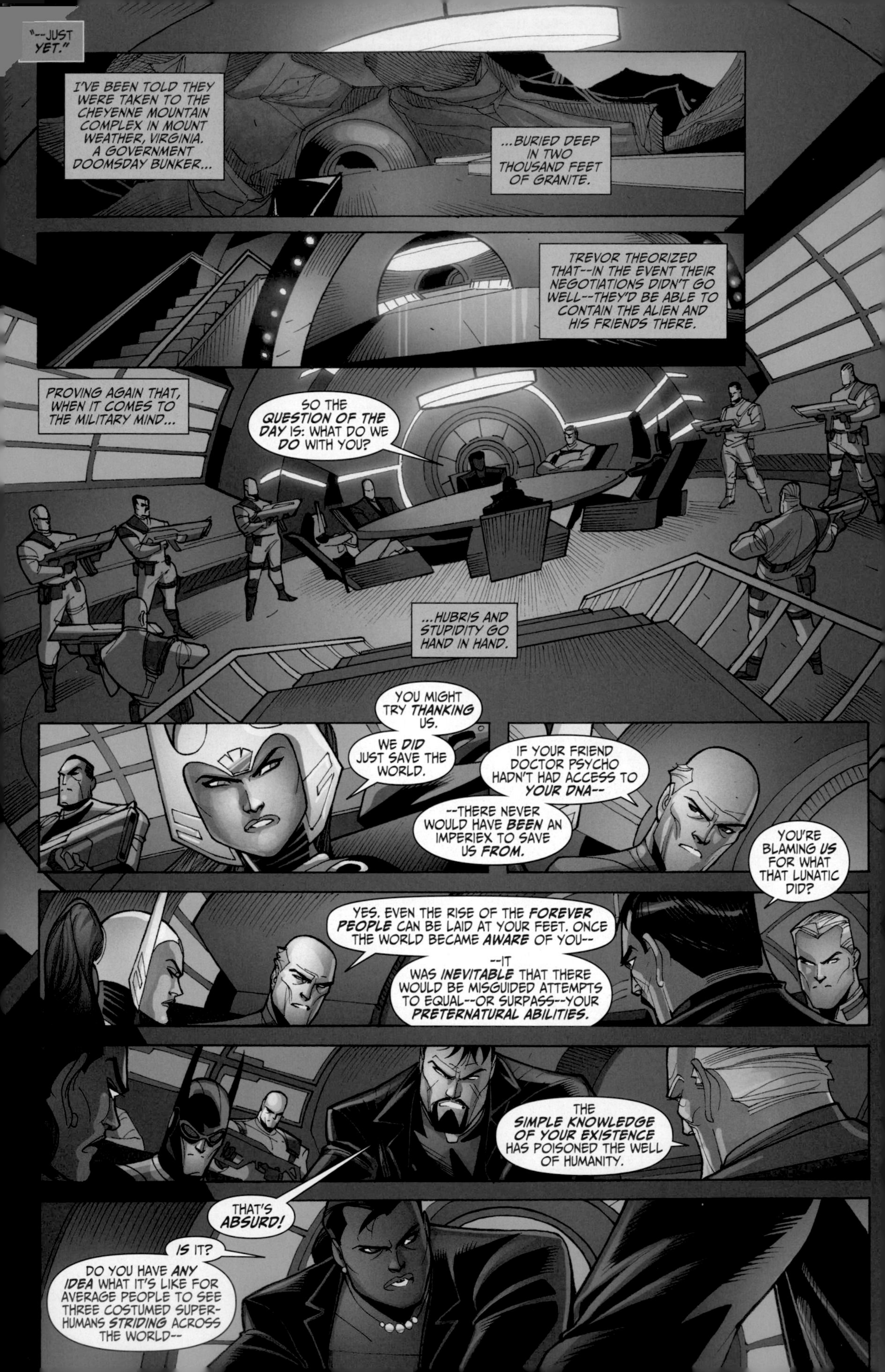
"--JUST YET."
I'VE BEEN TOLD THEY WERE TAKEN TO THE CHEYENNE MOUNTAIN COMPLEX IN MOUNT WEATHER, VIRGINIA. A GOVERNMENT DOOMSDAY BUNKER...
...BURIED DEEP IN TWO THOUSAND FEET OF GRANITE.
TREVOR THEORIZED THAT--IN THE EVENT THEIR NEGOTIATIONS DIDN'T GO WELL--THEY'D BE ABLE TO CONTAIN THE ALIEN AND HIS FRIENDS THERE.
PROVING AGAIN THAT, WHEN IT COMES TO THE MILITARY MIND...
SO THE QUESTION OF THE DAY IS: WHAT DO WE DO WITH YOU?
...HUBRIS AND STUPIDITY GO HAND IN HAND.
YOU MIGHT TRY THANKING US.
WE DID JUST SAVE THE WORLD.
IF YOUR FRIEND DOCTOR PSYCHO HADN'T HAD ACCESS TO YOUR DNA--
--THERE NEVER WOULD HAVE BEEN AN IMPERIEX TO SAVE US FROM.
YOU'RE BLAMING US FOR WHAT THAT LUNATIC DID?
YES. EVEN THE RISE OF THE FOREVER PEOPLE CAN BE LAID AT YOUR FEET. ONCE THE WORLD BECAME AWARE OF YOU--
--IT WAS INEVITABLE THAT THERE WOULD BE MISGUIDED ATTEMPTS TO EQUAL--OR SURPASS--YOUR PRETERNATURAL ABILITIES.
THE SIMPLE KNOWLEDGE OF YOUR EXISTENCE HAS POISONED THE WELL OF HUMANITY.
THAT'S ABSURD!
IS IT?
DO YOU HAVE ANY IDEA WHAT IT'S LIKE FOR AVERAGE PEOPLE TO SEE THREE COSTUMED SUPER-HUMANS STRIDING ACROSS THE WORLD--

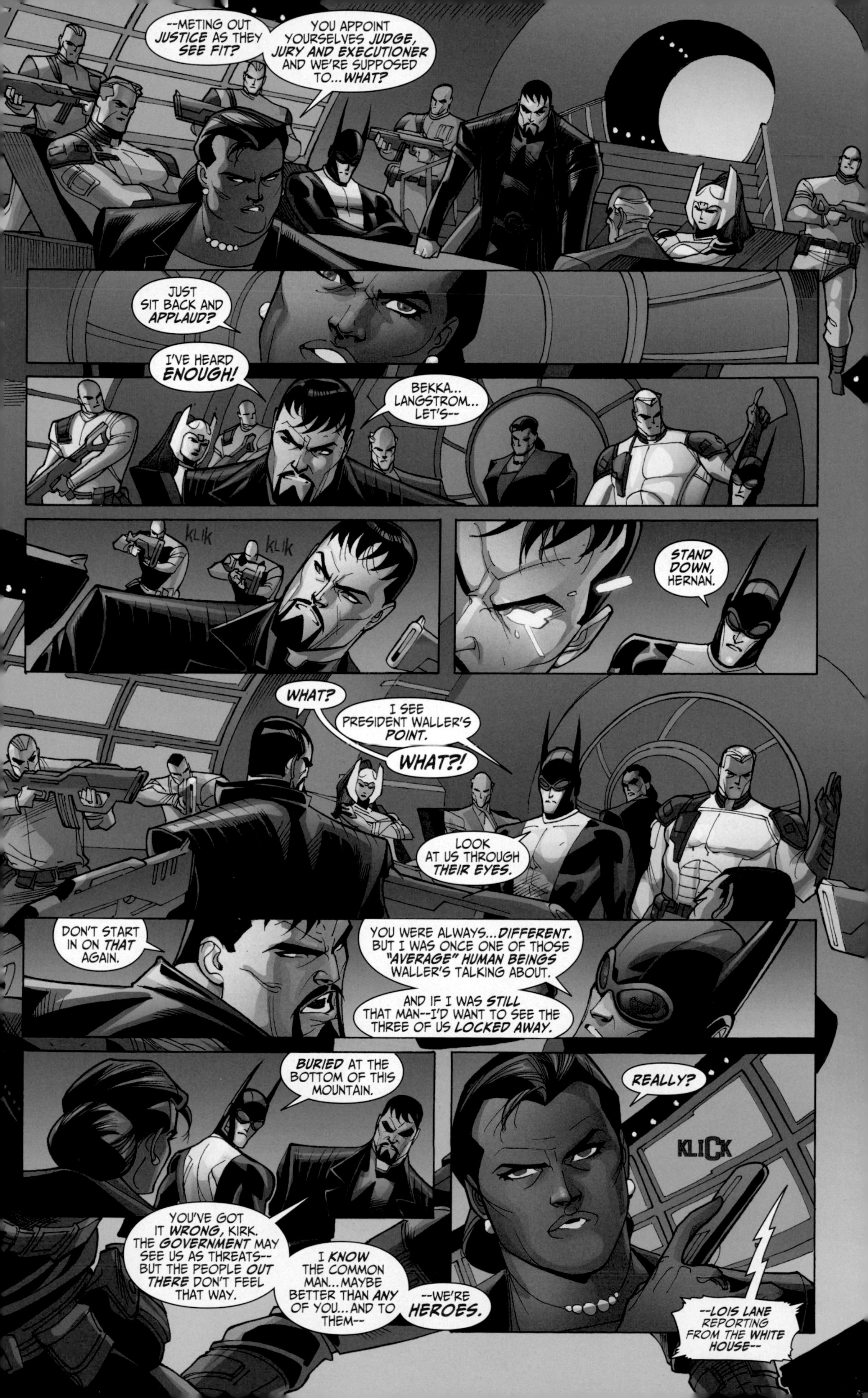
--METING OUT JUSTICE AS THEY SEE FIT?
YOU APPOINT YOURSELVES JUDGE, JURY AND EXECUTIONER AND WE'RE SUPPOSED TO... WHAT?
JUST SIT BACK AND APPLAUD?
I'VE HEARD ENOUGH!
BEKKA... LANGSTROM... LET'S--
KLIK
KLIK
STAND DOWN, HERNAN.
WHAT?
I SEE PRESIDENT WALLER'S POINT.
WHAT?!
LOOK AT US THROUGH THEIR EYES.
DON'T START IN ON THAT AGAIN.
YOU WERE ALWAYS... DIFFERENT. BUT I WAS ONCE ONE OF THOSE "AVERAGE" HUMAN BEINGS WALLER'S TALKING ABOUT.
AND IF I WAS STILL THAT MAN--I'D WANT TO SEE THE THREE OF US LOCKED AWAY.
BURIED AT THE BOTTOM OF THIS MOUNTAIN.
YOU'VE GOT IT WRONG, KIRK. THE GOVERNMENT MAY SEE US AS THREATS-- BUT THE PEOPLE OUT THERE DON'T FEEL THAT WAY.
I KNOW THE COMMON MAN... MAYBE BETTER THAN ANY OF YOU... AND TO THEM--
--WE'RE HEROES.
REALLY?
KLICK
--LOIS LANE REPORTING FROM THE WHITE HOUSE--

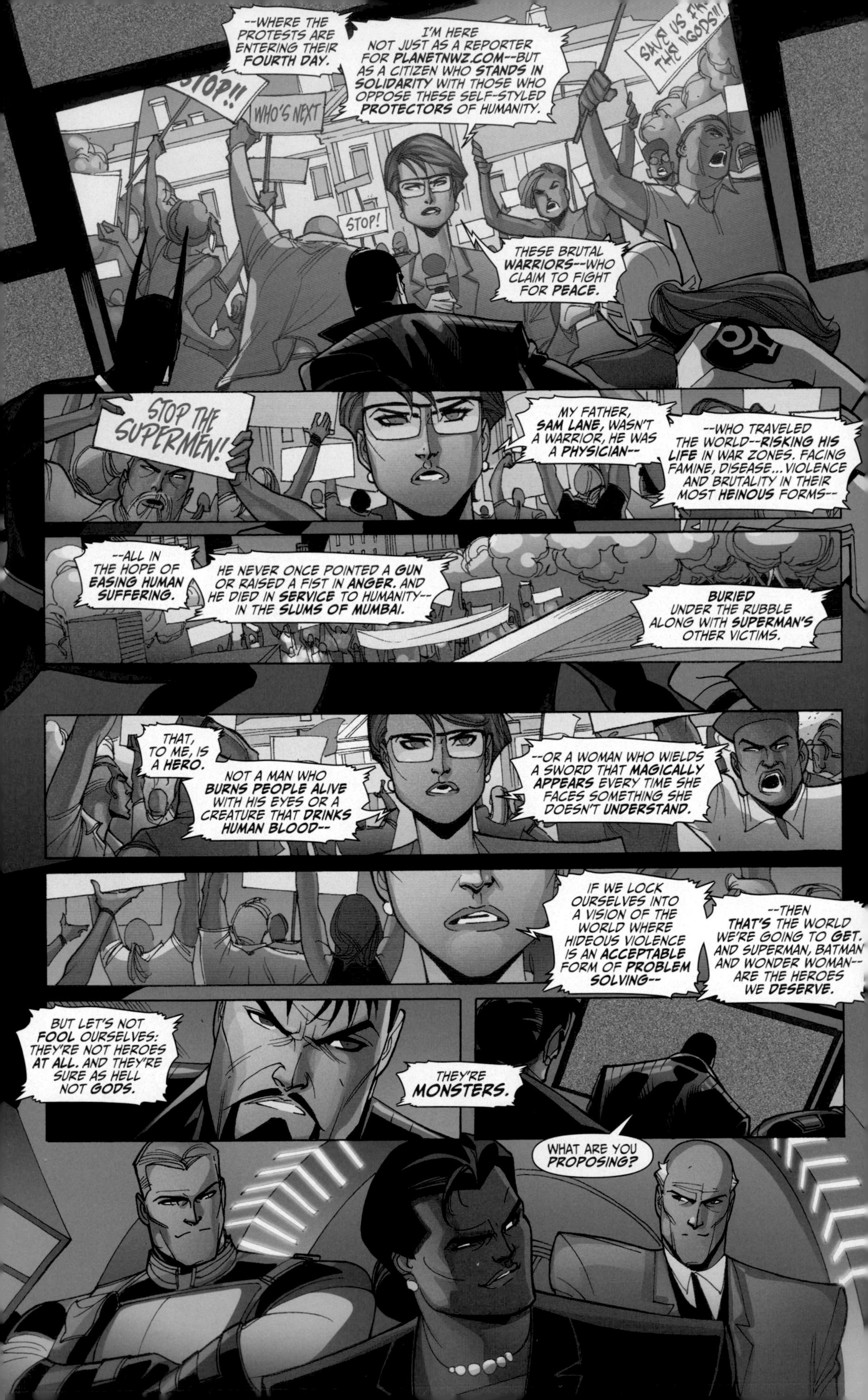
--WHERE THE PROTESTS ARE ENTERING THEIR FOURTH DAY.
I'M HERE NOT JUST AS A REPORTER FOR PLANETNWZ.COM--BUT AS A CITIZEN WHO STANDS IN SOLIDARITY WITH THOSE WHO OPPOSE THESE SELF-STYLED PROTECTORS OF HUMANITY.
STOP!!
WHO'S NEXT
STOP!
THESE BRUTAL WARRIORS--WHO CLAIM TO FIGHT FOR PEACE.
STOP THE SUPERMEN!!
MY FATHER, SAM LANE, WASN'T A WARRIOR, HE WAS A PHYSICIAN--
--WHO TRAVELED THE WORLD--RISKING HIS LIFE IN WAR ZONES. FACING FAMINE, DISEASE...VIOLENCE AND BRUTALITY IN THEIR MOST HEINOUS FORMS--
--ALL IN THE HOPE OF EASING HUMAN SUFFERING.
HE NEVER ONCE POINTED A GUN OR RAISED A FIST IN ANGER. AND HE DIED IN SERVICE TO HUMANITY--IN THE SLUMS OF MUMBAI.
BURIED UNDER THE RUBBLE ALONG WITH SUPERMAN'S OTHER VICTIMS.
THAT, TO ME, IS A HERO.
NOT A MAN WHO BURNS PEOPLE ALIVE WITH HIS EYES OR A CREATURE THAT DRINKS HUMAN BLOOD--
--OR A WOMAN WHO WIELDS A SWORD THAT MAGICALLY APPEARS EVERY TIME SHE FACES SOMETHING SHE DOESN'T UNDERSTAND.
IF WE LOCK OURSELVES INTO A VISION OF THE WORLD WHERE HIDEOUS VIOLENCE IS AN ACCEPTABLE FORM OF PROBLEM SOLVING--
--THEN THAT'S THE WORLD WE'RE GOING TO GET. AND SUPERMAN, BATMAN AND WONDER WOMAN--ARE THE HEROES WE DESERVE.
BUT LET'S NOT FOOL OURSELVES: THEY'RE NOT HEROES AT ALL. AND THEY'RE SURE AS HELL NOT GODS.
THEY'RE MONSTERS.
WHAT ARE YOU PROPOSING?

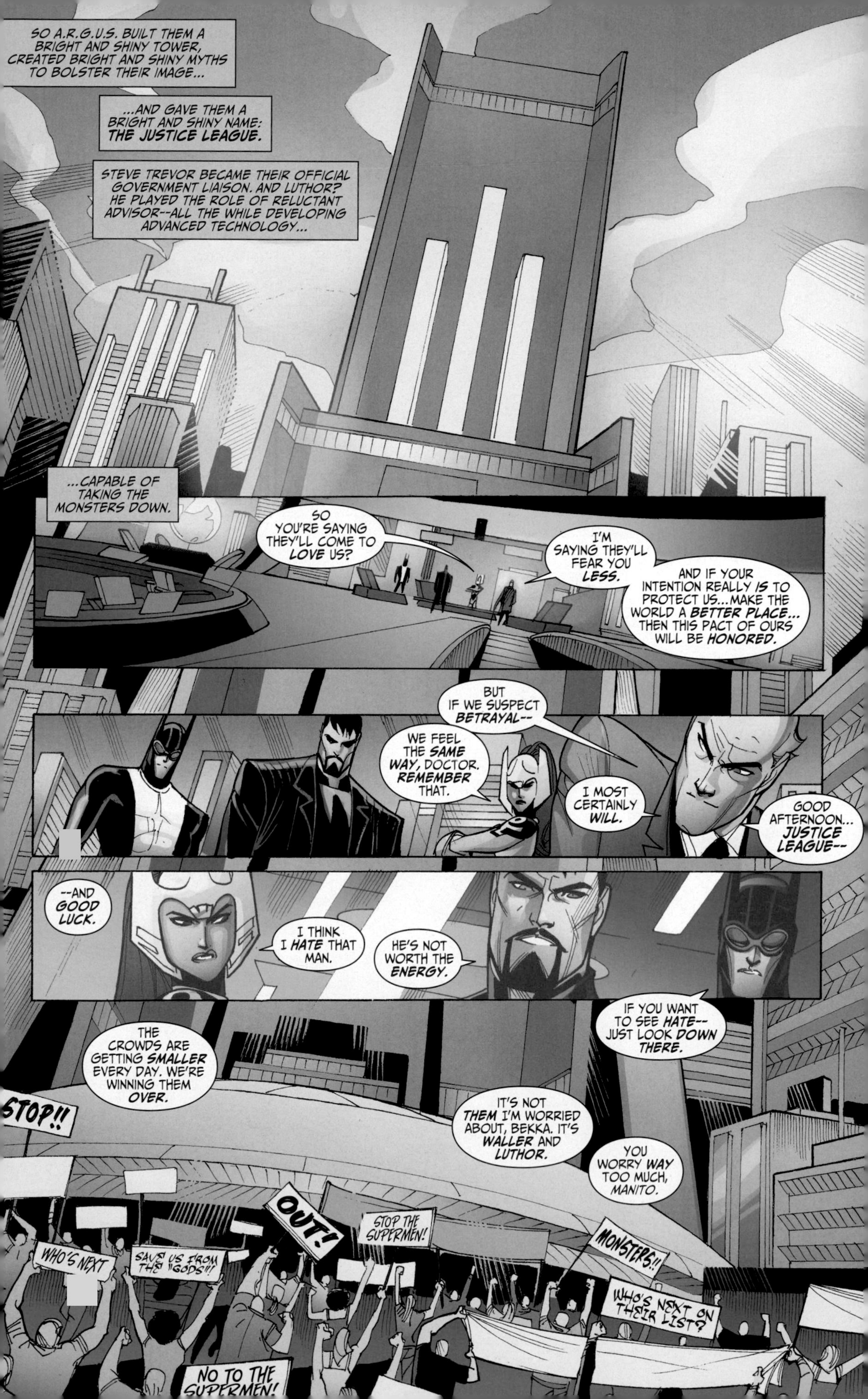
SO A.R.G.U.S. BUILT THEM A BRIGHT AND SHINY TOWER, CREATED BRIGHT AND SHINY MYTHS TO BOLSTER THEIR IMAGE...
...AND GAVE THEM A BRIGHT AND SHINY NAME: THE JUSTICE LEAGUE.
STEVE TREVOR BECAME THEIR OFFICIAL GOVERNMENT LIAISON. AND LUTHOR? HE PLAYED THE ROLE OF RELUCTANT ADVISOR--ALL THE WHILE DEVELOPING ADVANCED TECHNOLOGY...
...CAPABLE OF TAKING THE MONSTERS DOWN.
SO YOU'RE SAYING THEY'LL COME TO LOVE US?
I'M SAYING THEY'LL FEAR YOU LESS.
AND IF YOUR INTENTION REALLY IS TO PROTECT US...MAKE THE WORLD A BETTER PLACE... THEN THIS PACT OF OURS WILL BE HONORED.
BUT IF WE SUSPECT BETRAYAL--
WE FEEL THE SAME WAY, DOCTOR. REMEMBER THAT.
I MOST CERTAINLY WILL.
GOOD AFTERNOON... JUSTICE LEAGUE--
--AND GOOD LUCK.
I THINK I HATE THAT MAN.
HE'S NOT WORTH THE ENERGY.
IF YOU WANT TO SEE HATE-- JUST LOOK DOWN THERE.
THE CROWDS ARE GETTING SMALLER EVERY DAY. WE'RE WINNING THEM OVER.
STOP!!
IT'S NOT THEM I'M WORRIED ABOUT, BEKKA. IT'S WALLER AND LUTHOR.
YOU WORRY WAY TOO MUCH, MANITO.
OUT!
STOP THE SUPERMEN!
MONSTERS!!
WHO'S NEXT
SAVE US FROM THE "GODS"!!
WHO'S NEXT ON THEIR LIST?
NO TO THE SUPERMEN!

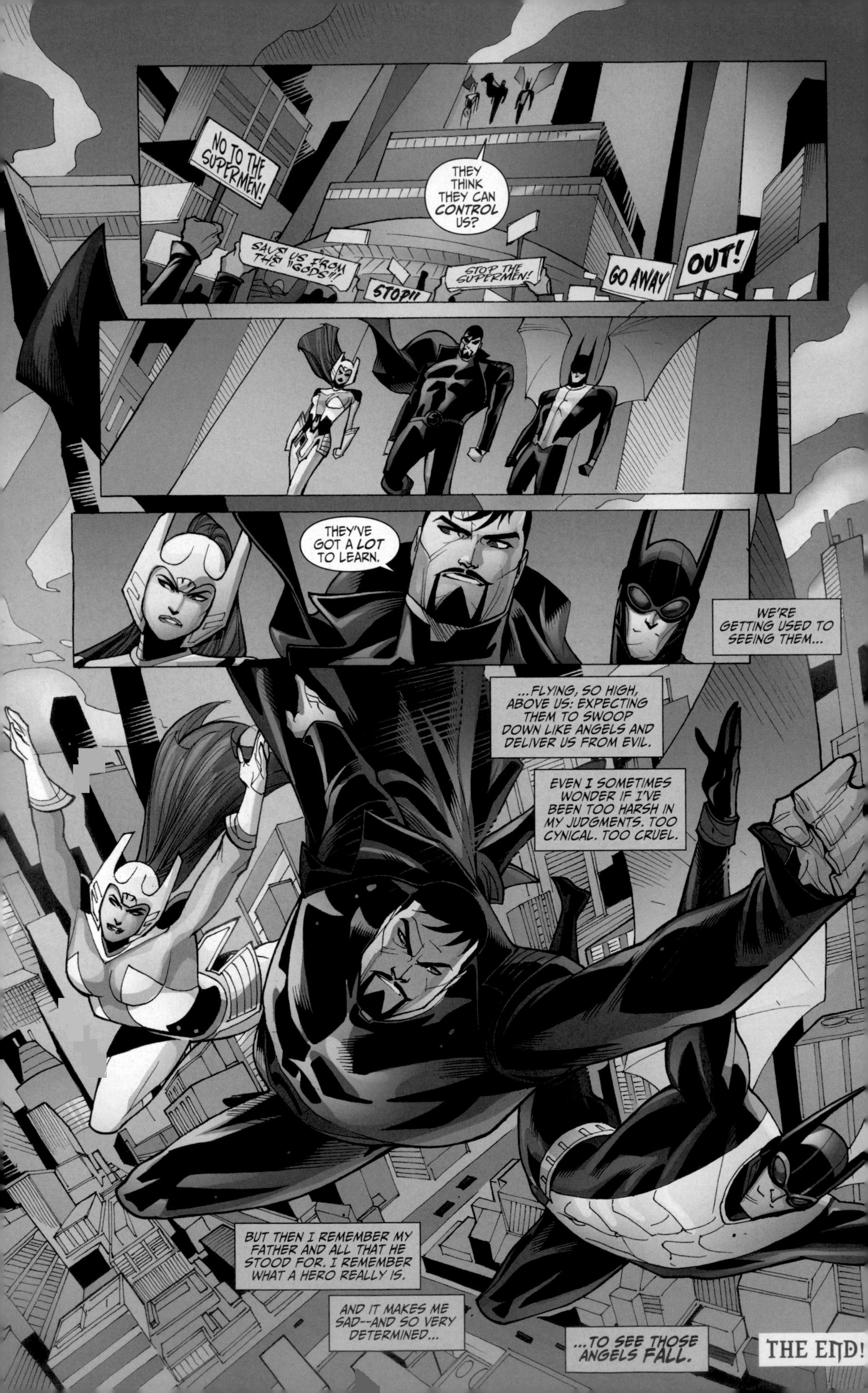
NO TO THE SUPERMEN!
THEY THINK THEY CAN CONTROL US?
SAVE US FROM THE "GODS"!
STOP!!
STOP THE SUPERMEN!
GO AWAY
OUT!
THEY'VE GOT A LOT TO LEARN.
WE'RE GETTING USED TO SEEING THEM...
...FLYING, SO HIGH, ABOVE US: EXPECTING THEM TO SWOOP DOWN LIKE ANGELS AND DELIVER US FROM EVIL.
EVEN I SOMETIMES WONDER IF I'VE BEEN TOO HARSH IN MY JUDGMENTS. TOO CYNICAL. TOO CRUEL.
BUT THEN I REMEMBER MY FATHER AND ALL THAT HE STOOD FOR. I REMEMBER WHAT A HERO REALLY IS.
AND IT MAKES ME SAD--AND SO VERY DETERMINED...
...TO SEE THOSE ANGELS FALL.
THE END!

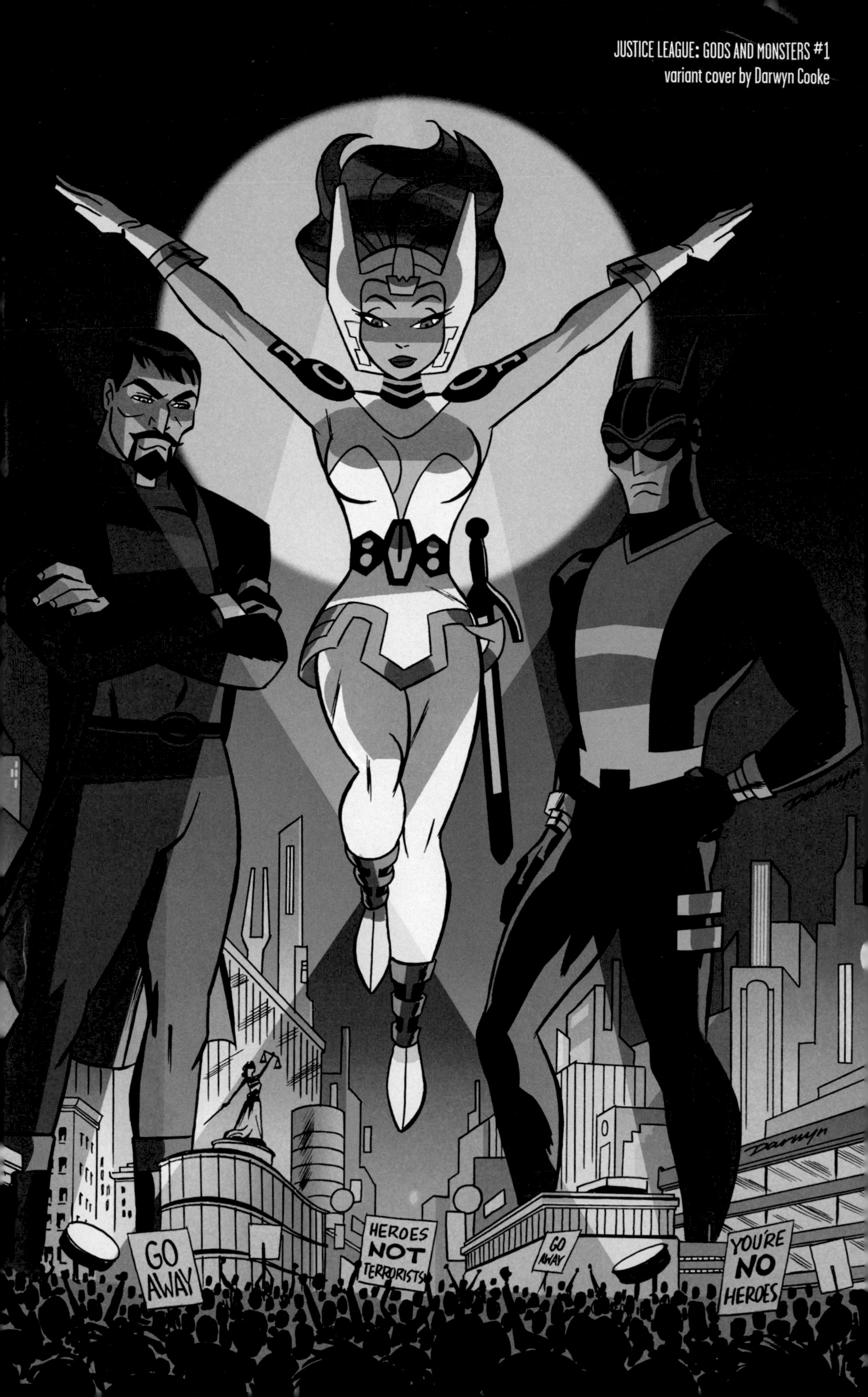
GO AWAY
HEROES NOT TERRORISTS
GO AWAY
YOU'RE NO HEROES
Darwyn
JUSTICE LEAGUE: GODS AND MONSTERS #1
variant cover by Darwyn Cooke

JUSTICE LEAGUE: GODS AND MONSTERS—SUPERMAN #1
variant cover by Darwyn Cooke

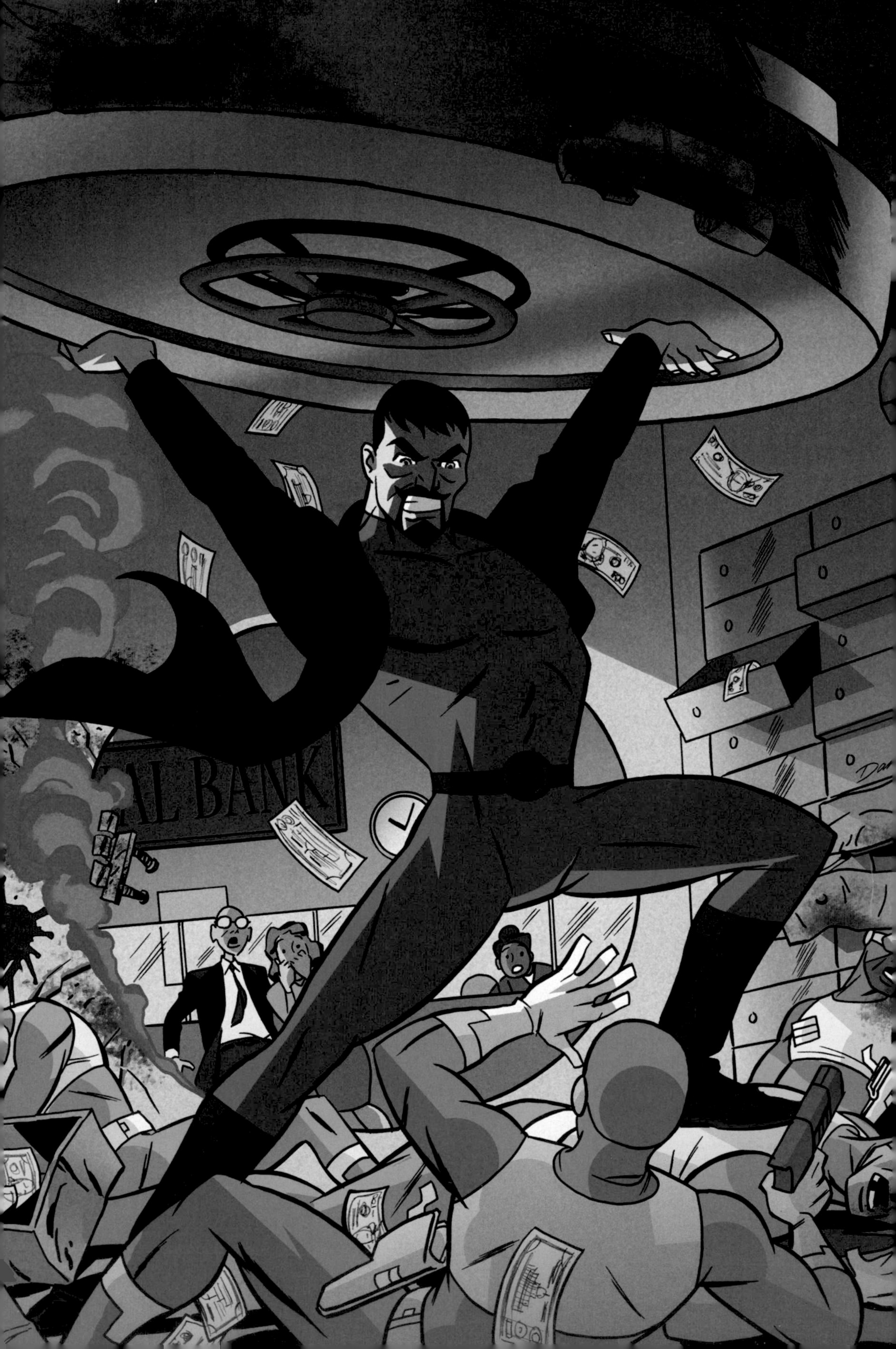
AL BANK

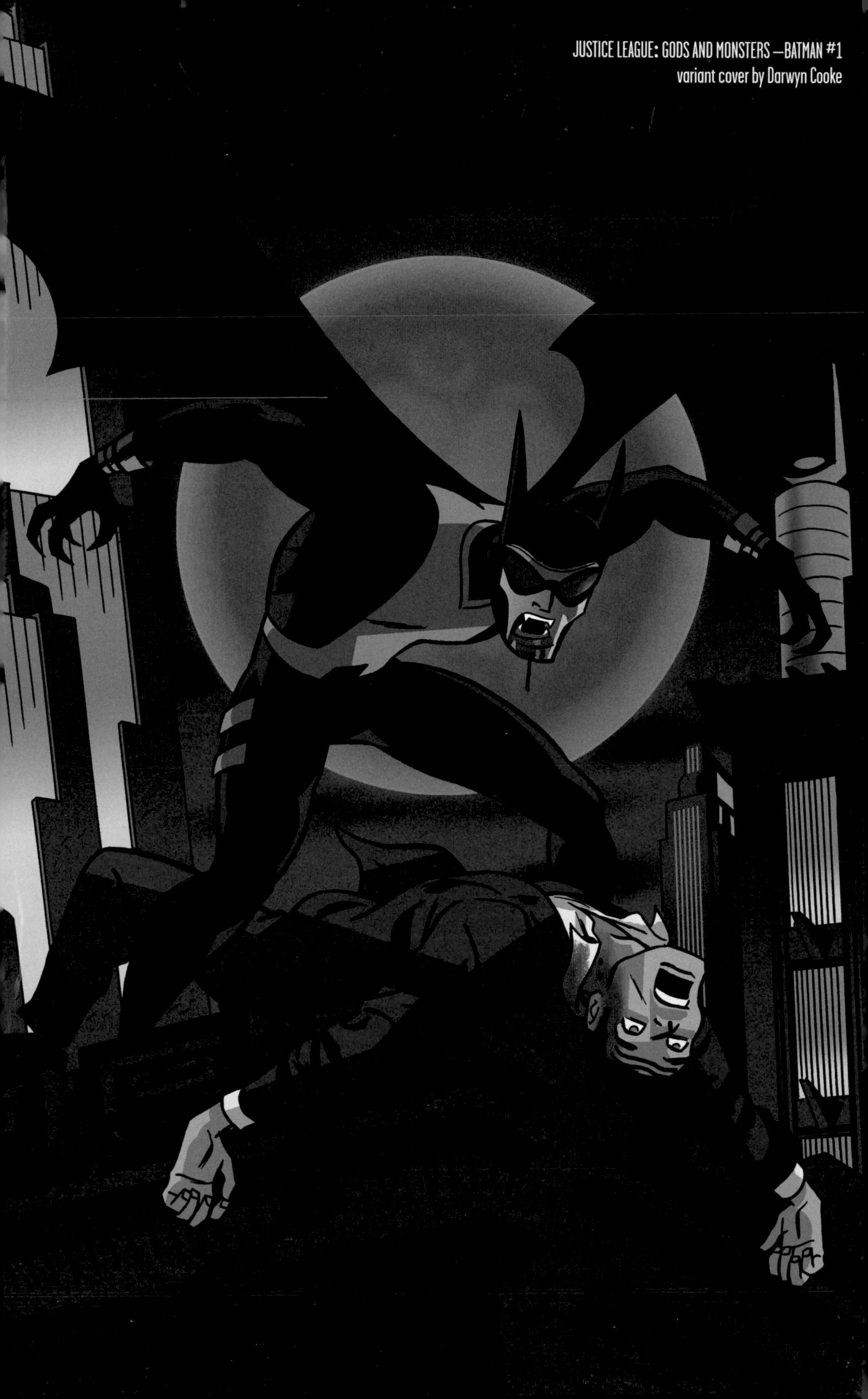

JUSTICE LEAGUE: GODS AND MONSTERS—BATMAN #1
variant cover by Darwyn Cooke

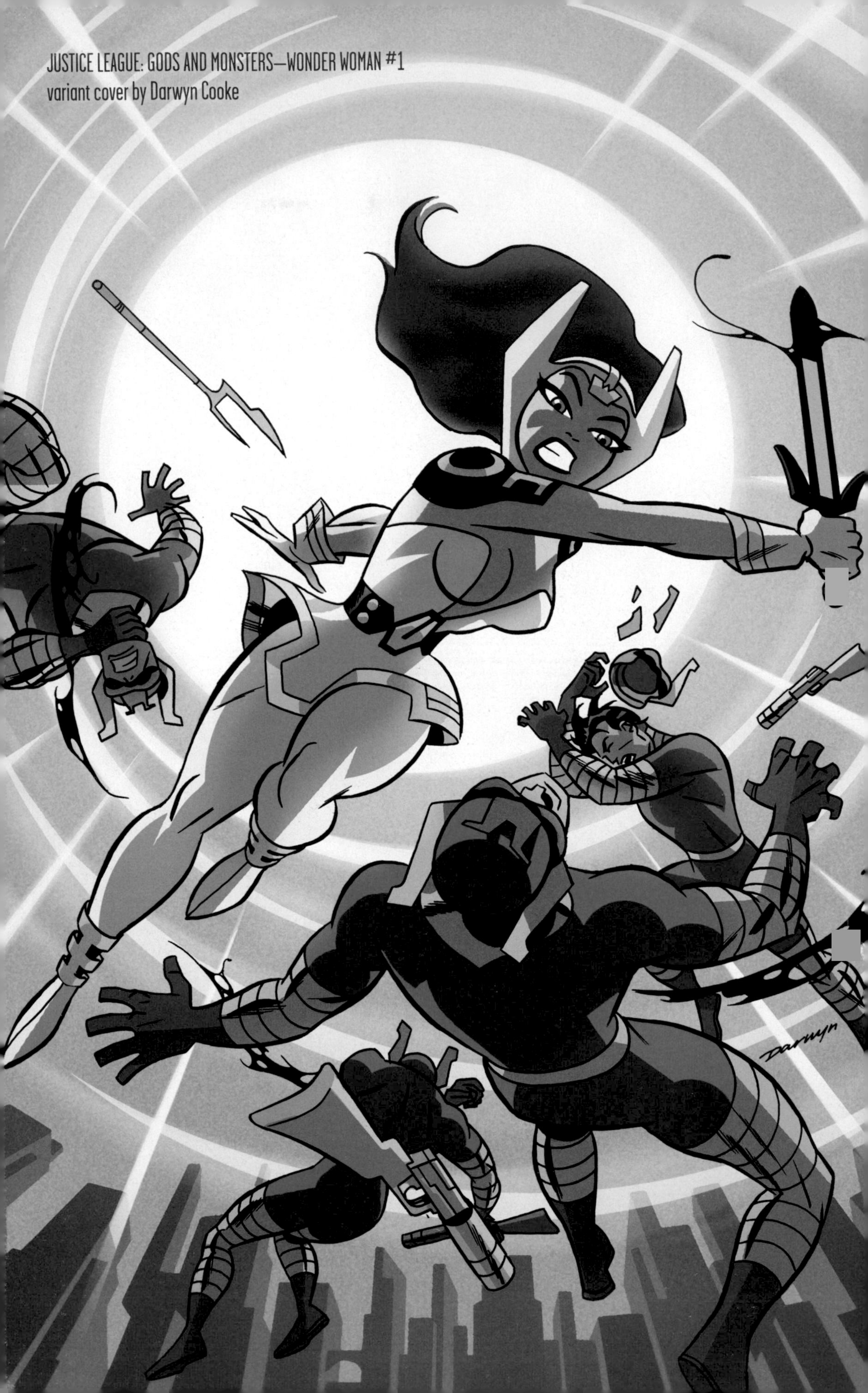
Darwyn

JUSTICE LEAGUE: GODS AND MONSTERS—WONDER WOMAN #1
variant cover by Darwyn Cooke